Chri

and Magical Rituals

Agostino Taumaturgo

THAVMA Publications
http://thavmapub.com

ISBN-10: 153282873X
ISBN-13: 978-1532828737

Cover Image: *Swedish Lutherans celebrate Halloween.*
Source: *Wikipedia, image declared public domain*
https://en.wikipedia.org/wiki/Halloween#/media/File:Halloween_S
weden.png

Table of Contents

This Page Intentionally Left Blank

About the Author

Agostino Taumaturgo (Brother A.D.A.) has been a student of Christian spirituality and magic for almost 30 years, specializing in theology and orthodox methods of manifestation. His father was a metaphysics teacher, and Agostino learned much from him. After being ordained a traditionalist Catholic priest in 2002 and consecrated a bishop in 2007, he learned even more but returned to the magical community because exoteric ministry just wasn't for him.

Agostino now writes, teaches, and lectures on spirituality, magic, and manifestation within a Christian paradigm, and is available for workshops, speaking engagements and one-on-one coaching. He can be reached at agostino@thavmapub.com.

When off-duty, Agostino lives in Dayton, Ohio, with his cats Melainos and Gray Lady.

Introduction

As magicians, we live in a world filled with literature and ritual. Sometimes we want to peruse the literature and learn something, while other times we want to find a ritual to help us get things done.

This book is meant for the latter purpose. In it the reader will find all the exercises, meditations, prayers, and rituals found in my writings to date, with the express purpose of easy reference and practical accessibility.

I've also included original material by way of the treatises on Rosary Magic and Exorcism, and a section on church services with an eye to those who shepherd small congregations. These are actual worship services I used during my latter years of exoteric ministry, and through techniques I plan to detail in a future work, I've found it's as possible to raise energy with the most "low church" service in the world, as it is with all the "smells and bells" to which ceremonial magicians are so accustomed.

In the future, I also intend to publish the entire Missal our congregation used in its worship, along with our hymnal and other worship aids.

It is my hope this volume finds you well, and that you find in it a useful resource for your ritual needs.

Other Books by Agostino Taumaturgo

Is Magic Wrong? An Historical and Religious Exploration

The Magic of Catholicism

Ritual Magic for Conservative Christians

Christian Candle Magic

Guide to Meditation

We Pray the Rosary

The Magic of Effective Prayer

I. Regular Prayers, Exercises, and Meditations

This section contains basic prayers, meditations, and ritual exercises that can be used on a daily basis as part of one's spiritual regimen. These exercises rate from the simple to the mildly complex, and are aimed at improving one's concentration, their ritual skill, their connection with God Almighty, and their ability to tap into spiritual energy.

1. The Sign of the Cross
Make the Sign of the Cross with the right hand, saying as you touch:
a. Forehead: **In the name of the Father,**
b. Breast or navel: **and of the Son,**
c. Left Shoulder: **and of the Holy**
d. Right Shoulder: **Ghost** (or **Spirit**)
e. Join hands in front of breast: **Amen.**

2. The Lord's Prayer
Our Father who art in heaven, hallowed be thy name.
Thy kingdom come. Thy will be done
on earth as it is in heaven.
Give us this day our daily bread,
and forgive us our trespasses,
as we forgive those who trespass against us,
and lead us not into temptation,
but deliver us from evil.
[Optional: For thine is the kingdom, and the power,
and the glory, for ever and ever. Amen.*]*

3. Invocatio Nominis Domini
Almighty God, in the Name of Jesus Christ Thine only-begotten Son I beseech Thee, to grant me the power to command all spirits, good or evil, without unintentionally causing harm to myself or to anybody else. Through our same Lord Jesus Christ, Thy Son, who liveth and reigneth

in the unity of the Holy Ghost, God, forever and ever.
Amen.

4. Prayer when Rising in the Morning

Loving God, as I awake this morning I give myself to you.
I thank and praise you for the many gifts you have given
me, and in a spirit of firm faith and childlike trust I know
you will protect me this day from all danger. Look also
upon me, Heavenly Father, and bring fill my life with love,
prosperity, wisdom, and fortitude. Forgive my
shortcomings and help me turn my weaknesses into
strength. Guide my words that they may be always true and
glorify you, O God. Through your Son, Jesus Christ our
Lord, who lives and reigns with you in the unity of the
Holy Spirit, one God, forever and ever. Amen.

5. Prayer when Retiring in the Evening

Almighty Living God, in a spirit of thanks I come to you
for guiding me through another day. As I lie down to sleep
this night, I ask that you place your holy angels to guard
and protect me:
Raphael before me,
Gabriel behind me,
Michael at my right hand,
And Uriel at my left.
May your love and protection surround me as a circle of
flaming stars, and above me and below me, within me and
without me, may the power of your Son envelop and
increase me as I seek to live each day in your name.
Through the same Christ our Lord. Amen.

6. Prayer for Sundays

Almighty God in the World of Knowledge, in the name of
your Son who rose from the dead on the first day of the
week, we come to you in thanks and praise for your glory.
We ask you to look after us in mind in body, in health and

in all matters of success and fortune. We ask also for illumination in matters of knowledge we may seek, and that you send the Archangel Michael to be our guide and our protector. We ask this through the same Christ our Lord. Amen.

7. Prayer for Mondays
Almighty Living God, we glorify you this day in all our works, and we ask that you help us to be in the right place at the right time for opportunity, to help us understand whatever messages you send us in our dreams, and send your Archangel Gabriel to help us understand both the messages and the opportunities you provide. Through Christ our Lord. Amen.

8. Prayer for Tuesdays
God of Strength and Power, this day we thank you for all the graces you have bestowed upon us, and we ask that you help us to edge out competition in our endeavors, grant us the energies to see our project through to completion, the strength of will to persevere to the end, and lend us the sword of your Archangel Camael against all who would see us undone. Through Jesus Christ, our Lord, your Son, who lives and reigns with you in the unity of the Holy Spirit, one God, forever and ever. Amen.

9. Prayer for Wednesdays
God of Hosts, we give you praise for your bounty throughout creation, and ask that our communications with our fellow human beings be accurate and effective, that our technology continues to work without fail, that we reach our destinations while traveling, and that we learn the lessons of today's experiences toward building a better tomorrow. With the staff of your Archangel Raphael to guide us and inform us, may we seek to praise and glorify you forever. Through Christ our Lord. Amen.

10. Prayer for Thursdays

God, we come before you this day in a spirit of love and jubilation. We give thanks for the abundance of your creation and praise for your giving us life to be part of that abundance. And we ask that you help us increase that abundance in our lives and our possessions, and that your righteous Archangel Sachiel will assist us in growth and prosperity. We ask this through Jesus' name. Amen.

11. Prayer for Fridays

You are holy, Lord of Hosts, and we praise the majesty of your victory and glory. We ask also that you will watch over and strengthen our relationships: personal, romantic, and professional. Make our relationships strong and help us to reach out and form new ones not only for our happiness and prosperity, but also for the glorification of your name. Through Jesus Christ, our Lord, your Son, who lives and reigns with you in the unity of the Holy Spirit, one God, forever and ever. Amen.

12. Prayer for Saturdays

Lord God, on a Saturday your Son waited in the tomb before rising up from the dead, and on that day he descended into Limbo to free the noble souls who were there constrained. We see in this that a flower's beauty is constrained within a seed, and for it to become a flower the seed must be ended and changed forever. Create in us this change, bringing about an end to old conditions that no longer suit us that we may blossom in new life. Send forth your Archangel Cassiel to end our loneliness, our sickness, our poverty, and our ignorance, that we may live lives filled with love, with health, with prosperity, and with knowledge, in so doing we may glorify you day by day, more and more. Through the same Christ our Lord. Amen.

13. Lesser Banishing Ritual of the Pentagram

1. Stand in the center of the room, facing east. Begin by making the sign of the Cross. As you touch each point, say the doxology of the Lord's Prayer in Hebrew, Greek, Latin, or English:

a. Forehead: כִּי לְךָ
(Ki Lekha, "For Thine is")

b. Breast: הַמַּלְכוּת
(Ha'Malkus, "the Kingdom")

c. Left Shoulder: וְהַגְּבוּרָה
(Va-Ha'Gevurah, "and the Power")

d. Right Shoulder: וְהַגְּדֻלָה
(Va-Ha'Gedulah, "and the Glory")

e. Clasp Hands: לְעוֹלְמֵי עוֹלָמִים אָמֵן
(Le-Olemei Olamim. Amen. "forever and ever. Amen.")

The Latin and Greek are as follows:

Latin:
Quia tuum est
regnum
et potéstas
et glória
in sáecula. Amen.

Greek:
῞Οτι σοῦ ἐστιν
ἡ βασιλεία
καὶ ἡ δύναμις
καὶ ἡ δόξα
εἰς τοὺς αἰῶνας. ᾿Αμήν.

2. Go to the east wall of the room. Hold out your right hand and draw a banishing pentagram, visualizing it in blue flame.

Once the pentagram is drawn, point your hand at the center and vibrate: **Yod Heh Vav Heh**.

3. Holding your arm out, walk in a circle toward the south. As you walk, visualize an arc of blue flame being created.

4. At the south wall, draw the pentagram again, this time saying: **Adonai**.

5. Repeat the process moving toward the west. **Eheieh**.

6. Repeat the process toward the north. **AGLA**.

7. Return to the East with your arm outstretched, completing the arc of blue flame. What you should now have visualized is a circle of blue flame studded with a blazing pentagram at each of the cardinal points:

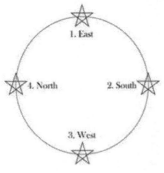

8. Return to the center of the circle, facing east, and stretch your arms out to your sides with palms upward, such that your body is in the shape of a cross.

9. Visualize the Archangel Raphael forming outside the circle at the east, and vibrate:
Ante me stat Ráphaël.
(Before me is Raphael.)

10. Visualize the Archangel Gabriel forming outside the circle at the west, and vibrate:
Post me stat Gábriel.
(Behind me is Gabriel.)

11. Visualize the Archangel Michael forming outside the circle at the south, and vibrate:
Ad déxteram meam stat Míchaël.
(At my right hand is Michael.)

12. Visualize the Archangel Uriel forming outside the circle at the north, and vibrate:
Atque ad sínistram meam stat Uriel.
(And at my left hand is Uriel.)

13. Lastly, visualize all this around you, and a brilliant gold-white six-rayed star at your back. Say:
Circumscríbor cum pentagrammátibus flammántibus, et post me stella radiórum sex lucet!
(About me flame the pentagrams, and behind me shines the six-rayed star!)

14. Close the ritual with the Sign of the Cross, as given in step 1.

14. Meditation to Increase Focus

Practice the rhythmic breath, feel your body relaxing, and empty your mind. If a stray thought pops up, do not try to fight it. Passively let it go about its way, and you'll find it the stray thought doesn't last long.

As your mind empties, you see nothing but blackness, like the void of space. Suddenly you see a faraway star, a bright dot in a sea of darkness. Fix your attention on that star, seeing it move closer or further away in your mind. It may change color, or it may change shape into a geometric design or religious symbol. But your focus stays on that object.

This exercise is harder than it looks, but don't let yourself be discouraged. If you haven't practiced concentration exercises before, it can take a week before you're able to focus on the object for more than a few minutes. In fact, the longer you stick with this exercise, the stronger you'll find your concentration in other areas of life as well.

15. Guardian Angel Meditation

1. Assume your usual meditation posture.

2. Begin the rhythmic breathing and relax yourself.

3. Once your mind is clear and your body feels relaxed, imagine yourself in a dark void, as if floating in space.

4. Off in the distance you see a white dot, like a faraway star. Imagine yourself moving toward that star.

5. The star gets larger as you move toward it. Eventually you find that it's not a star at all, but a large round door.

6. Walk through the door and feel it gently close behind you. You find yourself in a brightly-lit room with a table and two chairs.

7. You sit down on one of the chairs. Soon a figure enters the room from another door, made of light and wearing a flowing robe of pure energy.

8. The figure looks at you, and you say test it. You say to it: "Confess the name of the Lord! Confess that his coming in the flesh!"

NOTE: If the figure responds back with the name of Jesus and saying he came in the flesh, then the being is legitimate. If the being dissolves or tries to evade, then it was an impostor. When this happens you end the meditation by making the Sign of the Cross over the entity to bind it away from you, and then proceed immediately to step 10.

9. The test is passed, and the figure sits in the other chair. You begin to converse, discussing what's going on in your life while the figure talks about what it's like being a Guardian Angel and passes along any information it thinks important. Do not ask for anything; just enjoy each other's company and the conversation.

10. When the conversation is over, you thank your Guardian Angel for taking the time to talk to you, and then exit the room the way you came in, retracing your steps back to yourself.

11. Finally, you take a few breaths to center yourself, open your eyes, and the meditation is completed.

This exercise is best done regularly (once a week or so).

16. Saints Meditation

1. On your mensa or home altar, place a holy card or a statue of the Saint of your choice in the center. Either before or to the side of the image, place a candle of the Saint's color on the mensa, and you may also have a plate with food or with herbs proper to the Saint.

2. Cross yourself in the usual manner, and light the candle, saying: **I offer this candle and this food (or this herb) to Saint N., that we may come to know each other in friendship and in co-operation. Saint N., may we become fast friends, that I may follow your example here on earth, and in heaven may you intercede on my behalf before the throne of the Almighty Father.**

3. Sit comfortably in a chair and relax, using whatever relaxative/meditative procedure you desire. After that, mentally greet the Saint in your own words, or pray a chaplet to that Saint (if he or she has one), or some other suitable devotion.

4. After as long a time as feels appropriate (usually 10-20 minutes), feel free to close the meditation. **Saint N., I have enjoyed our time together. May almighty God richly bless you, and may we again meet soon.**

5. Cross yourself in the usual manner, completing the exercise.

Through this exercise, we can become closer with the Saints by talking to them as friends, inviting them into our lives to help us, and offering our help to them. This can be considered a hallmark of Christian piety, and definitely a practical application of the doctrine of the Communion of Saints.

17. Meditation on Christ's Divine Presence

This meditation works along the lines of what's called an "Act of Spiritual Communion," in that you meditate on the presence of the Triune God within you, filling you with love, and empowering you.

You begin by standing, lying down, or sitting – whichever is comfortable for you – and beginning meditation as usual with the rhythmic breath and emptying your mind.

If you are overcome with negativity, a bad mood or distraction, try this: when you exhale, visualize your negativity or distraction being breathed out through your forehead and forming into a dark grayish cloudy ball. Once you feel all the negativity has left you and formed part of that ball, visualize the ball descending through the floor and into the earth, or through the ceiling and up into space.

When you feel yourself free and relaxed, it's time to begin the meditation:

Imagine God the Father as a large, brilliant white flame filling and enveloping you. Focus on this image over the next three breaths, while saying mentally:

1st breath: **"God the Father of heaven * fills me with His power and with His love."**

2nd breath: **"The Creator of heaven and earth * Who shall judge both on the Last Day."**

3rd breath: **"Fills me * with His power and with His love."**

Afterwards, imagine God the Son in the same manner, as a large, brilliant, golden flame. Hold this image for the next three breaths, while saying mentally:

1st breath: **"Jesus Christ, Redeemer of the world * fills me with His power and with His love."**

2nd breath: "**Who died for love of us, * and Whose blood made us free.**"

3rd breath: "**Fills me * with His power and with His love.**"

Thirdly, imagine God the Holy Ghost as a large, brilliant, rose-gold flame. Hold this image for the next three breaths, while saying mentally:

1st breath: "**God, the Holy Ghost, the Paraclete * fills me with His power and with His love.**"

2nd breath: "**Who descended on the Apostles * and gives power to the Church.**"

3rd breath: "**Fills me * with His power and with His love.**"

Now concentrate on these three flames as they course through you, and feeling them fill your entire being.

Continue the rhythmic breathing while the image fades slowly from your consciousness.

Practice this meditation each day from here on out, for a minimum of three weeks; the key is to create permanent change by imprinting a permanent impression on the mind and soul. Afterwards you may continue with this exercise once a day or once every other day, whichever works best for you.

II. Prayers to Jesus, Mary, and the Saints

This chapter contains a collection of prayers and novenas both classical and contemporary, directed toward Jesus, Mary, and the Saints for their help in manifesting one's intentions. The subject matter may render this chapter more amenable to Catholic than to Protestant readers.

18-22. In Honor of Our Lord
18. Novena of Confidence to the Sacred Heart
O Lord Jesus Christ, to Thy most Sacred Heart, I confide this intention *(here mention your request)*. Only look upon me, then do what Thy Sacred Heart inspires. Let Thy Sacred Heart decide. I count on It. I trust in It. I throw myself on Its mercy. Lord Jesus! Thou wilt not fail me. Sacred Heart of Jesus, I trust in Thee. Sacred Heart of Jesus, I believe in Thy love for me. Sacred Heart of Jesus, Thy kingdom come.

O Sacred Heart of Jesus, I have asked Thee for many favors, but I earnestly implore this one. Take it, place it in Thy open, broken Heart; and when the Eternal Father looks upon it, covered with Thy Precious Blood, He will not refuse it. It will be no longer my prayer, but Thine, O Jesus, O Sacred Heart of Jesus, I place all my trust in Thee. Let me not be disappointed. Amen.

19. Novena in urgent Need to the Infant Jesus of Prague
To be said at the same time for nine consecutive hours, or for nine days.

O Jesus, who hast said, "Ask and you shall receive, seek and you shall find, knock and it shall be opened to you," through the intercession of Mary, Thy most holy Mother, I knock, I seek, I ask that my prayer be granted.
Mention your request

O Jesus, who hast said, "All that you ask of the Father in My Name, He will grant you," through the intercession of Mary, Thy most holy Mother, I humbly and urgently ask Thy Father in Thy Name that my prayer be granted.
Mention your request

O Jesus, who hast said, "Heaven and earth shall pass away, but My word shall not pass," through the intercession of Mary, Thy most holy Mother, I feel confident that my prayer will be granted.
Mention your request

20. Prayer for the Sick

Dear Jesus, Divine Physician and Healer of the sick, we turn to you in this time of illness. O dearest comforter of the troubled, alleviate our worry and sorrow with your gentle love, and grant us the grace and strength to accept this burden. Dear God, we place our worries in your hands. We place our sick under your care and humbly ask that you restore your servant to health again. Above all, grant us the grace to acknowledge your will and know that whatever you do, you do for the love of us. Amen.

21. Make Me an Instrument of Your Peace

Lord, make me an instrument of Your peace. Where there is hatred, let me sow love; where there is injury, pardon; where there is doubt, faith; where there is despair, hope; where there is darkness, light; where there is sadness, joy. O, Divine Master, grant that I may not so much seek to be consoled as to console; to be understood as to understand; to be loved as to love; For it is in giving that we receive; it is in pardoning that we are pardoned; it is in dying that we are born again to eternal life.

22. Prayer before Study or Instructions

Incomprehensible Creator, the true Fountain of light and only Author of all knowledge: deign, we beseech Thee, to enlighten our understanding, and to remove from us all darkness of sin and ignorance. Thou, who makest eloquent the tongues of those who lack utterance, direct our tongues, and pour on our lips the grace of thy blessing. Give us a diligent and obedient spirit, quickness of apprehension, capacity of retaining, and the powerful assistance of Thy holy grace; that what we hear or learn we may apply to Thy honor and the eternal salvation of our own souls. Amen.

23-24. To the Holy Family
23. Prayer in Honor of the Holy Family
LORD Jesus Christ, who, being made subject to Mary and Joseph, didst consecrate domestic life by Thine ineffable virtues; grant that we, with the assistance of both, may be taught by the example of Thy Holy Family and may attain to its everlasting fellowship. Who livest and reignest forever. Amen.

24. Prayer for a Good Husband or Wife
O Jesus, lover of the young, the dearest Friend I have, in all confidence I open my heart to You to beg Your light and assistance in the important task of planning my future. Give me the light of Your grace, that I may decide wisely concerning the person who is to be my partner through life. Dearest Jesus, send me such a one whom in Your divine wisdom You judge best suited to be united with me in marriage. May her/his character reflect some of the traits of Your own Sacred Heart. May s/he be upright, loyal, pure, sincere and noble, so that with united efforts and with pure and unselfish love we both may strive to perfect ourselves in soul and body, as well as the children it may please You to entrust to our care. Bless our friendship before marriage, that sin may have no part in it. May our mutual love bind us so closely, that our future home may ever be most like Your own at Nazareth.

O Mary Immaculate, sweet Mother of the young, to your special care I entrust the decision I am to make as to my future wife/husband. You are my guiding Star! Direct me to the person with whom I can best cooperate in doing God's Holy Will, with whom I can live in peace, love and harmony in this life, and attain to eternal joys in the next. Amen.

25-27. In Honor of Mary

25. To our Lady of Perpetual Help

O Mother of Perpetual Help! Grant that I may ever invoke your most powerful name, which is the safeguard of the living and the salvation of the dying. O purest Mary! O sweetest Mary! Let your name henceforth be ever on my lips. Delay not, O Blessed Lady, to succor me whenever I call on you. In all my temptations, in all my needs, I will never cease to call on you ever repeating your sacred name. Mary, Mary. Oh, what a consolation, what sweetness, what confidence, what emotion fills my soul when I utter your sacred name, or even only think of you! I thank the Lord for having given you, for my good, so sweet, so powerful, so lovely a name. But I will not be content with merely uttering your name. Let my love for you prompt me ever to hail you Mother of Perpetual Help.

Mother of Perpetual Help, pray for me and grant me the favor I confidently ask of you.
Hail Mary *(3 times)*.

26. Hail, Most Venerable Queen of Peace

Hail, most venerable Queen of Peace, most holy Mother of God, through the Sacred Heart of Jesus, thy Son, the Prince of Peace, procure for us the cessation of His anger, that so He may reign over us in peace. Remember, O most gracious Virgin Mary, that never was it known that anyone who sought thy intercession was left forsaken. Inspired with this confidence, I come unto thee. Despise not my petitions, O Mother of the Word, but graciously here and grant my prayer. O merciful, O kind, O sweet Virgin Mary. Amen.

27. Novena to the Blessed Virgin Mary
In the name of the Father, and of the Son, and of the Holy Ghost. *R.* Amen.

We fly to thy patronage, O holy Mother of God; despise not our petitions in our necessities, but deliver us always from all dangers, O glorious and blessed Virgin. *R.* Amen.

V. Hail, Mary, full of grace, the Lord is with thee.
R. Thou hast brought forth Him who made thee, and ever remain a virgin.

Memorare to Mary
Remember, O most gracious Virgin Mary, that never was it known that anyone who fled to thy protection, implored thy help, or sought thy intercession, was left unaided. Inspired with this confidence, we fly unto thee, O Virgin of virgins and Mother; to thee do we come; before thee we stand, sinful and sorrowful; O Mother of the Word Incarnate, despise not our petitions, but in thy mercy hear and answer us. *R.* Amen.

V. Blessed art thou among women.
R. And blessed is the fruit of thy womb.
O pure and immaculate and likewise blessed Virgin, who art the sinless mother of thy Son, the mighty Lord of the universe, thou who art inviolate and altogether holy, the hope of the hopeless and sinful, we sing thy praises. We bless thee as full of every grace, thou who borest the God-Man: we all bow low before thee; we invoke thee and implore thy aid. *R.* Amen.

Pause here to name your petitions.

V. O Mary, conceived without sin,
R. Pray for us who have recourse to thee.
Let us pray.
Holy Mary, succor the miserable, help the faint-hearted, comfort the sorrowful, pray for the people, plead for the clergy, intercede for all women consecrated to God; may all who keep thy holy commemoration feel now thy help and protection. Be ever ready to assist us when we pray, and bring back to us the answers to our prayers. Make it thy continual care to pray for the people of God, thou who, blessed by God, merited to bear the Redeemer of the world, who lives and reigns for ever and ever. *R.* Amen.

28-30. In Honor of St. Joseph
28. To thee, O blessed Joseph
To thee, O blessed Joseph, do we come in our tribulation, and having implored the help of thy most holy Spouse, we confidently invoke thy patronage also. Through that charity which bound thee to the immaculate Virgin Mother of God and through the paternal love with which thou embraced the Child Jesus, we humbly beg thee to graciously regard the inheritance which Jesus Christ has purchased by his Blood, and with thy power and strength to aid us in our necessities.

O most watchful Guardian of the Holy Family, defend the chosen children of Jesus Christ; O most loving father, ward off from us every contagion of error and corrupting influence; O our most mighty protector, be propitious to us and from heaven assist us in our struggle with the power of darkness; and, as once thou rescued the Child Jesus from deadly peril, so now protect God's Holy Church from the snares of the enemy and from all adversity; shield, too, each one of us by thy constant protection, so that, supported by thy example and thy aid, we may be able to live piously, to die holy, and to obtain eternal happiness in heaven. Amen.

29. Remember, O Most Pure Spouse of the Virgin Mary

Remember, o most pure Spouse of the Virgin Mary, my sweet Protector Saint Joseph, never was it heard that anyone who implored thy help nor sought thy intercession was left unaided. Inspired by this confidence I come to thee and to thee do I fervently commend myself. Despise not my petitions, I beseech thee, foster Father of the Redeemer, but graciously hear them. Amen.

30. Prayer for Success in Work

Glorious St. Joseph, model of all those who are devoted to labor, obtain for me the grace to work conscientiously, putting the call of duty above my many sins; to work with thankfulness and joy, considering it an honor to employ and develop, by means of labor, the gifts received from God; to work with order, peace, prudence and patience, never surrendering to weariness or difficulties; to work, above all, with purity of intention, and with detachment from self, having always death before my eyes and the account which I must render of time lost, of talents wasted, of good omitted, of vain complacency in success so fatal to the work of God. All for Jesus, all for Mary, all after thy example, O Patriarch Joseph. Such shall be my motto in life and death. Amen.

31-41. In Honor of the Angels

Michael
31. Prayer to Saint Michael
St. Michael the Archangel, defend us in battle; be our defense against the wickedness and snares of the devil. May God rebuke him, we humbly pray. And do thou, O prince of the heavenly host, by the power of God thrust into hell Satan and all the evil spirits who prowl about the world for the ruin of souls. Amen.

32. O Most Glorious Prince
O most glorious Prince, Saint Michael the Archangel, I, thy most humble servant, salute thee through the most beloved Heart of Jesus Christ which I lovingly offer for the increase of thy joy and thy glory. I give thanks to God for the blessedness which He brings to thee and with which He wishes to honor and exalt thee above all the other Angels. I especially commend myself to thy care in life and death. Be with me now and always, especially at the end of my life. Kindly console me, strengthen me, and protect me. Obtain for me an increase in faith, hope, and charity. Do not permit me to stray from the holy faith, nor fall into the snare of desperation, nor to take for granted good works, which I am engaged in through the grace of God. Obtain for me pardon of my sins, humility, patience and the other virtues, true perseverance in goodness, and the final grace that I may give glory to God with thee forever. Amen.

Gabriel
33. O Strength of God
O strength of God, Saint Gabriel, thou who announced to the Virgin Mary the incarnation of the only-begotten Son of God, I praise thee and honor thee, O elect spirit. I humbly beg thee, with Jesus Christ our Savior and with His Blessed Mother, to be my advocate. I also pray that thou wouldst

comfort me and strengthen me in all my difficulties, lest at any time I may be overcome by temptation and I might offend God by sinning. Amen.

34. Prayer to St. Gabriel, for Intercession
O Blessed Archangel Gabriel, we beseech thee, do thou intercede for us at the throne of divine Mercy in our present necessities, that as thou didst announce to Mary the mystery of the Incarnation, so through thy prayers and patronage in heaven we may obtain the benefits of the same, and sing the praise of God forever in the land of the living. Amen.

35. Prayer to St. Gabriel, for Others
O loving messenger of the Incarnation, descend upon all those for whom I wish peace and happiness. Spread your wings over the cradles of the new-born babes, O thou who didst announce the coming of the Infant Jesus. Give to the young a lily petal from the virginal scepter in your hand. Cause the Ave Maria to re-echo in all hearts that they may find grace and joy through Mary. Finally, recall the sublime words spoken on the day of the Annunciation – "Nothing is impossible with God," and repeat them in hours of trial – to all I love – that their confidence in Our Lord may be reanimated, when all human help fails. Amen.

Raphael
36. O Heavenly Doctor
O heavenly doctor and most faithful companion, saint Raphael, thou who didst restore sight to the elder Tobit, and didst escort the younger Tobias throughout his appointed journey and kept him safe and sound, be the doctor of my body and soul. Dispel the darkness of my ignorance, and assist me in the dangerous journey of this life always, until thou leadeth me to my heavenly homeland. Amen.

37. Prayer to Saint Raphael, the Archangel

Glorious Archangel, Saint Raphael, great prince of the heavenly Court, you are illustrious for your gifts of wisdom and grace. You are a guide of those who journey by land, or sea, or air, consoler of the afflicted, and refuge of sinners. I beg you, assist me in all my needs and in all the sufferings of this life, as once you helped the young Tobias on his travels. Because you are the "medicine of God" I humbly pray you to heal the many infirmities of my soul and the ills that afflict my body. I especially ask of you the favor of *(here name your request)* and the great grace of purity to prepare me to be the temple of the Holy Ghost. Amen.

38. Prayer to St. Raphael, Angel of Happy Meetings

O Raphael, lead us towards those we are waiting for, those who are waiting for us! Raphael, Angel of Happy Meetings, lead us by the hand towards those we are looking for! May all our movements, all their movements, be guided by your Light and transfigured by your Joy. Angel Guide of Tobias, lay the request we now address to you at the feet of Him on whose unveiled Face you are privileged to gaze. Lonely and tired, crushed by the separations and sorrows of earth, we feel the need of calling to you and of pleading for the protection of your wings, so that we may not be as strangers in the Province of Joy, all ignorant of the concerns of our country. Remember the weak, you who are strong--you whose home lies beyond the region of thunder, in a land that is always peaceful, always serene, and bright with the resplendent glory of God. Amen.

Guardian Angels
39. Angel of God (Guardian Angel Prayer)

Angel of God, my guardian dear,
To whom his love commits me here;
Ever this night be at my side,
To light and guard, to rule and guide. Amen.

40. Prayer to One's Guardian Angel

I believe that thou art the holy angel appointed by almighty God to watch over me. On this account, I beg and humbly implore thee, through Him who hast ordained thee to this task, that in this life thou wouldst always and everywhere guard me, wretched, weak, and unworthy that I am. Protect and defend me from all evil, and when God has bid my soul to leave this world, permit not the devil to have any power over it. Rather that thou wouldst gently take it from my body and lead it sweetly unto the bosom of Abraham with the biding and assistance of God our Creator and Savior, who is blessed for ever. Amen.

41. Prayer before Starting on a Journey

My holy Angel Guardian, ask the Lord to bless the journey which I undertake, that it may profit the health of my soul and body; that I may reach its end, and that, returning safe and sound, I may find my family in good health. Do thou guard, guide and preserve us. Amen.

42-95. In Honor of the Saints

42. St. Alphonsus De Liguori's Conclusion to a Short Treatise on Prayer

Let us pray, then, and let us always be asking for grace, if we wish to be saved. Let prayer be our most delightful occupation; let prayer be the exercise of our whole life. And when we are asking for particular graces, let us always pray for the grace to continue to pray for the future; because if we leave off praying we shall be lost. There is nothing easier than prayer. What does it cost us to say, Lord, stand by me! Lord, help me! Give me Thy love! And the like? What can be easier than this? But if we do not do so, we cannot be saved. Let us pray, then, and let us always shelter ourselves behind the intercession of Mary: "Let us seek for grace, and let us seek it through Mary," says St. Bernard. And when we recommend ourselves to Mary, let us be sure that she hears us and obtains for us whatever we want. She cannot lack either the power or the will to help us, as the same saint says: "Neither means nor will can be wanting to her." And St. Augustine addresses her: "Remember, O most pious Lady, that it has never been heard that any one who fled to thy protection was forsaken." Remember that the case has never occurred of a person having recourse to thee, and having been abandoned. Ah, no, says St. Bonaventure, he who invokes Mary, finds salvation; and therefore he calls her "the salvation of those who invoke her." Let us, then, in our prayers always invoke Jesus and Mary; and let us never neglect to pray.

I have done. But before concluding, I cannot help saying how grieved I feel when I see that though the Holy Scriptures and the Fathers so often recommend the practice of prayer, yet so few other religious writers, or confessors, or preachers, ever speak of it; or if they do speak of it, just touch upon it in a cursory way, and leave it. But I, seeing the necessity of prayer, say, that the great lesson which all spiritual books should inculcate on their readers, all preachers on their hearers, and all confessors on their penitents, is this, to pray always; thus they should admonish them to pray; pray, and never give up praying. If you pray, you will be certainly saved; if you do not pray, you will be certainly damned.

St. Anne
43. To Saint Anne
Good St. Anne, you were especially favored by God to be the mother of the most holy Virgin Mary, the Mother of our Savior. By your power with your most pure daughter and with her divine Son, kindly obtain for us the grace and the favor we now seek. Please secure for us also forgiveness of our past sins, the strength to perform faithfully our daily

duties and the help we need to persevere in the love of Jesus and Mary. Amen.

44. For the Sick
O Good Saint Anne, so justly called the Mother of the infirm, the health of those who suffer from disease, look kindly upon the sick person for whom I pray. Alleviate their sufferings, cause them to sanctify them by patience, and by complete submission to divine will. Finally deign to obtain health for them and with it the firm resolution to honor Jesus, Mary and yourself by the faithful performance of their Christian duties. Amen.

St. Anthony
45. Unfailing Prayer to St. Anthony
"Blessed be God in His Angels and in His Saints"
O Holy St. Anthony, gentlest of Saints, your love for God and Charity for His creatures, made you worthy, when on earth, to possess miraculous powers. Encouraged by this thought, I implore you to obtain for me *(request)*. O gentle and loving St. Anthony, whose heart was ever full of human sympathy, whisper my petition into the ears of the sweet Infant Jesus, who loved to be folded in your arms; and the gratitude of my heart will ever be yours. Amen.

46. Saint Anthony of Padua
Holy Saint Anthony, gentle and powerful in your help, your love for God and charity for His creatures, made you worthy, when on earth, to possess miraculous powers. Miracles waited on your word, which you were always ready to request for those in trouble or anxiety. Encouraged by this thought, I implore you to obtain for me (request). The answer to my prayer may require a miracle. Even so, you are the Saint of miracles. Gentle and loving Saint Anthony, whose heart is ever full of human sympathy, take my petition to the Infant Savior for whom you have such a

great love, and the gratitude of my heart will ever be yours.
Amen.

47. Saint Anthony, Consoler of the Afflicted
Dear St. Anthony, comforting the sorrowful is a Christian
duty and a work of mercy. By word, attitude, and deed I
should try to brighten their days and make their burden
easier to bear. St. Anthony, Consoler of the Afflicted, may I
remember when helping someone in sorrow that I am
helping Christ Himself. Kindly mention my pressing needs
to Him. *(Name your petitions)*.

48. Saint Anthony, Disperser of Devils
Dear St. Anthony, it is still as St. Peter said: The devil
prowls about, lion-like, looking for someone to devour. I
confess that I don't always resist him; I sometimes toy with
temptation. St. Anthony, Disperser of Devils, remind me of
my duty to avoid all occasions of sin. May I always pray in
temptation that I may remain loyal to my Lord Jesus. Pray
for my other intentions, please. *(Name them.)*

49. Saint Anthony, Example of Humility
Dear St. Anthony, after all these years in the school of
Christ, I still haven't learned the lesson of true humility.
My feelings are easily ruffled. Quick to take offense, I am
slow to forgive. St. Anthony, Example of Humility, teach
me the importance and necessity of this Christian virtue. In
the presence of Jesus, who humbled Himself and whom the
Father exalted, remember also these special intentions of
mine. *(Name them.)*

50. Saint Anthony, Generator of Charity
Dear St. Anthony, God wants us to see Christ, our brother,
in everyone and love Him truly in word and in deed. God
wills that we share with others the joy of His boundless
love. St. Anthony, Generator of Charity, remember me in

the Father's presence, that I may be generous in sharing the joy of His love. Remember also the special intentions I now entrust to you. (*Name them.*)

51. Saint Anthony, Guide of Pilgrims
Dear St. Anthony, we are all pilgrims. We came from God and we are going to Him. He who created us will welcome us at journey's end. The Lord Jesus is preparing a place for all His brothers and sisters. St. Anthony, Guide of Pilgrims, direct my steps in the straight path. Protect me until I am safely home in heaven. Help me in all my needs and difficulties. (*Name them.*)

52. Saint Anthony, Liberator of Prisoners
Dear St. Anthony, I am imprisoned by walls of selfishness, prejudice, suspicion. I am enslaved by human respect and the fear of other people's opinions of me. St. Anthony, Liberator of Prisoners, tear down my prison walls. Break the chains that hold me captive. Make me free with the freedom Christ has won for me. To your powerful intercession I also recommend these intentions. (*Name them.*)

53. Saint Anthony, Martyr of Desire
Dear St. Anthony, you became a Franciscan with the hope of shedding your blood for Christ. In God's plan for you, your thirst for martyrdom was never to be satisfied. St. Anthony, Martyr of Desire, pray that I may become less afraid to stand up and be counted as a follower of the Lord Jesus. Intercede also for my other intentions. (*Name them.*)

54. Saint Anthony, Model of Perfection
Dear St. Anthony, you took the words of Jesus seriously, "Be perfect, even as your heavenly Father is perfect." The Church honors you as a Christian hero, a man wholly dedicated to God's glory and the good of the redeemed. St.

Anthony, Model of Perfection, ask Jesus to strengthen my good dispositions and to make me more like you, more like Him. Obtain for me the other favors I need. (*Name them.*)

55. Saint Anthony, Performer of Miracles

Dear St. Anthony, your prayers obtained miracles during your lifetime. You still seem to move at ease in the realm of minor and major miracles. St. Anthony, Performer of Miracles, please obtain for me the blessings God holds in reserve who serve Him. Pray that I may be worthy of the promises my Lord Jesus attaches to confident prayer. (*Mention your special intentions.*)

56. Saint Anthony, Restorer of Sight to the Blind

Dear St. Anthony, you recall the Gospel episode about the blind man who, partly healed, could see men "looking like walking trees." After a second laying-on of Jesus's hands, he could see perfectly. St. Anthony, Restorer of Sight to the Blind, please sharpen my spiritual vision. May I see people, not as trees or numbers, but as sons and daughters of the Most High. Help me in my pressing needs. (*Name your special intentions.*)

57. Saint Anthony, Restorer of Speech to the Mute

Dear St. Anthony, how tongue-tied I can be when I should be praising God and defending the oppressed. My cowardice often strikes me dumb; I am afraid to open my mouth. St. Anthony, Restorer of Speech to the Mute, release me from my fears. Teach me to praise God and to champion the rights of those unjustly treated. Please remember also all my intentions. (*Name them.*)

58. Saint Anthony, Zealous for Justice

Dear St. Anthony, you were prompt to fulfill all justice. You gave God and His creation the service He required from you. You respected other people's rights and treated them with kindness and understanding. St. Anthony, Zealous for Justice, teach me the beauty of this virtue. Make me prompt to fulfill all justice toward God and toward all creation. Help me also in my pressing needs. (*Name them.*)

St. Blase

59. O glorious Saint Blase, who by thy martyrdom has left to the Church a precious witness to the faith, obtain for us the grace to preserve within ourselves this divine gift, and to defend, without human respect, both by word and example, the truth of that same faith, which is so wickedly attacked and slandered in these our times. Thou who didst miraculously cure a little child when it was at the point of death by reason of an affliction of the throat, grant us thy powerful protection in like misfortunes; and, above all, obtain for us the grace of Christian mortification together with a faithful observance of the precepts of the Church, which may keep us from offending Almighty God. Amen.

St. Christopher

60. St. Chistopher, patron of travellers, to you I entrust myself and those who will accompany me on my journey, praying you to keep us from all harm and to bring us safely to our destination. O great saint, true Christ-bearer, who converted multitudes to the Christian faith and who for love of Jesus Christ suffered cruel torments in your martyrdom, I implore your intercession to enable me to avoid every sin, the only real evil. Preserve me and those dear to me against the forces of the elements, such as earthquakes, tornadoes, lightning, fire and flood, and guide us safely through the dangers of this life to the eternal shores. Amen.

61. Patron of Motorists

Dear Saint, you have inherited a beautiful name – Christopher – as a result of a wonderful legend that while carrying people across a raging stream you also carried the Child Jesus. Teach us to be true "Christ-bearers" to those who do not know Him. Protect all drivers who often transport those who bear Christ within them. Amen.

St. Dymphna
62. Prayer to St. Dymphna – Charity
You are celebrated St. Dymphna, for your goodness to others. Both in your lifetime, and even more in the ages since, you have again and again demonstrated your concern for those who are mentally disturbed or emotionally troubled. Kindly secure for me, then, some measure of your own serene love, and ask our Lord to give us a share in His life and boundless charity. Amen.

63. Prayer to St. Dymphna – Chastity
Most pure virgin, St. Dymphna, we live at a time when many are intent on satisfying every carnal appetite. Your single-minded dedication to Christ alone is providential and inspiring. Please help us by your power with God to see life in proportion as you did. With your aid we propose to perform all our actions for a pure motive, and promptly to resist all our evil inclinations. Amen.

64. Prayer to St. Dymphna – Faith
Dear St. Dymphna, you gave us an example in your own life of firm faith. Neither flattery, earthly rewards nor the threat of death caused you to waver in your fidelity to God. Please help us then, amid the uncertainties of life, to imitate your wholehearted dedication to Christ. Be good enough to come to our aid in our need, and pray for us to God. Amen.

65. Prayer to St. Dymphna – Fortitude
Courageous St. Dymphna, your strength was from God. His grace enabled you to resist evil, and to prefer exile to a life of sinful luxury. Christ's own power preserved you faithful

to Him in life and in death. In your kindness help us to imitate your example in little things, and gain for us fortitude to bear with the misfortunes we meet, and strength to overcome our weakness. Amen.

66. Prayer to St. Dymphna – Hope
Good St. Dymphna, you placed all your hope in Christ's promises, and sacrificed even your life in that hope. The Lord, God, rewarded your constancy by making your name known and loved over many centuries by the thousands whom you have aided in time of difficulty. Please assist us now in our present necessity, and intercede before God for our intentions. Obtain for us a firm hope like your own in God's unfailing protection. Amen.

67. Prayer to St. Dymphna – Justice
Admirable St. Dymphna, how just you were to all whom you encountered, and how careful you were to give every person his due, and more than he might desire or expect. By your power with God please come to assist us to be just to all we meet, and even to be generous in giving everyone more than strict justice requires. Amen.

68. Prayer to St. Dymphna – Perseverance
Most faithful St. Dymphna, you remained true to your baptismal promises to the very end. You are, therefore, honored, known, and loved after 1,400 years by people you have aided all over the world. We do not know how long or short a time is left to us of this life here, but help us in any case to be faithful to God to the end. Please gain for us the grace to live one day at a time as if each were to be our last. Amen.

69. Prayer to St. Dymphna – Prudence
You were marked in life, St. Dymphna, by a high degree of prudence. You sought and followed the advice of your

confessor and spiritual guide. You fled from temptation even when it meant exile and poverty. In your last extremity you chose to die rather than offend God. Please help us now by your merits not only to know what is right, but procure for us also the strength to do it. Amen.

70. Prayer to St. Dymphna – Temperance

Generous St. Dymphna, like all Christ's martyrs you gained this crowning grace because you prepared for it by a life of self denial. By faithfulness in smaller things you were ready for your final trial. Please teach us by your example and help to use the good things of life so that we may not miss our chance for life eternal. Help us, too, to watch and pray for ourselves and others. Amen.

71. Saint Dymphna

Lord, our God, you graciously chose St. Dymphna as patroness of those afflicted with mental and nervous disorders. She is thus an inspiration and a symbol of charity to the thousands who ask her intercession. Please grant, Lord, through the prayers of this pure youthful martyr, relief and consolation to all suffering such trials, and especially those for whom we pray. (*Here mention those for whom you wish to pray*). We beg you, Lord, to hear the prayers of St. Dymphna on our behalf. Grant all those for whom we pray patience in their sufferings and resignation to your divine will. Please fill them with hope, and grant them the relief and cure they so much desire. We ask this through Christ our Lord who suffered agony in the garden. Amen.

St. Francis of Assisi

72. Dear Saint, once worldly and vain, you became humble and poor for the sake of Jesus and had extraordinary love for the Crucified, which showed itself in your body by the stigmata, the imprints of Christ's Sacred Wounds. In our

selfish and sensual age, how greatly we need your secret that draws countless men and women to imitate you. Teach us also great love for the poor and unswerving loyalty to the Vicar of Christ, our Holy Father the Pope. Amen.

St. Francis Xavier Cabrini

73. Great St. Francis, well beloved and full of charity, in union with you I reverently adore the Divine Majesty, and since I specially rejoice in the singular gifts of grace bestowed on you in life and of glory after death, I give thanks to God, and beg of you, with all the affection of my heart, that by your powerful intercession you may obtain for me above all things the grace to live a holy life and die a holy death. Moreover, I beg of you to obtain for me (*here mention special spiritual or temporal favor*); but if what I ask does not tend to the glory of God and the greater good of my soul, do you, I beseech you, obtain for me what will more certainly attain these ends. Amen.
(Our Father, Hail Mary, Glory Be).

St. Gerard Majella

74. For Motherhood

Good St. Gerard, powerful intercessor before the throne of God, wonder-worker of our day, I call upon you and seek your aid. You know that my husband and I desire the gift of a child. Please present our fervent plea to the Creator of life from whom all parenthood proceeds and beseech him to bless us with a child whom we may raise as his child and heir of heaven. Amen.

75. In thanks for a Safe Delivery

Good St. Gerard, patron of mothers, assist me in thanking God for the great gift of motherhood. During the months of my waiting, I learned to call upon you and placed the safety of my child and myself under your powerful protection. The great lesson of your trust in God sustained me; your slogan, "God will provide," became my hope and consolation. I thank God for a healthy and normal baby and my own good health. Help me to prize the great treasure of motherhood and obtain for me the grace to raise my child as a child of God. In gratitude, I will continue to call upon you and will tell other mothers about their special patron and friend. Amen.

76. For Special Intentions

Almighty and loving Father, I thank you for giving St. Gerard to us as a most appealing model and powerful friend. By his example, he showed us how to love and trust you. You have showered many blessings on those who call upon him. For your greater glory and my welfare, please grant me the favors which I ask in his name. (*Here mention them privately*) And you, my powerful patron, intercede for me before the throne of God. Draw near to that throne and do not leave it until you have been heard. O good saint, to you I address my fervent prayers; graciously accept them and let me experience in some way the effects of your powerful intercession. Amen.

77. Prayer of the Expectant Mother to Saint Gerard Majella

O Great Saint Gerard, beloved servant of Jesus Christ, perfect imitator of thy meek and humble Savior, and devoted Child of the Mother of God: enkindle within my heart one spark of that heavenly fire of charity which glowed in thine and made thee a seraph of love. O glorious Saint Gerard, because when falsely accused of crime, thou didst bear, like thy Divine Master, without murmur or complaint, the calumnies of wicked men, thou hast been raised up by God as Patron and Protector of expectant mothers. Preserve me from danger and from excessive pains accompanying childbirth, and shield the child which I now carry, that he or she may see the light of day and receive the lustral waters of baptism, through Jesus Christ our Lord.

(*say nine Hail Mary's, one for each month of pregnancy*).

78. For a Sick Child

St. Gerard, who, like the Savior, loved children so tenderly and by your prayers freed many from disease and even death, listen to us who are pleading for our sick child. We thank God for the great gift of our son (daughter) and ask him to restore our child to health if such be his holy will. This favor, we beg of you through your love for all children and mothers. Amen.

St. John Bosco

79. O glorious Saint John Bosco, who in order to lead young people to the feet of the divine Master and to mould them in the light of faith and Christian morality didst heroically sacrifice thyself to the very end of thy life and didst set up a proper religious Institute destined to endure and to bring to the farthest boundaries of the earth thy glorious work, obtain also for us from Our Lord a holy love for young people who are exposed to so many seductions in order that we may generously spend ourselves in supporting them against the snares of the devil, in keeping them safe from the dangers of the world, and in guiding them, pure and holy, in the path that leads to God. Amen.

St. Jude

80. Prayer to Saint Jude - Patron of Desperate Causes
Saint Jude, apostle of Christ, the Church honors and prays to you universally as the patron of hopeless and difficult cases. Pray for us in our needs. Make use, we implore you, of this powerful privilege given to you to bring visible and speedy help where help is needed. Pray that we humbly accept trials and disappointments and mistakes which are apart of human nature. Let us see the reflection of the

sufferings of Christ in our daily trials and tribulations. Let us see in a spirit of great faith and hope the part we even now share in the joy of Christ's resurrection, and which we long to share fully in heaven. Intercede that we may again experience this joy in answer to our present needs if it is God's Will. *(Make request here...)* Amen

81. Most holy Apostle St. Jude, faithful servant and friend of Jesus, the name of the traitor who delivered the beloved Master into the hands of His enemies has caused you to be forgotten by many, but the Church honors and invokes you universally as the patron of hopeless cases, of things despaired of. Pray for me who am so miserable; make use, I implore you, of this particular privilege accorded to you, to bring visible and speedy help, where help is almost despaired of. Come to my assistance in this great need, that I may receive the consolations and succor of Heaven in all my necessities, tribulations and sufferings, particularly *(here make your request)*, and that I may bless God with you and all the elect forever. I promise you, O blessed St. Jude, to be ever mindful of this great favor, and I will never cease to honor you as my special and powerful patron and to do all in my power to encourage devotion to you. Amen.

82. St. Jude, glorious Apostle, faithful servant and friend of Jesus, the name of the traitor has caused you to be forgotten by many, but the true Church invokes you universally as the Patron of things despaired of; pray for me, that finally I may receive the consolations and the succor of Heaven in all my necessities, tribulations, and sufferings, particularly (here make your request), and that I may bless God with the Elect throughout Eternity. Amen.

St. Lucy
83. Saint Lucy, whose beautiful name signifies light, by the light of Faith which God bestowed upon you, increase and

preserve his light in my soul, so that I may avoid evil, be zealous in the performance of good works, and abhor nothing so much as the blindness and the darkness of evil and sin. Obtain for me, by your intercession with God, perfect vision for my bodily eyes and the grace to use them for God's greater honor and glory and the salvation of souls. St. Lucy, virgin and martyr, hear my prayers and obtain my petitions. Amen.

St. Martin de Porres

84. To you Saint Martin de Porres we prayerfully lift up our hearts filled with serene confidence and devotion. Mindful of your unbounded and helpful charity to all levels of society and also of your meekness and humility of heart, we offer our petitions to you. Pour out upon our families the precious gifts of your solicitous and generous intercession; show to the people of every race and every color the paths of unity and of justice; implore from our Father in heaven the coming of his kingdom, so that through mutual benevolence in God men may increase the fruits of grace and merit the rewards of eternal life. Amen.

St. Monica

85. Prayer to St. Monica - Patroness of Mothers Exemplary
Mother of the great Augustine, for 30 years you perseveringly pursued your wayward son with love and affection and pardon and counsel and powerful cries to Heaven. Intercede for all mothers in our day so that they may learn to draw their children to God and to His Holy Church. Teach them how to remain close to their children, even the prodigal sons and daughters who have sadly gone so far astray. Amen.

St. Patrick

<u>86. Lorica of Saint Patrick (By St. Patrick, c.a. 377)</u>

I arise today
Through a mighty strength, the invocation of the Trinity,
Through a belief in the Threeness,
Through confession of the Oneness
Of the Creator of creation.

I arise today
Through the strength of Christ's birth and His baptism,
Through the strength of His crucifixion and His burial,
Through the strength of His resurrection and His ascension,

Through the strength of His descent
    for the judgment of doom.

I arise today
Through the strength of the love of cherubim,
In obedience of angels,
In service of archangels,
In the hope of resurrection to meet with reward,
In the prayers of patriarchs,
In preachings of the apostles,
In faiths of confessors,
In innocence of virgins,
In deeds of righteous men.

I arise today
Through the strength of heaven;
Light of the sun,
Splendor of fire,
Speed of lightning,
Swiftness of the wind,
Depth of the sea,
Stability of the earth,
Firmness of the rock.

I arise today
Through God's strength to pilot me;
God's might to uphold me,
God's wisdom to guide me,
God's eye to look before me,
God's ear to hear me,
God's word to speak for me,
God's hand to guard me,
God's way to lie before me,
God's shield to protect me,
God's hosts to save me
From snares of the devil,
From temptations of vices,
From every one who desires me ill,
Afar and anear,
Alone or in a mulitude.

I summon today all these powers between me and evil,
Against every cruel merciless power that opposes
     my body and soul,
Against incantations of false prophets,
Against black laws of pagandom,
Against false laws of heretics,
Against craft of idolatry,
Against spells of women and smiths and wizards,
Against every knowledge that corrupts
     man's body and soul.
Christ shield me today
Against poison, against burning,
Against drowning, against wounding,
So that reward may come to me in abundance.

Christ with me,
Christ before me,
Christ behind me,
Christ in me,

Christ beneath me,
Christ above me,
 Christ on my right,
Christ on my left,
Christ when I lie down,
Christ when I sit down,
Christ in the heart of every man who thinks of me,
Christ in the mouth of every man who speaks of me,
Christ in the eye that sees me,
Christ in the ear that hears me.
I arise today
Through a mighty strength, the invocation of the Trinity,
Through a belief in the Threeness,
Through a confession of the Oneness
Of the Creator of creation

St. Peregrine, the "Cancer Saint"

87. Glorious Wonder-Worker, St. Peregrine, you answered
the divine call , with a ready spirit, and forsook all the
comforts of the world to dedicate yourself to God in the
Order of His most Holy Mother. You labored manfully for
the salvation of souls; and in union with Jesus Crucified
you endured the most painful sufferings with such patience
as to deserve to be healed miraculously of an incurable
cancer-in your leg by a touch of His divine hand. Obtain for
me the grace to answer every call of God and to fulfill His
will in all the events of life. Enkindle in my heart a
consuming zeal for the salvation of souls; deliver me from
the infirmities that afflict my body (*especially...*). Obtain
for me also perfect resignation to the sufferings it may
please God to send me, so that, imitating our Crucified
Savior and His Sorrowful Mother, I may merit eternal glory
in heaven. Amen.

St. Peregrine, pray for me and for all who invoke your aid.
(3 times).

St. Peter

88. O glorious Saint Peter, who, in return for thy strong and generous faith, thy profound and sincere humility, and they burning love, wast rewarded by Jesus Christ with singular privileges, and, in particular, with the leadership of the other Apostles and the primacy of the whole Church, of which thou wast made the foundation stone, do thou obtain for us the grace of a lively faith, that shall not fear to profess itself openly, in its entirety and in all of its manifestations, even to the shedding of blood, if occasion should demand it, and to sacrifice of life itself rather than surrender. Obtain for us likewise, a sincere loyalty to our holy mother, the Church; grant that we may ever remain most closely and sincerely united to the Roman Pontiff, who is the heir of thy faith and of thy authority, the one, true, visible Head of the Catholic Church, that mystic ark outside of which there is no salvation. Grant, moreover, that we may follow, in all humility and meekness, her teaching and her advice, and may be obedient to all her precepts, in order to be able here on earth to enjoy a peace that is sure and undisturbed, and to attain one day in heaven to everlasting happiness. Amen.

V. Pray for us, Saint Peter the Apostle,
R. That we may be made worthy of the promises of Christ.

Let us pray.
O God, who hast given unto Thy blessed Apostle Peter the keys to the kingdom of heaven, and the power to bind and loose: grant that we may be delivered, through the help of this intercession, from the slavery of all our sins: Who livest and reignest world without end. Amen.

St. Pius X

89. Glorious Pope of the Eucharist, St. Pius X, who sought to restore all things in Christ, obtain for me a true love of Jesus that I may live only for Him. Help me, that, with lively fervor and a sincere will to strive for sanctity of life, I may daily avail myself of the riches of the Holy Eucharist in Sacrifice and Sacrament. By your love for Mary Mother and Queen of all, inflame my heart with tender devotion to her. Blessed model of the priesthood, obtain for us holy and zealous priests and increase vocations to the religious life. Dispel heresy and incline hearts to peace and concord, that all nations may place themselves under the sweet reign of Christ. Amen.

St. Pius X, pray for me, that (*mention any particular intention*).

Prayer to St Rita - Patroness of Impossible Cases

90. Holy Patroness of those in need, Saint Rita, your pleadings before your divine Lord are irresistible. For your lavishness in granting favors you have been called the "Advocate of the Hopeless" and even of the "Impossible." You are so humble, so mortified, so patient, so compassionate in love for your crucified Jesus that you can obtain from Him anything you ask if it is His Holy Will. Therefore, all confidently have recourse to you in hope of comfort or relief. Be propitious toward your suppliants and show your power with God in their behalf. Be generous with your favors now as you have been in so many wonderful cases for the greater glory of God, the spread of your devotion, and the consolation of those who trust in you. We promise, if our petition be granted, to glorify you by making known your favor, and to bless you and sing your praises. Relying then on your merits and power before the Sacred Heart of Jesus, we ask you (*Name your request*). Amen.

St. Teresa of Avila

91. O Saint Teresa, seraphic Virgin, beloved spouse of thy crucified Lord, thou who on earth didst burn with a love so intense toward thy God and my God, and now dost glow with a brighter and purer flame in paradise: obtain for me also, I beseech thee, a spark of that same holy fire which shall cause me to forget the world, all things created, and even myself; for thou didst ever avidly desire to see Him loved by all men. Grant that my every thought and desire and affection may be continually directed to doing the will of God, the supreme Good, whether I am in joy or in pain, for He is worthy to be loved and obeyed forever. Obtain for me this grace, thou who art so powerful with God; may I be all on fire, like thee, with the holy love of God. Amen.

St. Therese of Lisieux

92. I greet you, Saint Therese of the Child Jesus, lily of purity, ornament and glory of Christianity! I salute you, great saint, seraph of Divine Love. I rejoice at the favors our Blessed Lord Jesus has liberally bestowed on you. In humility and confidence I entreat you to help me, for 1 know that God has given you charity and pity as well as power. Oh then, behold my distress, my anxiety, my fears. Oh, tell Him now my wants. One sigh from you will crown my success, will fill me with joy. Remember your promise to do good on earth. Obtain for me from God the graces of our Divine Lord, especially (*Name your request*). Amen.

93. O wondrous Saint Theresa of the Child Jesus, who, in thy brief earthly life, didst become a mirror of angelic purity, of courageous love and of whole-hearted surrender to Almighty God, now that thou art enjoying the reward of thy virtues, turn thine eyes of mercy upon us who trust in thee. Obtain for us the grace to keep our hearts and minds pure and clean like unto thine, and to detest in all sincerity whatever might tarnish ever so slightly the luster of a virtue

so sublime, a virtue that endears us to they heavenly Bridegroom. Ah, dear Saint, grant us to feel in every need the power of thy intercession; give us comfort in all the bitterness of this life and especially at its latter end, that we may be worthy to share eternal happiness with thee in paradise. Amen.

V. Pray for us, O blessed Theresa,
R. That we may be made worthy of the promises of Christ.

Let us pray.
O Lord, who has said: "Unless you become as little children, you shall not enter into the kingdom of heaven;" grant us, we beseech Thee, so to walk in the footsteps of thy blessed Virgin Theresa with a humble and single heart, that we may attain to everlasting rewards: Who livest and reignest world without end. Amen.

Prayer to One's Patron or Any Saint
94. O Glorious Saint N. (*my beloved Patron*), you served God in humility and confidence on earth and are now in the enjoyment of His beatific Vision in heaven because you persevered till death and gained the crown of eternal life. Remember now the dangers that surround me in the vale of tears, and intercede for me in my needs and troubles (*Name your request*).

To the Holy Souls in Purgatory
95. O Holy Souls in Purgatory, who are the certain heirs of heaven, souls most dear to Jesus as the trophies of His Precious Blood and to Mary, Mother of Mercy, obtain for me through your intercession the grace to lead a holy life, to die a happy death and to attain to the blessedness of eternity in heaven. Dear Suffering Souls, who languish in your prison of pain and long to be delivered in order to praise and glorify God in heaven, by your unfailing pity

help me at this time, particularly (*Name your request*), that I may obtain relief and assistance from God. In gratitude for your intercession I offer to God on your behalf the satisfactory merits of all my works and sufferings of this day (*week, month, or whatever space of time you wish to designate.*)

III. Prayers for Various Needs

This chapter will likely be more amenable to Protestant readers, and contains prayers directed toward specific needs and intentions: Love, Healing, Prosperity, Strength, Knowledge, Protection, and for the sake of Children. These prayers are directed toward God alone instead of toward this or that Saint; it is possible to use prayers from both chapters in conjunction with one another.

96-103. Prayers for Love

96. Prayer to find love
Lord of Hosts: you have searched me, and you know me. You hear my thoughts, you know my needs and breathe your life into my dreams.

I know that you understand my longing to find love, and I know you will lead me to meet someone special. You are a loving Parent, and I can share with you my every hope, feeling and dream.

I pray that I would meet someone soon whom I can love and who will love me, with whom I can have a close relationship, marry, and share my life.

Through Christ our Lord. Amen.

97. Prayer to Find a Companion
Lord of Hosts, hear this relationship prayer. As you are first in my heavenly heart, mind, and spirit, so do I desire a companion for my earthly heart, mind, and being. Guide me to the partner you know is perfect for me. Help me walk in faith until that time of our first meeting.

Show me how I can become a partner worthy of love, and then guide me through every stage of our relationship, so that, as we move ever closer to you, we grow closer to each other in Love, in Joy, and in Faith.

Through Christ our Lord. Amen.

98. Prayer for true love and happiness
Dear Lord, your heart is full of wisdom, truth and love. You lead us to enjoy the beauty in creation and to engage each day with love in our hearts. You teach us to live lives brimming with your love and goodness.

We are so blessed to live in your care, and we thank you for guiding us into true love and happiness by your gentle hand. We choose to give you our lives each day, through Christ our Lord. Amen.

99. Finding a Life Partner
Heavenly Father, you created this world and all its inhabitants. You found it is not good for a person to be alone. I therefore pray this to you, O Lord, because I seek a partner for my life.

In the Bible you show us that finding the right partner brought numerous couples to live a happy life. Bless me, Father, that I may build a family like theirs. I believe, Lord, that you do not deny joy and happiness to your children.

I pray that the loneliness in my heart will be gone soon. I pray this to You, O Lord. Amen.

100. Prayer for love to return
O Lord, each moment of everyday I trust my loved one to you. May you cover them with protection, carry them through the hard times, and lead them to return in love and

happiness. I ask that you rekindle the fire of our love. Come inspire my mind and show me if there is anything I can do to care for my loved one.

I can not always be there for them, but you are forever besides them. Each moment of everyday I trust my loved one to you. Through Christ our Lord. Amen.

101. Prayer to Heal a Relationship

Dear Lord, I offer you this prayer to help me with my current relationship situation. Please take away all the pain and hurt in my heart. Fill it with love, joy, patience, and understanding.

Bless my partner and me, so we may never surrender to whatever challenges come our way. Fill our hearts with love for one another, and make each of us realize the other's worth. Please touch the heart of my partner, *(name)*, and fill it with much love for me.

Make our complicated relationship become uncomplicated. For this I seek for your mercy and blessing to overcome all problems that confront us. Fill us with mutual love for one another, guide us wherever we go, and lead us away from temptations; put us always in each other's hearts and mind. Thank you, Lord, for hearing my prayer in Christ our Lord. Amen.

102. Rekindling a Relationship

Lord, help us to remember when we first met, and remember the strong love that grew between us.
Help us to work that love into practical things so nothing can divide us. We ask for words both kind and loving, and for hearts always ready to ask forgiveness as well as forgive. We ask this through Jesus the Lord. Amen.

103. Miscommunication in a Marriage

Dear Lord, you know what path I am on right now, and you know the disharmony in my married life. You once instituted marriage because you found it is not good for a person to be alone.

I deeply believe that you have given me this person to love and to hold for the rest of our days. Come and be with us, Lord, for only you can make two broken hearts understand each other. You are the King of Peace, and I know you are able to change any sad situation in my life.

Father, I know it is your will that we should lead a loving and peaceful life together. Fill us both with more love and help us better to understand each other, bringing unity to our relationship. Help me become more understanding to my partner's needs and feelings.

Grant me wisdom that I may know how to deal with this situation and build a house in your glory. In Jesus' name I pray, O Lord. Amen.

104-114. Prayers for Healing

104. Prayer for Healing

Dear Lord of Mercy and Father of Comfort: to you I turn for help in times of weakness and need. I ask you to be with your servant during this illness, because I know you send out your Word and heal. I thus ask you to send your healing Word to your servant, and in the name of Jesus to drive out all infirmity and sickness from this body.

I ask you to turn this weakness into strength, suffering into compassion, sorrow into joy, and pain into comfort for others. May your servant trust in your goodness and hope in your faithfulness, even in the middle of this suffering.

Let him *(her)* be filled with patience and joy in your presence as he *(she)* waits for your healing touch.

Restore your servant to full health, dear Lord. Remove all fear and doubt from his *(her)* heart by the power of your Holy Spirit, and may you, O Lord, be glorified through his *(her)* life.

As you heal and renew your servant, Lord, may he *(she)* bless and praise you.

I pray for this in the name of Jesus Christ. Amen.

105. For Healing

Lord, you invite all who are burdened to come to you. Allow your healing hand to heal me. Touch my soul with your compassion for others. Touch my heart with your courage and infinite love for all. Touch my mind with your wisdom, that my mouth may always proclaim your praise. Teach me to reach out to you in my need, and help me to lead others to you by my example. Most loving Heart of Jesus, bring me health in body and spirit that I may serve you with all my strength. Touch gently this life which you have created, now and forever. Amen.

106. Prayer before Surgery

Loving Father, I entrust myself to your care this day; guide with wisdom and skill the minds and hands of the medical people who minister in your Name, and grant that every cause of illness be removed, I may be restored to soundness of health and learn to live in more perfect harmony with you and with those around me. Into your hands, I commend my body and my soul through Jesus Christ our Lord. Amen.

107. Prayer after Surgery

Blessed Savior, I thank you that this operation is safely past, and now I rest in your abiding presence, relaxing every tension, releasing every care and anxiety, receiving more and more of your healing life into every part of my being. In moments of pain I turn to you for strength, in times of loneliness I feel your loving nearness. Grant that your life and love and joy may flow through me for the healing of others in your name. Amen.

108. Prayer for Doctors and Nurses

O merciful Father, who have wonderfully fashioned man in your own image, and have made his body to be a temple of the Holy Spirit, sanctify, we pray you, our doctors and nurses and all those whom you have called to study and practice the arts of healing the sick and the prevention of disease and pain. Strengthen them in body and soul, and bless their work, that they may give comfort to those for whose salvation your Son became Man, lived on this earth, healed the sick, and suffered and died on the Cross. Amen.

109. Prayer for Healing

Lord, look upon me with eyes of mercy, may your healing hand rest upon me, may your life-giving powers flow into every cell of my body and into the depths of my soul, cleansing, purifying, restoring me to wholeness and strength for service in your Kingdom. Amen.

110. Prayer for Healing

O God who are the only source of health and healing, the spirit of calm and the central peace of this universe, grant to me such a consciousness of your indwelling and surrounding presence that I may permit you to give me health and strength and peace, through Jesus Christ our Lord. Amen.

111. Renew My Mind, Body and Soul

Lord, I come before you today in need of your healing hand. In you all things are possible. Hold my heart within yours, and renew my mind, body, and soul

I am lost, but I am singing. You gave us life, and you also give us the gift of infinite joy. Give me the strength to move forward on the path you've laid out for me. Guide me towards better health, and give me the wisdom to identify those you've placed around me to help me get better

In your name I pray, Amen.

112. To Heal a Friend

Think, O God, of our friend who is ill, whom we now commend to your compassionate regard.

Comfort him *(her)* upon his *(her)* sickbed, and ease his *(her)* suffering. We ask for deliverance, and submit that no healing is impossible for you, if it be your will.

We therefore pray that you bless our friend with your loving care, renew his *(her)* strength, and heal what ails him *(her)* in Your loving name.

We thank you for this through Christ our Lord. Amen.

113. A Prayer to Jesus for Healing

Dear Lord, you are the Just judge, Holy and True. You are the Most High God. You give us life. You hold all power in your hands. You are the Mighty one who carries the world, and are ruler over all the earth. You, O Most Blessed One, are the giver of life. In you are only good things. In you is mercy and love. In you is healing for the nations. In you is freedom from worry and freedom from pain.

Lord Almighty, you loved us so much. You were sent to save us from destruction, and you were sent to earth to help us.

Lord full of mercy and grace, forgive us for our faults. Lord Jesus, in you all healing is performed. You, Lord, are the miracle worker. In your Spirit, your gift of healing is alive. In you we can put our trust that you can heal us. We believe you can protect us from the enemy, and from death to our soul.

You, Lord, are a miracle worker for the sick and for lost souls. You, Lord, forgive us and save us from condemnation. You cleanse us and make us born anew. You give us a clean heart full of peace. You are the Lord of Light.

In you is all truth. Your way is the way to Heavenly Hope. Your hands created the universe. You are the true Giver of Life. Every child is a miracle of Life, and Life rests in your Hands.

Wrap us as a close knit family and draw us near to you. Bind us with your Loving Hands and let us be drawn closer to you. You are the Vine, and we are the branches. You carry all knowledge and all power, for you are our medicine. Your words are Truth and Life.

Help us put our trust in you, for you are the greatest physician. You heal, you protect, you care, you love, you are kind, you are patient, you are thoughtful, and you are strength. You, O Lord, are our Creator.

You know our thoughts, our sighings and our cryings and every hair on our head. You are Wonderful and make all good things for us. Heal us, Lord, if it be your will. Amen.

114. A Prayer against Disease

Lord, your scripture says that you heal all diseases and whoever believes in you will not perish but have eternal life. Strengthen your servant, Lord, in this time of illness. Sustain him *(her)* as he *(she)* lays sick in his *(her)* bed. When you were on earth, you did all things good and healed all kinds of sickness.

You healed those who had diseases. You died and rose for our sins that we may have eternal life. I believe in my heart that you are here with us today and that with your most holy power will remove all sicknesses and evils that roam the earth. Let it be done in your glory, Lord.

We praise and glorify your name, O Lord, for you live and reign forever and ever. Amen.

115-122. Prayers for Prosperity

115. Prosperity Prayer

Dear God, thank you so much for all you have given me; I am happy and grateful for the abundance I already have. You amaze me with the love, blessings and rewards we receive everyday without even asking or realizing what we receive.

God of Abundance, I give you my life and today surrender all my financial concerns to you. You've told me I needn't worry fear for anything. Your Scriptures have told us you take care of everything, and we need only to trust and have faith.

I completely trust that my finances and debts will be paid, and that I'll have a constant flow of money in my life starting today.

I only think of the positive now, never looking at the past. I believe my prosperity is here and I thank you for it now. I also want to thank you for showing me how to handle my finances carefully and for teaching me how my prosperity can be of help to your kingdom.

Father, thank you for all your great rewards! I will continue to work diligently and strive to do my best in all that I do. In Jesus' name. Amen.

116. Debt prayer

Heavenly Father, I come before you today to ask for a financial blessing to improve my life. My faith keeps me strong, and I know you will provide for me and the people I love.

I do not seek a large sum of money. I do not trouble you for unneeded comforts or luxury. I only ask for enough money to relieve my financial woes and ease this stress.

Give me the means to do your work, and spread your Love. I have so much to give, if only I were allowed the chance. In Jesus' name I pray. Amen

117. Debt Removal Prayer

Lord, I confess I've made mistakes. I have accumulated too much debt, and now I can not imagine overcoming it without your help.

Please Lord, I beg of you to intercede on my behalf. Provide me with the financial means to be able to breathe again.

Please forgive my sins, Lord. Walk with me and help me to make the right decisions throughout my life. In Jesus' name I pray, Amen

118. Giver of Bread

Lord God, giver of bread, we bless you for your Heavenly kindness. When we forget your infinite kindness, help us remember there can be no famine while the Bread of Heaven endures. How blessed it is to know we shall not want forever, and that you will not allow your children to go without nourishment. However long the day or hard the work, we have the rest, the bounty, and the bread. Happy and grateful are we, for you plan your daily feast for us! As we eat of the Bread of Heaven we shall continue to prosper on earth. Feed me, Kind Lord, until I shall want no more!

119. Make Us Worthy of Your Blessings

O God, we thank you for your generosity and kindness, and ask that you hear us in this hour of financial need. Make us worthy of your blessing and keep us from further want. Help us restore our abundance here on earth, so that we may turn more attention to your divine kingdom. We have worked so hard, and yet there is no end to our lacking. Grant us this wish, and make us worthy of its fulfillment through Christ our Lord. Amen.

120. Supply All My Needs

I give thanks to God for this day, in which my dream will flourish, my plans will succeed, my destiny will be assured, and the desire of my heart will be granted in Jesus' name.

The money I need will know my name and address before the end of this month.

As I awake this morning, may my life be clean, calm, and clear as the early morning dew. May the grace of the Almighty support, sustain and supply all my needs according to his riches in glory.
Through Christ our Lord. Amen!

121. Prosper in a New Job

Loving God, I cast all my worries upon you. I have so much anxiety and fear in my heart about this new job I have. Fill my heart with desire to do great things and bless the work of my hands, for I completely trust you and have deep faith in You.

Let all that I do be pleasing to you. Grant me wisdom and knowledge that I may do what is good and true in all the days of my life. Let me feel your mighty presence, dear God, as I give you my praise and thanks.

Through Christ our Lord. Amen.

122. Prosper in School and Work

Dear God, I praise and glorify you. I pray that you help me in my studies. I know that you want me, your child, to prosper in all my endeavors.

Give me your knowledge and wisdom as I study for my lessons and exams. Let me learn my lessons properly and understand them completely. I pray that I overcome all my academic weaknesses.

Bless me with this, O Lord, for your greater glory. Let me be a blessing to my family that I love so much, and I thank you in advance for answering my prayer.

In Jesus' name I pray. Amen.

123-131. Prayers for Knowledge

123. Prayer for the Gift of Knowledge

Absolute and all-knowing God, nothing is hidden from your sight. In your prescience since the beginning, all knowledge has existed within you.

Kindly share your knowledge with me, making me aware of what is meant to be, permitting my soul to understand it, and wisdom to agree with its outcome.

Provide me with the gift of discretion to prudently apply received knowledge and ensure the fulfillment of Your Will. In Jesus' name, your knowledge shines forth forever!

124. Prayer for Students

God of Light and Wisdom, thank you for giving me a mind that can know and a heart that can love.

Help me to keep learning every day of my life – no matter what the subject may be. Let me be convinced that all knowledge leads to you and let me know how to find you and love you in all the things you have made.

Encourage me when the studies are difficult and when I am tempted to give up, enlighten me when my brain is slow, and help me to grasp the truth held out to me.

Grant me the grace to put my knowledge to use in building the kingdom of God on earth so that I may enter your kingdom in heaven. In Jesus' name. Amen.

125. Prayer for Wisdom and Discernment

Lord God, We come before you and desire that our lives to be like an open book. Come write your story of love across every page, and may we hear your voice of guidance in all we do. We trust that with you we will always see the way ahead, and may our every move be at one with your will.

We know that you protect us, and keep us as we travel. Come reveal to us all that we need to see along the way, as we journey on this incredible adventure with you. Through Christ our Lord. Amen.

126. Prayer for wisdom and knowledge

Lord of heaven and earth, I pray that as I search for knowledge in study that I would discover divine treasure. May I be able to sift through all I read to find the gems of your kingdom.

Lord, I long not for the wisdom that leads to power or fortune but the wisdom that leads to faith and love.

Guide my pathway as I thirst for your truths. May I drink from your word and pour out this heavenly water on others – your water of life, faith, hope, truth and love – into the hearts and lives of all I meet. In Jesus' name I pray. Amen.

127. Prayer for Knowledge

Incomprehensible Creator, the true Fountain of light and only Author of all knowledge: vouchsafe, we beseech Thee, to enlighten our understandings, and to remove from us all darkness of sin and ignorance. Thou, who makest eloquent the tongues of those that want utterance, direct our tongues, and pour on our lips the grace of Thy blessing. Give us a diligent and obedient spirit, quickness of apprehension, capacity of retaining, and the powerful assistance of Thy holy grace; that what we hear or learn we may apply to Thy honor and the eternal salvation of our own souls. We ask this through Christ our Lord. Amen.

128. Prayer before Studies

Holy Spirit, Giver of all good gifts, enter into my mind and heart. Give me the gift of knowledge and the grace to use it wisely. Help me in all my endeavors. Give me perseverance and fortitude. Help my memory, that I may remember what I learn and recall it when necessary. Guide me in the classroom. You who are the Way, the Truth, and the Life, let me not be deceived by false teaching. Our Lady of Good Studies, pray for me. Amen.

129. Prayer for Knowledge of God's Creation

Almighty and everlasting God, You made the universe with all its marvelous order: its atoms, worlds, and galaxies, and the infinite complexity of living creatures.

Grant that, as we probe the mysteries of your creation, we may come to know you more truly, and more surely fulfill our role in your eternal purpose; in the name of Jesus Christ our Lord. Amen.

130. Prayer for the Gift of Knowledge

Holy Spirit, give yourself to me so that I may distinguish evil from evil, wrong from wrong, and what hurt each one does.

Grant me, Spirit of knowledge, the blessing of this gift. This spirit makes a person mindful of the past, wary about the future, and guarded in the present. It brings forth honey from the rock. It turns difficult things to pleasantness, pains to delight, and sins to profit. It is a lantern that illuminates your ways, O Lord, a light for my path; without it, everyone who walks the road of repentance goes astray.

This is the spirit that rescued Israel from slavery in Egypt and freed Joseph from prison. To Job it gave back gifts of many kinds. It made Moses the friend of God.

But see! When the enemy who is set against the human race sees that no resistance is being offered, he wages another war in the hope of victory. He stirs up pride, urges revenge, and provokes scorn, so that in this way he may overcome us. Though he promises strength, weakness is the prize that he gives.

Against this enemy, O Sweetness of the Lord, give us the gift of knowledge, that by union with the Word of God, we may have the power to stand firmly and resist strongly. In Jesus' name we pray. Amen.

131. Prayer for Hidden Knowledge

O Lord God, Holy Father, Almighty and Merciful One, you have created all things, you know all things and can do all things. Nothing is hidden from you, and to you nothing is impossible. We ask, by your sacred Mercy, that you will give us the ability to penetrate into the knowledge of hidden things, and permit that we may arrive at this understanding of secret things by your aid, of whatever nature they may be. Through Jesus Christ your Son, our Lord, who lives and reigns with you and the Holy Spirit, one God, and to whose kingdom and power shall have no end unto the ages of the ages. Amen.

132-141. Prayers for Strength

132. For Strength and Wisdom

Thank you, Lord, for being there for me in my times of need. It's amazing to me that the Lord of the Universe would take time to listen to me and care about what I say.

God, there are things happening around me right now that I do not understand. Some of these things make me feel weak, helpless, and afraid.

Even in the midst of this, I know that you are the Lord. I know that the situation is in your hand, and I trust you.

I ask you for the strength and wisdom to endure this situation and handle it in a way that brings glory to your name.

I ask this through Christ our Lord. Amen.

133. Prayer for Overcoming Life's Hardships

Lord, we call upon you in our time of sorrow, asking you to give us the strength and willpower to bear our heavy burdens, until we can again feel the warmth and love of your divine compassion. Be mindful of us and have mercy on us while we struggle to comprehend life's hardships.

Keep us ever in your watch, till we can walk again with light hearts and renewed spirits. In Jesus' name. Amen.

134. Strength for a Friend

God of Might, I come before you today knowing that all power is in your hand. I know that you are the Lord and that you care for your people. Right now, my friend is struggling with a difficult trial. I can see his *(her)* strength is faltering, and I know you have all the strength that he *(she)* needs.

I pray that you will reach down and touch him *(her)* right now wherever he *(she)* is at this moment. Let your presence fill the room where he *(she)* is and let him *(her)* feel an extra portion of your strength that can help him *(her)* get through this day.

He *(she)* needs you now, Lord, and I thank you in advance for meeting him *(her)* where he *(she)* is and shoring up his *(her)* strength during this difficult time. In Jesus' name. Amen.

135. Prayer for Guidance and Help

Dear Lord, I call upon you today for your divine guidance and help. I am in crisis and need a supporting hand to keep me on the right and just path.

My heart is troubled but I strive to keep it set on you, because your infinite wisdom will show me the right way to a just resolution. Thank you for hearing my prayer and for staying by my side. In Jesus' name. Amen.

136. Short Prayer for Strength at Work
As I go to work,
Be with me Lord.
Be the patience when I'm frustrated.
Be the endurance when I am tired.
Be the wisdom when I am uncertain.
Be the inspiration when I'm out of ideas.
Be the peacemaker when I feel hurt.
Be the comforter when I feel overwhelmed.
Be the energy when I am weary.
Be the guide when I am confused.
Be the forgiver when I get it wrong.
Be with me Lord, today.

137. Give Me Strength, Lord
Lord, you are Holy above all others, and all of the strength that I need is in your hands.

I am not asking, Lord, that you take this trial away. Instead, I simply ask that your will be done in my life. Whatever that means, that is what I want. But I admit that it's hard, Lord.

Sometimes I feel like I can't go on. The pain and the fear are too much for me, and I know that I don't have the strength on my own to get through this.

I know that I can come to you, Jesus, and that you will hear my prayer. I know that it is not your intent to bring me to this point just to leave me in the wilderness alone.

Please, Lord, give me the strength that I need to face today. You don't have to worry about tomorrow.

If you just give me the strength that I need today, that is all I need.

Keep me from sinning during this trial. Instead, help me to keep my eyes on you. You are the Holy Lord, and all of my hope rests in you.

Thank you for hearing my prayer in Jesus' name. Amen.

138. Prayer for Strength from Isaiah
O Lord,
You are the everlasting God,
the Creator of the ends of the earth.
You do not grow faint or weary;
your understanding is unsearchable.
You give power to the weak,
and strengthen the powerless.
Even the young will grow weary,
and will fall exhausted;
but those who wait for you
shall renew their strength,
and shall mount up with wings like eagles;
they shall run and not be weary;
they shall walk and not faint. Amen
Adapted from Isaiah 40:28-31

139. Prayer for Strength during Pain
Lord Jesus Christ, by your patience in suffering you made holy earthly pain and gave us the example of obedience to your Father's will: Be near me in my time of weakness and pain; sustain me by your grace, that my strength and courage may not fail; heal me according to your will; and help me always to believe that what happens to me here is of little account if you hold me in eternal life, my Lord and my God. Amen.

140. Prayer for Quiet Confidence

O God of peace, who taught us that in returning and rest we shall be saved, and in quietness and confidence shall be our strength. By the might of your Spirit lift us, we pray, to your presence, where we may be still and know that you are God; through Jesus Christ our Lord. Amen.

141. Prayer for Strength When Grieving

Lord, at the moment nothing seems able
   to help the loss I feel.
My heart is broken and my spirit mourns.
All I know is that your grace is sufficient.
This day, this hour, moment by moment
I choose to lean on you.
For when I am at my weakest, your strength is strongest.
I pour out my grief to you and praise you that
   on one glorious day,
When all suffering is extinguished and love has conquered,
We shall walk together again.
In Jesus' name. Amen.

142-154. Prayers for Protection

142. Hear Us, Holy Lord

Hear us, Holy Lord, Almighty Father, Eternal God: and send your holy angel from heaven to guard, watch over, protect, and remain with all who dwell in this house. Through Christ our Lord. Amen.

143. Be with Me Christ

The cross of Christ be with me;
The cross of Christ overcomes all water and every fire;
The cross of Christ overcomes all weapons;
The cross of Christ is a perfect sign and blessing
   to my soul.
May Christ be with me and my body during all my life

At day and at night. Now I pray, I *(name)*, pray
    to God the Father
For the soul's sake, and I pray God the Son
    for the Father's sake,
And I pray God the Holy Ghost
    for the Father's and Son's sake,
That the Holy Trinity of God may bless me
    against all evil things, words and works. Amen.

144. The Cross of Christ

The cross of Christ open unto me future bliss;
The cross of Christ be with me, above me, before me,
Behind me, beneath me, aside of me and
Everywhere, and before all my enemies,
Visible and invisible; these all flee from me
As soon as they but know or hear.
Enoch and Elijah, the two prophets, were never
Imprisoned, nor bound, nor beaten and came
Never out of their power; thus no one of my enemies
Must be able to injure or attack me in my body
Or my life,
(Here make the Sign of the Cross.)
In the name of God the Father, the Son, and the Holy
Ghost. Amen!

145. Guard Me

Like unto the cup and the wine, and the holy supper which
our dear Lord Jesus Christ gave unto his dear disciples.
On each day, may the Lord Jesus guard me in daytime, and
at night, that:
No dog may bite me,
No wild beast tear me to pieces,
No tree fall upon me,
No water rise against me,
No firearms injure me,
No weapons, no steel, no iron cut me,

No fire burn me, No false sentence fall upon me,
No false tongue injure me,
No rogue enrage me, and that no fiends,
No witchcraft or enchantment can harm me.
Amen.

146. Protect my Day
Blessed be my protection when I go out
    during day or night,
That thou mayest not let any of my enemies,
    or thieves, approach me,
If they do not intend to bring me what was
    intended from your Holy Altar.
Because God the Lord Jesus Christ is ascended into Heaven
    in his living Body,
And so shall my body and wellbeing be protected
    on this journey.
O Lord, bless me and watch over me day and night.
In the name of the Father, the Son and the Holy Spirit.
Amen.

147. Protect my Journey
In the name of God I go on this journey.
May God the Father be with me,
God the Son protect me, and
God the Holy Ghost be by my side.
Whoever is stronger than these three persons
May approach my body and my life; yet
Whoso is not stronger than these three
Would much better let me be!

148. Guard over Me
Jesus, I will arise; Jesus do thou accompany me;
Jesus, do thou lock my heart into thine,
And let my body and my soul
Be commended unto thee.

The Lord is crucified.
May God guard and protect my senses
So that misfortunes may not overcome me.
(Here make the Sign of the Cross.)
In the name of God the Father, Son, and the Holy Ghost.
Amen!

149. Let No Evil Befall Us (before Traveling)

O God, you are the preserver of all humanity and the keeper of our lives. We commit ourselves to your perfect care on the journey that awaits us. We pray for a safe and auspicious journey.

Give your angels charge over us to keep us in all our ways. Let no evil befall us, nor any harm come to our dwelling that we leave behind. Although we are uncertain of what the days may bring, may we be prepared for any event or delay, and greet such with patience and understanding.

Bless us O Lord, that we may complete our journey safely and successfully under your ever watchful care. In Jesus' name we pray. Amen.

150. Prayer for Protection against Fires

Almighty and eternal God, we ask your protection against destroying fire. Fire is necessary for our existence, and yet, when it gets out of control, it can be more damaging than anything else. Keep our homes, buildings, woods, and fields safe from this scourge. Help us always to be most careful in our use of it. Help us especially in the wintertime when need and use it most. For if our homes are destroyed by fire, we suffer more than ever.

Give us, too, we humbly pray you, a saving fear of the fires of passion, and the help of your grace to control them. Help us also to fear the fires of hell, that we may always keep

away from serious sin, and live lives of goodness and
virtue, through Christ our Lord. Amen.

151. Protection from Thieves
God be with you, brethren; stop, ye thieves,
Robbers, murderers, horsemen and soldiers,
In all humility, for we have tasted
The rosy blood of Jesus.
Your rifles and guns will be stopped up with the
Holy blood of Jesus; and all swords and arms
    are made harmless
By the five holy wounds of Jesus.
There are three roses upon the heart of God;
The first is beneficent,
The other is omnipotent,
The third is his holy will.
You thieves must therefore stand under it,
Standing still as long as I will.
In the name of God the Father, Son and Holy Ghost,
You are commanded and made to stop!

152. Prayer for Protection for Those in the Military
O God, I beseech you, watch over those exposed to the
horror of war, and the spiritual dangers of a soldier's or
sailor's life. Give them such a strong faith that no human
respect may ever lead them to deny it, nor fear ever to
practice it. By your grace, O God, fortify them against the
contagion of bad example, that being preserved from vice,
and serving you faithfully, they may be ready to meet you
face to face when they are so called: through Christ our
Lord. Amen.

153. The Light of God
The light of God surrounds us,
The love of God enfolds us,
The power of God protects us,

The presence of God watches over us,
Wherever we are, God is,
And where God is, all is well.
St. Matthew, St. Mark, St. Luke, St. John,
Like unto the prophet Jonah, as a type of Christ,
Who was guarded for three days and
Three nights in the belly of a whale,
Thus shall the Almighty God,
As a Father, guard and protect me from all evil.

154. Grant me Protection

Grant, O Lord, Thy protection
And in protection, strength
And in strength, understanding
And in understanding, knowledge
And in knowledge, the knowledge of justice
And in the knowledge of justice, the love of it
And in the love of it, the love of all existences
And in that love, the love of spirit and all creation.

155-161. Prayers for Children

155. A Short Prayer for a Child

Strength and wholeness. I shall run and not be weary. I shall walk and not faint.

Come Gracious Spirit, Heavenly Dove, With light and comfort from above.

Be Thou our Guardian, Thou our Guide, Stay close by every child's side. Amen!

156. For a Rebellious Youth

Dear Lord, you have witnessed the rebelliousness of youth since the very beginnings of time.

You understand a parent's anguish and helplessness over the actions of his child.

Please help us to transform our anger and frustration into loving care for our child who has gone astray. Help us begin to mend our broken fences and heal our broken hearts. Bless our child and also help him to mend the error of his ways. Help and bless us all to do right in your name and restore us to peace and tranquility. Through Christ our Lord. Amen.

157. For an Angry or Depressed Child
Heavenly Father, my child is your greatest gift, and my biggest challenge! I know my child is truly distressed, and yet I am at my wit's end to find a peaceful resolution.

I feel helpless and frustrated. I ask myself, "What would my Heavenly Father do in His infinite wisdom and beneficence?"

Lord, come into my heart and mind, and share your loving wisdom with me! Help my child to heal his *(her)* pain, and help me to become as loving and wise a parent, as you are for us your children. Thank You Lord, for hearing me and coming to my aid! Bring your loving Peace to me and my child today. Amen.

158. Bring Healing to Our Child
Lord, you love our child as you love all children, Bring healing to our child who is not well. Stay by his *(her)* side and comfort him *(her)* through this trying time. Keep us ever mindful of your loving presence. Bless us with your powerful healing and comfort us also. Thank you for hearing our prayer, in Jesus' name. Amen.

159. Restore My Child to Health

O Lord God, I come to you for help and succor. You have afflicted my child *(child's name)*. Help me to understand that you mean well.

Give me grace to bear my child's affliction with patience and strength. Bless me, O Father, and restore my child *(child's name)* to health. Do not forsake us, but give us an assurance of your loving Kingdom. Bless this illness to me and my child *(child's name)*, and help us both to be better children of yours because of it. In the name of your Holy Son Jesus Christ. Amen!

160. A Child's Morning Prayer

Lord, I awake and see your light,
For you have kept me through the night,
To you I lift my hands and pray,
Keep me from sin throughout this day,
And if I die before it's done,
Save me through Jesus Christ, your Son.
Amen.

161. A Child's Nighttime Prayer

Now I lay me down to sleep,
I pray the Lord my soul to keep.
And if I die before I wake.
I pray the Lord my soul to take.
Amen.

IV. Religious and Church Services

This chapter is devoted to Ministers and lay leaders who serve in a small church setting. These are actual orders of service I've used during the course of a seven-year multi-denominational ministry, and are recommended for small groups in an intimate setting. Likewise these service orders can be used as a template for those looking to plant a magically-oriented church or "outer order" congregation, either as written or with a little rewording of the prayers.

162. Service of the Word
A service of prayer and preaching for use by ordained or lay worship leaders, for informal services on Sundays or during the week.

Greeting
Good *(morning/afternoon/evening)*, brothers and sisters. I'm *(name)* and welcome to today's service.

We're here to *worship* God the Father who created us!

We're here to *thank* God the Son who redeemed us!

We're here to *invoke* God the Holy Spirit who sanctifies us!

And while we praise, while we thank, and while we invoke, let us all sing our opening song, *(title)*.

Opening Song

(After the Song, the worship leader says:)
My friends, let us pray.

And then the **Opening Prayer** *(also called a* **Collect***)*

Bible Readings
(Can be from one to three readings from Scripture. For continuity with the mainstream churches, use of the Revised Common Lectionary is recommended.)

Doxology
(After the readings, all sing:)
Praise God, from whom all blessings flow,
Praise him, all creatures here below.
Praise him above, ye heav'nly host,
Praise Father, Son, and Holy Ghost. Amen.

Message or Guided Meditation
(Should be based on the readings.)

Hymn of the Day
(This Hymn is tied with the theme for the day.)

General Prayer
(This is an ex tempore or pre-written prayer for all gathered at the Service, and for all conditions of people.)

Lord's Prayer
All: Our Father, who art in heaven,
hallowed by thy name,
Thy kingdom come,
thy will be done, on earth as it is in heaven.
Give us this day our daily bread;
and forgive us our trespasses,
As we forgive those who trespass against us;
And lead us not into temptation,
but deliver us from evil.
For thine is the kingdom, and the power,
and the glory, forever and ever. Amen.

Blessing
Leader: May the blessing of almighty God
Father, Son, and Holy Spirit
descend upon us and remain for all time.
People: Amen.

*The service ends with the **Closing Song.***

163. A Short Order for Holy Communion
This service order is for ordained ministers who wish to preside over a sacramental Eucharist, and is designed with "mid-" or "broad-church" congregations in mind.

Prelude (Instrumental or Hymn)

A Brief Order for Confession and Forgiveness
Minister: In the name of the Father, and of the Son, and of the Holy Spirit.

People: Amen.

Minister: Almighty God, to whom all hearts are open, all desires known and from whom no secrets are hid: Cleanse the thoughts of our hearts by the inspiration of your Holy Spirit, that we may perfectly love you and worthily magnify your holy name, through Jesus Christ our Lord.

People: Amen.

Minister: If we say we have no sin, we deceive ourselves and the truth is not in us. But if we confess our sins, God who is faithful and just will forgive our sins and cleanse us from all unrighteousness.

Minister: Most merciful God.

All: We confess that we are in bondage to sin and cannot free ourselves. We have sinned against you in thought, word, and deed, by what we have done and by what we have left undone. We have not loved you with our whole heart; we have not loved our neighbors as ourselves. For the sake of your Son, Jesus Christ, have mercy on us. Forgive us, renew us, and lead us, so that we may delight in your will and walk in your ways, to the glory of your holy name. Amen.

Minister: Almighty God, in His mercy, has given His Son to die for us, and for His sake forgives us all our sins. As a called and ordained minister of the Church of Christ, and by His authority, I therefore declare to you the entire forgiveness of all your sins, in the name of the Father, and of the Son, and of the Holy Spirit.
People: Amen.

*(Then all sing the **Opening Hymn**.)*

(After the hymn is sung, the minister shall say:)

Minister: The Grace of our Lord Jesus Christ, the love of God, and the communion of the Holy Spirit be with you all.
People: And also with you.

Minister or Assistant: In peace, let us pray to the Lord.
People: Lord, have mercy.

Minister or Assistant: For the peace from above, and for our salvation, let us pray to the Lord.
People: Lord, have mercy.

Minister or Assistant: For the peace of the whole world, for the well-being of the Church of God and for the unity of all, let us pray to the Lord.
People: Lord, have mercy.

Minister or Assistant: For this holy house, and for all who offer here their worship and praise, let us pray to the Lord.
People: Lord, have mercy.

Minister or Assistant: Help, save comfort, and defend us, gracious Lord.
People: Amen.

Hymn of Praise: *(Omitted during Advent and Lent)*
All: Glory to God in the highest,
and peace to His people on earth.

Lord God, heavenly King,
Almighty God and Father,
We worship you, we give you thanks,
we praise you for your glory.

Lord Jesus Christ, only Son of the Father,
Lord God, Lamb of God,
you take away the sins of the world: have mercy on us;
You are seated at the right hand of the Father:
receive our prayer.

For you alone are the Holy One,
you alone are the Lord,
You alone are the Most High, Jesus Christ,
with the Holy Spirit, in the glory of the Father. Amen.

Collect or Opening Prayer
Minister: The Lord be with you.
People: And also with you. *(or* And with your spirit.*)*

(The minister says the prayer for the day.)
People: Amen.

Readings from the Bible

Reader: The first lesson for today is
from_____.
(The first lesson is read.)

Reader: The Psalm for today is _____.
(The psalm for the day is read responsively or in unison by all).

Reader: The second lesson for today is
from_____.
(The second lesson is read.)

Minister: The gospel for today is from
St._____.
People: Glory to you, O Lord.

(The Holy Gospel is read.)

Minister: The Gospel of the Lord.
People: Praise to you, O Christ.

Sermon or Guided Meditation
(Should be based on the readings.)

Hymn of the Day

The Prayers
Minister or Assistant: Let us pray for the whole people of God in Christ Jesus, and for all people according to their needs.

(The prayers are prayed responsively. After each portion of the Prayers:)
Assistant: Let us pray to the Lord.
People: Lord, hear our prayer.

(The prayers conclude:)
Minister: Into your hands, O Lord, we commend all for whom we pray, trusting in your mercy, through your Son, Jesus Christ our lord.
People: Amen.

The Sign of Peace
Minister: The peace of the Lord be with you always.
People: And also with you. *(or* And with your spirit.*)*

(The minister and people greet each other with a customary greeting.)

Offering Prayer
Minister: Let us pray. Merciful Father:

People with Minister: We offer with joy and thanksgiving what you have first given us – our selves, our time, and our possessions, signs of your gracious love. Receive them for the sake of him who offered himself for us, Jesus Christ our Lord. Amen.

Great Thanksgiving
(The minister says the Prayer of Thanksgiving.)
Blessed are you, Lord of heaven and earth. In mercy for our fallen world you gave your only Son, that all those who believe in him should not perish, but have eternal life. We give thanks to you for the salvation you have prepared for us through Jesus Christ. Send now your Holy Spirit into our hearts, that we may receive our Lord with a living faith as he comes to us in his holy supper.

In the night in which he was betrayed, our Lord Jesus took bread, and gave thanks; and broke it, and gave it to his disciples, saying: TAKE AND EAT; THIS IS MY BODY, GIVEN FOR YOU.

Do this for the remembrance of me.

Again, after supper, he took the cup, gave thanks, and gave it for all to drink, saying:
FOR THIS IS THE CHALICE OF MY BLOOD, OF THE NEW AND EVERLASTING COVENANT, THE MYSTERY OF FAITH: WITH SHALL BE SHED FOR YOU AND FOR MANY, UNTO THE REMISSION OF SINS.

Do this for the remembrance of me.

For as often as we eat of this bread and drink from this cup, we proclaim the Lord's death, until he comes.

The Lord's Prayer
Minister (optional): Let us pray with confidence to the Father, in the words our Savior taught us:

All: Our Father, who art in heaven, hallowed by thy name, Thy kingdom come, thy will be done, on earth as it is in heaven. Give us this day our daily bread; and forgive us our trespasses, As we forgive those who trespass against us; And lead us not into temptation, but deliver us from evil. For thine is the kingdom, and the power, and the glory, forever and ever. Amen.

(Minister invites people to receive communion.)

(The minister and assistant distribute communion.
They say these words to each communicant:)
The body of Christ, given for you.
The blood of Christ, shed for you.

(After all have received communion, the minister may say:)
Minister: The body and blood of our Lord Jesus Christ
strengthen you and keep you in his grace.
People: Amen.

Post-Communion Hymn

Prayer after Communion
Minister: Let us pray.

*(The minister says the prayer after communion. May be
extempore.)*
People: Amen.

ANNOUNCEMENTS
*(If there are any announcements,
the Minister makes them now.)*

Benediction
(The minister blesses the people.)
The Lord bless you and keep you.
The Lord make his face shine on you
and be gracious to you.
The Lord look upon you with favor and give you peace.
People: Amen.

Dismissal (Sending Forth)
Minister: Go in peace. Serve the Lord.
People: Thanks be to God.

Closing Hymn

V. Blessings and Consecrations

These are the formulas for blessing and consecrating one's tools according to the magical system I use and teach in my books.

164. Order for Creating Holy Water
The first tool we're going to talk about is Holy Water, because it's used when blessing all your other implements. Holy Water is used for chasing away anything bad, hence its association with healing (chasing away sickness), exorcism (chasing away evil spirits), and reminding us of our baptism (chasing away sin).

There are a few forms for making Holy Water, and I prefer mine the old-fashioned way: first by exorcising the salt and water, then blessing them, and then combining them. I have no qualm if you prefer to use the Novus Ordo formula or any other rite in existence, and encourage you to pursue that. I simply choose to stick with the way I was raised and trained.

1. Whenever you need Holy Water, have some water and a small quantity of salt in your working-space. If you're a cleric, wear a purple stole (if you're not, then don't worry about this part). You begin the blessing by making the sign of the cross while saying:
V. **Our help is in the name of the Lord.**

Your assistant responds:
R. **Who made heaven and earth.**

NOTE 1: In future, note that "V" means "versicle" (you say it) and "R" means "response" (your assistant or those present say it). If you're working alone, then you say all the responses yourself.

2. You then say the Exorcism and Blessing of the salt:
I exorcise thee, creature of salt, by the living + God, by the true + God, by the holy + God, by God who ordered you to be thrown into the water-spring by the prophet Elisha to heal it of its barrenness. May you be a purified salt, a means of health for those who believe, a medicine for body and soul for all who make use of you. May all evil fancies of the foul fiend, his malice and cunning, be driven afar from the place where you are sprinkled. And let every unclean spirit be repulsed by Him who is coming to judge both the living and the dead and the world by fire. R. Amen.

NOTE 2: When you see a + in the text, make the sign of the cross over the person or object.

Let us pray.
Almighty everlasting God, we humbly appeal to your mercy and goodness to graciously bless + and sanctify + this creature of salt, which you have given for mankind's use. May all who use it find in it a remedy for body and mind. And may everything that it touches or sprinkles be freed from uncleanness and any influence of the evil spirit; through Christ our Lord.
R. **Amen.**

Next the Exorcism and Blessing of the water:
I exorcize you, creature of water, in the name of God +the Father almighty, in the name of Jesus +Christ, His Son, our Lord, and in the power of the Holy +Spirit. May you be a purified water, empowered to drive afar all power of the enemy, in fact, to root out and banish the enemy himself, along with his fallen angels. We ask this through the power of our Lord Jesus Christ, who is coming to judge both the living and the dead and the world by fire. R. Amen.

Let us pray.

O God, who for man's welfare established the most wonderful mysteries in the substance of water, hearken to our prayer, and pour forth your blessing +on this element now being prepared with various purifying rites. May this creature of yours, when used in your mysteries and endowed with your grace, serve to cast out demons and to banish disease. May everything that this water sprinkles in the homes and gatherings of the faithful be delivered from all that is unclean and hurtful; let no breath of contagion hover there, no taint of corruption; let all the wiles of the lurking enemy come to nothing. By the sprinkling of this water may everything opposed to the safety and peace of the occupants of these homes be banished, so that in calling on your holy name they may know the well-being they desire, and be protected from every peril; through Christ our Lord. R. Amen.

3. Afterward you put the salt in the water while making three signs of the cross, while saying the following only once:

May this salt and water be mixed together; in the name of the Father +, and of the Son, + and of the Holy + Spirit. R. Amen.

NOTE 3: You only need to add a pinch of salt.

The rite is finished by these versicles and the final prayer.

V. **The Lord be with you.**

R. **And with your spirit.**

Let us pray.

God, source of irresistible might and king of an invincible realm, the ever-glorious conqueror; who restrain the force of the adversary, silencing the uproar of his rage, and valiantly subduing his wickedness; in

awe and humility we beg you, Lord, to regard with favor this creature thing of salt and water, to let the light of your kindness shine upon it, and to hallow it with the dew of your mercy; so that wherever it is sprinkled and your holy name is invoked, every assault of the unclean spirit may be baffled, and all dread of the serpent's venom be cast out. To us who entreat your mercy grant that the Holy Spirit may be with us wherever we may be; through Christ our Lord.
R. Amen.

165. Rite for Consecrating Oil
Some Christians are suspicious of Holy Water because they believe it unscriptural, and may prefer to use oil instead. Since the symbols and gestures were explained in the blessing of water, I give the text without annotations:

V. **Our help is in the name of the Lord.**
R. **Who made heaven and earth.**
I exorcise you, creature of oil, through God + the Father almighty, who made the heaven, the earth, the sea, and all things contained therein. May all power of the adversary, all the devil's hosts and incursions, every phantasm of Satan be eradicated, and take flight from this creature of oil, that it may be unto all who make use of it a healing remedy of mind and body; in the name of God + the Father almighty, and of Jesus + Christ His Son our Lord, and of the Holy + Ghost, the Paraclete, and in the love of our same Lord Jesus Christ, who shall come again to judge the living and the dead, and the world by fire. R. Amen.

V. **Lord, hear my prayer.**
R. **And let my cry come to you.**
V. **The Lord be with you.**
R. **And with your spirit.**

Let us pray
Lord God almighty, unto whom the hosts of Angels
stand in awe, and whose spiritual service is recognized:
vouchsafe, we beseech you, to look upon, +bless, and
+sanctify this creature of oil which you hast brought
forth from the sap of olives, and which you have
commanded for anointing the infirm: so that, insofar as
they have been made well, they shall give thanks to you,
O Living and True God. Grant, we ask you, that they
who will use this oil which we +bless in your name, may
be delivered from all suffering, all infirmity, and all the
wiles of the enemy: let it be a means of averting any
kind of adversity from man, made in your image and
redeemed by the precious Blood of your Son, so that
they may never again suffer the sting of the ancient
serpent. Through the same Lord, Jesus Christ, your
Son, who lives and reigns in the unity of the Holy Ghost,
God, forever and ever. R. Amen.

166. Blessing Your Altar or Mensa

*In the last chapter we discussed the symbolism of the altar,
and elsewhere I've explained my preference to call it a
mensa or "table-top." No matter what name we call it,
your mensa is both a Table of Light and a Table of Art, a
focal point where contact between and divine takes place.
The following formula can be used when blessing it:*

V. **Our help is in the name of the Lord.**
R. **Who made heaven and earth.**
V. **The Lord be with you.**
R. **And with your spirit.**
Let us pray.
O Lord Jesus Christ, through your life, death, and
resurrection you opened for us the heavenly light, *[and
upon your altars the sacrifice of your Body, Blood, soul
and divinity illuminates our spiritual lives:]* vouchsafe to

+**bless and +sanctify this table, that it may be a table of divine light, upon which may manifest every purpose, which is in the minds of those who shall use it for praying to you to glorify your name, and to the greater manifestation of the presence of the Holy +Ghost throughout the entire world. You who live and reign forever and ever.** R. **Amen.**

You may then sprinkle it with Holy Water.

This sprinkling with Holy Water is optional, and so is all text inside brackets.

167. Blessing Your Cross or Crucifix

What would a Christian's magical space be if he didn't have a cross? The cross represents the focus of your work and the symbol of a higher ideal the Christian wishes to attain. The blessing is as follows, and can be used either for a crucifix or a plain cross with no image:

V. **Our help is in the name of the Lord.**
R. **Who made heaven and earth.**
V. **The Lord be with you.**
R. **And with your spirit.**
Let us pray.
Holy Lord, Father almighty, eternal God: we ask you to +bless this sign of the Cross, that it may be a saving help to mankind; let it be a bulwark of faith, an encouragement to good works and the redemption of souls; let it be a consolation and a protection, and a shield against the cruel darts of the enemy; through Christ our Lord. R. **Amen.**

Let us pray.
Lord Jesus Christ, +Bless this Cross, by which you
delivered the world from the power of demons, and by
your suffering you conquered the tempter of sin; who
rejoiced in the first man's fall in eating from the
forbidden tree. Here he may sprinkles the Cross with
Holy Water. May this sign of the Cross be +hallowed in
the name of the +Father, and of the +Son, and of the
Holy + Ghost; that those who pray in honor of you
before this Cross may find health in body and soul.
You who live and reign forever and ever. R. Amen.

The blessed cross may be placed on your mensa or hung on
the wall.

168. Blessing for Candles
*Candles are a symbol of light shining in the darkness, and
likewise a symbol of ourselves being consumed by the Lord
who is "a consuming fire." (Deuteronomy 4:24)*

*The blessing for candles is simple, and aims to make them a
protection against the powers of darkness, the same as a
candle's light dispels darkness from a room:*

V. **Our help is in the name of the Lord.**
R. **Who made heaven and earth.**
V. **The Lord be with you.**
R. **And with your spirit.**
Let us pray.
Lord Jesus Christ, Son of the living God, +bless these
candles at our humble request. Endow them, Lord, by
the power of your holy +Cross and by a heavenly
blessing; you gave them to humankind to dispel the
darkness, now let this blessing they receive by the sign
of your holy +Cross be so powerful that, wherever they
are lighted or placed, the princes of darkness may

tremble and depart from these places, and flee in fear, along with all their legions, and never more dare to disturb or molest those who serve you, almighty God; who live and reign forever and ever. R. Amen.

And they may be sprinkled with holy water.

169. Blessing for an Altar Pentacle

This form of pentacle is unique to the system I use and teach, and consists of a 9-inch diameter brass hoop into which is threaded a pentagram out of brass wire. Its purpose is to provide a point of concentration where energy may be drawn into a talisman or other focus of a working.

V. **Our help is in the name of the Lord.**
R. **Who made heaven and earth.**
I exorcize you, creature of metal, by the true + God, by the living + God, by the holy + God, by God who made the heavens, the earth, the sea, and all things therein. By Jesus + Christ his only-begotten Son, and by the Holy + Ghost the Paraclete. Be delivered from every evil, every fraud, every malice, and every snare of the adversary, that you may become an instrument fit for the rites of Christ's faithful, for concentrating the power of almighty God into whatsoever is placed within your borders: through the same Jesus Christ our Lord, who shall come again to judge the living and the dead, and the world by fire. R. Amen.

V. **Lord, hear my prayer.**
R. **And let my cry come to you.**
V. **The Lord be with you.**
R. **And with your spirit.**

Let us pray.
Almighty God, +bless and +sanctify this pentacle, that
whatsoever is placed within it may be saturated and
infused with your divine power: make it an instrument
fit for the rites of Christ's faithful, and in any rite in
which it is used, may that rite succeed in bringing forth
those events the Operator desires. Through our Lord
Jesus Christ, your Son, who lives and reigns with you in
the unity of the Holy Ghost, God, forever and ever.
R. **Amen.**

You may then anoint with oil or sprinkle with holy water.

170. Constructing a Talisman

While amulets are normally constructed out of sturdy (or
sturdy-ish) materials, both amulets and talismans can be
constructed out of any substance: metal, wood, crystal,
bone, leather, cloth, and even paper. In fact, it's not
uncommon for folk magicians to take talisman designs
from the old grimoires (which required silver, gold, or the
skin of an animal the Operator killed himself) and draw
them on paper for use in their magic workings.

When describing talismans, they're considered to have two
sides: the obverse and the reverse. These terms are
analogous to "front side" and "back side," but we'll sound
smarter if we say these words.

On the obverse side, it's common to write your desire in a
symbolic language. Geometric shapes, colors, planetary
symbols, however you deem appropriate. I learned long ago
that overloading a talisman with symbols is like playing too
many songs at one time, so I have a preference for
simplicity and clarity; your mileage may vary, and you may
have to explore to find the right balance.

On the reverse you write the name(s) of the person or people you wish to affect; write your own name if you're doing magic for yourself. When two or more people are involved, the name of the person you're affecting the most goes on top.

For example if you want to keep your teenage daughter away from a bad crowd, do you want this to happen by your daughter staying away from them or by the crowd shunning her? You would determine this based on the circumstances of the situation and which is easier to affect for the desired outcome.

If you don't wish to create your own talismanic designs, there are many designs available in centuries' worth of magical literature, in various books on the subject, and even on the internet. The variety is endless, and I would only caution that if you buy a pre-made talisman online, know who you're buying it from and a little something about what they're into.

Once you've constructed or selected you amulet or talisman, you can then consecrate it with a blessing and anointing it with essential oils. Which oil should be used for which intention(s) is common knowledge and readily found on the internet, so I won't go into any detail here.

171. General Exorcism of Amulets and Talismans

This exorcism is used before consecrating an amulet or talisman, to make sure the object is cleansed before you charge it. Once it's exorcized, you proceed immediately to the appropriate form of consecration.

1. This exorcism may be done before blessing any pentacle or amulet, for whatsoever purpose.

V. **Our help is in the name of the Lord.**
R. **Who made heaven and earth.**

Then say the General Exorcism:
I exorcise you, creature of metal *(or wood, leather, papyrus, paper, or whatever)*, **by the true + God, the living +God, the holy + God, the God who made heaven and earth, the sea and all things therein: through Jesus + Christ, his Son, at whose name every knee shall bend and every head shall bow, by whose name every demon and power of the enemy shall flee with terror: and by the Holy + Ghost, the Paraclete, through whose gifts the Christian faithful expel demons and perform wonders: that you become be a pure material, a stainless material into which the grace of God may be imparted, and from which the same God's power shall radiate forth, that in the world may be accomplished any intentions of the operator who consecrates you, or of whosoever shall carry or possess you. Through our Lord Jesus Christ, who shall come again to judge the living and the dead, and the world by fire. R. Amen.**

172. Consecration for a Love/Relationship Talisman
This is for talismans geared toward love, attraction, friendship, family, and restoring harmony in your personal or professional relationships.

Immediately after the General Exorcism, you say:
V. **Lord, hear my prayer.**
R. **And let my cry come to you.**
V. **The Lord be with you.**
R. **And with your spirit.**
Let us pray.
Most benign and almighty God, Lord of Hosts who watches over relationships and loves: take note of the humbleness of this creature of metal *(or wood, or*

leather, or papyrus, or paper, or whatever), **and impart to it the + blessing of your divine power, that in keeping with the spirit of the sigils and characters inscribed upon its surface, it may attract to the operator, or towards whomever carries or possesses this amulet: great love, physical as well as spiritual, and the spirit of attraction persons. Through our Lord Jesus Christ, your Son, who lives and reigns with you in the unity of the Holy Ghost, God, forever and ever. R. Amen.**

Next you anoint the amulet or talisman by making the sign of the cross over it with an appropriate oil (I suggest an olive oil base to which rose and a few drops of cinnamon oil are added), while saying:

By this holy anointing, and His most loving mercy, may the Lord of Hosts impart to this amulet the power of amorous attraction. In the name of the Father, and of the + Son, and of the Holy Ghost. Amen.

173. Consecration for a Money/Business Talisman

Use this formula for talismans intended to give your financial life a push in the right direction. Where it says "United States of North America," replace it with the name of your country as applicable.

Immediately after the General Exorcism, you say:

V. Lord, hear my prayer.
R. And let my cry come to you.
V. The Lord be with you.
R. And with your spirit.
Let us pray.
Hear me, O holy Lord, Father Almighty, God of blessings; grant me the power to manifest much money into the life of *(name)*, and vouchsafe also to send your holy Archangel Sachiel from heaven, together with the Heavenly Choir of Angels: that, through the +

consecration of this talisman, they may physically manifest much money into the life of *(name)* **May** *(name)***'s pocketbook be filled with gold, silver, and money of every type legal in the United States of North America, that the purse of** *(name)* **maybe always full. Through our Lord Jesus Christ, your Son, who lives and reigns with you in the unity of the Holy Ghost, God, forever and ever. R. Amen.**

After the consecration you may anoint the talisman with olive oil (the futures market was invented because of olives!), while saying nothing.

174. Consecration for a Health Talisman

I'll admit it; I don't like health and healing magic. I don't like it because there are people who think it a substitute for proper medical attention; such people fail to understand how magic works, and in the process make all magic-users look bad.

I've seen healing magic achieve wonderful results used in conjunction with modern medicine. On the other hand, I've seen magic and faith-healing by itself lead to deaths that could've been avoided. So if you're going to do healing magic, remember that magic either pushes results through established channels, or creates opportunites to establish those channels. It's like the Good Book says: "Honor physicians for their services, for the Lord created them; for their gift of healing comes from the Most High, and they are rewarded by the king." (Sirach 38:1-2/NRSV)

Immediately after the General Exorcism, you say:
V. **Lord, hear my prayer.**
R. **And let my cry come to you.**
V. **The Lord be with you.**
R. **And with your spirit.**

Let us pray.
God of Hosts, you who preside above the hosts of
heaven: humbly I pray and humbly do I come before
you, that you will look favorably upon this amulet
dedicated and consecrated to healing members of the
human race. Look favorably upon it, O Lord, and send
into it the essence of your Archangel Raphael, the
Divine Physician. + Bless and + consecrate this amulet,
O God, that once filled with Raphael's spirit, whosoever
places this amulet upon *his* forehead, or in *his* hand, or
in *his* clothing, or uses it in rites for healing the sick or
places it in the room where a sick person is staying, may
find health of body and firmity of soul, for *himself* or
for whomever *he* does the work. Through Christ our
Lord. R. Amen.

If desired, this talisman may be anointed with olive oil or
any oil geared toward healing.

VI. Candle Magic

175-178. Candle Magic for Love

<u>175. To Find a Suitable Mate:</u>
Let's face it: many of us are in situations where we're lonely and just not able to find that right person. In fact we may be convinced that right person doesn't exist in our local area. The internet's proven itself an equally dismal place to search, since the male/female distribution isn't the greatest. So in this situation, what do you do?

Materials:
Red male or female figure candle
Vase of Roses (as many as you want, but at least six)
Image or Statue of St. Therese, to the right of figure candle.
Image of Holy Family, to the left of the figure candle.
Medal of St. Therese

This ritual should ideally be performed on a Friday, and calls upon both the Holy Family and St. Therese for help.

1. Before beginning the rite, you should spend some time in meditation before the mensa. Light the altar candles and proceed to meditate on your goal, visualizing yourself as having found you perfect mate and spending time with her, going to a movie or out to dinner, planning a marriage, or whatever. The important thing is to keep it simple. You may also want to perform the "Meditation on the Divine Presence" at this space as well.

2. After your meditation, arise and proceed to the mensa, and state your Declaration of Intent:
I do this that I may find the perfect mate. Holy Family, bring this perfect person to me now. St. Therese, send

down your roses from heaven that the spouse of my
dreams shall soon be in mine arms!

3. Take the red figure candle into your left hand and hold
your right hand over it, saying:
**This candle is my perfect mate, lover, and spouse,
whoever and wherever she** *(he)* **may be. May almighty
God +bless and +sanctify this candle, imbuing it with
the dew of heavenly sweetness, that by this work which
I am about to perform, the burning of this candle shall
call to her** *(him)* **and swiftly bring her** *(him)* **into my
arms.**
Sprinkle the candle three times with holy water.

4. Light the candle, saying:
**As I light this red candle, so does it become a burning
flame within the heart of my perfect mate, calling her**
(him) **to me and drawing her** *(him)* **into my arms.**

5. Looking at the image of the Holy Family, recite prayer
#24 from Chapter II:
**O Jesus, lover of the young, the dearest Friend I have,
in all confidence I open my heart to You to beg Your
light and assistance in the important task of planning
my future. Give me the light of Your grace, that I may
decide wisely concerning the person who is to be my
partner through life. Dearest Jesus, send me such a one
whom in Your divine wisdom You judge best suited to
be united with me in marriage. May her/his character
reflect some of the traits of Your own Sacred Heart.
May s/he be upright, loyal, pure, sincere and noble, so
that with united efforts and with pure and unselfish love
we both may strive to perfect ourselves in soul and
body, as well as the children it may please You to
entrust to our care. Bless our friendship before
marriage, that sin may have no part in it. May our**

**mutual love bind us so closely, that our future home
may ever be most like Your own at Nazareth.
O Mary Immaculate, sweet Mother of the young, to
your special care I entrust the decision I am to make as
to my future wife/husband. You are my guiding Star!
Direct me to the person with whom I can best cooperate
in doing God's Holy Will, with whom I can live in peace,
love and harmony in this life, and attain to eternal joys
in the next. Amen.**

6. Pick up the roses and place them next to the image of St.
Therese, if they are not there already. Say:
**St. Therese, Little Flower of the Child Jesus, who said
you would send down roses from Heaven to those who
call upon you. Receive this offering of roses now, and
intercede alongside the Holy Family on my behalf,
bringing to me the one with whom I am to properly
share my life and my love. I am tired of (going to bars,
searching the internet, being set up with friends of
friends, etc., as applies to your personal situation), and
now seek only to find the one with whom my life is to be
shared. Intercede for me, Little Flower, that this person
shall come to me, and be known to me, and be in my
arms quickly. Through Christ our Lord. Amen.**

7. Pick up the medal and place it around your neck, saying:
**As I place this medal around my neck, so too do I place
my confidence in the intercession of the Little Flower of
the Child Jesus, that she shall steer me correctly to my
perfect love. Amen.**

8. You should now sit, stand, or kneel (whichever is your
usual custom) and pray five decades of the Rosary, using
the Mysteries proper to that day and meditating on your
petition. Offer this Rosary to the Holy Family for their

assistance; next to the Mass, the Rosary is the sweetest and most powerful offering that can possibly be made.

9. When you are finished, say a prayer of Thanks to almighty God and the Saints for having assisted you in this endeavor. Now, every day for the next nine days, you will repeat this entire operation, thus making it a novena. The only exception to this is that you will not repeat the blessing and sprinkling of the candle in step 3.

10. While you perform this novena and even afterward, wear the medal around your neck and keep the roses watered and as well cared-for as your ability will allow. These roses are an offering, and therefore should not be allowed to rot and wither away before their time. When the ritual is finished, go to the nearest shrine of St. Therese and place them as close as possible to her image, relic, or side altar, thus completing the offering.

176. To Keep or Restore Peace in a Marriage

I like to think that we're all realists, and reality is even the best marriages have their snags where communication just isn't happening or the partners are at each other's throat. When this occurs, you can work this operation in order to create an atmosphere where the problem can be brought into the open and dealt with in a more constructive manner.

This rite calls upon the intercession of Blessed Luigi and Maria Beltrame Quattrocchi, who were beatified by Pope John Paul II in 2002 and are looked upon as the patrons of the married estate.

It should be noted from the onset, however, that this operation will only work if both spouses honestly and truly want the marriage to heal. There are times where one or the other spouse is causing problems and trying to force a break-up, instead of being a responsible adult and openly communicating with his or her partner. In cases like these, there's no magic that'll fix the situation, and in the long run it may be better for both parties to let the marriage die.

Materials:
White 7-Day Candle
Image of Blessed Luigi and Maria Quattrocchi
Picture of wife (to left of candle)
Picture of husband (to right of candle)
Piece of paper

1. In front of your mensa, sit in meditation upon your goal, that the problems in your (or your friend's or client's) marriage may be solved. Imagine the two of them sitting in a lavender room with white lace curtains, a cool gentle breeze coming through the window and cooling them off, while they sit and gently discuss the issues at hand. Having come to a working resolution, imagine them holding one another in their arms, and giving each other a kiss, signifying that love has once again returned and the problem is overcome. Finally, a brilliant white light, the light of God's blessing, comes in through the window and envelops the couple as they stand in loving embrace.

2. Arise and approach the mensa. Make your Declaration of Intent in your own words, an example of which follows:
I do this because the marriage of N. and N.N. has come to trouble. Blessed Luigi and Maria Quattrocchi, intercede on behalf of my petitions before the Father, that this marriage shall become fresh, loving, and free of these adversities as you both loved one another.

Now place the pictures of husband and wife on top of one another. Whether wife-over-husband or husband-over-wife doesn't matter, just do what feels right.

3. On the paper in front of you, write:
N. and N.N. have conquered the obstacles to a happy marriage.
Place this paper on the mensa, on top of the pictures.

4. Picking up the white 7-Day candle in your left hand, bless it with the right, saying:
+Bless, O Lord of Hosts, this candle which we in thy name +bless, that its oily wax shall symbolize the grease and filth of the obstacles keeping peace from returning to the marriage of N. and N.N., and so as it is burned away by this purifying flame which is the light of thy Son, so too shall all obstacles be burned away from the marriage of N. and N.N. Through Christ our Lord. Amen.

And sprinkle the candle three times with holy water, saying nothing. Place the candle on top of the paper and the pictures and light it.

5. Fixating on the flame of the candle, say this prayer:
Blessed Luigi and Maria Quattrocchi, come to my aid and intercede on behalf of my petitions before the Father! Help restore peace and harmony to this troubled marriage between N. and N.N., and may they again remember the meaning and purpose of this holy Sacrament through which their souls are both entwined. Bring them peace, bring them harmony, bring them comfort, and help them join together to crush any obstacles in the way to their happy union. Through Jesus Christ our Lord, who with the Father lives and reigns in the unity of the Holy Ghost, God, forever and ever. Amen.

6. Now sit back and meditate again on your objective, visualizing as you did in step 1. If possible, you may also want to say a Rosary here for your intentions.

7. Say this prayer of thanks:

Blessed Luigi and Maria Quattrocchi, I give you thanks for your intercession, that you have helped to heal the marriage of N. and N.N. Amen.

8. You are finished for this night. Now leave the candle burning until it burns out on its own, and for each day that it burns, repeat steps 5 to 8 inclusive.

177. To Construct a Love Charm

Common wisdom has it that the best charm for attracting love is within yourself: work on yourself, improve yourself, and make yourself inwardly attractive, and people will be more drawn to you; this is similar to the late-nineteenth century concept of the "Law of Attraction." There is a great deal of truth in this, but sometimes we need a little extra help to point us in the right direction.

Sometimes all we need is something to make us feel more attractive: a shave, a change in wardrobe, just bathing more often, or even going to a new location where you can meet available people. Other times we might just be like Linus and need a "security blanket," which in this case would be a piece of jewelry that helps us to feel more confident and beautiful (which is the only non-superstitious way to explain how most love talismans work). And other times, we just need divine guidance outright.

For these times, I propose the consecration and use of a love charm which can be worn around the neck or placed in the pocket while going out. This won't help you to go out to a bar and "get laid," but is instead intended to help you keep your focus on the divine guidance as to how you yourself can become and feel more attractive, and in response others will find themselves more attracted to you. While there's no miracle that will do this overnight, the idea here is to help accelerate the process.

Materials:
Love charm (described in step 1)
Red 7/8" straight candle
Green 7/8" straight candle
Optional: Holy Water or Rose oil mixed with cinnamon.

1. Procure the love charm itself, which can be anything from a charm on a bracelet or necklace, a copper nugget with the symbol of Venus etched upon it, or a piece of jewelry that you feel has an especial connection with attraction and attractiveness.

2. Place the red and green candles side-by-side, upon the center of your mensa. The green candle should be on the left, the red on the right. Place the charm in front of the candles.

3. Make your Declaration of Intent, which may be something like the following:
I perform this work that this talisman of love may be consecrated, thus shall love and romance be brought into the life of N. Amen.

4. Now we begin the rite of blessing the talisman, saying:
Our help is in the name of the Lord.

Then either you or an assistant respond:
Who made the heaven and the earth.

You say:
The Lord be with you.

Then either you or an assistant respond:
And with your spirit.

Finally, you say Let us pray, and then place left hand on the mensa, right hand over the talisman, while saying the prayer of blessing:
Most benign and almighty God, Lord of Hosts who watches over relationships and loves: take note of the humbleness of this creature of metal *(or wood, or leather, or papyrus, or paper, or whatever)*, and impart to it the + blessing of your divine power, that in keeping with the spirit of the sigils and characters inscribed upon its surface, it may attract to the operator, or towards whomever carries or possesses this amulet: great love, physical as well as spiritual, and the spirit of attraction persons. Through our Lord Jesus Christ, your Son, who lives and reigns with you in the unity of the Holy Ghost, God, forever and ever.

After the prayer is concluded, either you or an assistant finalize the blessing by saying: **Amen.**

5. Now that the blessing has been given, you have the option of sprinkling it with holy water thrice in the form of a cross (in silence), or you may anoint it with a mixture of rose and cinnamon oil, also in the form of a cross, while saying:
By this holy anointing, and His most loving mercy, may the almighty Lord impart to this amulet the power of amorous attraction.

Here you anoint the amulet, saying:
In the name of the Father, and of the +Son, and of the Holy Ghost. Amen.

178. To Get Someone to Think About You

In a relationship, there may be times when you're separated from your beloved over a great distance or for a period of time, and you may have no way of getting in touch to see how they're doing or even say "I love you." This can be painful and even agonizing, so here's something to send them a message and get them to contact you.

The general principle of this rite rests in working with guardian angels as intermediaries between you and your beloved. It's been said that if you cannot reach another person or are having a problem with a person, you should ask your guardian angel to talk it over with his or her guardian angel, and then things will start to move in a more positive direction.

Of course, the drawback is that if you're dealing with someone who's dense as a ton of bricks, then neither this nor any other operation will be successful; since magic is an art of dealing with subtle energies, those who have no receptivity or sensitivity to energy will simply not be effected one way or the other.

Materials:
One red candle (7/8" straight or figure candle).
Usual mensa candles (7/8" straight, 2 white and 1 red).
Piece of Paper.
Pen with either red or black ink.
Mixture of rose and rosemary oil.

1. Place your red figure candle in the center of the mensa, with the piece of paper in front of it; do not light the candle. Your mensa candles should be in the usual place.

2. With hands joined upon the mensa, make your Declaration of Intent, which could be like this:
I do this that I may enjoy the thoughts of N., that N. shall think about me pleasantly and contact me presently.

3. Anoint the red candle with the oil mixture, by whatever method you prefer. On the piece of paper, write the name of the person you wish to think about you. Write nine times:
(Name), think about me and come to me.

4. After writing this out, anoint the paper with a mixture of rose and rosemary oil in the form of a cross, and then fold it into quarters. Place the paper underneath the red candle.

5. Light the red candle, praying as you do so:
Almighty God, unto whom all secrets are known and by whom the hearts of the human race are bestirred. Send forth thine Holy Spirit and transmit thy power into this my work. By the intercession of St. Gabriel, whom thou sent as a messenger to Daniel and to the Blessed Virgin Mary; by the intercession of St. Martha, one of whose charges is to keep us on our lover's minds; and by the actions of mine and N.'s guardian angels, I seek that the heart of N. be such bestirred, that N. shall keep me in his/her thoughts, and that N. shall contact me at the first possible opportunity. Through our Lord Jesus Christ thy Son, who liveth and reigneth in the unity of the same Holy Ghost, God, world without end. Amen.

6. Once you finish this prayer, say the following address to Sts. Gabriel and St. Martha:

O glorious St. Gabriel, thou who wast chosen by Almighty God to bring messages to the sons and daughters of men, so too do I call upon thee to bring N. the tidings of my love. O wondrous St. Martha, sister of Lazarus who was called back from death by our Lord. It is said that one of your provinces is the closeness between lovers. Thus I seek thee, thus I ask thee, thus I come before thee to draw N. closer to me. Keep me in his/her thoughts, keep me in his/her dreams, keep me in his/her fantasies, that he/she shall come to me or call me at the first possible opportunity. Through Christ our Lord. Amen.

And finally, the Guardian Angel prayer:

Angel of God, my guardian dear, to whom his love commits me here; ever this day *(night)* be at my side, to light and guard, to rule and guide.

If you know your guardian Angel's name, you may say "Angel N" in the above prayer, in place of "Angel of God."

7. Keeping your hands joined, continue the prayer thus:

O holy Guardian Angel, deputed from birth to guide and to protect me to the end of my years: guide me, advocate for me, and present my case for me now. Go, I ask you, to the guardian Angel of N., and persuade him to place my countenance in N.'s thoughts, my voice in N.'s dreams, and my touch in N.'s fantasies. Persuade him so to make my image, my voice, and my touch so compellingly real and palpable to N, that N. shall come to me straightaway, or at the first possible opportunity. I seek this through the power of our Lord Jesus Christ, who with the Father liveth and reigneth in the unity of the Holy Ghost, God, world without end. Amen.

8. Remain standing for a few minutes, imagining your loved one thinking, dreaming, and fantasizing about you. Then imagine him or her calling you and getting back in touch with you.

When the time comes that you feel is right – and it's important not to rush this step – inhale, while separating your hands and holding them over the candle. As you exhale, imagine the energy from these visualizations going out from the palms of your hands and into the candle, giving the ritual fuel to draw your beloved back to you.

9. When you are finished, leave the candle burning, and say a prayer of thanksgiving to Almighty God, to Sts. Gabriel and Martha, and to your Guardian Angel for the work they have accomplished on your behalf. Amen.

179-181. Candle Magic for Prosperity

179. To gain money in a hurry
Is it just me, or do we all have those times when we need to stretch to pay the bills? Of course, you can go to those check-cashing places for a "fast payday loan," but then you'll just get caught up in a vicious web of debt that's nigh impossible to escape. You can take up a second job, but then you'll have no time for the kids and it'll be up to three weeks before you see your first paycheck! You need the money now, so here's a suggestion:

Materials:
1 Green light bulb
1 Green 7-day candle
1 Brown 7-day candle
2 White 7-day candles
2 Green votive glass candle-holders
14 tealights

Pen with Green Ink
Piece of unlined paper
Piece of Paper Currency ($1, $5, $10, or $20 bill)

1. This rite assumes a room where your materials will be undisturbed for the duration of the working, no matter what else is done in that room. So start by unscrewing whatever light bulb is currently in use, and replace it with the green bulb. This bulb is to be kept lit constantly for the duration of the ritual.

2. The two white 7-Day candles will be your mensa candles for this operation, so bless them and set them up accordingly.

3. Place the money on the center of the mensa, and on the piece of paper write nine times:
Much money comes quickly to N.,
where "N." is your name. Place this on top of the currency.

4. Place the Brown and Green 7-day candles on top of the paper, with the brown to the left and the green to the right. The green candle represents the energy of wealth that you wish to manifest, and the brown candle represents the channel of speedy manifestation for that energy. Bear this in mind as you proceed.

5. Place the votive glasses in front of the 7-day candles, with a tea light in each.

6. Make your Declaration of Intent:
I do this because I need money, in the amount of x inside the next y days. Almighty God, through your Angels and through your Saints I draw nigh that you will grant this to me.

In this statement, x is the amount of money you need, and y is the amount of time in which you need it.

7. Light your mensa candles, saying nothing as you do so, but thinking about the money you need. Visualize yourself already having it and happily holding it in your hands. Picture yourself paying your bills, getting out of debt, and investing and growing your future.

8. Now light the Green and Brown 7-day candles, in that order, saying:

At the green: **From spiritual force.**
At the brown: **Unto physical form be manifest.**

9. Light the tea lights, also from right to left, in silence. Then, bowing with hands joined upon the mensa, say this prayer:
Almighty Eternal God, you who preside over the sphere of plenty and prosperity: by the intercession of St. Joseph, the Foster-Father of thy Son our Lord and patron of workers, and by the rising up of Sadkiel, the Archangel of prosperity: I call unto thee, I draw nigh unto thee, and I invoke thee. I invoke thee into this my work that thou wilt give ear unto my plea, and that by sending forth thy light and thy grace this work shall be successful. Help me, O Lord, to gain x amount of dollars in y day's time, that my physical needs and those of my loved ones shall be met, and that we shall thus be able to turn our whole minds, hearts, and souls to the contemplation of thy glory. Through our same Lord, Jesus Christ, thy Son, who liveth and reigneth with thee in the unity of the Holy Ghost, God, forever and ever. Amen.

10. Afterwards, go about your daily business while leaving the candles to burn. Each day, you will replace the tea lights with fresh ones, light them, and say the above prayer; the money you seek should be in your hands by the end of the ritual.

180. To Bring Money into a Business Venture

Okay, so you've shelled out for all necessary and legal and licensing requirements, you've got the building or office space, and you've got the product, whatever that may be. It's your first day on the job, and you want customers! Here's a short and simple operation to be carried out daily, to help draw customers (and revenue) into your sphere of availability.

This rite invokes the Holy Family and especially the Infant Jesus of Prague. In traditional Benedicaria practice, it is believed that to the Infant of Prague can ensure a steady flow of income into the home. We elaborate on this, and also encourage the practitioner to place a statue or image of the Infant facing the door of his place of business.

Materials:
1 Virgin Mary 7-day Candle (in any of her titles)
1 St. Joseph 7-day Candle
1 Infant Jesus of Prague 7-day Candle
1 Piece of Unlined Paper
1 Pen with Green Ink

1. As above, and as in all rites, we assume that your mensa will be set up in a place where it won't be disturbed for the entire time of the operation.

2. The mensa is to be set up as follows: on the left, far corner shall be placed the candle of the Virgin Mary; on the right, far corner the candle of St. Joseph; and in the center,

front shall be placed the candle of the Infant Jesus. Under the "Jesus Candle" you place the piece of paper, with the saying **I want money to come to my business** written on it nine times.

3. Light the "Mary Candle," then recite Prayer #25 from Chapter II:

O Mother of Perpetual Help! Grant that I may ever invoke your most powerful name, which is the safeguard of the living and the salvation of the dying. O purest Mary! O sweetest Mary! Let your name henceforth be ever on my lips. Delay not, O Blessed Lady, to succor me whenever I call on you. In all my temptations, in all my needs, I will never cease to call on you ever repeating your sacred name. Mary, Mary. Oh, what a consolation, what sweetness, what confidence, what emotion fills my soul when I utter your sacred name, or even only think of you! I thank the Lord for having given you, for my good, so sweet, so powerful, so lovely a name. But I will not be content with merely uttering your name. Let my love for you prompt me ever to hail you Mother of Perpetual Help. Mother of Perpetual Help, pray for me and grant me the favor I confidently ask of you, that my business shall generate enough money to pay my bills, my expenses, and all the needs of survival, that through thee I may glorify thy Son more and more.

4. From this, we light the "Joseph Candle," while praying the oration for Success in Work, which is #30 from Chapter II:

Glorious St. Joseph, model of all those who are devoted to labor, obtain for me the grace to work conscientiously, putting the call of duty above my many sins; to work with thankfulness and joy, considering it an honor to employ and develop, by means of labor, the

gifts received from God; to work with order, peace, prudence and patience, never surrendering to weariness or difficulties; to work, above all, with purity of intention, and with detachment from self, having always death before my eyes and the account which I must render of time lost, of talents wasted, of good omitted, of vain complacency in success so fatal to the work of God. All for Jesus, all for Mary, all after thy example, O Patriarch Joseph. Such shall be my motto in life and death. Amen.

Follow with this prayer:
Glorious St. Joseph, pray for me and grant me the favor I confidently ask of you, that my business shall generate enough money to pay my bills, my expenses, and all the needs of survival, that through thee I may glorify Our Lord more and more.

5. Finally, we come to the "Jesus Candle," which we light while reciting the Novena to the Infant Jesus of Prague, which is #19 from Chapter II:
O Jesus, who hast said, "Ask and you shall receive, seek and you shall find, knock and it shall be opened to you," through the intercession of Mary, Thy most holy Mother, I knock, I seek, I ask that my prayer be granted.

Here mention your request:
Holy Infant of Prague, come to me and grant me the favor I confidently ask of you, that my business shall generate enough money to pay my bills, my expenses, and all the needs of survival, that I may humbly glorify Thee more and more.

Continue the Novena prayer:

O Jesus, who hast said, "All that you ask of the Father in My Name, He will grant you," through the intercession of Mary, Thy most holy Mother, I humbly and urgently ask Thy Father in Thy Name that my prayer be granted.

Again mention your request:

Holy Infant of Prague, come to me and grant me the favor I confidently ask of you, that my business shall generate enough money to pay my bills, my expenses, and all the needs of survival, that I may humbly glorify Thee more and more.

Continue the Novena prayer:

O Jesus, who hast said, "Heaven and earth shall pass away, but My word shall not pass," through the intercession of Mary, Thy most holy Mother, I feel confident that my prayer will be granted.

Again mention your request:

Holy Infant of Prague, come to me and grant me the favor I confidently ask of you, that my business shall generate enough money to pay my bills, my expenses, and all the needs of survival, that I may humbly glorify Thee more and more.

6. Meditate in front of the candles, contemplating the Holy Family and how they have helped you in your life; know now that they are helping you now, and will continue to do so. You wish to follow their example, so let them know that by reciting Prayer #23 from Chapter II:

Lord Jesus Christ, who, being made subject to Mary and Joseph, didst consecrate domestic life by Thine ineffable virtues; grant that we, with the assistance of both, may be taught by the example of Thy Holy Family

and may attain to its everlasting fellowship. Who livest and reignest forever. Amen.

7. Now give thanks to the Holy Family for their assistance, in your own words, and say it devoutly and sincerely. The Holy Family love you and will help you as a result of that love. It's only right to love them back and freely express that love, the same way you would express love for your own family.

8. This ends the first day. Now for each day that the candles burn, sit and meditate in front of them, and say the prayers indicated throughout the text of this rite. Once the candles burn down, replace them and begin the rite over again, making this a daily devotion.

181. Finding a New Job

Back in the 90's, nobody had problems finding a job. You could grab something and if you didn't like it, you'd have another job within an hour's time. It's not like that anymore, and no matter how much recovery we might see in the stock markets, a lot of people still don't have jobs and the market's still tough.

Sometimes, we just need a little lift.

The following exercise is aimed at doing just that: finding new employment quickly. It may not be the best-paying job or a job with the most dignity, but you'll find something to support yourself and your family, which can give you a springboard to move on to something better before long.

Materials:
1 Yellow or (preferably) St. Joseph 7-day Candle
1 Blue or (preferably) Virgin Mary 7-day Candle
28 Tea lights or Votive Candles

2 Yellow Votive Candleholders
2 Blue Votive Candleholders
Altar Candles (see Chapter 4, p. 104)
1 Green Light Bulb.
Rosary

1. Light the light bulb, which should be the only light in the room.

2. On your mensa, place the Altar Candles first (Chapter IV, figure 4-1). Then place the Virgin Mary and St Joseph Candles in the center, with Mary on the left and Joseph on the right. Finally, place the blue Votive holders in front of Mary and the Yellow ones in front of Joseph. Place tea lights or Votive candles in these.

3. For a few seconds, quietly meditate on your purpose for doing this, and visualize yourself being employed and supporting yourself and your family. Your bills are paid, your rent or mortgage is current, and debt collectors are off your back. After formulating your intention, say out loud why you're doing this. Use your own words and keep it simple.

4. Light the Saint Joseph candle, saying:
St. Joseph, patron of workers and foster-father of Our Lord, intercede for me and help me to find a decent job.

5. Light the Blessed Mother candle, saying:
O Most Sorrowful and Immaculate Blessed Virgin Mary, Mother of God and Mother of the whole Church, interceded for me and help me find a decent job.

6. Light the Candles in the yellow holders, saying:
St. Joseph, pray for us, and intercede for us in the sight of Almighty God.

7. Light the candles in the blue holders, saying:
O Holy Mother of God, pray for us.
That we may be made worthy of the promises of Christ.

8. Take the Rosary in your hands, and assume the position you do when normally praying the Rosary (standing, sitting, or kneeling, as you find most comfortable and best for your mental concentration). Before starting, hold the Rosary in your hands and say:
May this offering of the Most Holy Rosary be found acceptable to Our Lady, and may she earnestly intercede on behalf of my petitions before the Father.

9. Pray the Rosary in the usual manner, meditating upon the Mysteries proper to that day of the week. There is a technique with the Mysteries in which the Mystery is said in the middle of the Hail Mary, right after the name of Jesus. Here, we would insert the purpose of our working, such as:
"... blessed is the fruit of thy womb, Jesus.
<u>Who helped me find suitable employment.</u>
Holy Mary, Mother of God ..."

Finish out the Rosary saying the usual prayers in the usual manner.

10. After the Rosary is finished, end with this prayer:
O most Sorrowful and Immaculate Blessed Virgin Mary, Mother of God and Mother of men, thou who wast found worthy to carry God himself in thy womb, and thou who has crushed him who is at once the enemy of God and man in common under thy heel. Humbly do I, *(name)*, approach thee, through these Joyful *(or Sorrowful, or Glorious)* Mysteries of this thy Most Holy Rosary, asking that this offering may be acceptable to thee, and that thou wilt earnestly intercede on behalf of

my petitions before the Father, namely that thou, with the help of St. Joseph, thy Spouse, and Jesus Christ, thy Son, will help me to find suitable employment. Through our same Lord Jesus Christ thy Son, who with the Father liveth and reigneth in the unity of the Holy Ghost, God, forever and ever. Amen.

11. Finish this day by saying thanks for all the good you have received, and all the help you have received in finding a job. On all subsequent days, repeat step three to form your intention, and then repeat steps 6-11 every day.

Please realize that this ritual will not automatically make a job drop into your lap, as God helps them who help themselves. You must comb the papers, look for "Help Wanted" signs, search the internet high and low, and fill out your own job applications. However, this will be of great help (I've used it myself in the past!) finding employment when market is tight.

182-183. Candle Magic for Health

182. To Restore One's Health
In the first place, the Bible tells us to honor the medical profession (Sirach 38:1), and we're not about to argue against Sacred Scripture. However, the Church also encourages us to seek out the intercession of the Saints during our trials in this life, especially in the more difficult cases.

Materials: Altar Candles
1 Yellow Taper Candle
1 St. Raphael Holy Card
1 St. Raphael Medal

1. Procure the St. Raphael Medal and have it blessed by your priest. If he asks why, do not lie to him. Tell him that it is for yourself or for a friend or family member (such as the case may actually be), and that you believe St. Raphael's intercession will help him or her to get better.

2. Once the medal is blessed, you may place it around your neck or the neck of the person for whom you're praying. If possible, you may also set it down on your mensa when you pray, as a symbol of uniting your prayers with the medal.

3. Place the yellow candle in the center of your mensa, and light the Altar Candles in the usual fashion. Place the St. Raphael Holycard in front of the candle.

4. With hands joined, pray for St. Raphael's intercession, using Prayer #37 from Chapter II:
Glorious Archangel, Saint Raphael, great prince of the heavenly Court, you are illustrious for your gifts of wisdom and grace. You are a guide of those who journey by land, or sea, or air, consoler of the afflicted, and refuge of sinners. I beg you, assist me in all my needs and in all the sufferings of this life, as once you helped the young Tobias on his travels. Because you are the "medicine of God" I humbly pray you to heal the many infirmities of my soul and the ills that afflict my body. I especially ask of you the favor of healing N of the affliction the affects him/her, *(here name the affliction)***, and the great grace of purity to prepare me to be the temple of the Holy Ghost. Amen.**

5. Now quietly meditate in front of the candle, and in your mind, imagine Raphael going up to the Seat of grace with your request and presenting it at the feet of God the Father. He then comes down, whether to you or to the person for

whom you are praying, wraps his wings around him, and heals him or her. Don't just watch it, but feel it happening and believe that it's already happened. Remember what our Lord says in Mark 11:24: *"So I tell you, whatever you ask for in prayer, believe that you have received it, and it will be yours."*

6. Once finished, extinguish the candle and thank St. Raphael for helping you in this work. For nine days, keep lighting the candle, praying, and meditating.

183. For a Safe Childbirth
We all wish that our pregnancies, or those of our wives, would have a smooth and easy run from conception to delivery. Yet unfortunately, this isn't always the case.

In times like this, when there are complications with the pregnancy or the birth itself, or even just to ensure that all goes as it should, we look to the intercession of St. Gerard Majella and/or St. Anne to help us in these delicate times. Of course, the expectant mother should always be under the care of an obstetrician during the course of the pregnancy, and it's recommended that this procedure be done both by mother and father as soon as they find out she's expecting.

Materials:
I White seven-day candle
2 White taper candles (other than the altar candles)
Images of St. Anne and of St. Gerard Majella
Holy Water

1. Set it up and light the altar candles in the usual manner, and place the white 7-day candle in the center of the mensa, with one of the white tapers to either side. Place the image of Saint Anne in front of the left-hand taper, and the image of St. Gerard in front of the right-hand taper.

2. Mother and father should both make the sign of the Cross, if both are working together. In the case that either is working in solitude without the other present, the he or she makes the Sign of the Cross, and adapts everything below to the use of a single practitioner.

3. Operator makes the following Declaration of Intent: **Almighty God, truly hast Thou granted us a marvel in the form of this unborn child. And now, in this hour, we draw nigh to Thee, seeking that Thou wilt be favorable to our supplications, to ensure that this child shall be born healthily and without complications, that the world may wonder upon seeing this manifestation of Thine ineffible glory. Amen.**

4. The mother (or father, if he's working alone) then lights the 7-day candle, praying as she does so: **As I light this candle on this day/night, so doth it represent my desire to see my child born into the world, healthy and without complications.**

The father continues this prayer (or mother, if alone): **May Almighty God, Father, Son, and Holy Ghost, who has given us this wonderful child, assist us in bringing to term this pregnancy. For His wonder is seen in the eyes of every child, and to be as a little child is to enter into the kingdom of Heaven. Amen.**

5. The mother (or father, if he is alone) lights the left-hand taper candle, and prays an adaptation of Prayer #43 from Chapter II: **Good St. Anne, you were especially favored by God to be the mother of the most holy Virgin Mary, the Mother of our Savior. By your power with your most pure daughter and with her divine Son, kindly obtain for us the grace and the favor we now seek, that this our child**

shall be allowed to be born into the world healthily and without complications. Please secure for us also forgiveness of our past sins, the strength to perform faithfully our daily duties and the help we need to persevere in the love of Jesus and Mary. Amen.

6. The father (or mother, if she is alone) lights the right-hand taper candle, and prays this adapted form of prayer #77 from Chapter II:

O Great Saint Gerard, beloved servant of Jesus Christ, perfect imitator of thy meek and humble Savior, and devoted Child of the Mother of God: enkindle within my heart one spark of that heavenly fire of charity which glowed in thine and made thee a seraph of love. O glorious Saint Gerard, because when falsely accused of crime, thou didst bear, like thy Divine Master, without murmur or complaint, the calumnies of wicked men, thou hast been raised up by God as Patron and Protector of expectant mothers. Preserve my wife from danger and from excessive pains accompanying childbirth, and shield the child which she now carries, that he or she may see the light of day and receive the lustral waters of baptism, through Jesus Christ our Lord. Amen.

7. Both parents should now kneel (the mother may stand, sit, or lie down as her condition requires), and say one Our Father, followed by nine Hail Marys, one for each month of pregnancy. When done, they should reflect in silence upon what they've requested, then rise and say in unison the following prayer of thanksgiving:

Almighty God, St. Anne, St. Gerard, we give thanks to all of you, for you have aided us in delivering this our child, healthily and without complications. Through Christ our Lord. Amen.

8. The father should make the sign of the Cross over the mother's womb (blessing his child), and then sprinkle the mother's womb with Holy Water. The taper candles are extinguished, the two then make the sign of the Cross, and the rite is concluded.

9. Every day while the 7-day candle continues to burn, the couple should repeat the following:
Declaration of Intent.
Light the taper candles, and repeat steps 5-8.

This operation can also be adapted as a Pro-Life devotion, by praying for an unborn infant that you know or for the unborn in general.

184. Candle Magic for Protection
We all have moments when we could use a little help, whether we need protection against evil spirits, our crabby neighbors, a mean-spirited supervisor, meddling in-laws, or any host of other evils, be they intentionally or unintentionally inflicted on us.

Were one to look through the various magical literature extant, there would be found numerous formulae for every kind of protection: against storms, against sorcery, and so on and so forth. These take the form of "hardening the aura," of making a circle of salt around oneself, of charging and wearing talismans, and any other thing that one can possibly imagine.

For myself, I'd say many of the operations found in these books are overly drawn-out, and some are just plain absurd.

However, there are many prayers and even Masses employed to invoke divine protection, and a number of

Saints are patrons for protection against one or other kind of tribulation. So here's an all-around general procedure:

1. Research the Saints on the internet and find one whose patronage includes your situation. For example, St. Christopher is for safe travel or St. Benedict for protection against spiritual evil. You'll also find a number of protection prayers in Chapter III, while the *Lorica of St. Patrick* (Prayer #86 from Chapter II) serves as an excellent protection against all manner of persons and conditions.

2. Get an image of that Saint and a white candle.

3. Light the candle and say a prayer to that Saint asking his or her intercession to protect you from whatever circumstance.

4. Thank the Saint for having interceded on your behalf.

5. Sprinkle yourself with Holy Water. In addition, you can wear a medal of the Saint in question, or carry a holycard in your purse or coat pocket.

Now, know that you are protected (repeat if you feel it necessary) and amend your life to live as a good Christian.

VII. Rosary Magic

185. Fifteen Promises of the Holy Rosary

It's said that the Blessed Virgin Mary made these fifteen promises to St. Dominic and Blessed Alan de la Roche for all who pray the Rosary every day.

While we don't know for a fact whether the Blessed Mother actually made these promises (and it's doubtful considering scholars date the Rosary to 300 years after Dominic's death), those who would practice Rosary Magic would do well to familiarize themselves both with these promises and with St. Louis de Montfort's little book The Secret of the Rosary, *because experience shows these form a spiritual contract of sorts between the Court of Heaven and the Rosary magician.*

1. To all those who will recite my Rosary devoutly, I promise my special protection and very great graces.

2. Those who will persevere in the recitation of my Rosary shall receive some signal grace.

3. The Rosary shall be a very powerful armor against hell; it shall destroy vice, deliver from sin, and shall dispel heresy.

4. The Rosary shall make virtue and good works flourish, and shall obtain for souls the most abundant divine mercies; it shall substitute in hearts love of God for love of the world, elevate them to desire heavenly and eternal goods. Oh, that souls would sanctify themselves by this means!

5. Those who trust themselves to me through the Rosary, shall not perish.

6. Those who will recite my Rosary piously, considering its Mysteries, shall not be overwhelmed by misfortune nor die a bad death. The sinner shall be converted; the just shall grow in grace and become worthy of eternal life.

7. Those truly devoted to my Rosary shall not die without the consolations of the Church, or without grace.

8. Those who will recite my Rosary shall find during their life and at their death the light of God. the fullness of His grace, and shall share in the merits of the blessed.

9. I will deliver very promptly from purgatory the souls devoted to my Rosary.

10. The true children of my Rosary shall enjoy great glory in heaven.

11. What you ask through my Rosary, you shall obtain.

12. Those who propagate my Rosary shall obtain through me aid in all their necessities.

13. I have obtained from my Son that all the confreres of the Rosary shall have for their brethren in life and death the saints of heaven.

14. Those who recite my Rosary faithfully are all my beloved children, the brothers and sisters of Jesus Christ.

15. Devotion to my Rosary is a special sign of predestination.

186. How to Do Basic Rosary Magic

When properly done, the Rosary is an exercise both in visualization and repetitive prayer. Because of this, it's also an excellent weapon for magical working.

To do this, you pray the Rosary as usual, visualizing your goal accomplished by the power of Jesus, through the Blessed Mother's intercession. During the prayers, you insert your intentions in the middle of each Hail Mary, like this:

Hail Mary, full of grace, the Lord is with thee.
Blessed art thou amongst women, and blessed is the fruit of thy womb, Jesus.
(Here name your intentions.)
Holy Mary, Mother of God, pray for us sinners now and at the hour of our death. Amen.

Remember that you name your intention after the word "Jesus," so you can say it in a way that Jesus already did this for you in the past tense. For example, *"Who healed me of whatever ails me."* Keep your intention short and sweet, and know in faith that your prayer is being answered.

After you've finished the entire Rosary or just the five Mysteries for that day, say a prayer from Chapter III that best expresses your intention, and then conclude with this prayer:
O most Sorrowful and Immaculate
Blessed Virgin Mary,
Mother of God and Mother of men,
thou who wast found worthy
to carry God himself in thy womb,
and thou who hast crushed him
who is at once the enemy
of God and man in common under thy heel.

Humbly do I, N., approach thee,
through these Joyful (Sorrowful, or Glorious) Mysteries
of this thy Most Holy Rosary,
asking that this offering may be acceptable to thee,
and that thou wilt earnestly intercede
on behalf of my petitions before the Father,
namely that (here name your petitions).
Through our Lord Jesus Christ thy Son,
who with the Father liveth and reigneth
in the unity of the Holy Ghost, God,
forever and ever. Amen.

Do this daily until your intention is manifested, pray in the
past tense as though your intention has already been
manifested, and keep your eyes peeled for opportunities
that can lead to exactly that.

187. Magical Uses of the Fifteen Mysteries
The Mysteries of the Rosary are symbolic of steps on one's
spiritual path, and resonate with energy that can helps
fulfill your magical intentions. Yet even though the
individual Mysteries may have applications to particular
magical purposes, it is best that we not pick and choose
each Mystery for its relevance to our operations.

Rather, it's better that we pray the entire Rosary as directed
by the Church, praying those Mysteries on the days in
which they are associated: *Joyful* on Monday and
Thursday, *Sorrowful* on Tuesday and Friday, and *Glorious*
on Wednesday and Saturday. Sundays are divided amongst
the three sets: Joyful between *Advent and Ash Wednesday*,
Sorrowful between *Ash Wednesday and Easter*, and
Glorious between *Easter and Advent*.

To better understand this, perhaps it would benefit us to
think of the Rosary as the visible spectrum of light, and the

Mysteries as colors in that spectrum. Now as to color, Faber Birren argues that the skin must contain cells which pick out the colors the body needs from white light and applies it to its needs (*Color Psychology and Color Therapy*, p. 132). Arguing from this logic, the Entire Rosary would be as a ray of sunlight, from which our operations will pick out the appropriate "colors" and apply them to our lives. Thus we get the benefit not only of the one or two Mysteries that most apply, but rather of all the Mysteries, which will help keep us in balance and maybe even help avoid the side-effects which sometimes come with magical operations.

188. The Joyful Mysteries (Mysteria Gaudiosa)
The First Joyful Mystery, the **Annunciation**, is associated with humility and acceptance of the divine will. That the Annunciation is the beginning of Jesus' journey in the flesh connects it with the beginning of one's spiritual journey, or beginnings or journeys in general.

The **Visitation** is associated with the spiritual fruit of charity, and as such is connected with works of love, harmony, friendship, and also of sacrificing of one's time and comfort for the sake of others. This is exemplified by the fact that Mary was pregnant, and for six months of her pregnancy she worked around Elizabeth's house and gave of herself so that her cousin may be more comfortable.

The **Nativity**, the Mystery where God manifests on earth in physical form, brings the spiritual fruit of indifference to the world and its physical conditions. St. Ignatius, in his Spiritual Exercises, tells us that we should become indifferent to heat or cold, wealth or poverty, and so on and so forth, and while praying the Rosary back on the Feast of the Immaculate Conception in 2000, I remember meditating upon this Mystery and I heard a voice saying to me:

"Indifference is power." I interpreted this as saying that when we are passionate or care inordinately about something or someone, then we allow ourselves to be controlled.

When the time prescribed by the Law had come, the infant Jesus was **Presented in the Temple**, in obedience to Divine Law. Obedience as a virtue is connected with piety and spiritual love, which are the purposes for which God made man: "To know Him, to serve Him, and to love Him." Through obedience to the Law, we grow in our relationship with God and in our own personal spirituality. Thus this Mystery also figures into all operations where you would wish to grow or expand something.

The Fifth Joyful Mystery, the **Finding in the Temple**, centers on the episode in Luke's Gospel where Jesus was left behind in the Temple and confounded the Priests and the Doctors with his knowledge and discourse about God. When Mary and St. Joseph finally found him and asked what he was doing, he simply responded he was about "my Father's business." The spiritual fruit of this Mystery is conversion to Christ-ward, with Christ as the Sun around which our spiritual lives are in perpetual orbit. Many of us are in a distant orbit around that Sun, separating ourselves through sin and self-interest. This Mystery also contains another layer, because in being converted, we are likewise communicating with and being taught by God Himself. Magically this figures into purposes involving enlightenment, knowledge, and conversion to the faith.

189. The Sorrowful Mysteries (Mysteria Dolorosa)
In the First Sorrowful Mystery, the **Agony in the Garden**, we see a higher analogue of the Fourth Joyous, because obedience to Divine Law takes its logical conclusion in submission to the Divine Will. This submission, in order to

be a true act of submission, must be given out of trust and pious love. It also goes further than this, because to bring oneself to obey, it requires a purgation of the urge to disobey. In fact, all the Sorrowful Mysteries are purgative in character, as they all involve purging something. From a magical perspective, this can be associated with purposes involving submission, restraint, or resolve.

The Second Sorrowful Mystery, the **Scourging at the Pillar**, has the spiritual fruit of gaining control over one's lower and carnal nature. This ties it in with purposes where self-control is needed in matters of the flesh, which can include prayers for your teenage son not to be controlled by his raging hormones!

The Third Sorrowful Mystery, the **Crowning with Thorns**, has for its fruit the gaining of control over one's thoughts and emotions. This Mystery is especially handy when striving not only to remove pride and unwanted thoughts/emotions from one's psyche, but also in the pursuit of peace, be it peace within oneself or peace within a community. I say this because its focus is the remove (or at least control) that which would cause contention, and thus has a side effect of creating an environment conducive to peaceful relations.

The Fourth Sorrowful Mystery, the **Carrying of the Cross**, has for its object perseverance exemplified by Our Lord patiently carrying the Cross. From this Mystery we learn patience (the root word of which is the Latin *pati*, "to suffer") and gain the courage to persevere, even in times of the most heinous persecution and suffering. This can be applied to purposes involving suffering, endurance, patience, silence (as Our Lord didn't complain as he carried the Cross), and to some degree strength and empowerment through the ability to persevere.

The Fifth Sorrowful Mystery, the **Crucifixion**, teaches us to die unto ourselves, and the mutual forgiveness both of those we have offended and those who have offended us. This brings into play intentions of penance, desensitization to the physical condition (thus a higher analogue of the Third Joyous Mystery), working through sorrow, and the strength to overcome crises and forgive those who caused them.

190. The Glorious Mysteries (Mysteria Gloriosa)

As we progress from the Joyful to the Sorrowful Mysteries, there's a shift of mood from one of beginning and initiation, to one of pain and purgation. As we progress from the Sorrowful and into the Glorious Mysteries, we see the mood change from one of suffering and purgation and into one of happiness, joy, and completion.

This transition of mood is very much brought forth in the First Glorious Mystery, the **Resurrection**, in which the Son has come back from the dead and is now the Sun of our spiritual lives. St. Paul tells us that if the Resurrection didn't happen, then our faith is all nothing but make-believe nonsense (1 Corinthians 15:14), and so this Mystery's fruit is the strengthening and continued firmness of that faith. This Mystery lends itself well to applications involving the defense of one's faith, the protection of loved ones from being influenced by those want them to abandon their faith, and for an increased knowledge and love of Christ and the economy of salvation.

The process of fulfillment continues in the Second Glorious Mystery, the **Ascension of Jesus**. Here we have the completion of the Third Joyous, in which not only are we indifferent and have we died to the physical world, but we have now shown our mastery over it to such a point that we've transcended it. This Mystery can teach us that if we wish to enter our spiritual home, we must first conquer and transcend the temptations, influences, and limitations of this one. It is only after we've conquered that we enter into the habitations of the Church Triumphant.

After Jesus ascended into Heaven, ten days later he sent the Holy Ghost to come down upon the Blessed Mother and the Apostles. This, the Third Glorious Mystery, the **Descent of the Holy Ghost**, is a completion of the Fifth Joyous because, as the Doctors and Priests were confounded by the prepubescent Christ, we now see the adult, conquering, and reigning Christ send down the Holy Ghost to lead us into all truth. This Mystery applies to the intentions of truth-finding, of gaining profound knowledge, and of seeking an amplification of the gifts of the Holy Ghost, which is the spiritual fruit of this Mystery.

For another fifteen years, the Blessed Mother is said to have remained upon this earth, until such time that God saw fit to call for her. Here, as God had done with Enoch, Moses, and Elijah, He chose to bring her body and soul directly into Heaven, which we call the **Assumption**. The spiritual fruit of this Mystery is a happy death, and this brings the sense of rest after labor, completion of work, and the peace of a well-earned reward. This Mystery can therefore be applied to works involving retirement, prayers for the souls in Purgatory, or anything else involving the peace and reward that should come after a prolonged period of hard work and right living.

This whole process comes to completion in the fifteenth and last Mystery, the **Coronation of Mary**. Here we have the final completion of a cycle that began with a fifteen-year old girl consenting to bear God Himself in her womb, and now she receives the full reward of her answer:

"Behold the handmaid of the Lord! Be it done to me according to thy word!" In the Forty-Eighth chapter of St. Louis' book, he tells us that there's also a crown that awaits us in heaven should we persevere in the good fight, and the spiritual fruit is the reception of this crown. This can apply to all works of spiritual unity, spiritual reward, and completion, much as the Assumption would apply to these things on the physical level.

VIII. Talismans

The following are samples of talismans I've constructed over the years, based on the symbolic language described in Ritual Magic for Conservative Christians. *A cursory glance at the grimoires and other magical literature will show that pretty much any set of symbols can be translated sort of pictographic language for your talismans.*

191. Separatio Populi Duorum Talisman

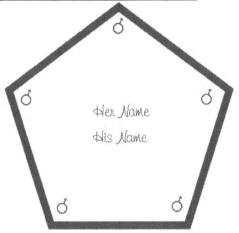

I did my first magical operation when I was sixteen years old, and it was something I can't say I'm proud of. At the time, I had a friend involved with a guy a little too old for her (she was 16 and he was 21), had her pawning her stuff to make his car payments, and more than a few other red flags. After a few phone conversations with her mother, I did what any young and dumb aspiring magician would do: my first "spell" was to break up their relationship.

The operation was successful. I learned a lot from that experience, and it's not something I would do again without good reason. In any case, this is the talisman I used in that ritual almost 26 years ago, and it's the first talisman I ever designed.

The first thing to notice is the pentagon, which is drawn in red ink. While a pentagram represents concentration of energy, is used to concentrate, a pentagon is symbolic of that energy being set into motion and dispersed. The red is the color of Mars, again represented by the symbols in each vertex.

I did the ritual by aiming at her to come to her senses (I'm happy to report that she did!), which is why her name was written on top and his name on the bottom. The symbolic language is that "She kicks him to the curb."

192. Hexagram of Shemesh

Another of my early designs, this came about when my sister had taken ill in the early 90's. It can be drawn in yellow or orange ink (orange gives greater visibility), or can be drawn in black ink on yellow paper.

The colors and planetary symbol are those of the Sun, to promote good health and harmony of the entire person. The hexagram is both a star representing the sun's rays and a traditional Jewish symbol to chase away evil influences. The name "Shemesh" is likewise Hebrew for the Sun, and the Hebrew names written in the center are likewise associated.

The person's name can be written either on the reverse of this talisman, or it can be written inside the symbol of the Sun in the center.

193. Pentacle of Nogah

You may notice that my talismanic designs tend towards Hebrew names and planetary themes. I do that because there's an element of convenience to it, and this pentacle is no exception. It is drawn in green ink, with the only exception being the heart in the center (drawn in pink).

The word "Nogah" is Hebrew for "Venus," and the color green bears out this association along with the planetary symbols. The pentagram is used both to show concentration of will and to represent that this talisman involves a human being (in fact most of my designs use pentagrams for that exact reason). If you're working to get a certain person interested in you, then on the reverse you would write that person's name on top of your own.

As to its use, I published this design a long time ago on the Christian Occultism and Magic in General website, where I gave the caption: "Wear or carry it to gain love or friendship. You may also hold it in your right hand while meditating on the love you would like to find."

194. Protectio Pecuniae Talisman

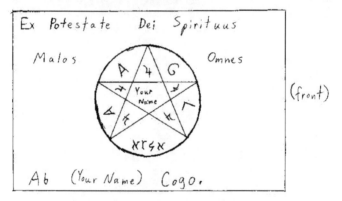

Drawn in green ink, this talisman was created a little later in my magical "career," with the intention of protecting a business venture while simultaneously drawing a regular income. As we can see, the obverse is about protection and the reverse *(next page)* about money.

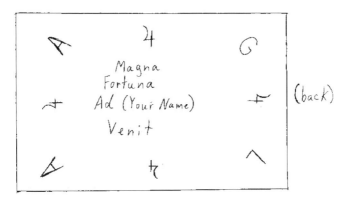

The green is the color of fertility and growth, and Jupiter is the planet associated with prosperity, with the pentagram employed as a protective symbol.

The word AGLA is short for the Hebrew phrase Atah Gavor Le-Olam Adonai, a phrase from the Jewish weekday prayer Tefilas Amidah and translating: "Thou art mighty forever, O Lord." The Latin – obverse and reverse, respectively – translate "By the power of God I bind all evil spirits away from *(name)*" and "Great fortune comes to *(name)*."

195. Financial Assistance Talisman

I constructed this Talisman in 2003, in conjunction with the original draft of the Money Ritual used as a sample in *Ritual Magic for Conservative Christians.*

This talisman is constructed along the lines of the pentagram representing the person whom this will benefit, with the Hebrew names of God, the Archangels, Angels, and planetary Spheres of the Kabbalistic Sefiros *Chesed* and *Malkhus* inside the circle (another book I plan on writing some day). The Hebrew in the upper-left translates "Water and Earth bring the money." The Latin inside the pentagram's points translates "Big money always comes to me," and the symbols and person's name in the center show that the money's intended to enter one's personal sphere, not fall all around that person while being inaccessible to him or her.

On the reverse of this talisman, write the following prayer: **Deus benévolens, Dne terrae et Rex universórum: per bráchia archangelórum tuórum Sáchiel et Sándalphon**

dona mihi pecúniam pro necessáriis desideriísque meis. Per Xm Dnm Nm. Amen.

In English this reads:
"God the benevolent, Lord of the earth and King of the universe: by the arms of Thine archangels Tzadkiel and Sandalphon grant me money for my necessities and my desires. Through Christ our Lord. Amen."

Charge and use according to your preferred method for talismanic magic, and the prayer may be said as a daily mantra.

196. Sleeping Pill

Sometimes necessity is the mother of invention. In this case I couldn't sleep and nothing I tried would help: counting sheep, watching TV until I was tired, nothing. One day I created this talisman and put it under my pillow; I slept like a baby and woke up refreshed the next day.

The talisman is drawn in purple ink, and the pentagram denotes the person it's intended to affect. The signs of the

Moon reference the Moon's affinity for the body's natural rhythms, in this case the sleep/wake cycle. The Greek letters spell "hypnos," which means sleep (my intention was sleep as in the word "sleep," not Hypnos as in the god of sleep; the word means both).

IX. Ritual Magic

197. Ritual for Drawing Money
This rite is geared toward entrepreneurs and others who can use a little help generating income.

0. Pre-Ritual Preparation
In the chamber of Art, there should be a small mensa with a blue or green candle upon its surface. This mensa stands in the center of the room, facing north (meaning that the Operator may stand at its south side, facing north across it). If the Operator shall use an amulet or talisman designed for drawing money, then let him place it upon the table, beneath the candle (talisman #195 was designed specifically for this ritual).

The ritual has places where you say the specific amount, of money you're looking for. I advise using a realistic number, based on your circumstances, employment prospects, professional and social network, etc. While magic can powerfully move things in the right direction, it still has its limits especially in the hands of a beginning practitioner.

1. Declaration of Intent
Stand at the mensa facing north, and then say the Declaration of Intent, using this form or your own words:
I proclaim this rite to the heavens and to the earth, because more money is needed in the life of *(name).*

Then make the Sign of the Cross, saying:
In the name of the Father, and of the Son, and of the Holy Spirit. Amen.
Or
For Thine is the Kingdom, and the Power, and the Glory, forever and ever. Amen.

2. Purification of the Working Space
Cleanse the working area using your banishing ritual or choice. Whether by sprinkling holy water around the area, by visualizing, by the Lesser Banishing Ritual of the Pentagram, or some other rite of your preference.

> Optional: Opening Hymn
Here you may sing a hymn or secular song pertaining to you desires if you wish. This is recommended more for group settings than for solitaries, yet may be done in either. *[The ideal Opening Hymn for any ritual is* Veni Creator Spiritus *or* Creator Spirit, Heavenly Dove, *#199 or #52 in the Hymnal.]*

3. First Address
In the First Address, you raise your hands into the Orans posture, talking to God about what you're doing, why you're doing this, and whose help you seek in order to get it done.

Hear me, Holy Lord, Father Almighty, eternal God, who preside over the abundance of your faithful; grant me the power to bring more money into the life of (name), and send also your holy Archangel Sachiel from the heavens alongside the Choir of the Angels, manifesting this money into the life of (name), dwelling here on earth below. To this end, may they be helped by your Archangel Sandalfon, the prayers of the entire Church Triumphant, and every entity and power responsible for bringing good things to the lives of your faithful. Through our Lord Jesus Christ, your Son, who lives and reigns with you in the unity of the Holy Ghost, one God, forever and ever. Amen.

4. Invocatio Nominis Domini
You then stand or kneel and say the Invocatio Nominis Domini:

Almighty God, in the Name of Jesus Christ Thine only-begotten Son I beseech Thee, to grant me the power to command all spirits, good or evil, without unintentionally causing harm to myself or to anybody else. Through our same Lord Jesus Christ, Thy Son, who liveth and reigneth in the unity of the Holy Ghost, God, forever and ever. Amen.

5. Reading of the Verse and Lighting of the Candles
Here you read the Verse, which in this case is an excerpt from the 11th poem of the Carmina Burana:
**On the earth right now the highest king is cash.
Cash do kings admire, and cash do they worship.
Cash that lifts the poor man up from the dung-heap.
Without cash no one is loved, no one admired.
Therefore cash must I acquire!**

Then you light the candle on the mensa. While you light it, you identify it with the subject of your working by saying these or similar words:
This candle is *(name)*, whose purse shall be filled with *(quantity of money)* through one week, every week through the remainder of his/her life, thence the money shall transfer on to his/her heredity. Amen.

6. The Lighting and Censing with Incense (Optional)
If you choose to use incense, you bless it by saying:
By the intercession of Sachiel the Archangel, standing at the right hand of the altar of incense, and of all His elect, may the Lord vouchsafe to +bless this incense, and in an odor of sweetness to receive it. Through Christ our Lord. Amen.

After the incense is blessed and place on the charcoal – or a stick or cone is lit, etc. – proceed to cense the mensa. Say this formula from the Latin Mass:
Lord, guide my prayer as incense to your sight: the lifting-up of my hands like the evening sacrifice.

7. Completing the Circle
NOTE: If incense is not used, this part may be done by walking to the appropriate part of the room, holding your hands out as in greeting, and saying the words.

Take the incense to the north part of the room. Censing to the north a few times, you say:
The purse of *(name)* is filled from the north, with more than *(quantity)* per week.

Walk in a quarter-circle from the north to the east of the room. When you get there, cense in that direction and say:
The purse of *(name)* is filled from the east, with more than *(quantity)* per week.

Proceed then to the south and after that to the west, censing each direction and saying the same formula.

Afterwards you go from the west to the north, censing again (completing the circle) while saying:
The purse of *(name)* is filled from from every direction, with more than *(quantity)* per week.

Finally you return back to the mensa and cense it one last time, saying:
And in the center, from within and from without, from above and from below, the purse of *(name)* is filled with more than *(quantity)* per week.

Afterwards you return your incense burner to its proper place, saying:
The circle is now complete,
That the pockets of *(name)* may be replete
With at least *(quantity)* per week.

Then make the Sign of the Cross, saying:
In the name of the Father, and of the Son, and of the Holy Spirit. Amen.
Or
For Thine is the Kingdom, and the Power, and the Glory, forever and ever. Amen.

8. Calling on God, Hierarchies, and Entities
We near the climax of the ritual, which starts by praying to God before calling the powers directly:
Almighty God, Benevolent Father of heaven, earth, the sea, and all things contained within, and whose hand distributes gifts to all your children; I come before you by the intercession of your Archangels Sachiel and Sandalfon, the Heavenly Choir of Angels and all the Saints of the Church Triumphant, that much money, more than (quantity) per week, be manifest physically into the purse of (name), towards helping him/her in his/her daily life, for necessity and for desire. May he/she enjoy peace in life, and eternal joy in death, that by word and example (name) will come to glorify you more and more. Through our Lord Jesus Christ your Son, who lives and reigns in the unity of the Holy Ghost, one God, forever and ever. Amen.

Next the Archangel is called. If calling on more than one (as in this rite), they are invoked separately.

Holy Sachiel the Archangel, prince of the heavenly Shining Ones deputed by God to administer his generosity: through the same God I call and invoke you into this my work. Come, Sachiel, and enter into the life of *(name)*; **bring with you every host, angel, intelligence, saint, spirit, and entity you find necessary for this task, and fill the purse of** *(name)* **with money of every type legal in** *(country)*. **May the purse of** *(name)* **be always full throughout all his/her days, and after his/her death may it transfer to his/her heredity, with** *(quantity)* **throughout each week. Through God's power I approach you, and by the pain of survival do I labor. Come forth, therefore, you who stand before God's throne, and help me in manifesting your power here on this physical plane. Now and forever. Amen.**

Afterwards the prayer to Saint Sandalphon:
And you, Archangel Sandalfon, who stand before the Lord Who Is King and whose heart beats near to our earthly affairs: I call upon you as well, that that in this earthly realm be manifest more money in the purse of *(name)*, **to wit more than** *(quantity)* **per week. Be it manifest by you, with the help of every angel, intelligence, saint, spirit, power, and entity you find necessary for this task. Now and forever. Amen.**

After the Archangels, you invoke the Angelic Choir(s):
Heavenly Choir of the Angels, you dwell close to the earth and help those in need; by the name of the God of Blessings do I call you forth from your heavenly abodes and into this my work, that the purse of *(name)* **shall be filled with much money legal in** *(country)*, **in the denomination of over** *(amount)* **per week. Bring with you every intelligence, saint, spirit, and entity you find necessary for this task, that the Wheel of Fortune be turned in** *(name)***'s favor, and the seed be implanted in**

heaven, money manifest in the purse of *(name)* **upon earth.**

And finally you invoke the Saints, mentioning by name those most appropriate to the task. In this case we name Saints Expedite, Nicholas, and Martin Caballero for their patronage of fast results, generosity, and making money: **All ye Saints in the Church Triumphant – especially Expedite, Nicolas, and Martin Caballero – be my prayers lifted up unto the heavens by your intercession, manifest on earth by the power of Almighty God and through every Archangel, Angel, Saint, Intelligence, Spirit, and Entity that he so wills, and by whatever means he commands it. That the life and heredity of** *(name)* **shall be free from all concerns of money in the physical, and able to contemplate the spiritual life and the mysteries of heaven, to be with God in heaven at the hour of his/her death. Now and forever. Amen.**

9. Order of Sending Out the Powers
Now that all entities have been called, we proceed to send them to work on our objective. We do this in the reverse order in which we called them – i.e. we called them starting from the highest and ending with the lowest. When sending, we send them starting with the lowest rank and moving upwards.

We begin by prayer:
God of Blessings, Eternal Father and Benefactor to all your children: look upon me in your generosity and grant me a part of your divine power, that I may send every entity and power just called to complete this work, to fill the purse of *(name)*. **I ask that you move the heavens, that the seed planted above be made fruitful here below. Through Christ our Lord. Amen.**

NOTE: In the sections that follow, the Sign of the Cross is made over the candle (or the talisman, if used) any time you see the + symbol. This represents sending them forth into the work and sealing their power into your goal.

Here the actual sending begins. You hold your right hand over the candle (and/or talisman, if you use one) and say:
All Intelligences, Spirits, Entities, and Powers deemed necessary to complete this work, by the God of Mercy and Blessing I send you to + fill the purse of *(name)*. **Amen.**

All ye Saints of the Church Triumphant, especially Expedite, Nicholas, and Martin Caballero, by the God of Mercy and Blessing I send you to + fill the purse of *(name)*. **Amen.**

Heavenly Choir of the Angels, by the God of Mercy and Blessing I send you to + fill the purse of *(name)*. **Amen.**

Archangels Sachiel and Sandalfon, by the God of Mercy and Blessing I send you to + fill the purse of *(name)*. **Amen.**

The sending is now complete. You seal it by declaring the result in these or similar words:
The purse of *(name)* **is now filled with** *(amount)* **per week, every week up until the hour of** *(name)*'**s death. Amen.**

10. Thanksgiving and Dismissal of Entities
You're almost finished, and all that's left is to thank the entities who help you. Speak as though the goal has already been accomplished, using these or similar words:
I thank you Almighty and Eternal God, Father of generosity who gives gifts to your children: you also,

**holy Archangels Sachiel and Sandalfon; Heavenly
Choir of the Angels; All ye Saints of the Church
Triumphant; and all intelligences, spirits, entities, and
powers necessary to complete this task: for you have
helped me in this my work, and filled the purse of
(name) to overflowing. The peace of Christ be with you,
and be there peace and between us now and forever.
Amen.**

The Dismissal takes a simple form and can be said as
follows:
**All you who have helped, and all you who were
attracted by this my rite: the time has come for us to
depart. Be there goodwill between us, and in gladness
come again when you are called.**

Then you may say or chant the Announcement of Ending:
Bene, consummátum est. (Good, it is finished.)

If you have assistants, they respond (or yourself if alone):
Deo grátias. (Thanks be to God.)

11. Final Banishing
Now you banish and cleanse your working area as before,
and the rite is technically done. Unless you wish to sing a:

> *Optional: Closing Hymn*
As before, you may sing a hymn or secular song pertaining
to you desires if you wish. This is recommended more for
group settings than for solitaries, yet may be done in either.

[A good general-purpose Closing Hymn would be Lord,
Dismiss Us with Your Blessing, *#110 in the Hymnal.]*

199. Money and Business: the Protectio Pecuniae

This Ritual's main intention is to protect a business or financial enterprise while at the same time drawing income.

This is also a good example of ritual magic's flexibility, since it demonstrates a synthesis of high magical ritual procedure combined with the more informal practices of Candle Magic.

Materials
4 Green Candles
5 White Candles
1 Purple Candle
Pen w/ Green Ink
Paper (unruled)
Blue Chalk
Green Chalk
Straight Pin (optional)

0. Pre-Ritual Preparation
The purple candle represents you, or the person for whom you're working; you may want to scratch the first and last name on it with the straight pin. Likewise, the five white candles represent Christ and the four Archangels Uriel, Michael, Raphael, and Gabriel.

1. On the floor, or on your mensa if it's big enough, draw a circle about 3 feet in diameter with the blue chalk, and in the middle of that circle draw another one, about 9 inches in diameter with the green chalk.

Candle Layout: Candle 1 is Purple, 2-6 are White, 7-10 are Green (2-6 form a Pentagram, 7-10 form a cross)

2. Once you finish placing the candles, your altar/floor should look like the above diagram. Place them in the numbered order, and formulate the Declaration of Intent in your own words. Follow this with your preferred banishing rite and then the **Invocatio Nominis Domini**.

Next, begin lighting the candles, and as you light each one, say the following:

Lighting the Candles in the Pentagram:
a. **This is** *(name)*. **Le-Olam Amen.**

b. **Archangel Uriel, by the Name of God our King I license and compel thee to dispel all from the North who desire to harm the success of** *(name)*. **Amen.**

c. **My Lord and Savior Jesus Christ, I ask thee to shed the Light of thy blessing upon** *(name)*, **and to dispel all dark forces that desire to harm the success of** *(name)*. **Amen.**

d. **Archangel Michael, by the Name of God our King I license and compel thee to dispell all from the South who desire to harm the success of** *(name)*. **Amen.**

e. **Archangel Raphael, by the Name of God our King I license and compel thee to dispel all from the East who desire to harm the success of** *(name)*. **Amen.**

f. **Archangel Gabriel, by the Name of God our King I license and compel thee to dispel all from the West who desire to harm the success of** *(name)*. **Amen.**

Lighting the Candles in the Cross:
g. **Atah. From the North may only success come to** *(name)*. **AGLA Le-Olam Amen.**

h. **Gavor. From the East may only success come to** *(name)*. **AGLA Le-Olam Amen.**

i. **Le-Olahm. From the South may only success come to** *(name)*. **AGLA Le-Olam Amen.**

j. **Adonai. From the West may only success come to** *(name)*. **AGLA Le-Olam Amen.**

3. Now your candle setup is complete. Say:
Uriel in the North, Michael in the South, Raphael in the East and Gabriel in the West. In the Name of our God-Who-Is-King and his Christ I call You. To guard, protect, and bring profitable income to this undertaking of *(name)*, **that this undertaking shall not perish until** *(name)* **wills it. Amen.**

4. Now say:
Atah gavor le-olam, Adonai! May only success come to this undertaking of *(name)*. **AGLA Le-Olam Amen.**

5. While all the candles are still burning, take the pen and paper, draw talisman #194 from Chapter VII, and read the inscriptions aloud. The inscription on the front translates:
By the power of God I compel all evil spirits away from *(name)*.

The inscription on the back says:
Much fortune comes to *(name)*.

6. At this point you could either extinguish your candles (in the reverse of the order in which they were lit, going from j to a), or let them burn all the way down. In either case, when they do go out, perform the Banishing ritual to which you are most accustomed, and conclude by giving thanks to the Lord for His services.

>Follow-Through in the Real World
Now every morning before you go to work, read the talisman aloud (front and back), then fold it up and put it in your pocket.

199. Ritual for Love: The Ama Me

1. On the floor, trace a pentagram large enough for two people to stand in the center. The top angle of the pentagram should face to the north.

2. Create a talisman of the Pentagram of Nogah, writing it in Green ink on unlined paper, with the heart colored pink.

3. Enter the pentagram and kneel, facing north. In this position you say the Declaration of Intent and the **Invocatio Nominis Domini** (Prayer #3 from Chapter I). Afterward you stand up and perform your preferred banishing rite.

4. The banishing rite finished, place the Pentagram of Nogah (Talisman #193 from Chapter VIII) inside the center of the pentagram on the floor. The upmost point should face north.

5. Extend you arms in front of you, palms down, and standing at the south of the pentagram, walk around your working area seven times clockwise. As you do this, imagine the circle you walk as filling up with an intensifying green light.

6. After finishing the seventh circle, return to the south of the pentagram and stand, facing north, pointing to the talisman with your index finger. Repeat this prayer seven times:

Archangel Anael, angel of love, by the name of Yahveh I call thee, into this pentagram, and into the heart of *(name)***; to fill the** *(name)***'s mind with the image of** *(other name)***'s face, to fill the heart of** *(name)* **with intimate passions for** *(other name)***. Now and forever. Amen.**

7. Seal your prayer by making the Sign of the Cross over yourself, saying the Protestant ending to the Lord's Prayer: **For thine is the kingdom, and the power, and the glory, forever and ever. Amen.**

8. Step into the pentagram, standing with the talisman between both feet. Then say: **As I have entered this pentagram, so has** *(other name)* **entered into the heart of** *(name)***. Now and forever. Amen.**

Again make the Sign of the Cross, as above.

9. Exit the pentagram, pick up the talisman and move it to another place (like a side table, for example). Then perform your preferred banishing rite.

10. Lastly, say a prayer giving thanks to God and to the Archangel Anael for helping you. Use your own words and keep it simple. Then keep the talisman on your person (if you did this for someone else, have them keep the talisman on their person), until attaining your objective.

11. Once your objective is attained, burn the talisman in the flame of a green candle while again giving thanks in prayer.

Field testing with this rite has shown it to be successful on multiple occasions, both when performing the rite as written or when using the prayers by themselves. It also helps to do this under green light, by placing a green light bulb in the room's overhead light socket, or in lamps if you don't have an overhead light on your ceiling.

200. Justice. The Revelatio Innocentiae

I composed this rite in my early 20's, for what seems a minor reason: one of my friends (we'll call him "O") had accused another friend ("N") of stealing a movie from his anime collection. Something felt really off to me even though the (circumstantial) evidence was pretty damning. Until I did some magic on the situation, that is.

A day after I performed this ritual, I got a phone call from O asking me to relay apologies to N. Turns out that N didn't steal anything, but O's girlfriend put a piece of tape over the recording tab (this was back in the VHS days) and then taped her soap operas over the movie! As the cool kids today might say, facepalm.

Further experimentation has shown this rite useful when you or the person you're working for is falsely accused and the truth can use some help coming to light, preferably in conjunction with proper legal representation in cases involving a court of law. What this rite won't do is help you "beat the rap" if you are in fact guilty.

1. Set up your mensa as follows: your metal pentacle in the center, and inside it a red pillar candle. Place a bloodstone in front of the candle.

2. Begin by stating exactly why you are performing this operation, keeping it simple and using your own words (e.g. "I do this because...").

3. Perform the Banishing ritual to which you are most accustomed.

4. Assuming the orans posture, recite the First Address combined with an alternate form of the Invocatio Nominis Domini:
Almighty God, you are the Prime Mover and First Cause of the universe, and you revealed yourself to Moses in the Burning Bush: through the Name of Jesus Christ the Savior I ask that you see this ritual fit to be performed, and that you will grant me the power to manifest proof of the innoccence of *(name)*. Amen.

5. Take the bloodstone in your left hand, cup your hands around the stone, and then put your hands to your breast, as in a praying position. In this posture, recite the *Lavabo inter innocentes* (Psalm 26:6-12):
I wash my hands in innocence,
   and go about your altar, Lord,
proclaiming aloud your praise
   and telling of all your wonderful deeds.
Lord, I love the house where you live,
   the place where your glory dwells.
Do not take away my soul along with sinners,
   my life with those who are bloodthirsty,
in whose hands are wicked schemes,
   whose right hands are full of bribes.
I lead a blameless life;
   deliver me and be merciful to me.
My feet stand on level ground;
   in the great congregation I will praise the Lord.
Glory be to the Father, *etc.*

6. Light the candle on the mensa. Then extend your arms with the palms downward and walk clockwise around the

working area five times. As you walk, visualize the circle as filling up with an intensifying red light.

7. At the end of the fifth circle, you face the mensa and kneel, saying the following prayer five times:
God of Power and Might, in the Name of Jesus Christ the Savior I ask you to send your Archangel Camaël, to intercede and show that *(name)* **is innoccent of the charge of** *(accusation)*. **Through the same Christ our Lord. Amen.**

8) While still kneeling, at the end of the fifth prayer seal yourself with the Sign of the Cross. As you do, you may say either "In the name of the Father, etc." or the Protestant ending to the Lord's Prayer.

9. Hold your hands slightly above the bloodstone, but not touching it. Keeping your eyes fixed on it, address the Archangel Camaël:
Archangel Camael, in the name of God the Mighty One I send you, to go forth and prove that *(name)* **is innocent of** *(accusation)*.

10. Make the Sign of the Cross over the stone, saying the invocation "In the name of the Father, etc."

11. Say the following prayer of thanksgiving:
I-Am-Who-I-Am, Eternal and Mighty God, I heartily thank you for your help in proving *(name)* **is innocent of** *(accusation)*.
    You too, Archangel Camaël, for your assistance in bringing this proof to light. Be there good will between us, my friend, and come again in gladness when you are called.

12. Close this with the Sign of the Cross, saying either the invocation "In the Name of" or the Protestant ending to the Lord's Prayer.

13. Extinguish candle and perform the Banishing ritual to which you are most accustomed.

14. If the accused is open to it, have him or her wear the bloodstone until their case is finally dismissed.

201. Health. The Vocatio Salutis
I've said before that I really don't like healing magic, and I've also said why. Yet I also believe in an ancient principle of Christian jurisprudence: The abuse does not take away the use, and there are plenty of magical practitioners responsible enough to use common sense.

Materials:
Light Yellow Paper, Yellow Pen, Yellow Candle

1. With your pen, draw the following talisman on one side of the paper:

NOTE: The Hexagram of Shemesh (#192 from Chapter VII) may be used instead.

2. Place the talisman in the center of your mensa, face up. Place the candle on top of that and light it.

3. Facing the mensa, say your Declaration of Intent, followed by the banishing rite of your choice.

4. Assume the orans posture and make the First Address as follows:
Lord God, giver of knowledge and health to the world: *(name)* **has been afflicted with** *(illness)*. **I call to you to send your Archangel Raphael and the Heavenly Choir of the Powers to rid** *(name)* **of** *(illness)*. **Through Christ our Lord. Amen.**

5. After the First Address, kneel or stand in the orans posture while you say the **Invocatio Nominis Domini**.

6. Hold your arms out with your right palm down and your left palm up. Walk clockwise in a circle around the altar. Do this six times. As you walk, imagine the circle filling up with an intensifying yellow light.

7. At the end of your sixth circle, kneel before the altar and say this invocation six times:
Archangel Raphael, Healer of God: in the name of the God of Knowledge and Healing do I call you, that you will gather up the Heavenly choir of Powers and heal *(name)* **of the injury** *(ailment)* **that afflicts** *(name)*. **Amen.**

Seal this evocation with the Sign of the Cross. As you do, you may say either "In the name of the Father, etc." or the Protestant ending to the Lord's Prayer.

8. Pick up the candle and pour its molten wax over the talisman until it's covered completely. As you do this, say:
As I send this wax onto this talisman, so has Almighty God sent the Archangel Raphael and the Choir of Powers to heal *(name)* **of** *(illness)*. **Amen.**

9. Say thanks to Almighty God, to Raphael, and the Choir of Powers for what they've done (remember to speak as if the deed has already been done!), extinguish your candle, and perform your banishing ritual. Keep the talisman close to yourself or the person for whom you're working.

> Follow-Through

10. Once the injury is healed or the ailment cured, say another prayer of thanks while burning the talisman in the flame of the same yellow candle.

X. Magical Advice

202. Considerations for Success

By now we've dropped enough meditation exercises and ritual theory in your lap to keep you busy for quite some time. Yet it's all meaningless if we don't spend some time talking about what can go wrong and what you can do to make it right.

I've said more than once that magic won't manifest something out of thin air. This has to do with how magic works.

"Magic, like water, always seeks the easiest route to the sea." – Donald Tyson

At its most basic level, magic is a calling on the energy of God's grace and conscious direction of that energy to further your goals. The thing to understand, though, is that energy must have a channel by which to manifest your goals, or it can help you find an opportunity for you to create that channel. If there's no channel available and no opportunity within reach to create one, then your magical work is likely to fail.

203. Non-Magical Collaboration

"Pray as though everything depended on God. Work as though everything depended on you." – St. Augustine

If magic is all about channels and opportunities, this brings us to an excellent question: what are you doing non-magically to reach your goals?

If you're working to increase your wealth, then ideally you should study every piece of money and finance-related information you can get your hands on. Then you should implement that new knowledge to the best of your understanding and ability.

If you're working to increase your success with love or just getting along with people in general, then ideally you should read books on communication, relationships, and exercises to improve your charisma. You also want to go to friends' parties and put yourself in social situations where you'll actually meet people instead of staying at home like a couch potato.

The point of this is that by learning and growing, you make yourself better able to create channels through which your magic can manifest, and you'll certainly be better prepared to perceive the opportunities around you when they knock on your door. Or to create them.

Just remember that magic works best in collaboration with non-magical action, and try always to make a thorough assessment of the situation, its available resources and opportunities, what you need magically for the desired outcome to manifest, and what you'll need to do non-magically to help that happen.

204. Too Little, Too Late
There are times when no amount of magic will bring the desired goal. For example, I once had an apartment where I'd lost my job and had fallen behind on the rent. The property manager let it slide for a few months, during which I scrambled to find another job and get the money together. I found the job but by then I owed $1500 in back rent plus the current month, and the building's owners wouldn't let her be lenient anymore.

I resorted to magic work, and it was too little too late: *I'd let so much pile on for so long that there was neither channel nor opportunity for me to keep the apartment.* Fortunately, however, an opportunity did open up for another place to live and a better job.

The moral of the story is that if you let a situation go on for too long, then all the magic in the universe isn't going to help you. As the situation drags on, you'll find that opportunities vanish, networks and contact lists might grow smaller, and the window for change eventually closes. In this case, oftentimes the best you can do is find or create a way out where you'll land on your feet, or may land on your feet in the foreseeable future.

So I implore you never to let things get that bad if it's in your power to do so. Especially if you have children or loved ones hanging in the balance. An ounce of prevention in these matters can be worth much more than a kiloton of cure!

205. When Magic Doesn't Work

"Sometimes the answer is 'No.'" – Anonymous

It doesn't matter how long you've been doing this or how good you are at it. There will eventually come a time when every circumstance is perfect and everything lines up, but you can't get results no matter what you throw into it. It feels like you've just come up against an impenetrable wall.

When this happens, it usually means something or someone is working against you. It could be an unforeseen factor that's just an obstacle in the way. It could also be another person actively working against you.

For example, consider magic being worked to find a new job. You check the ads and find something that looks perfect. You do some magic and get the interview. The interview goes perfectly, they say they're planning to schedule the next interview, and then you don't get the job!

Sometimes that's just how the ball rolls. I long ago learned that interviewers are good at making it sound like they want you when you were never really a candidate to begin with; you can learn to fish those out with practice. Other times, you're not the only person doing magic to get that position.

Consider this: if two people are doing magic to get the same job, or the same house, etc., then it's a foregone conclusion that one of them is going to lose. Nobody in this situation is casting curses on anybody, and it's not a question of God loving you or the other person more; it's simply a question of which one of you was able to gather the most energy in your favor.

Other times you'll have people working against you intentionally and perhaps even maliciously. In these cases you may never even find out who the person is, though sometimes they may tip their hand. In a case like this, you could work banishing rituals to break any "curse" that's taken hold, you can work a binding (involving the Archangel Cassiel and the Choir of Thrones) to prevent them from doing it to you again, and you can then try your magic another time to see if it works.

Lastly, it's equally possible your magic isn't working because you're jinxing yourself. It could be that you're not serious about your undertaking, or you have a problem seriously believing your results can happen, or your subconscious may realize you're asking for something that's not right for you.

Whenever your magic doesn't work, don't panic. Instead remain calm and size up your situation. See if you can isolate the problem, deal with it accordingly, and then try again. If you need help, I offer magical coaching services and can be reached at agostino@thavmapub.com.

206. Interference from Entities
Likewise, there are times when an entity may interfere with your magic and keep it from working. Most of the time it's not a demon or anything inherently "evil," so much as looking for entertainment which usually happens at humans' expense. Unfortunately, one of the dangers of practicing magic is that these spirits will start to take more notice of you.

Everybody has their own way of detecting when an entity's messing with them, and for me I notice feeling of frustration, depression, and a short temper. You'll have your own way of noticing, and eventually you'll learn to listen to the signals your emotions and your body give you.

If you find out that an entity is messing with you, most are so weak they can be dispelled with a simple banishing ritual. Others will require stronger stuff; I typically use the "Exorcism Against Satan and the Rebellious Angels" from the *Rituale Romanum* (#219 in Chapter XI) and it solves the problem quickly.

Of course, there are entities that take more than just a banishing rite to repel, and some people tend to be targeted by these entities simply for breathing. If you fit under this category, then magic will only serve to make you a bigger target. For your own good I ask you to put this book down, walk away, and leave all practice of magic alone.

XI. Rites of Exorcism

Our English word "exorcism" comes from the Greek ἐξορκισμός, meaning "binding by oath." While the word can be found used referring to conjurations, in modern Christian parlance the word refers almost exclusively to ridding a person, place, or thing of the influence of some or other entity.

207. Who May Perform an Exorcism
Before we go further, it may be useful to discuss *who* may perform an exorcism. There's a debate on this with one side saying only a priest or bishop can cast out entities, while the other side says anyone, including a layperson, may perform exorcism.

First I'm going to give the short answer, and then I'm going to go into the reasoning leading to the long answer (and it's *long*!)

208. Short Answer:
1. Yes, laypeople are capable of successfully performing exorcism.
2. The restriction to priests is part of a well-intentioned power grab spanning centuries.
3. The power to perform exorcism does not come from ordination but from baptism.

As a sort of postscript, I should point out that I'm answering this question from a Catholic perspective because Protestants don't seem to have this level of debate over hierarchical authority when it comes to exorcism. Catholics, on the other hand, tend to have hang-ups about authority mainly because "pay, pray, and obey" was pounded into their brains since childhood.

209. Long Answer: Validity versus Liceity

The question of whether only a priest can perform an exorcism boils down to a concept a lot of the faithful don't seem to understand: the question of *validity* versus *liceity*.

In essence, *validity* refers to whether the action "works" or if it's successful, while *liceity* refers to whether the person doing the deed has permission from an institution's leaders. My favorite example is driving a car: you can drive from point A to point B validly even without a license, but it's not licit unless you have that license. When dealing with Church law, this is an important distinction a lot of people don't seem to understand.

210. The Order of Exorcists

I successfully performed exorcisms for nine years before being ordained, thus **I know a layperson may validly perform an exorcism** even if it's not licit. In fact for most of the Church's history exorcism was not only the province of the priesthood but also of commissioned Exorcists (a "minor order" several steps below the priesthood), and the rite for commissioning an exorcist specifically tells the exorcist-to-be:

"You receive, therefore, the power to lay your hands upon the possessed; and by the imposition of your hands, the grace of the Holy Spirit, and the words of the exorcism, the unclean spirits shall be cast out from the bodies of the possessed."

Later in the rite, as the bishop says to each new exorcist as they come forward:

"Receive, and commit to memory, and have the power to lay your hands upon the possessed, be they baptized or catechumens."

And finally the bishop prays over the new exorcists:

"Let us, dearly beloved brethren, humbly beseech God, the Father Almighty, that He may graciously + bless these His servants for the office of exorcist. May they be spiritual commanders, to cast out of the bodies of the possessed the evil spirits with all their manifold wickedness. Through His only-begotten Son, Jesus Christ, our Lord, who lives and reigns with Him in the unity of the Holy Spirit, God, forever and ever. Amen."

211. Canon Law, 1917

Over time the Order of Exorcist became less a function in itself but a step on the way to the priesthood (those steps consisting of four "minor orders" and the three "major orders"), and the action of exorcism became the purview of the priesthood and then only with permission of their bishop.

We see this spelled out clearly in the 1917 Code of Canon Law, in Canon 1151. There's an important distinction here, so I'm first going to quote the original Latin and then give an English translation:

§1. Nemo, potestate exorcizandi praeditus, exorcismos in obsessos proferre legitime potest, nisi ab Ordinario peculiarem et expressam licentiam obtinuerit.

"§1. No one, endowed with the power of exorcizing, can legitimately perform exorcisms on those obsessed, unless he shall have obtained especial and express license from the Ordinary."

§2. Haec licentia ab Ordinario concedatur tantummodo sacerdoti pietate, prudentia ac vitae integritate praedito; qui ad exorcismos ne procedat, nisi postquam diligenti

*prudentique investigatione compererit exorcizandum esse
revera a daemone obsessum.*

"§2. This license from the Ordinary may only be conceded
to a priest endowed with piety, prudence, and integrity of
life; who may not proceed to exorcisms except after having
determined the person is obsessed by way of diligent and
prudent investigation."

We gain a few pieces of insight from this piece of legal
code. First and foremost we see that it doesn't say only a
priest may validly perform an exorcism, it says those
people *endowed with the power of exorcism* must have
permission from the bishop. Then it restricts that
permission to priests, but there's clearly no assumption that
only a priest may validly perform exorcisms. The
references to "legitimately" and "license" in the Code make
it clear this is an issue of *liceity*.

(SIDE NOTE: For anyone with questions, "legitime" in the
framework of Canon Law refers specifically to liceity. If
the text were addressing validity, the word would be
"valide.")

Another thing we notice is that the Code explicitly limits
itself to possessed *persons*, with no reference to exorcizing
places or objects. In practice the exorcism of a person (I
called them "human cases" in my exorcist days) is a
relatively rare thing, and it's mostly places and objects that
will occupy the exorcist's attention.

Thus far, the Code neither states non-priests are not capable
of performing an effective exorcism, nor does the Code
require the bishop's permission to exorcise anything that's
not a human being.

212. Exorcism Allowed to Laity

These conclusions are further corroborated by the publication of the *Exorcismus in Satanam et Angelos Apostaticos* by Leo XIII – also called the "St. Michael Exorcism" or the "Exorcism Against Satan and the Rebellious Angels" and directed at exorcizing objects and places. This exorcism was published in English translation in several pamphlets each bearing the *imprimatur* (official permission) of various bishops, and explicitly stated this exorcism was allowed to the laity so long as they omitted a small handful of words.

213. Canon Law, 1983

Eighteen years after Vatican II, the 1983 Code of Canon Law retains a shortened form of this law in Canon 1172. Again, I give the text in the original Latin and in English translation.

§ 1. Nemo exorcismos in obsessos proferre legitime potest, nisi ab Ordinario loci peculiarem et expressam licentiam obtinuerit.

"§1. No one can perform exorcisms legitimately upon the possessed unless he has obtained special and express permission from the local ordinary."

§ 2. Haec licentia ab Ordinario loci concedatur tantummodo presbytero pietate, scientia, prudentia ac vitae integritate praedito.

"§2. The local ordinary is to give this permission only to a presbyter who has piety, knowledge, prudence, and integrity of life."

Again, we see this applies only to possessed people and speaks only of liceity, not validity. The terms "legitime" and "licentia" (with the lack of "valide") are our indicators here. What's also missing is the requirement for diligent investigation before performing the exorcism, but that's such an established practice it's not an issue for argument here.

So our take-aways thus far: 1) a non-priest can *validly* perform exorcisms over possessed people as well as places or things, 2) a non-priest can *validly and licitly* perform exorcisms over places and things, and 3) a non-priest may *not licitly* perform exorcisms over a person.

Well, not so fast. That window was closed in 1984.

214. The Power Grab Is Complete
In 1984 then-Cardinal Ratzinger published *Inde ab Aliquot Annos*, in which he revoked any and all permissions for laypersons to use the Leo XIII exorcism or any other form "*...in the course of which the demons are directly disturbed and an attempt is made to determine their identity.*"

Like most post-Vatican II pronouncements, this document only addresses liceity and not validity. While there's a reference to "those who lack the requisite power" (*ii qui debita potestate carent*), there's no delineation for who has and who doesn't have that power.

In fact the general rule is that the Church can only legislate concerning liceity; she can't legislate validity but can only recognize the conditions leading to it (this is why modern-day Rome is careful to avoid pronouncing on the validity of schismatic and non-canonical ordinations, usually saying "whatever the validity may be, we don't recognize their authority within our institution.")

In any case, as of 1984 – and I find it ironic the year *was* 1984 – the transference of exorcism out of the hands of the laity and everyone else outside the priesthood is complete, and non-priests are left with only the scraps of asking "please God, take this evil away from me" and told they're not allowed to stand up and take care of the problem like a grown-up.

I don't think this power grab was made without reason, though. It's not uncommon to hear of cases where people die in the course of exorcisms, and what can happen when an unqualified would-be exorcist confronts a spiritual power that's more than they bargained for.

Love her or hate her, the fact stands that Roman Catholic Church is a dictatorship and not a democracy, and a dictatorship that demands docility of its subjects (*Catechism*, n. 87, and the word "subject" is the term found in Canon Law). When you seek to subjugate those under you and tell them they must be docile, you automatically take on the duty of protecting those people from themselves.

215. Whence the Power Comes
In the last verses of Mark 16, Jesus was very clear that those who believe will be able to cast out demons. We also find Jesus sending out the 72 disciples in Luke 10 and telling them they're able to cast out demons. Remember that all bishops and priests descend from the Twelve Apostles, not the 72 disciples, meaning that we had non-priests doing exorcism from the very beginning of Christianity.

This indicates to me that the power to perform exorcism doesn't come from ordination. This power can only come from Baptism.

But I'm not finished. I'm not finished because of the Order of Exorcists. While it became so later, the Order of exorcist was not originally a step on the way to the priesthood. And even in the latter days, the exorcist did not share any part in the Sacramental Character (the imprint on the soul) of Ordination.

So let's break out our theology textbooks, in this case Ott's *Fundamentals of Catholic Dogma*. When discussing the Minor Orders, he says:

"*The four Minor Orders and the Subdiaconate are not Sacraments but merely Sacramentals.*

"*The Minor Orders and the subdiaconate are not of Divine institution, but were only gradually introduced by the Church to meet special requirements. The lectorate is first attested to by Tertullian (De praescr. 41), the subdiaconate by St. Hippolytus of Rome (Traditio Apost.), all the Minor Orders (which up to the 12th century included the subdiaconate), by Pope St. Cornelius (D 45). The Greek Church knows only two Minor Orders: lectorate and hypodiaconate. The rite of consecration for these does not include the imposition of hands.*"

Though not a theology textbook, the 1911 *Catholic Encyclopedia* corroborates this and expands upon the reasoning:

"*Although several medieval theologians regarded minor orders as sacramental, this view is no longer held, for the fundamental reason that minor orders, also the subdiaconate, are not of Divine or Apostolic origin. The rites by which they are conferred are quite different from ordination to holy orders.*"

Perhaps what's most telling is the fact that the Minor Orders were altogether abolished by Paul VI in 1972, in the Motu Proprio *Ministeria Quaedam*. The motu says the following about the minors:

"*Nevertheless, since the minor orders have not always been the same and many functions connected with them, as at present, have also been exercised by the laity, it seems fitting to reexamine this practice and to adapt it to contemporary needs.*"

Now we need to contrast this with what If the minors were of divine institution and an actual Sacrament, then even the Pope wouldn't be able to abolish them, because as his predecessor Pius XII said in *Sacramentum Ordinis* some 25 years earlier: "*The Church has no power over the substance of the Sacraments.*"

In saying this, Pius XII was merely reiterating his own predecessors throughout the centuries, and the Council of Trent made the extent of the Church's power clear in its XXI session:

"*It furthermore declares, that this power has ever been in the Church, that, in the dispensation of the sacraments, **their substance being untouched**, it may ordain,--or change, what things soever it may judge most expedient, for the profit of those who receive, or for the veneration of the said sacraments, according to the difference of circumstances, times, and places.*" – (emphasis mine)

We again see that the Church has a lot of latitude with her Sacred Rites, but no latitude whatsoever with the substance of the Sacraments. The reason is that the substance of the Sacraments (though not their exact rituals) were given directly by Christ and therefore cannot be altered or abolished altogether.

Yet a minor order is abolished altogether, and the historical and theological consensus is that the minors are not a Sacrament. So what does this mean? It means that if the Church is able to abolish the minors entirely, then the minors were not a Sacrament and therefore imparted no Sacramental Character onto the recipient's soul.

Which, in turn, leads us to only one conclusion: the minor orders are not a Sacrament and therefore confer no spiritual power onto whoever receives them. Thus we can only conclude that if the power to perform exorcism does not come from Ordination, then the power can only come from one other place: **Baptism**.

Which in turn brings us back to Jesus' own words that casting out spirits is a sign "that will follow those who believe." Again corroborating my "short answer" that even though formal permission may be extended only to priests, exorcism may be successfully performed by any baptized Christian.

Whether the individual baptized Christian wants to break their church's rules or is even knowledgeable or qualified to perform an exorcism, however, is a different conversation entirely.

216. Potential Issues with Exorcism

A lot of people think exorcism can be a great and wonderful thing. It's like they've been drawn in by what we see in the movies and on TV. I'm here to tell you firsthand that there's nothing wonderful about it.

If you're considering performing an exorcism or becoming an exorcist, then I want you to read this section and take it very seriously.

I speak as a battle-scarred veteran and can tell you most entities are weak and easily evicted from wherever they're found. Either that or I have an extraordinary gift for this sort of thing. I have no idea one way or the other.

What I do know is that if you're planning on doing an exorcism, you need to come prepared. Even if most entities are weak, you absolutely cannot go in there with a sense of overconfidence. Confidence is a key to success, while overconfidence is a swift ticket to failure. Especially if the entity you face is not a weakling.

When you address the spirit, they may laugh, they may hide, they may be silent, or they may try to taunt you. But know this: in all cases, they will attempt to read your mind in hopes of finding a way to retaliate.

One way to block a spirit from reading your mind is to say the *Ave Maria* in your mind over and over again. It's a short prayer that's easily memorized and can be mentally repeated over and over without interrupting your thoughts or your concentration. You can do it in English, but make sure to learn it in Latin. Pronounce it in Church Latin, because for some reason it irritates the entities even more. (I don't know why, I just know that it works.)

If the spirit finds a way to retaliate, it can be anything from minor inconveniences to car accidents to finding yourself losing your home and your job. They generally try to scan your life and find the weakest possible point, the point most vulnerable to attack.

If you're financially struggling and in real risk of losing your home or apartment, that can become a point of attack. If your car has a tie rod on its way out or a transmission gasket a hair's breadth away from leaking, that becomes a point of attack. If you have an inordinate tendency for sexual desire, that can become a point of attack. If you have a naturally closed-minded or bigoted personality, that likewise becomes a point of attack. They will inconvenience you if they can, ruin your life if they can, or outright manipulate you if they can.

If you have any of these weaknesses, you should not attempt to perform an exorcism. Doubly so if you have severe mental illness and refuse to take medication.

If they find they can't get to you directly, then they'll try to work through those around you. Relationships may grow bitter, friendships may grow cold, your supervisors at work may become a little frosty. In essence everyone you know becomes a potential weakness, a potential vulnerability, and a potential liability.

You need to examine your relationships with people before you try an exorcism. You need to figure out who's weak-minded, mentally imbalanced, most vulnerable, and whether these relationships can't afford to be sabotaged (supervisors at work, for example).

If you have liabilities in this department, it doesn't mean you shouldn't go forward with the exorcism. It does mean you should be aware of any possible directions for counter-attack and have a strategy at hand.

There are times where you may be facing a strong spirit and getting the upper hand. At that point the spirit may try to offer you a deal. Do not take it, it's a trap. Such deals need to be navigated with extreme precision; otherwise the spirit will find some loophole to cheat you out of what you ask for.

There will be other times when you defeat the spirit only to see it turn friendly and even appear years later to advise you on some or other matter. This is a highly specialized matter where I can't advise on a "one size fits all" basis. In some cases the spirit is showing honest respect and in others looking for revenge, so I can only suggest rejecting or ignoring such attempts at friendship at least in your beginning years.

Once you learn to get a feel for how the spirit realm works (and only so much of it can be taught), use your judgment and come to your own decisions on a case-by-case basis. I would urge using extreme caution and being very careful when giving the benefit of the doubt. In fact don't give that benefit at all. Verify, verify, verify.

While I may have written a long treatise on why one doesn't have to be a priest to perform an exorcism, it by now be obvious why leaving exorcism to the priesthood is a good idea. It's one thing to have the *power* to do it, but another thing entirely to be in a position of freedom from the troubles into which it can get you.

217. General Rubrics for Exorcism

1. A priest - one who is expressively and particularly authorized by the ordinary - when he intends to perform an exorcism over persons tormented by the devil, must be properly distinguished for his piety, prudence and integrity of life. He should fulfill this devout undertaking in all constancy and humility, being utterly immune to any striving for human recognition, and relying, not on his own,

but on the divine power. Moreover, he ought to be of mature years, and revered not alone for his office but for his moral qualities.

2. In order to exercise his ministry rightly, he should resort to a great deal more study of the matter (which has to be passed over here for the sake of brevity), by examining approved authors and cases from experience; on the other hand, let him carefully observe the few more important points enumerated here.

3. Especially, he should not believe too readily that a person is possessed by an evil spirit; but he ought to ascertain the signs by which a person possessed can be distinguished from one who is suffering from some illness, especially one of a psychological nature. Signs of possession may be the following: ability to speak with some facility in a strange tongue or to understand it when spoken by another. The faculty of divulging future and hidden events; display of powers which are beyond the subject's age and natural condition; and various other indications which, when taken together as a whole, build up the evidence.

4. In order to understand these matters better, let him inquire of the person possessed, following one or the other act of exorcism, what the latter experienced in his body or soul while the exorcism was being performed, and to learn also what particular words in the form had a more intimidating effect upon the devil, so that hereafter these words may be employed with greater stress and frequency.

5. He will be on his guard against the arts and subterfuges which the evil spirits are wont to use in deceiving the exorcists. For often times they give deceptive answers and make it difficult to understand them, so that the exorcist

might tire and give up, or so it might appear that the afflicted one is in no wise possessed by the devil.

6. Once in a while, after they are already recognized, they conceal themselves and leave the body practically free from every molestation, so that the victim believes himself completely delivered. Yet the exorcists may not desist until he sees the signs of deliverance.

7. At times, moreover, the evil spirits place whatever obstacles they can in the way, so that the patient may not submit to exorcism or they try to convince him that his affliction is a natural one. Meanwhile, during the exorcism they cause him to fall asleep and dangle some illusion before him, while they seclude themselves, so that the afflicted one appears to be freed.

8. Some reveal a crime which has been committed and the perpetrators thereof, as well as the means of putting an end to it. Yet the afflicted person must beware of having recourse on this account to sorcerers or necromancers or to use any parties except the ministers of the Church, or of making any use of superstitious or forbidden practice.

9. Sometimes the devil will leave the possessed person in peace and even allow him to receive the holy Eucharist, to make it appear that he has departed. In fact, the arts and frauds of the evil one for deceiving a man are innumerable. For this reason the exorcist must be on his guard not to fall into this trap.

10. Therefore, he will be mindful of the words of our Lord (Matthew 17:20), to the effect that there is a certain type of evil spirit who cannot be driven out except by prayer and fasting. Therefore, let him avail himself of these two means above all for imploring the divine assistance in expelling

demons, after the example of the holy fathers; and not only himself, but let him induce others, as far as possible, to do the same.

11. If it can be done conveniently the possessed person should be led to church or to some other sacred and worthy place, where the exorcism will be held, away from the crowd. But if the person is ill, or for any valid reason, the exorcism may take place in a private home.

12. The subject, if in good mental and physical health, should be exhorted to implore God's help, to fast, and to fortify himself by frequent reception of penance and Holy Communion, at the discretion of the priest. And in the course of the exorcism he should be fully recollected, with his intention fixed on God, whom he should entreat with firm faith and in all humility. And if he is all the more grievously tormented, he ought to bear this patiently, never doubting the divine assistance.

13. He ought to have a crucifix at hand or somewhere in sight. If relics of the saints are available, they are to be applied in a reverent way to the breast or the head of the person possessed (the relics must be properly and securely encased and covered). One will see to it that these sacred objects are not treated improperly or that no injury is done them by the evil spirit. However, one should not hold the holy Eucharist over the head of the person or in any way apply it to his body, owing to the danger of desecration.

14. The exorcist must not digress into senseless prattle nor ask superfluous questions or such as are prompted by curiosity, particularly if they pertain to future and hidden matters, all of which have nothing to do with his office. Instead, he will bid the unclean spirit keep silence and answer only when asked. Neither ought he to give any

credence to the devil if the latter maintains that he is the spirit of some saint or of a deceased party, or even claims to be a good angel.

15. But necessary questions are, for example: the number and name of the spirits inhabiting the patient, the time when they entered into him, the cause thereof, and the like. As for all jesting, laughing, and nonsense on the part of the evil spirit - the exorcist should prevent it or contemn it, and he will exhort the bystanders (whose number must be very limited) to pay no attention to such goings on; neither are they to put any question to the subject. Rather they should intercede for him to God in all humility and urgency.

16. Let the priest pronounce the exorcism in a commanding and authoritative voice, and at the same time with great confidence, humility, and fervor; and when he sees that the spirit is sorely vexed, then he possesses and threatens all the more. If he notices that the person afflicted is experiencing a disturbance in some part of his body or an acute pain or a swelling appears in some part, he traces the sign of the cross over that place and sprinkles it with holy water, which he must have at hand for this purpose.

17. He will pay attention as to what words in particular cause the evil spirits to tremble, repeating them the more frequently. And when he comes to a threatening expression, he recurs to it again and again, always increasing the punishment. If he perceives that he is making progress, let him persist for two, three, four hours, and longer if he can, until victory is attained.

18. The exorcist should guard against giving or recommending any medicine to the patient, but should leave this care to physicians.

19. While performing the exorcism over a woman, he ought always to have assisting him several women of good repute, who will hold on to the person when she is harassed by the evil spirit. These assistants ought if possible to be close relatives of the subject, and for the sake of decency the exorcist will avoid saying or doing anything which might prove an occasion of evil thought to himself or to the others.

20. During the exorcism he shall preferable employ words from Holy Writ, rather than forms of his own or of someone else. He shall, moreover, command the devil to tell whether he is detained in that body by necromancy, by evil signs or amulets; and if the one possessed has taken the latter by mouth, he should be made to vomit them; if he has them concealed on his person, he should expose them; and when discovered they must be burned. Moreover, the person should be exhorted to reveal all his temptations to the exorcist.

21. Finally, after the possessed one has been freed, let him be admonished to guard himself carefully against falling into sin, so as to afford no opportunity to the evil spirit of returning, lest the last state of that man become worse than the former.

218. Exorcizing Those Obsessed by the Demon
This rite is also called the "solemn" or "major" exorcism, as it's intended specifically for a person being troubled by a spirit.

1. The exorcist shall have gone to confession, or at least elicited an act of contrition, and offered the Holy Sacrifice of the Mass if it is possible so to do; he ought, moreover, to have implored God's help in devout prayer.

Vested in surplice and purple stole, and having before him the person possessed (in fetters if there is any danger – remembering to comply with governmental law and medical prudence), he traces the sign of the Cross over him, over himself, and the bystanders, then sprinkles them with holy water. Kneeling down he prays the Litany of the Saints, excluding the prayers which follow it, with the others making the responses.

After the Litany the priest says (prays):

Antiphon: **Remember not, O Lord, our offenses, nor those of our parents: neither take retribution on our sins.**

Our Father (inaudibly until)

V. **And lead us not into temptation,**
R. **But deliver us from evil.**

Psalm 54
SAVE me, O God, by thy name,
 and further my cause by thy power,
O God, hear my prayer;
 give ear to the words of my mouth.
For proud men have risen against me,
 and men of violence have sought my life;
 they have not set God before their eyes.
But see -- God is my helper;
 the Lord supporteth my life.
Let the evil recoil upon my foes,
 and cut them off in thy faithfulness.
Gladly will I sacrifice unto thee.
 I will praise thy name, O Lord, for it is good.
In every need He hath delivered me,
 and mine eye hath seen the confusion of my foe.

Glory be to the Father, and to the Son,
  and to the Holy Spirit.
R. As it was in the beginning, is now, and ever shall be,
  world without end. Amen.

V. Save thy servant (handmaid),
R. Who places his (her) trust in thee, my God.
V. Be unto him (her), O Lord, a fortress of strength.
R. In the face of the enemy.
V. Let the enemy have no power over him (her).
R. And the son of evil do nothing to harm him (her).
V. Send him (her), Lord, aid from on high.
R. And from Sion watch over him (her).
V. O Lord, hear my prayer.
R. And let my cry come unto thee.
V. The Lord be with you.
R. And with thy spirit.

Let us pray.
O GOD, Whose nature it is ever to show mercy and to
spare, receive our petition, that this thy servant
(handmaid), bound by the fetters of sin, may by thy
sweet forgiveness be pardoned.

O HOLY Lord, almighty Father, eternal God and
Father of our Lord Jesus Christ, Who didst one time
consign that fugitive and fallen tyrant to everlasting hell
fire, Who didst send thy Sole-Begotten into the world to
crush that spirit of evil with his bellowing, do thou
speedily give heed and hasten to snatch from ruination
and from the noonday demon a human being, created in
thine image and likeness. Strike terror, O Lord, into the
beast that lays waste thy vineyard. Grant confidence to
thy servants to fight most manfully against that
reprobate dragon, lest he dare despise them who put
their trust in thee, and least he say with Pharaoh, who

once declared: "I know not God, neither will I let Israel go!" Let thy powerful right hand prevail upon him to depart from thy servant, N. (Thy handmaid N.), + so that he may no longer hold captive him (her) whom it has pleased thee to make in thine image and to redeem through thy Son. Thou Who livest and reignest in the unity of the Holy Spirit, God forever and ever. R. Amen.

2. Then he gives the command to the evil spirit as follows: **I COMMAND thee, unclean spirit, whosoever thou art, along with all thine associates who have taken possession of this servant (handmaid) of God, that, by the mysteries of the Incarnation, Passion, Resurrection, and Ascension of our Lord Jesus Christ, by the descent of the Holy Spirit, by the coming of our Lord unto judgment, thou shalt tell me by some sign or other thy name and the day and the hour of thy departure. I command thee, moreover, to obey me to the letter, I who, though unworthy, am a minister of God; neither shalt thou be emboldened to harm in any way this creature of God, nor the bystanders, nor any of their possessions.**

3. Next he reads over the possessed person these selections from the Gospel, or at least one of them.

A Reading From the Holy Gospel According to Saint John *(John 1:1-14)*

Saying this, he signs himself and the possessed on the brow, lips, and breast.

IN THE beginning was the Word: and the Word was with God: and the Word was God. The same was in the beginning with God. All things were made by him: and without him was made nothing that was made. In him

was life: and the life was the light of men. And the light shineth in darkness: and the darkness did not comprehend it. There was a man sent from God, whose name was John. This man came for a witness, to bear witness of the light, that all men might believe through him. He was not the light, but was to give testimony of the light. That was the true light, which enlighteneth every man that cometh into this world. He was in the world: and the world was made by Him: and the world knew Him not. He came unto his own: and His own received Him not. But as many as received Him, He gave them power to be made the sons of God, to them that believe in His name. Who was born, not of blood, nor of the will of the flesh, nor of the will of man, but of God (genuflect). And the Word was made flesh, and dwelt among us, and we saw His glory, the glory as it were of the Only-Begotten of the Father, full of grace and truth.

R. Thanks be to God.

A Reading From the Holy Gospel According to Saint Mark *(Mark 16:15-18)*

AND He said to them: Go ye into the whole world, and preach the gospel to every creature. He that believeth and is baptized shall be saved: but he that believeth not shall he condemned. And these signs shall follow them that believe: In my name they shall cast out devils. They shall speak with new tongues. They shall take up serpents; and if they shall drink any deadly thing, it shall not hurt them. They shall lay their hand upon the sick, and they shall recover.

A Reading From the Holy Gospel According to Saint Luke *(Luke 10:17-20)*

AND the seventy-two returned with joy, saying: Lord, the devils also are subject to us in thy name. And he said to them: I saw Satan like lightning falling from heaven. Behold, I have given you power to tread upon serpents and scorpions and upon all the power of the enemy, and nothing shall hurt you. But yet rejoice not in this, that spirits are subject unto you; but rejoice in this, that your names are written in heaven.

A Reading From the Holy Gospel According to Saint Luke *(Luke 11:14-22)*

AND HE was casting out a devil, and the same was dumb. And when He had cast out the devil, the dumb spoke: and the multitudes were in admiration at it. But some of them said: He casteth out devils by Beelzebub, the prince of devils. And others tempting, asked of Him a sign from heaven. But He seeing their thoughts, said to them: Every kingdom divided against itself shall be brought to desolation, and house upon house shall fall. And if Satan also be divided against himself, how shall his kingdom stand? Because you say that through Beelzebub I cast out devils. Now if I cast out devils by Beelzebub, by whom do your children cast them out? Therefore, they shall be your judges. But if I by the finger of God cast out devils, doubtless the kingdom of God is come upon you. When a strong man armed keepeth his court, those things are in peace which he possesseth. But if a stronger than he come upon him and overcome him, he will take away all his armour wherein he trusted, and will distribute his spoils.

V. **O Lord, hear my prayer.**
R. **And let my cry come unto thee.**
V. **The Lord be with you.**
R. **And with thy spirit.**

Let us pray.
O Almighty Lord, Word of God the Father, Christ Jesus, God and Lord of all creation! Who didst give to thine apostles the power to trample underfoot serpents and scorpions; who along with the other mandates to work miracles hast deigned to say: "You shall drive out evil spirits!" Whose mighty command caused Satan to fall like lightning from heaven. Wherefore, in fear and trembling I suppliantly call upon thy holy name: grant unto me, thy most unworthy servant, pardon for all my sins; bestow on me steadfast faith and the power to attack this cruel demon with assurance and fearlessness, fortified by the might of thy holy arm. Through thee, Jesus Christ, our Lord and God, Who shalt come to judge the living and the dead and the world by fire.
R. **Amen.**

4. Then he fortifies himself and the one possessed with the sign of the Cross, he places the end of the stole on the neck of the latter and, with his right hand laid on the person's head, he says what follows with constancy and firm faith:

V. **Behold the Cross of the Lord; begone ye hostile powers!**
R. **The Lion of Juda's tribe hath conquered, He Who is the rod of David.**
V. **O Lord, hear my prayer.**
R. **And let my cry come unto thee.**
V. **The Lord be with you.**
R. **And with thy spirit.**

Let us pray.

O God and Father of our Lord Jesus Christ, I call upon thy holy name and humbly entreat thy clemency, that thou wouldst graciously assist me in the assault against this as well as every unclean spirit who now torments the creature fashioned by thy hands. Through the selfsame Jesus Christ, thy Son, our Lord, Who liveth and reigneth with thee in the unity of the Holy Spirit, God, forever and ever. R. Amen.

Exorcism #1

I CAST thee out, thou unclean spirit, along with the least encroachment of the wicked enemy, and every phantom and diabolical legion. In the name of our Lord Jesus + Christ, depart and vanish from this creature of God. + For it is He who commands thee, He Who ordered thee cast down from the heights of heaven into the nethermost pit of the earth. He it is Who commands thee, Who once ordered the sea and the wind and all the storm to obey. Hence, pay heed, Satan, and tremble, thou enemy of the faith, thou foe of the human race! For thou art the carrier of death and the robber of life; thou art the shirker of justice and the root of all evil, the formenter of vice, the seducer of men, the traitor of the nations, the instigator of envy, the font of avarice, the source of discord, the exciter of sorrows! Why tarriest thou resisting, when thou knowest that Christ the Lord doth bring thy plans to naught? Him shalt thou fear, Who in Israel was sacrificed, in Joseph was sold, in the lamb was slain, was crucified as man, and finally triumphed over hell. (The three signs of the Cross which follow are traced on the brow of the one possessed.) Wherefore, get thee gone in the name of the Father, + and of the Son, + and of the Holy + Spirit. Make way for God the Holy Spirit through the sign of the holy + Cross of our Lord Jesus Christ. Who liveth and reigneth with the Father and the selfsame Holy Spirit, God, forever and ever. R. Amen.

V. O Lord, hear my prayer.
R. And let my cry come unto thee.
V. The Lord be with you.
R. And with thy spirit.

Let us pray.
O GOD, Creator and Defender of the human race, Who hast formed man in thine image, look down with pity upon this thy servant, N. (Thy handmaid, N.), for he (she) has fallen a prey to the craftiness of an evil spirit. The ancient adversary, the archenemy of the earth enshrouds him (her) in shuddering fear. He renders his (her) mental faculties befuddled; he keeps him (her) bewildered by making him (her) sore afraid; he holds him (her) in a state of perturbation, as he strikes terror within him (her). Drive out, O Lord, the power of the devil, and banish his artifices and frauds. Let him, the wicked tempter, be routed afar. By the sign + (on the brow) of thy name let thy servant (handmaid) be protected and safeguarded in both body and soul. (The three Crosses which follow are traced on the breast of the subject.) Keep watch over his (her) + reason, rule thou over his (her) + emotions, bring cheer into his (her) + heart. Let there vanish from his (her) soul the temptations of the mighty adversary. O Lord, as we call upon thy holy name, graciously grant that the evil spirit, who hitherto terrorized over us, may now himself be terror-stricken and may he depart vanquished.

Thus let this servant (handmaid) of thine offer thee with steadfast heart and sincere mind the meed that is thy due. Through Jesus Christ, thy Son, our Lord, Who liveth and reigneth with thee in the unity of the Holy

Spirit, God forever and ever. R. **Amen.**

Exorcism #2

I ADJURE thee, thou ancient serpent, by the Judge of the living and the dead, by thy own Creator, by the Creator of the world, by Him Who has the power to consign thee to hell, that thou speedily depart in trembling, along with thy raving followers, from this servant (handmaid) of God, N., who seeks refuge in the bosom of the Church.

I adjure thee once more + (on the brow), not by my own weakness but by the might of the Holy Spirit, begone from this servant (handmaid) of God, N., whom the Almighty has made in His image. Yield, therefore, yield, not to myself but to the minister of Christ! For it is the power of Christ that compels thee, Who brought thee under the subjection of His Cross. Quake before His arm, for it is He Who silenced the groans of hell, and brought forth the souls unto light. Be afraid of the body of man + (on the breast), be in dread of the image of God + (on the brow). Make no resistance, neither delay in leaving this person, for it has pleased Christ to take up his dwelling in man. Let it not occur to thee to despise my command, because thou dost recognize in me a poor sinner.

It is God Himself Who commands + thee! The majesty of Christ commands + thee! God the Father commands + thee, God the Son commands thee, God the Holy Spirit commands + thee! The mystery of the Cross commands + thee! The faith of the holy apostles Peter and Paul and the other saints commands + thee! The blood of the martyrs commands + thee! The constancy of the confessors commands + thee! The devout intercession of all holy men and women commands +

thee! The power of the mysteries of Christian faith commands + thee! Go out, then, thou transgressor, go out, thou seducer full of deceit and perfidy, thou enemy of virtue and persecutor of the innocent. Make way, thou horrible creature, make way, thou monster, make way for Christ, in whom thou has found nothing of thy works.

For He has stripped thee of thy might and laid waste thy kingdom; He has overcome thee and put thee in chains, and has blown up thy war materials. He has cast thee out into exterior darkness, where ruination is being made ready for thee and thine abettors. But to what purpose dost thou resist in thy insolence? To what purpose dost thou brazenly refuse? Thou art guilty before the almighty God, Whose laws thou hast transgressed. Thou art guilty before His Son, our Lord Jesus Christ, Whom thou didst presume to tempt, Whom thou wast emboldened to nail to the Cross. Thou art guilty before the human race, for through thy blandishments thou didst proffer it the poisoned cup of death.

I adjure thee, therefore, thou profligate dragon, in the name of the spotless + Lamb, Who walked upon the asp and the basilisk and tread underfoot the lion and the dragon, depart from this man + (on the brow), depart from the Church of God + (signing the bystanders). Quake and fly afar, as we call upon the name of the Lord, before Whom hell trembles, to Whom the heavenly Virtues and Powers and Dominations are subject, Whom the Cherubim and Seraphim praise with unending voice as they sing: Holy, holy, holy, Lord God of Sabaoth!

The Word made flesh commands + thee. He Who was born of a Virgin commands + thee. Jesus + of Nazareth commands thee. For when thou didst mock His disciples, He did shatter and humble thy pride, and did order thee out of a certain man; and when He had cast thee forth, thou didst not even dare except by His leave to enter into a herd of swine. And now as I adjure thee in His + name, vanish from this man whom He has created. It is hard for thee to want to resist. + It is hard for thee to kick against the goad. + For the longer thou dost delay thy departure, the heavier thy punishment shall be; since it is not men thou dost contemn, but rather Him, the Ruler over the living and the dead, Who shall come to judge the living and the dead and the world by fire. R. Amen.

V. O Lord, hear my prayer.
R. And let my cry come unto thee.
V. The Lord be with you.
R. And with thy spirit.

Let us pray.
O GOD of heaven and God of earth, God of the angels and God of the archangels, God of the Prophets and God of the apostles, God of martyrs and God of Virgins, thou hast the power to bestow life after death and rest after toil; for there is no other God beside thee, nor could there be a true God apart from thee, the Creator of heaven and earth, Who art truly the King of Whose kingdom there shall be no end. Hence I humbly implore thy sublime Majesty, that thou wouldst vouchsafe to deliver this thy servant (handmaid) from the unclean spirits. Through Christ our Lord. R. Amen.

Exorcism #3

I CAST thee out, every unclean spirit, every phantom, every encroachment of Satan, in the name of Jesus Christ + of Nazareth, Who, after John baptized Him, was lead into the desert and vanquished thee in thy citadel. Cease thy attack on man, whom He has made for His honor and glory out of the slime of the earth. Tremble before wretched man, not in the condition of human frailty but in the likeness of almighty God. Yield thee to God, + for it is He Who in Pharaoh and his army did drown thee and thy malice through His servant, Moses, in the depths of the sea.

Yield to God, + Who, by the singing of holy canticles on the part of David, His faithful servant, banished thee from the heart of King Saul. Yield to God, + Who condemned thee in the traitor Judas Iscariot. For He menaces thee with a divine + scourge, before Whose countenance thou didst tremble and cry out, saying: "What have we to do with thee, Jesus, Son of the Most High? Hast thou come hither before the time to torture us?" He threatens thee with everlasting fire, Who at the end of time will say to the wicked: "Depart from me, ye cursed, into everlasting fire which has been prepared for the devil and his angels."

For thee, O evil one, and for thy followers there will be worms which never perish. For thee and for thine angels is made ready an unquenchable fire, because thou art the prince of accursed murder, thou the author of lechery, thou the leader in sacrilege, thou the model of vileness, thou the teacher of heretics, thou the inventor of every obscenity. Depart then, + O evil one, depart + accursed one, depart with all thy falsity, for God has desired that man be His temple. But why dost thou linger here yet longer?

Give honor to God the Father + Almighty, before Whom every knee bows. Give place to the Lord Jesus + Christ, Who shed for men His most precious blood. Give place to the Holy + Spirit, Who, through His holy apostle, Peter, struck thee down openly in Simon; Who afflicted thee in King Herod, because he had not given the honor to God; Who smote thee with the night of blindness in Elymas, the magician, at the word of the apostle, Paul, and at his command bade thee likewise to go out of Pythonissa, the soothsayer.

Begone, + now! Begone, + thou seducer! Thy place is in solitude; thy dwelling in the serpent. Humble thyself, and fall prostrate! This matter brooks no delay. For behold, the Lord, the Ruler comes quickly, and fire will burn before Him, and it will go on ahead and set flames round about His enemies. Man thou canst betray, but God thou canst not mock. It is He that drives thee out, from Whose eyes nothing is hidden. By Him art thou cast forth, to Whose might all things are subject. By Him art thou expelled, Who hath prepared unending hell for thee and thine angels, from Whose mouth there shall come forth a pointed sword, Who shall come to judge the living and the dead and the world by fire. R. Amen.

5. All that precedes can be repeated as necessary until the possessed one is fully liberated.

6. In addition, it will be very helpful to say devoutly over and over again the Our Father, Hail Mary, and the Creed, as well as all that follows.

7. The canticles Magnificat and Benedictus concluding with Glory be to the Father.

7a. The Athanasian Creed

7b. Psalm 91; psalm 68; psalm 70; psalm 54; psalm 118; psalm 35; psalm 31; psalm 22, psalm 3; psalm 10; psalm 13.

Prayer Following Deliverance
WE BESEECH thee, O almighty God, that the spirit of iniquity may no longer have any power over thy servant N. (Thy handmaid N.), but rather that he may depart afar and nevermore return. At thy command, O Lord, let there enter into this man (woman) a disposition to goodness and the peace of our Lord Jesus Christ, by Whom we have been redeemed, and let us fear no evil, because the Lord is with us. Who liveth and reigneth with thee in the unity of the Holy Spirit, God, forever and ever. Amen.

219. Against Satan and the Rebellious Angels
While the previous rite is intended for a person who labors under a spirit's influence, this rite is geared toward purging a building or geographic location.

Experience has shown me this rite can be used in human cases, and in fact I've had better results with this rite than with the rite for Solemn Exorcism. In fact this is pretty much my go-to rite for every occasion.

In the name of the Father, and of the Son, and of the Holy Ghost. Amen.

Prayer to St. Michael the Archangel
O MOST illustrious prince of the heavenly hosts, holy Michael the Archangel, from thy heavenly throne defend us in the battle against the princes and powers, against the rulers of this world's darkness.

Come to the assistance of humankind, whom God has created in His own image and likeness, and whom He has purchased at a great price from Satan's tyranny. Thee the holy Church does venerate as her patron and guardian. To thee the Lord has entrusted the service of leading the souls of the redeemed into heavenly blessedness. Intercede for us to the God of peace, that He would crush Satan under our feet, lest he any longer have power to hold men captive and to do harm to the Church. Present our prayers at the throne of the Most High, so that He may all the more speedily favor us with His mercy. Lay hold of the dragon, the ancient serpent, no other than the demon, Satan, and cast him bound into the abyss, so that he may no longer seduce mankind.

Exorcism

IN THE name of Jesus Christ, our Lord and God, with confidence in the intercession of the Virgin Mary, Mother of God, of blessed Michael the Archangel, of the holy apostles Peter and Paul, and all the saints, *[a layperson omits these words:* **and with assurance in the sacred power of our ministry***,]* we steadfastly proceed with the task of expelling the molestations of the devil's frauds.

Psalm 68

Let God arise, and let his enemies be scattered: and let them that hate him flee from before his face.
As smoke vanisheth, so let them vanish away: as wax melteth before the fire, so let the wicked perish at the presence of God.

[NOTE: In human cases, or in cases where it's felt necessary to bind the spirit, the exorcist may say the Praecipio tibi *found in the rite of Solemn Exorcism. We place it here for convenience:*

***I COMMAND** thee, unclean spirit, whosoever thou art, along with all thine associates who have taken possession of this servant (handmaid) of God, that, by the mysteries of the Incarnation, Passion, Resurrection, and Ascension of our Lord Jesus Christ, by the descent of the Holy Spirit, by the coming of our Lord unto judgment, thou shalt tell me by some sign or other thy name and the day and the hour of thy departure. I command thee, moreover, to obey me to the letter, I who, though unworthy, am a minister of God; neither shalt thou be emboldened to harm in any way this creature of God, nor the bystanders, nor any of their possessions.]*

V. **Behold the Cross of the Lord, begone, ye hostile powers!**
R. **The Lion of Juda's tribe hath conquered, He Who is the rod of Jesse.**
V. **Let thy mercy, O Lord, be upon us.**
R. **Even as we have trusted in thee.**

WE CAST thee out, every unclean spirit, every devilish power, every assault of the infernal adversary, every legion, every diabolical group and sect, by the name and power of our Lord Jesus + Christ, and command thee to fly far from the Church of God and from all who are made to the image of God and redeemed by the Precious Blood of the Divine Lamb. + Presume never again, thou cunning serpent, to deceive the human race, to persecute the Church of God, nor to strike the chosen of God and sift them as wheat. +

For the Most High God commands thee, + He to Whom thou didst hitherto in thy great pride presume thyself equal; He Who desireth that all men might be saved, and come to the knowledge of truth, God the Father + commandeth thee! God the Son + commandeth thee! God the Holy + Spirit commandeth thee! The majesty of Christ commands thee, the Eternal Word of God made flesh, + Who for the salvation of our race, lost through thine envy, humbled Himself and was made obedient even unto death; Who built His Church upon solid rock, and proclaimed that the gates of hell should never prevail against her, and that He would remain with her all days, even to the end of the world! The sacred mystery of the Cross + commands thee, as well as the powers of all mysteries of Christian faith! + The most excellent Virgin Mary, Mother of God + commands thee, who in her lowliness crushed thy proud head from the first moment of her Immaculate Conception! The faith of the holy apostles Peter and Paul and the other apostles + commands thee! The blood of the martyrs commands thee, as well as the pious intercession + of holy men and women!

Therefore, accursed dragon, and every diabolical legion, we adjure thee by the living + God, by the true + God, by the holy + God, by the God Who so loved the world that He gave His Sole-Begotten Son, that whosoever believeth in Him shall not perish, but shall have life everlasting - cease thy deception of men and thy giving them to drink of the poison of eternal damnation; desist from harming the Church and fettering her freedom! Get thee gone, Satan, founder and master of all falsity, enemy of mankind! Give place to Christ in Whom thou didst find none of thy works; give place to the one, holy, catholic, and apostolic Church which Christ Himself bought with His blood!

Be thou brought low under God's mighty hand; tremble
and flee as we call upon the holy and awesome name of
Jesus, before Whom hell trembles, and to Whom the
Virtues, Powers, and Dominations are subject; Whom
the Cherubim and Seraphim praise with unfailing
voices, saying: Holy, holy, holy, the Lord God of Hosts!

V. O Lord, hear my prayer.
R. And let my cry come unto thee.
V. The Lord be with you.
R. And with thy spirit.

Let us pray
O God of heaven and God of earth, God of the angels
and God of the archangels, God of the patriarchs and
God of the prophets, God of the apostles and God of
Martyrs, God of confessors and God of Virgins! O God,
Who hast the power to bestow life after death and rest
after toil; for there is no other God beside thee, nor
could there be a true God apart from thee, the creator
of all things visible and invisible, of Whose kingdom
there shall be no end. Hence we humbly appeal to thy
sublime Majesty, that thou wouldst graciously
vouchsafe to deliver us by thy might from every power
of the accursed spirits, from their bondage and from
their deceptions, and to preserve us from all harm.
Through Christ our Lord. R. Amen.

From the snares of the devil, deliver us, O Lord.
That thou wouldst assist thy Church to serve thee
    in all security and freedom, we beseech thee, hear us.
That thou wouldst vouchsafe to humble
    the enemies of holy Church, we beseech thee, hear us.

The surroundings are sprinkled with holy water.

220. Exorcism Prayers of St. Basil the Great

For those impassioned or imprisoned by demons, and every manner of demonic illness or control.

First Prayer of Exorcism
V. Let us pray to the Lord.
R. Lord, have mercy.
O God of gods and Lord of lords, Creator of the fiery ranks, and Fashioner of the fleshless powers, the Artisan of heavenly things and those under the heavens, Whom no man has seen, nor is able to see, Whom all creation fears: Into the dark depths of Hell You hurled the commander who had become proud, and who, because of his disobedient service, was cast down from the height to earth, as well as the angels that fell away with him, all having become evil demons.

Grant that this my exorcism being performed in Your awesome name, be terrible to the Master of evil and to all his minions who had fallen with him from the height of brightness. Drive him into banishment, commanding him to depart hence, so that no harm might be worked against Your sealed Image. And, as You have commanded, let those who are sealed receive the strength to tread upon serpents and scorpions, and upon all power of the Enemy. For manifested, hymned, and glorified with fear, by everything that has breath is Your most holy Name: of the Father +, and of the Son +, and of the Holy + Spirit, now and ever and into ages of ages. Amen.

Second Prayer of Exorcism
V. Let us pray to the Lord.
R. Lord, have mercy.
I expel you, primal source of blasphemy, prince of the rebel host, originator of evil. I expel you, Lucifer, who was cast from the brilliance on high into the darkness of the abyss

on account of your arrogance: I expel you and all the fallen hosts which followed your will: I expel you, spirit of uncleanness, who revolted against Adonai, Elohim, the omnipotent God of Sabaoth and the army of His angels. Be gone and depart from the servant (handmaid) of God N. .

I expel you in the name of Him Who created all things by His Word, His Only-Begotten Son, our Lord Jesus Christ, Who was ineffably and dispassionately born before all the ages; by Whom was formed all things visible and invisible, Who made man after His Image: Who guarded him by the angels, Who trained him in the Law, Who drowned sin in the flood of waters from above and Who shut up the abysses under the heaven, Who demolished the impious race of giants, Who shook down the tower of Babel, Who reduced Sodom and Gomorrah to ashes by sulfur and fire, a fact to which the unceasing vapors testify; and Who by the staff of Moses separated the waters of the Red Sea, opening a waterless path for the people while the tyrannical Pharaoh and his God-fighting army were drowned forever in its waves for his wicked persecution of them; and Who in these last days was inexplicably incarnate of a pure Virgin who preserved the seal of her chastity intact; and Who was pleased to purge our ancient defilement in the baptismal cleansing.

I expel you, Satan, by virtue of Christ's baptism in the Jordan, which for us is a type of our inheritance of incorruption through grace and sanctified waters: the same One Who astounded the angels and all the heavenly powers when they beheld God incarnate in the flesh and also revealed at the Jordan His beginningless Father and the Holy Spirit with Whom He shares the unity of the Trinity.

I expel you, evil one, in the name of Him Who rebuked the winds and stilled the turbulent sea; Who banished the legion of demons and opened the eyes of him who was born blind from his mother's womb; and Who from clay fashioned sight for him, whereby He re-enacted the ancient refashioning of our face; Who restored the speech of the speechless, purged the stigma of leprosy, raised the dead from the grave and Who Himself despoiled Hades by His death and Resurrection thereby rendering mankind impervious to death. I expel you, in the name of Almighty God Who filled men with the inbreathing of a divinely inspired voice and Who wrought together with the Apostles the piety, which has filled the universe.

Fear and flee, run, leave, unclean and accursed spirit, deceitful and unseemly creature of the infernal depths, visible through deceit, hidden by pretense.

Depart wherever you may appear, Beelzebub, vanish as smoke and heat, bestial and serpentine thing, whether disguised as male or female, whether beast or crawling thing or flying, whether garrulous, mute or speechless, whether bringing fear of being trampled, or rending apart, conniving, whether oppressing him (her) in sleep, by some display of weakness, by distracting laughter, or taking pleasure in false tears whether by lechery or stench of carnal lust, pleasure, addiction to drugs, divination or astrology, whether dwelling in a house, whether possessed by audacity, or contentiousness or instability, whether striking him with lunacy, or returning to him after the passage of time, whether you be of the morning, noonday, midnight or night, indefinite time or daybreak, whether spontaneously or sent to someone or coming upon him (her) unawares, whether from the sea, a river, from beneath the earth, from a well, a ravine, a hollow, a lake, a thicket of reeds, from matter, land, refuse, whether from a grove, a tree, a thicket, from a fowl, or thunder, whether from the precincts of a bath, a pool of water or from a pagan sepulcher or from any place where you may lurk; whether by knowledge or ignorance or any place not mentioned.

Depart, separate yourself from him (her), be ashamed before him who was made in the image of God and shaped by His hand. Fear the likeness of the incarnate God and no longer hide in His servant (handmaid) N.; rather await the rod of iron, the fiery furnace of Tartars, the gnashing of teeth as reprisal for disobedience. Be afraid, be still, flee, neither return nor hide in him some other kind of evil, unclean spirits. Depart into the uncultivated, waterless waste of the desert where no man dwells, where God alone vigilantly watches, Who shall bind you that dares with envy to plot against His image and Who, with chains of darkness shall hold you in Tartaros, Who by day and night and for a great length of time has devised all manner of evils, O devil; for great is your fear of God and great is the glory of the Father, of the Son and of the Holy Spirit. Amen.

Third Prayer of Exorcism
V. Let us pray to the Lord.
R. Lord, have mercy.
O God of the heavens, God of Light, God of the Angels and Archangels obedient to Thine Authority and Power; O God Who art glorified in Thy Saints, Father of our Lord Jesus Christ, Thine Only-begotten Son, Who delivered the souls which were bound to death and Who enlightened them that dwelt in darkness; He Who released us from all our misery and pain and Who has protected us from the assaults of the enemy. And Thou, O Son and Word of God, has purposed us for immortality by Thy death and glorified us with Thy glory; Thou Who loosed us from the fetters of our sins through Thy Cross, rendering us pleasing to Thyself and uniting us with God; Thou Who didst rescue us from

destruction and cured all our diseases; Thou Who set us on the path to heaven and changed our corruption to incorruption.

Hear Thou me who cry unto Thee with longing and fear, Thou before Whom the mountains and the firmament under the heavens do shrink; Thou Who makest the physical elements to tremble, keeping them within their own limits; and because of Whom the fires of retribution dare not overstep the boundary set for them but must await the decision of Thy Will; and for Whom all creation sighs with great sighs awaiting deliverance; by Whom all adverse natures have been put to flight and the legion of the enemy has been subdued, the devil is affrighted, the serpent trampled under foot and the dragon slain; Thou Who has enlightened the nations which confess and welcome Thy rule, O Lord; Thou through Whom life hath appeared, hope hath prevailed, through Whom the man of the earth was recreated by belief in Thee. For Who is like unto Thee, Almighty God? Wherefore we beseech Thee, O Father, Lord of mercies, Who existed before the ages and surpasses all good, calling upon Thy holy name, through the love of Thy Child, Jesus Christ, the Holy One, and Thine All-powerful Spirit.

Cast away from his (her) soul every malady, all disbelief, spare him (her) from the furious attacks of unclean, infernal, fiery, evil-serving, lustful spirits, the love of gold and silver, conceit, fornication, every shameless, unseemly, dark and profane demon. Indeed, O God, expel from Thy servant (handmaiden) N. every energy of the devil, every enchantment and delusion; all idolatry, lunacy, astrology, necromancy, every bird of omen, the love of luxury and the flesh, all greed, drunkenness, carnality, adultery, licentiousness, shamelessness, anger, contentiousness, confusion and all evil suspicion. Yea, O Lord our God, breathe upon him (her) the Spirit of Thy Peace, watch over him (her) and produce thereby the fruits of faith, virtue, wisdom, chastity, self-control, love, uprightness, hope, meekness, longsuffering, patience, prudence and understanding in Thy servant (handmaiden) that he (she) may be welcomed by Thee in the name of Jesus Christ, believing in the coessential Trinity, giving witness and glorifying Thy dominion, along with the Angels and Archangels and all the heavenly host, guarding our hearts by them; for all things are possible to Thee, O Lord.

Therefore, we ascribe glory to the Father, and to the Son and to the Holy Spirit, now and ever and unto the ages of ages. Amen.

221. Exorcism Prayers of St. John Chrysostom
For General Use

All four prayers are said.

<u>First Prayer</u>
O Eternal God, Who has redeemed the race of men from the captivity of the devil, deliver Thy servant (handmaid) N. from all the workings of unclean spirits. Command the evil and impure spirits and demons to depart from the soul and body of N. your servant (handmaid) and not to remain nor hide in him (her). Let them be banished from this the creation of Thy hands in Thine own holy name and that of Thine only begotten Son and of Thy life-creating Spirit, so that, after being cleansed from all demonic influence, he (she) may live holy, godly, justly and righteously and may be counted worthy to receive the Holy Mysteries of Thine only-begotten Son and our God with Whom Thou art blessed and glorified together with the all holy and good and life-creating Spirit now and ever and unto the ages of ages. Amen.

Second Prayer

O Thou Who hast rebuked all unclean spirits and by the power of Thy Word has banished the legion, come now, through Thine only begotten Son upon this creature, which Thou hast fashioned in Thine own image and deliver him (her) from the adversary that holds him (her) in bondage, so that, receiving Thy mercy and becoming purified, he (she) might join the ranks of Thy holy flock and be preserved as a living temple of the Holy Spirit and might receive the divine and holy Mysteries through the grace and compassion and loving kindness of Thine only-begotten Son with Whom Thou art blessed together with Thine all-holy and good and life-creating Spirit now and ever and unto the ages of ages. Amen.

Third Prayer

We beseech Thee, O Lord, Almighty God, Most High, untempted, peaceful King. We beseech Thee Who has created the heaven and the earth, for out of Thee has issued the Alpha and the Omega, the beginning and the end, Thou Who has ordained that the fourfooted and irrational beasts be under subjection to man, for Thou hast subjected them. Lord, stretch out Thy mighty hand and Thy sublime and holy arm and in Thy watchful care look down upon this Thy creature and send down upon him (her) a peaceful angel, a mighty angel, a guardian of soul and body, that will rebuke and drive away every evil and unclean demon from him (her), for Thou alone are Lord, Most High, almighty and blessed unto ages of ages. Amen.

Fourth Prayer

We make this great, divine, holy and awesome invocation and plea, O devil, for thine expulsion, as well as this rebuke for your utter annihilation, O apostate! God Who is holy, beginningless, frightful, invisible in essence, infinite in power and incomprehensible in divinity, the King of glory and Lord Almighty, He shall rebuke thee, devil! He Who composed all things well by his Word from nothingness into being; He Who walks upon the wings of the air. The Lord rebukes thee, devil! He Who calls forth the water of the sea and pours it upon the face of all the earth. Lord of Hosts is His name.

O devil: the Lord rebukes thee! He Who is ministered to and praised by numberless heavenly orders and adored and glorified in fear by multitudes of angelic and archangelic hosts.

O Satan: the Lord rebukes thee!

He Who is honored by the encircling Powers, the awesome six-winged and many-eyed Cherubim and Seraphim that cover their faces with two wings because of His inscrutable and unseen divinity and with two wings cover their feet, lest they be seared by His unutterable glory and incomprehensible majesty, and with two wings do fly and fill the heavens with their shouts of "Holy, holy, holy, Lord Sabaoth, heaven and earth are full of Thy glory!"

Attend devil, the Lord rebukes thee! He Who came down from the Father's bosom and, through the holy, inexpressible, immaculate and adorable Incarnation from the Virgin, appeared ineffably in the world to save it and cast thee down from heaven in His authoritative power and showed thee to be an outcast to every man.

Attend Satan, the Lord rebukes thee! He Who said to the sea, be silent, be still, and instantly it was calmed at His command. O devil: The Lord rebukes thee! He Who made clay with His immaculate spittle and refashioned the wanting member of the man blind from birth and gave him his sight.

Attend devil: The Lord rebukes thee! He Who by His word restored to life the daughter of the ruler of the synagogue and snatched the son of the widow out from the mouth of death and gave him whole and sound to his own mother. Devil: The Lord rebukes thee! The Lord Who raised Lazarus the four-days dead from the dead, undecayed, as if not having died, and unblemished to the astonishment of many.

Attend Satan: The Lord rebukes thee! He Who destroyed the curse by the blow on His face and by the lance in His immaculate side lifted the flaming sword that guarded Paradise. Devil: The Lord rebukes thee! He Who dried all tears from every face by the spitting upon His precious expressed image. Devil: The Lord rebukes thee! He Who set His Cross as a support, the salvation of the world, to thy fall and the fall of all the angels under thee.

Attend Devil: The Lord rebukes thee! He Who spoke from His Cross and the curtain of the temple was torn in two, and the rocks were split and the tombs were opened and those who were dead from the ages were raised up. Devil: The Lord rebukes thee! He Who by death put death to death and by His rising granted life to all men.

May the Lord rebuke thee, Satan! It is, He Who descended into Hades and opened its tombs and set free those held prisoner in it, calling them to Himself; before Whom the gatekeepers of Hades shuddered when they saw Him and, hiding themselves, vanished in the anguish of Hades. May the Lord rebuke thee, devil! It is, Christ our God Who arose from the dead and granted His Resurrection to all men.

May the Lord rebuke thee, Satan! He Who in glory ascended into heaven to His Father, sitting on the right of majesty upon the throne of glory. Devil: May the Lord rebuke thee! He Who shall come again with glory upon the clouds of heaven with His holy angels to judge the living and the dead. Devil: May the Lord rebuke thee! He Who has prepared for thee unquenchable fire, the unsleeping worm and the outer darkness unto eternal punishment.

Attend Devil: May the Lord rebuke thee! For before Him all things shudder and tremble from the face of His power and the wrath of His warning upon thee is uncontainable. Satan: The Lord rebukes thee by His frightful name! Shudder, tremble, be afraid, depart, be utterly destroyed, be banished! Thee who fell from heaven and together with thee all evil spirits: every evil spirit of lust, the spirit of evil, a day and nocturnal spirit, a noonday and evening spirit, a midnight spirit, an imaginative spirit, an encountering spirit, whether of the dry land or of the water, or one in a forest, or among the reeds, or in trenches, or in a road or a crossroad, in lakes, or streams, in houses, or one sprinkling in the baths and chambers, or one altering the mind of man.

Depart swiftly from this creature of the Creator Christ our God! And be gone from the servant (handmaid) of God N., from his (her) mind, from his (her) soul, from his (her) heart, from his (her) reins, from his (her) senses, from all his (her) members, that he (she) might become whole and sound and free, knowing God, his (her) own Master and Creator of all things, He Who gathers together those who have gone astray and Who gives them the seal of salvation through the rebirth and restoration of divine Baptism, so that he may be counted worthy of His immaculate, heavenly and awesome Mysteries and be united to His true fold, dwelling in a place of pasture and nourished on the waters of repose, guided pastorally and safely by the staff of the Cross unto the forgiveness of sins and life everlasting.

For unto Him belong all glory, honor, adoration and majesty together with Thy beginningless Father and His all-holy, good and life-giving Spirit, now and ever, and unto ages of ages. Amen.

222. Prayer Against Malefice

This is an example of what's called "epiclectic" or "deprecative" exorcism, meaning the exorcism's not done by addressing the entity directly but by praying to God and asking that he'll take the evil away.

God, our Lord, King of ages, All-powerful and All-mighty, You Who made everything and Who transform everything simply by Your will. You Who in Babylon changed into dew the flames of the 'seven-times hotter' furnace and protected and saved the three holy children. You are the doctor and the physician of our soul. You are the salvation of those who turn to You. We beseech You to make powerless, banish, and drive out every diabolic power, presence, and machination; every evil influence, malefice, or evil eye and all evil actions aimed against Your servant *[name of person/s]*. Where there is envy and malice, give us an abundance of goodness, endurance, victory, and charity. O Lord, You Who love man, we beg You to reach out Your powerful hands and Your most high and mighty arms and send the angel of peace over us, to protect us, body and soul. May he keep at bay and vanquish every evil power, every poison or malice invoked against us by corrupt and envious people. Then, under the protection of Your authority may we sing, in gratitude, 'The Lord is my salvation; whom should I fear? I will not fear evil because You are with me, my God, my strength, my powerful Lord, Lord of peace, Father of all ages."

Yes, Lord our God, be merciful to us, Your image, and save your servant *[name of person/s]* from every threat or harm from the evil one, and protect him/her by raising him/her above all evil. We ask You this through the intercession of our Most Blessed, glorious Lady, Mary ever Virgin, Mother of God, of the most splendid archangels and all Your saints. Amen!

223. Prayer Against Every Evil
Another epiclectic/deprecative exorcism

Spirit of our God, Father, Son, and Holy Spirit, Most Holy Trinity, Immaculate Virgin Mary, angels, archangels, and saints of heaven, descend upon me. Please purify me, Lord, mold me, fill me with yourself, use me.

Banish all the forces of evil from me, destroy them, vanish them, so that I can be healthy and do good deeds.

Banish from me all spells, witchcraft, black magic, malefice, ties, maledictions, and the evil eye; diabolic infestations, oppressions, possessions; all that is evil and sinful, jealously, perfidy, envy; physical, psychological, moral, spiritual, diabolical aliments. Burn all these evils in hell, that they may never again touch me or any other creature in the entire world.

I command and bid all the power who molest me – by the power of God all powerful, in the name of Jesus Christ our Savior, through the intercession of the Immaculate Virgin Mary – to leave me forever, and to be consigned into the everlasting hell, where they will be bound by Saint Michael the archangel, Saint Gabriel, Saint Raphael, our guardian angels, and where they will be crushed under the heel of the Immaculate Virgin Mary. Amen.

XII. The Hymnal

224. Introduction to the Hymnal

Music plays an important part in the life of any church or ministry. It plays an important part because people are drawn to music that is well-performed and beautiful, and away from music that is ugly. Music also plays an important part because it is the expression of the community, connecting the many into one through means of a common song, and thereby the community's common prayer. Likewise, the choice and style of music also becomes a statement about the community itself, sending forth its song and its message to the outside world so that others may hear.

In my last years of exoteric ministry, the community I pastored was made up of people from a number of diverse backgrounds and experiences, and as a result our hymnody was originally drawn from a number of sources. Now, one might say this is a wonderful thing, but it was not so wonderful having to juggle around three or four books during every service. As such, it was decided early on that our community needed its own hymnal.

The hymnal before you is a result of that decision, and is a compilation of hymns culled from the Baptist, Lutheran, Catholic, Anglican, and Methodist traditions, with an eye towards hymns that are singable and accessible to the greatest possible number of people, while still beautiful and of a stature suitable for reverent worship.

In the compilation of these hymns, we have taken pains not to include any that are still under copyright, in the hopes of producing a finished hymnal that could also be used by other small churches or faith communities who found themselves with a similar need. If, however, we have made an oversight in this matter, please bring it to our attention along with documentation of the copyright in question, and we will make haste to rectify the issue.

In closing, I would like to thank the members of my last congregation for sharing their favorite hymns and making this hymnal possible. I'd also like to thank and acknowledge all those generations of hymn-writers, living and dead, whose hymns have become near and dear to our hearts and on whose work churches around the world still draw to this day.

It is my fervent prayer that almighty God will approve of this hymnal, and make use of it wherever he may choose.

Peace and Blessings,
The Most Reverend Agostino Taumaturgo
April 18, 2016

225. A Hymn of Glory Let Us Sing

Text: *Hymnum Canamus Gloriae*, Venerable Bede, 673-735
Tr. Benjamin Webb, 1819-1885

Tune: Lasst Uns Erfreuen, L. M. with alleluias
Geistliche Kirchengesange, Cologne, 1623

1. A hymn of glo – ry let us sing New songs thru – out
2. The ho – ly a – po – sto – lic band Up – on the Mount
3. To whom the an – gels draw– ing nigh, "Why stand and gaze
4. "A – gain ye shall be – hold him so, As ye to – day
5. O grant us thi – ther– ward to tend And with un – wea–
6. Be thou our joy and strong de – fense, Who art our fu –
7. O ris – en Christ, a – scend– ed Lord, All praise to thee

1. the world shall ring Al – le – lu – ia! Al – le – lu – ia!
2. of Ol – ives stand Al – le – lu – ia! Al – le – lu – ia!
3. up – on the sky?" Al – le – lu – ia! Al – le – lu – ia!
4. have seen him go." Al – le – lu – ia! Al – le – lu – ia!
5. ried hearts a – scend, Al – le – lu – ia! Al – le – lu – ia!
6. ture Re – com – pense, Al – le – lu – ia! Al – le – lu – ia!
7. let earth ac – cord, Al – le – lu – ia! Al – le – lu – ia!

1. Christ, by a road be – fore un – trod A – scend– eth to
2. And with his fol – low – ers they see Je – sus' re – splen–
3. "This is the Sav – ior," thus they say. "This is his no –
4. "In glo – rious pomp a – scend– ing high Up to the por –
5. Un – to thy king– dom's throne, where thou As is our faith,
6. So shall the light that springs from thee Be ours through all
7. Who art, while end – less a – ges run, With Fa – ther and

1. the throne of God. Al – le – lu – ia! Al – le – lu – ia!
2. dent maj – es – ty. Al – le – lu – ia! Al – le – lu – ia!
3. ble tri – umph day." Al – le – lu – ia! Al – le – lu – ia!
4. tals of the sky." Al – le – lu – ia! Al – le – lu – ia!
5. art seat – ed now. Al – le – lu – ia! Al – le – lu – ia!
6. e – ter – ni – ty. Al – le – lu – ia! Al – le – lu – ia!
7. with Spir – it One. Al – le – lu – ia! Al – le – lu – ia!

1-7. Al – le – lu – ia! Al – le – lu – ia! Al – le – lu – ia!

226. A Mighty Fortress Is Our God

Text: *Eine Feste Burg,* Martin Luther, 1483-1546
Tr. Fredrick H. Hedge, 1805-1890

Tune: Eine Feste Berg – 87. 87. 66. 66. 7.
Martin Luther, 1483-1546

1. A might – y for – tress is our God, A bul – wark
2. Did we in our own strength con – fide, Our striv – ing
3. And though this world with de – vils filled, Should threat –en
4. That Word a – bove all earth – ly pow'rs, No thanks to

1. nev – er fail – ing; Our hel – per he, a – mid the flood,
2. would be los – ing. Were not the right man on our side,
3. to un – do us, We will not fear, for God hath willed;
4. them, a – bid – eth; The Spir – it and the gifts are ours,

1. Of mor – tal ills pre – vail – ing. For still our
2. The man of God's own choos – ing. Dost ask who
3. His truth to tri – umph through us. The Prince of
4. Through him who with us sid – eth. Let goods and

1. an – cient foe, Doth seek to work us woe,
2. that may be? Christ Je – sus, it is he!
3. Dark – ness grim, We trem – ble not for him;
4. kin – dred go, This mor – tal life al – so;

1. His craft and pow'r are great, And armed with
2. The Lord of Hosts his name, From age to
3. His rage we can en – dure, For, lo, his
4. The bod – y they may kill, God's truth a –

1. cru – el hate. On earth is not his e – qual.
2. age the same. And he must win the bat – tle.
3. doom is sure, One lit – tle word shall fell him.
4. bid – eth still, The King – dom is for – ev – er!

235

227. A Thousand Lights Their Glory Shed

Text: *Sacra Jam Splendent*, Pope Leo XIII, 1810-1903
Tr. Msgr. Hugh Thomas Henry, 1862-1946

Tune: O Filii et Filiae, 88.84.
Solesmes, 15th Century

1.	A	thou – sand	lights	their	glo – ry	shed
2.	Sweet– er	is	low – ly	Naz – a – reth,
3.	And	the	Child	grew	in	wis – dom's	ken
4.	At	Jo – seph's	bench,	at	Je – sus'	side,
5.	Glo – ry	to	you,	O	Je – sus	dear,

1.	On	shrines	and	al – tars	gar – land – ed:
2.	Where	Je – sus	drew	his	child – ish	breath
3.	And	years	and	grace	with	God	and	men;
4.	The	Mo – ther	sits,	the	Vir – gin	Bride:
5.	Mod – el	of	ho – ly	liv – ing	hear!

1.	While	swing – ing	cen – sers	dusk	the	air
2.	Sweet – er	the	sing – ing	that	en – dears
3.	And	in	his	step – fa – ther's	hum – ble	art
4.	Hap – py,	if	she	may	cheer	their	hearts
5.	You	reign	with	Fa – ther	and	Ho – ly	Ghost

1.	With	per – fumed	prayer.
2.	His	hid – den	years.
3.	Took	share	and	part.
4.	With	lov – ing	arts.
5.	O'er	hea – ven's	host.

228. Accept, Almighty Father

Text: Anonymous, 19th Century.

Tune: Gott Soll Gepriesen 76. 76. D.
Mohr's Psalterlein, 1877

1. Ac – cept, Al – might– y Fa – ther, This gift of bread and wine,
2. O God, by this com– ming – ling Of wa – ter and of wine,

1. Which now thy priest doth of – fer, To thee, O God, be – nign,
2. May he who took our na – ture Give us his life di – vine.

1. In hum – ble rep – a – ra – tion, For sins and fail – ings dread,
2. Come, thou who mak– est ho – ly, And bless this sac – ri – fice;

1. To win life ev – er – last – ing For liv – ing and for dead.
2. Then shall our gift be pleas– ing To thee a – bove the skies.

229. Adeste Fideles

Text: John Francis Wade, c. 1711-1786
ENGLISH: "O Come, All Ye Faithful"

Tune: Adeste Fideles – Irregular with Refrain
John Francis Wade, c. 1711-1786

1. A – dés – te fi – dé – les, lae – ti tri – um – phán – tes,
2. De – um de De – o, Lu – men de lú–mi – ne,
3. Can – tet nunc «I – o» cho– rus an – ge – ló – rum,
4. Er – go qui na – tus, di – e ho – di – ér – na,

1. Ve – ní – te, ve – ní – te in Béth – le – hem.
2. Ges – tant pu – él – lae ví – sce – ra.
3. Can – tet nunc au – la coe – lé – sti – um.
4. Je – su ti – bi sit gló – ri – a.

1. Na – tum vi – dé – te, Re – gem an – ge – ló – rum.
2. De – um ve – rum, Gé – ni – tum, non fa – ctum.
3. Gló – ri – a, gló – ria In ex – cél – sis De – o.
4. Pa – tris ae – tér – ni Ver – bum ca – ro fa – ctum.

Refrain:

Ve – ní – te a – do – ré – mus, ve – ní – te a – do – ré – mus,

Ve – ní – te a – do – ré – mus Dó – mi – num.

230. Adoro Te Devote

Text: St. Thomas Aquinas, 1227-1274   Tune: Adoro Te Devote 11. 11. 11. 11.
ENGLISH: "Godhead Here in Hiding"   Chant, Mode V

1. A – dó – ro te de – vó – te, la – tens Dé – i – tas,
2. Vi – sus, ta – ctus, gus – tus, in te fál – li – tur;
3. In cru – ce la – té – bat so – la Dé – i – tas,
4. Pla – gas, si – cut Tho – mas, non in – tú – e – or:
5. O me – mo – ri – á – le mor – tis Dó – mi – ni!
6. Je – su, quem ve – lá – tum nunc a – spí – ci – o,

1. Quae sub his fi – gú – ris, ve – re lá – ti – tas:
2. Sed au – dí – tu so – lo, tu – to cré – di – tur.
3. At hic la – tet si – mul et Hu – má – ni – tas,
4. De – um ta – men me – um te con – fí – te – or.
5. Pa – nis vi – vus, vi – tam prae – stans hó – mi – ni!
6. O – ro, fi – at il – lud quod tam sí – ti – o:

1. Ti – bi se cor me – um, to – tum súb – ji – cit,
2. Cre – do quid – quid dix – it, De – i Fí – li – us:
3. Am – bo ta – men cre – dens at – que cón – fi – tens,
4. Fac me ti – bi sem – per ma – gis cré – de – re,
5. Prae– sta me ae men – ti de te ví – ve – re,
6. Ut te re – ve – lá – ta cer – nens fá – ci – e,

1. Qui – a te con – tém – plans, to – tum dé – fi – cit.
2. Nil hoc ver – bo ve – ri – tá – tis vé – ri – us.
3. Pe – to quod pe – tí – vit la – tro poé – ni – tens.
4. In te spem ha – bé – re, te di – lí – ge – re.
5. Et te il – li sem – per dul – ce sá – pe – re.
6. Vi – su sim be – á – tus tu – ae gló – ri – ae.

231. Ah, Dearest Jesus

Text: *Herzliebster Jesu*, Johann Heermann, 1585-1647
Tr. Jeremiah Franklin Ohl, 1850-1941

Tune: Herzliebster Jesu, 11. 11. 11. 5.
Johann Crüger, 1598-1662

1. Ah, dear – est Je – sus, how hast thou of – fend –ed,
2. They have chas – tised thee, thorns the crown thou wear– est,
3. Whence come these sor – rows? Why art thou af – flict – ed?
4. O love un – fath – omed, that for my sal – va – tion,

1. That such fell judg – ment hath on thee de – scend – ed?
2. Thy face is smit – ten, cru – el taunts thou bear – est,
3. For me, a sin – ner, art thou, Lord, con – vict – ed;
4. Thou, Lord, dost suf – fer such hu – mil – i – a – tion!

1. What deeds of e – vil bring thee trib – u – la – tion,
2. Gall thou art giv – en, on the cross in an – guish,
3. All thou en – dur – est, while as vic – tim of – fered,
4. While as a world – ling, I loved mirth and glad – ness,

1. And con – dem – na – tion?
2. Thou, Lord, dost lan – guish.
3. I should have suf – fered.
4. Thine is the sad – ness.

232. Alas! And Did My Savior Bleed

Text: Isaac Watts, 1674-1748, alt.

Tune: Martyrdom, C. M.
Hugh Wilson, 1764-1824

1. A – las! And did my Sav – ior bleed,
2. Was it for sins that I had done
3. Well might the sun in dark – ness hide
4. Thus might I hide my blush – ing face
5. But tears of grief can – not re – pay

1. And did my sov – 'reign die?
2. He groaned up – on the tree?
3. And shut its glo – ries in
4. While his dear cross ap – pears,
5. The debt of love I owe;

1. Would he de – vote that sa – cred head
2. A – maz – ing pit – y, grace un – known,
3. When God, the might – y mak – er, died
4. Dis – solve my heart in thank – ful ness,
5. Here, Lord, I give my – self a – way:

1. For sin – ners such as I?
2. And love be – yond de – gree!
3. For his own crea – tures' sin.
4. And melt my eyes to tears.
5. It's all that I can do.

233. All Creatures of Our God and King

Text: *Laudato Si, Mi Signore*, St. Francis, 1182-1226 Tune: Lasst Uns Erfreuen, L. M. with alleluias
Tr. William H. Draper, 1855-1933   *Geistliche Kirchengesange*, Cologne, 1623

1. All crea – tures of our God and King,
2. Thou rush – ing wind that art so strong,
3. Thou flow – ing wa – ter, pure and clear,
4. Dear moth – er earth, who day by day
5. And all peo – ple of ten – der heart,
6. And thou, most kind and gen – tle death,
7. Let all things their Cre – a – tor bless,

1. Lift up your voic – es, let us sing:
2. Ye clouds that sail in heav'n a – long,
3. Make mu – sic for thy Lord to hear,
4. Un – fold – est bless – ings on our way,
5. For – giv – ing oth – ers, take your part,
6. Wait – ing to hush our lat – est breath,
7. And wor – ship him in hum – ble – ness,

1. Al – le – lu – ia! Al – le – lu – ia!
2. O – praise him, Al – le – lu – ia!
3. Al – le – lu – ia! Al – le – lu – ia!
4. O – praise him, Al – le – lu – ia!
5. O – sing ye, Al – le – lu – ia!
6. O – praise him, Al – le – lu – ia!
7. O – praise him, Al – le – lu – ia!

1. Thou burn – ing sun with gold – en beams,
2. Thou ris – ing morn, in praise re – joice,
3. Thou fire so mas – ter – ful and bright,
4. The flow'rs and fruits that in thee grow,
5. Ye who long pain and sor – row bear,
6. Thou lead – est home the child of God,
7. Praise, praise the Fa – ther, praise the Son,

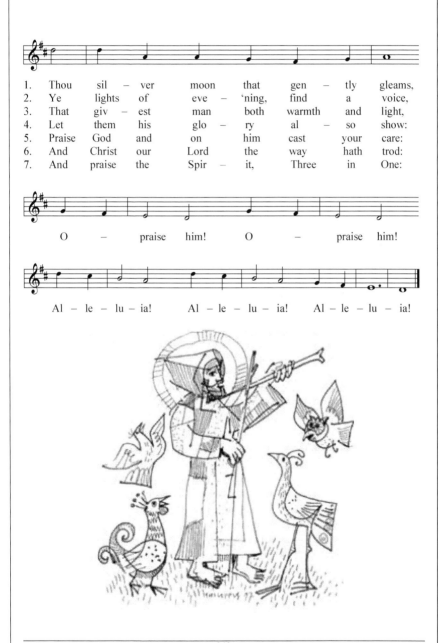

1.	Thou	sil – ver	moon	that	gen – tly	gleams,
2.	Ye	lights	of	eve – 'ning,	find	a	voice,
3.	That	giv – est	man	both	warmth and	light,
4.	Let	them	his	glo – ry	al – so	show:
5.	Praise	God	and	on	him	cast	your	care:
6.	And	Christ	our	Lord	the	way	hath	trod:
7.	And	praise	the	Spir – it,	Three	in	One:

O – praise him! O – praise him!

Al – le – lu – ia! Al – le – lu – ia! Al – le – lu – ia!

234. All Glory Be to God on High

Text: *Allein Gott*, Nikolaus Decius, c. 1485-1546   Tune: Allein Gott In Der Hoh, 87. 87. 88. 7.
Tr. Catherine Winkworth, 1827-1878   Nikolaus Decius, c. 1485-1546

1. All glo – ry be to God on high, Who hath our race
2. We praise, we wor – ship thee, we trust, And give thee thanks
3. O Je – sus Christ, our God and Lord, Be – got – ten of
4. O Ho – ly Spir – it, pre – cious gift, Thou Com– for – ter

1. be – friend – ed. To us no harm shall now come nigh,
2. for – ev – er, O Fa – ther, that thy rule is just
3. the Fa – ther, Who hast our fall – en race re – stored
4. un – fail – ing, Do thou our troub– led souls up – lift,

1. The strife at last is end – ed. He bends his ear
2. And wise and chang – es nev – er. Thy bound– less pow'r
3. And stray – ing sheep dost gath – er, Thou Lamb of God,
4. A – gainst the foe pre – vail – ing; Since Christ for us

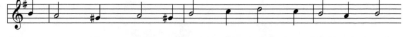

1. to ev – 'ry call, And of – fers peace, good will to all,
2. o'er all things reigns, Thou dost what – e'er thy will or – dains,
3. en – throned on high, Be – hold our need and hear our cry;
4. his blood hath shed, A – vert our woes and calm our dread;

1. O thank him for his good– ness.
2. 'Tis well thou art our Rul – er.
3. Have mer – cy on us, Je – sus.
4. Do thou in faith sus – tain us. A – – – – men.

235. All Glory Laud and Honor

Text: *Gloria Laus et Honor*, Theodulph of Orleans, c. 760-820
Tr. John Mason Neale, 1818-1866

Tune: St. Theodulph, 76. 76. D.
Melchior Teschner, 1584-1635

Refrain:

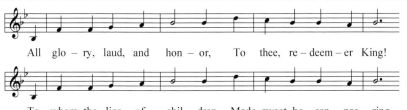

All glo – ry, laud, and hon – or, To thee, re – deem – er King!

To whom the lips of chil – dren, Made sweet ho – san – nas ring.

1.	Thou	art	the	King	of	Is – ra – el,
2.	The	com – pa – ny	of	an – gels,		
3.	The	peo – ple	of	the	He – brews,	
4.	To	thee	be – fore	thy	pas – sion,	
5.	Thou	didst	ac – cept	their	prais – es;	

1.	Thou	Da – vid's	roy – al	Son,		
2.	Are	prais – ing	thee	on	high;	
3.	With	palms	be – fore	thee	went:	
4.	They	sang	their	hymns	of	praise:
5.	Ac – cept	the	prayers	we	bring,	

1.	Who	in	the	Lord's	name	com – est,
2.	And	mor – tal	men,	and	all	things,
3.	Our	praise	and	prayers	and	an – thems,
4.	To	thee,	now	high	ex – alt – ed,	
5.	Who	in	all	good	de – light – est,	

1.	The	King	and	bless – ed	One.	
2.	Cre – a – ted	make	re – ply.			
3.	Be – fore	thee	we	pre – sent.		
4.	Our	mel – o – dy	we	raise.		
5.	Thou	good	and	gra – cious	King!	

236. All Hail the Power of Jesus' Name

Text: Edward Perronet, 1726-1792

Tune: Coronation C.M.
Oliver Holden, 1765-1844

1. All hail the pow'r of Je – sus' name!
2. Hail him, ye heirs of Da – vid's line,
3. Let ev – 'ry tongue and ev – ery tribe,
4. O that, with yon – der sa – cred throng,

1. Let an – gels pros – trate fall;
2. Whom Da – vid Lord did call,
3. On this ter – res – trial ball,
4. We at his feet may fall;

1. Bring forth the roy – al di – a – dem,
2. The God in – car – nate, Man di – vine,
3. To him all ma – jes – ty as – cribe,
4. We'll join the ev – er – last – ing song,

1-4. And crown him Lord of all;

1. Bring forth the roy – al di – a – dem,
2. The God in – car – nate, Man di – vine,
3. To him all ma – jes – ty as – cribe,
4. We'll join the ev – er – last – ing song,

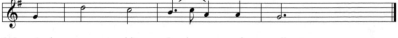

1-4. And crown him Lord of all.

237. All Praise to Thee, My God, This Night

Tune: Thomas Ken, 1637-1711

Tune: Tallis' Canon, L. M.
Thomas Tallis, 1505-1585

1. All praise to thee, my God, this night
2. For – give me, Lord, for thy dear Son,
3. Teach me to live that I may dread
4. Praise God, from whom all bless – ings flow;

1. For all the bless – ings of the light.
2. The ill that I this day have done
3. The grave as lit – tle as my bed.
4. Praise him, all crea – tures here be – low;

1. Keep me, oh, keep me, King of Kings,
2. That with the world, my – self, and thee
3. Teach me to die so that I may
4. Praise him a – bove ye heav'n – ly host:

1. Be – neath thine own al – might – y wings.
2. I, ere I sleep, at peace may be.
3. Rise glo – rious at that awe – full Day!
4. Praise Fa – ther, Son, and Ho – ly Ghost.

238. All Praise to you, O Lord

Text: Hyde W. Beadon, 1812-1891

Tune: Franconia, S.M.
Johann B. König, 1691-1758

1. All praise to you, O Lord,
2. You speak, and it is done;
3. Oh, may that grace be ours,
4. So, led from strength to strength,

1. Who by your might — y pow'r
2. O – be – dient to your word,
3. In you for – e'er to live,
4. Grant us, O Lord, to see

1. Did man – i – fest your glo – ry forth
2. The wa – ter red – d'ning in – to wine
3. And drink of those re – fresh – ing streams
4. The mar – riage sup – per of the Lamb,

1. In Ca – na's mar – riage hour.
2. Pro – claims the pre – sent Lord.
3. Which you a – lone can give.
4. The great E – piph – a – ny.

239. All Who Believe and Are Baptized

Text: *Enhver Som Tror*, Thomas H. Kingo, 1634-1703
Tr. George T. Rygh, 1860-1943, alt.

Tune: Es Ist Das Heil, 87. 87. 88. 7
Erlich christlich Lieder, Wittenberg, 1524

1. All who be – lieve and are bap – tized
2. With one ac – cord, O God, we pray,

1. Shall see the Lord's sal – va – tion;
2. Grant us your Ho – ly Spir – it;

1. Bap – tized in – to the death of Christ,
2. Help us in our in – fir – mi – ty

1. They are a new cre – a – tion;
2. Through Je – sus' blood and mer – it;

1. Through Christ's re – demp – tion they will stand
2. Grant us to grow in grace each day

1. A – mong the glor – ious heav'n – ly band
2. By ho – ly Bap – tism, that we may

1. Of ev – 'ry tribe and na – tion.
2. E – ter – nal life in – her – it.

240. Alleluia, Sing to Jesus

Text: William Chatterton Dix, 1837-1898

Tune: Hyfrydol, 87. 87. D
Rowland H. Prichard, 1811-1887

1,5. Al – le – lu – ia! Sing to Je – sus! His the scep – ter,
2. Al – le – lu – ia! Not to or – phans Are we left in
3. Al – le – lu – ia! Bread of An – gels, Thou on earth our
4. Al – le – lu – ia! King e – ter – nal, Thee the Lord of

1,5. his the throne; Al – le – lu – ia! His the tri – umph,
2. sor – row now; Al – le – lu – ia! He is near us,
3. food, our stay! Al – le – lu – ia! Here the sin – ful
4. lords we own; Al – le – lu – ia! Born of Ma – ry,

1,5. His the vic – to – ry a – lone; Hark! The songs of
2. Faith be – lieves, nor ques – tions how: Though the cloud from
3. Flee to thee from day to day: In – ter – ces – sor,
4. Earth thy foot – stool, heav'n thy throne: Thou with – in the

1,5. peace– ful Zi – on Thun – der like a might – y flood;
2. sight re – ceived him, When the for – ty days were o'er,
3. friend of sin – ners, Earth's Re – deem – er, plead for me,
4. veil hast en – tered, Robed in flesh, our great High Priest;

1,5. Je – sus out of ev – 'ry na – tion
2. Shall our hearts for – get his prom – ise,
3. Where the songs of all the sin – less
4. Thou on earth both Priest and Vic – tim

1,5. Hath re – deemed us by his blood.
2. "I am with you ev – er – more?"
3. Sweep a – cross the crys – tal sea.
4. In the Eu – cha – ris – tic feast.

241. Alleluia! Song of Sweetness!

Text: *Alleluia Dulce Carmen*, 11th Century
Tr. John Mason Neale, 1818-1866

Tune: St. Thomas, 87. 87. 87.
Cantus Diversi, John Francis Wade, c. 1711-1786

1. Al — le — lu — ia,   song   of   sweet – ness,
2. Al — le — lu — ia   thou   re – sound – est,
3. Al — le — lu — ia   can — not   al — ways
4. There – fore   in   our   hymns   we   pray   thee

1. Voice   of   joy   that   can — not   die;
2. True   Je — ru — sa — lem   and   free;
3. Be   our   song   while   here   be — low;
4. Grant   us   bless – éd   Tri — ni — ty,

1. Al — le — lu — ia   is   the   an — them
2. Al — le — lu — ia,   joy — ful   moth – er,
3. Al — le — lu — ia   our   trans – gres – sions
4. At   the   last   to   keep   thine   Eas – ter

1. Ev — er   dear   to   choirs   on   high;
2. All   thy   chil — dren   sing   with   thee;
3. Make   us   for   a   while   fore — go;
4. In   our   home   be — yond   the   sky,

1. In   the   house   of   God   a — bid — ing
2. But   by   Ba — by — lon's   sad   wa — ters
3. For   the   sol — emn   time   is   com — ing
4. There   to   thee   for — ev — er   sing — ing

1. Thus   they   sing   e — ter — nal — ly.
2. Mourn — ing   ex — iles   now   are   we.
3. When   our   tears   for   sin   must   flow.
4. Al — le — lu — ia   joy — ful — ly.   A – men.

242. Amazing Grace

Text: John Newton, 1725-1807

Tune: New Britain (Amazing Grace), C. M.
Columbian Harmony, 1829

1. A – maz – ing grace, how sweet the sound,
2. 'Twas grace that taught my heart to fear,
3. Through man – y dan – gers, toils, and snares
4. The Lord has prom – ised good to me;
5. Yea, when this flesh and heart shall fail,
6. When we've been here ten thou – sand years,

1. That saved a wretch like me!
2. And grace my fears re – lieved;
3. I have al – read – y come;
4. His Word my hope se – cures;
5. And mor – tal life shall cease,
6. Bright shin – ing as the sun,

1. I once was lost, but now am found;
2. How pre – cious did that grace ap – pear
3. 'Tis grace has brought me safe thus far,
4. He will my shield and por – tion be
5. I shall pos – sess, with – in the veil,
6. We've no less days to sing God's praise,

1. Was blind, but now I see.
2. The hour I first be – lieved!
3. And grace will lead me home.
4. As long as life en – dures.
5. A life of joy and peace.
6. Than when we'd first be – gun.

243. America the Beautiful

Text: Katherine L. Bates, 1859-1929

Tune: Materna, C.M.D.
Samuel A. Ward, 1848-1903

1. O beau – ti – ful for spa – cious skies, For am – ber
2. O beau – ti – ful for pil – grim feet, Whose stern, im –
3. O beau – ti – ful for he – roes proved In lib – er –
4. O beau – ti – ful for pa – triot dream That sees be –

1. waves of grain, For pur – ple moun – tain maj – es – ties
2. pas – sioned stress A thor – ough – fare for free – dom beat
3. a – ting strife, Who more than self their coun – try loved,
4. yond the years Thine al – a – bas – ter cit – ies gleam,

1. A – bove the fruit – ed plain! A – mer – i – ca!
2. A – cross the wil – der – ness! A – mer – i – ca!
3. And mer – cy more than life! A – mer – i – ca!
4. Un – dimmed by hu – man tears! A – mer – i – ca!

1. A – mer – i – ca! God shed his grace on thee,
2. A – mer – i – ca! God mend thine ev – 'ry flaw,
3. A – mer – i – ca! May God thy gold re – fine,
4. A – mer – i – ca! God shed his grace on thee,

1. And crown thy good with broth – er – hood
2. Con – firm thy soul in self con – trol,
3. Till all suc – cess be no – ble – ness,
4. And crown thy good with broth – er – hood

1. From sea to shin – ing sea.
2. Thy lib – er – ty in law.
3. And ev – 'ry gain di – vine.
4. From sea to shin – ing sea.

244. Amidst Us Our Beloved Stands

Text: Charles Spurgeon, 1834-1892

Tune: Hamburg, L.M.
Lowell Mason, 1792-1872

1. A – midst us our Be – lov – èd stands,
2. What gen – 'rous food a – dorns his board,
3. If now, with eyes de – filed and dim,
4. Our for – mer trans – ports we re – count,
5. Thou glo – rious Bride – groom of our hearts,

1. And bids us view his pier – cèd hands;
2. When at his ta – ble sits the Lord!
3. We see the signs, but see not him;
4. When with him in the ho – ly mount,
5. Thy pre – sent smile a heav'n im – parts!

1. Points to the wound – ed feet and side,
2. The wine how rich, the bread how sweet,
3. O may his love the scales dis – place,
4. These cause our souls to thirst a – new,.
5. Oh lift the veil, if veil there be,

1. Blest em – blems of the Cru – ci – fied.
2. When Je – sus deigns the guests to meet!
3. And bid us see him face to face!
4. His marred but love – ly face to view.
5. Let ev – 'ry – one thy beau – ties see!

245. Angels We Have Heard on High

Text: *Les Anges dans Nos Campagnes*, French Carol, 18th Century Tune: Gloria, 77. 77. with Refrain
Tr. *Crown of Jesus Music*, London, 1862   Traditional French Carol

1. An — gels   we   have   heard   on   high
2. Shep — herds,   why   this   ju — bi — lee?
3. Come   to   Beth — le — hem   and   see

1. Sweet — ly   sing — ing   o'er   the   plains,
2. Why   your   joy — ous   strains   pro — long?
3. Him   whose   birth   the   an — gels   sing;

1. And   the   moun — tains   in   re — ply
2. Say   what   may   the   tid — ings   be,
3. Come   a — dore   on   bend — ed   knee,

1. Ech — o   back   their   joy — ous   strains.
2. Which   in — spire   your   heav'n — ly   song.
3. Christ,   the   Lord,   the   new — born   King.

Glo– – – – – – – – – – – – – – – – ri – a   in   ex – cel – sis   De – o,

Glo– – – – – – – – – – – – – – – – ri – a   in   ex – cel–sis   De – o,

246. As with Gladness Men of Old

Text: Foliot S. Pierpoint, 1835-1917

Tune: Dix, 77. 77. 77.
Conrad Kocher, 1786-1872

1. As with glad – ness men of old Did the guid – ing
2. As with joy – ful steps they sped To that low – ly
3. As they of – fered gifts most rare At that man – ger
4. Ho – ly Je – sus, ev – 'ry day Keep us in the
5. In the heav'n – ly coun – try bright Need they no cre –

1. star be – hold; As with joy they hailed its light,
2. man – ger bed, There to bend the knee be – fore
3. rude and bare So may we with ho – ly joy,
4. nar – row way; And, when earth – ly things are past,
5. a – ted light; Thou its light, its joy, its crown,

1. Lead – ing on – ward, beam – ing bright; So, most gra –
2. Him whom heav'n and earth a – dore; So, may we
3. Pure and free from sin's al – loy, All our cost –
4. Bring our ran – somed souls at last Where they need
5. Thou its sun which goes not down; There for – ev –

1. cious God, may we Ev – er – more be led to thee.
2. with will – ing feet Ev – er seek thy mer – cy seat.
3. liest treas – ures bring, Christ, to thee, our heav'n–ly King.
4. no star to guide, Where no clouds thy glo – ry hide.
5. er may we sing Al – le – lu – ias to our King.

247. At Jesus' Feet Our Infant Sweet

Text: Matthias Loy, 1828-1915

Tune: Ellacombe, C.M.D.
Gesangbuch der Herzogl, Würtemberg, 1784

1. At Jesus' feet our infant sweet We lay with
2. We fail to see the Holy Three Concealed the
3. We bring our child by sin defiled, Then, dearest

1. all its* stain, That renders it* for heav'n unmeet
2. fount within, Mere water seems the mystery
3. Lord, to thee; Here clothe it* in thy nature mild,

1. Until 'tis* born again: We here embrace
2. That cleanses us from sin; But who may tell
3. From sin here make it* free; And buried here

1. his proffered grace In this baptismal wave,
2. what virtues dwell Through God's Word in that flood,
3. in death severe, To new life may it* rise,

1. Nor shall the world our trust efface
2. Or who the simple faith repel
3. And trained for thee, with thee appear

1. The bath its* soul will save.
2. That owns it Jesus' blood?
3. Immortal in the skies.

** Where the child is referred to as "it," the singers should replace this word with "he" or "she."
For convenience, each instance is marked by an asterisk.*

248. At the Cross Her Station Keeping

Text: *Stabat Mater Dolorosa*, Pope Innocent III or Jacopone da Todi   Tune: Stabat Mater, 8. 8. 7.
Tr. Edward Caswall, 1814-1878, alt.   *Mainz Gesanbuch*, 1661

1. At the cross her sta – tion keep – ing, Stood the mourn – ful

1. Mo – ther weep – ing, Close to Je – sus to the last.

2. Through her soul, of joy bereavéd,
Bowed with anguish deeply grievéd,
Now at length the sword had passed.

3. Oh, how sad and sore distresséd
Was that mother highly blesséd
Of the sole-begotten One!

4. Christ above in torment hangs;
She beneath beholds the pangs
Of her dying glorious Son.

5. Who, on Christ's dear mother gazing,
Pierced by anguish so amazing,
Born of woman, would not weep?

6. Who, on Christ's dear mother thinking,
Such a cup of sorow drinking,
Would not share her sorrows deep?

7. Bruised, derided, cursed, defiled,
She beheld her tender child
All with bloody scourges rent.

8. For the sins of His own nation,
Saw Him hang in desolation,
Till His spirit forth He sent.

9. In the passion of thy Maker,
Be my sinful soul partaker,
May I bear with her my part;

10. Of his passion bear the token,
In a spirit bowed and broken
Bear his death within my heart.

11. Wounded with His every wound,
Steep my soul till it hath swoon'd
In His very blood away.

12. May his wounds both wound and heal me,
He enkindle, cleanse, and heal me,
Be his cross my hope and stay.

13. May he, when the mountains quiver,
From the flame which burns forever;
Help me on that judgment day.

14. Jesus, may thy cross defend me,
And thy saving death befriend me,
Cherished by thy deathless grace:

15. When to dust my dust returneth,
Grant a soul that to thee yearneth,
In thy paradise a place.

249. At the Lamb's High Feast We Sing

Text: *Ad Regias Agni Dapes*, 4th Century
Tr. Robert Campbell, 1814-1868, alt.

Tune: Salzburg, 77. 77. D
Jakob Hintze, 1622-1702

1. At   the   Lamb's high   feast   we   sing   Praise to   our   vic –
2. Where   the   Pas – chal   blood is   poured, Death's dark an – gel
3. Might – y   vic – tim   from   the   sky,   Hell's fierce pow'rs be –
4. Eas – ter   tri – umph, Eas – ter   joy,   This   a – lone can

1. to – rious King. Who   has   washed us   in   the   tide
2. sheathes his   sword;   Is – rael's hosts tri – umph – ant go
3. neath   you   lie;   You   have   con – quered in   the   fight,
4. sin   de – stroy;   From   sin's pow'r, Lord, set   us   free

1. Flow – ing   from   his   pierc – éd   side;   Praise we   him
2. Through the   wave   that   drowns the   foe.   Praise we   Christ,
3. You   have   brought us   life   and   light;   Now   no   more
4. New – born   souls in   you   to   be.   Fa – ther, who

1. whose love   di – vine   Gives his   sa – cred   Blood for   wine,
2. whose blood was   shed,   Pas – chal vic – tim,   Pas – chal bread;
3. can   death ap – pall,   Now   no   more   the   grave en – thrall;
4. the   crown shall give,   Sa – vior, by   whose death we   live,

1. Gives his   Bod – y   for   the   feast,
2. With   sin – cer – i – ty   and   love
3. You   have   o – pened par – a – dise,
4. Spir – it,   guide through all   our   days,

1. Christ the   vic – tim,   Christ the   priest.
2. Eat   we   man – na   from   a – bove.
3. And   in   you   your   saints shall rise.
4. Three in   One,   your   name   we   praise.

250. Attend Our Prayer, O Lord

Text: *Attende Domine*, Mozarabic, 10th Century
Tr. Agostino Taumaturgo (b. 1974)

Tune: Attende Domine, 11. 11. 11. with Refrain
Chant, Mode V

Refrain (Sung first by the Cantor, then repeated by the Choir):

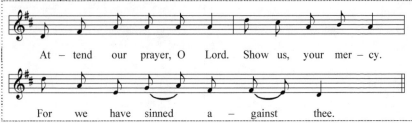

At – tend   our   prayer, O   Lord. Show us,   your mer – cy.

For   we   have   sinned   a – gainst   thee.

1. To   you   high – est   King,   Re – deem – er   of   us   all,
2. Right hand, of   the   Fa –ther, the   ho – ly   cor – ner – stone,
3. We   be – seech you,   God,   in   your   great   maj – es – ty:
4. To   you   we   con – fess,   we   ad – mit   of   our   sins:
5. In – no – cent   cap – tive,   not   re – fus – ing   to   be   led;

1. We   lift   up   our   eyes   in   weep – ing   and   sigh – ing:
2. Way   of   sal – va – tion,   O   true   gate   of   hea – ven,
3. With   your   ho – ly   ears   hear   our   tears   and   cry – ing:
4. With   a   con – trite   heart,   we   re – veal   things   hid – den:
5. By   false   wit – ness – es,   con – demned for   us   sin – ners:

1. Hear   the   prayers, O   Christ,   of   your   hum – ble   ser – vants.
2. Wash a – way   our   sins   and   the   stains   of   our crimes.
3. Do   not   be   wrath – ful;   please   for – give   us   our crimes.
4. O,   kind   Re – deem – er,   look   not   on   our   stray – ings.
5. O,   Christ,   keep   safe   those   whom   you   have   re – deem – éd.

251. Attende Domine

Text: Mozarabic, 10th Century

ENGLISH: "Attend Our Prayer, O Lord"

Tune: Attende Domine, 11. 11. 11. with Refrain

Chant, Mode V

Refrain (Sung first by the Cantor, then repeated by the Choir):

At – tén – de Dó – mi – ne, et mi – se – ré – re,

Qui – a pec – cá – vi – mus ti – bi.

1. Ad te Rex sum – me, ó – mni – um Re – dém – ptor,
2. Déx – te – ra Pa – tris, la – pis an – gu – lá – ris,
3. Ro – gá – mus, De – us, tu – am ma – jes – tá – tem:
4. Ti – bi fa – té – mur, crí – mi – na ad – mís – sa:
5. In – no – cens ca – ptus, nec re – pú – gnans du – ctus;

1. Ó – cu – los nos – tros sub – le – vá – mus flen – tes:
2. Vi – a sa – lú – tis já – nu – a coe – lé – stis,
3. Áu – ri – bus sa – cris gé – mi – tus ex – aú – di:
4. Con – trí – to cor – de pán – di – mus oc – cúl – ta:
5. Tés – ti – bus fal – sis, pro ím – pi-is da – mná – tus:

1. Ex – aú – di Chri – ste, sup – pli – cán – tum pre – ces.
2. Áb – lu – e no – stri má – cu – las de – lí – cti.
3. Crí – mi – na no – stra plá – ci – dus in – dúl – ge.
4. Tu – a Re – dém – ptor, pí – e – tas i – gnó – scat.
5. Quos re – de – mí – sti, tu con – sér – va, Chri – ste.

252. Audi, Benigne Conditor

Text: St. Gregory the Great, 540-604
ENGLISH: "O Kind Creator, Bow Thine Ear"

Tune: Audi Begnine Conditor, L.M.
Chant, Mode II

1. Au – di, be – ní – gne Cón – di – tor,
2. Scru – tá – tor al – me cór – di – um,
3. Mul – tum qui – dem pec – cá – vi – mus,
4. Con – cé – de no – strum cón – te – ri
5. Prae – sta be – á – ta Trí – ni – tas,

1. No – stras pre – ces cum flé – ti – bus,
2. In – fír – ma tu scis ví – ri – um:
3. Sed par – ce con – fi – tén – ti – bus:
4. Cor – pus per ab – sti – nén – ti – am
5. Con – cé – de sim – plex Ú – ni – tas:

1. In hoc sa – cro je – jú – ni – o
2. Ad te re – vér – sis éx – hi – be
3. Ad nó – mi – nis lau – dem tu – i,
4. Cul – pae ut re – lín – quant pá – bu – lum
5. Ut fru – ctu – ó – sa sint tu – is

1. Fu – sas qua – dra – ge – ná – ri – o.
2. Re – mis – si – ó – nis grá – ti – am.
3. Con – fer me – dé – lam lán – gui – dis.
4. Je – jú – na cor – da crí – mi – num.
5. Je – ju – ni – ó – rum mú – ne – ra.

253. Awake, My Soul, and with the Sun

Text: Thomas Ken, 1637-1711

Tune: Morning Hymn, L.M.
François H. Barthélémon, 1741-1808

1. A – wake, my soul, and with the sun
2. All praise to thee, who safe hast kept
3. Lord, I my vows to thee re – new.
4. Di – rect, con – trol, sug – gest, this day,
5. Praise God, from whom all bless – ings flow;

1. Thy dai – ly stage of du – ty run;
2. And hast re – freshed me while I slept.
3. Dis – perse my sins as mor – ning dew;
4. All I de – sign or do or say,
5. Praise him, all crea – tures here be – low;

1. Shake off dull sloth, and joy – ful rise
2. Grant, Lord, when I from death shall wake,
3. Guard my first springs of thought and will;
4. That all my pow'rs, with all their might,
5. Praise him a – bove, ye heav'n – ly host;

1. To pay thy morn – ing sac – ri – fice.
2. I may of end – less light par – take.
3. And with thy – self my spir – it fill.
4. In thy sole glo – ry may u – nite.
5. Praise Fa – ther, Son, and Ho – ly Ghost.

254. Away in a Manger

Text: St. 1-2, Anonymous
St. 3, Disputed. John T. McFarland or Charles H. Gabriel

Tune: Mueller, 11.11.11.11.
James R. Murray, 1841-1905

1. A – way in a man – ger, no crib for a bed,
2. The cat – tle are low – ing; the ba – by a – wakes,
3. Be near me, Lord Je – sus; I ask thee to stay

1. The lit – tle Lord Je – sus laid down his sweet head;
2. But lit – tle Lord Je – sus no cry – ing he makes.
3. Close by me for – ev – er and love me, I pray.

1. The stars in the sky . . . . looked down where he lay,
2. I love thee, Lord Je – sus; look down from the sky
3. Bless all the dear chil – dren in thy ten – der care

1. The lit – tle Lord Je – sus a – sleep on the hay.
2. And stay by my cra – dle till mor – ning is nigh.
3. And fit us for heav – en to live with thee there.

255. Be Joyful Mary

Text: *Regina Coeli Jubila*, Anonymous, 17th Century
Tr. Anonymous

Tune: Leisentritt 85.84.7.
Leisentritt's *Gesanbuch*, 1584

1. Be joy – ful, Mar – y, heav'n–ly Queen, be joy – ful, Mar – y!
2. The Son you bore by heav – en's grace, be joy – ful, Mar – y!
3. The Lord has ris – en from the dead, be joy – ful, Mar – y!
4. Then pray to God, O Vir – gin fair, be joy – ful, Mar – y!

1. Your grief has changed to joy se – rene,
2. Did by his death our guilt e – rase,
3. He rose in glo – ry as he said,
4. That he our souls to heav – en bear,

1. Al – le – lu – ia! Re – joice, re – joice, O Mar – y!
2. Al – le – lu – ia! Re – joice, re – joice, O Mar – y!
3. Al – le – lu – ia! Re – joice, re – joice, O Mar – y!
4. Al – le – lu – ia! Re – joice, re – joice, O Mar – y!

256. Beautiful Savior

Text: *Schönster Herr Jesu*, Münster Gesanbuch, 1677
Tr. Joseph A. Seiss, 1823-1904

Tune: Schonster Herr Jesu, 557. 558.
Silesian Folk Melody, 1842

1. Beau – ti – ful   Sav – ior,   King   of   cre – a – tion,
2. Fair   are   the   mead – ows,   Fair   are   the   wood – lands,
3. Fair   is   the   sun – shine,   Fair   is   the   moon – light,
4. Beau – ti – ful   Sav – ior,   Lord   of   the   na – tions,

1. Son   of   God   and   Son   of   Man!
2. Robed   in   flow'rs   of   bloom – ing   spring;
3. Bright   the   spar – kling   stars   on   high;
4. Son   of   God   and   Son   of   Man!

1. Tru – ly   I'd   love   thee,   Tru – ly   I'd   serve   thee,
2. Je – sus   is   fair – er,   Je – sus   is   pur – er,
3. Je – sus   shines   bright – er,   Je – sus   shines   pur – er,
4. Glo – ry   and   hon – or,   Praise, ad – o – ra – tion,

1. Light   of   my   soul,   my   joy,   my   crown.
2. He   makes   our   sor – r'wing   spir – it   sing.
3. Than   all   the   an – gels   in   the   sky.
4. Now   and   for – ev – er   more   be   thine!

257. Beneath the Cross of Jesus

Text: Elizabeth C. Clephane, 1830-1869

Tune: St. Christopher, 76. 86. 86. 86.
Fredrick Maker, 1844-1927

1. Be – neath the cross of Je – sus, I long to
2. Up – on the cross of Je – sus, My eye at
3. I take, O cross, your shad – ow, For my a –

1. make my stand; The shad – ow of a might – y rock,
2. times can see, The ver – y dy – ing form of one
3. bid – ing place; I ask no oth – er sun – shine than

1. With – in a wea – ry land, A home with – in
2. Who suf – fered there for me. And from my con –
3. The sun – shine of his face; Con – tent to let

1. a wil – der – ness, A rest up – on the way,
2. trite heart, with tears, Two won – ders I con – fess:
3. the world go by, To know no gain nor loss,

1. From-the burn – ing of the noon – tide heat,
2. The won – der of his glo – rious love
3. My sin – ful self my on – ly shame,

1. And bur – dens of the day.
2. And my un – wor – thi – ness.
3. My glo – ry all, the cross.

258. Benediction of Aaron (Birkhas Kohanim)

Text: *Birkhas Kohanim*, Numbers 6:24-26, with Invocation
Adapted from the *Confraternity Bible*, 1957

Tune: Aaronic Benediction
Prepared for this Hymnal

The   Lord   bless   you   and   keep   you.

The Lord let his face shine upon you and be gracious to   you.

The   Lord look upon you with fa – vor and give you peace.

In the name of the Father, and of the Son, and of the   Ho – ly   Spir – it.

After the blessing, the people respond:

A – men.

259. Blessed Be the Lord (Benedictus)

Text: *Benedictus Dominus Deus Israel*, Luke 1:68-79
Tr. *The Book of Common Prayer*, 1662, alt.

Tune: Psalm Tone II
Chant, Mode I

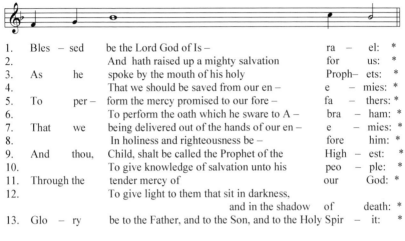

1.	Bles – sed		be the Lord God of Is –	ra	–	el:	*
2.			And hath raised up a mighty salvation	for		us:	*
3.	As	he	spoke by the mouth of his holy	Proph–	ets:		*
4.			That we should be saved from our en –	e	–	mies:	*
5.	To	per –	form the mercy promised to our fore –	fa	–	thers:	*
6.			To perform the oath which he sware to A –	bra	–	ham:	*
7.	That	we	being delivered out of the hands of our en –	e	–	mies:	*
8.			In holiness and righteousness be –	fore		him:	*
9.	And	thou,	Child, shalt be called the Prophet of the	High	–	est:	*
10.			To give knowledge of salvation unto his	peo	–	ple:	*
11.	Through the		tender mercy of	our		God:	*
12.			To give light to them that sit in darkness,				
			and in the shadow	of		death:	*
13.	Glo – ry		be to the Father, and to the Son, and to the Holy Spir	–	it:		*

1.	for he hath visited, and redeemed	his	peo –	ple;
2.	in the house of his ser –	vant	Da –	vid;
3.	which have been since the	world	be –	gan;
4.	and from the hands of all	that	hate	us;
5.	and to remember his holy	Cov –	e –	nant;
6.	that he	would	give	us;
7.	might serve him	with –	out	fear;
8.	all the days	of	our	life.
9.	for thou shalt go before the face of the Lord to pre –	pare	his	ways;
10.	for the remission	of	their	sins,
11.	whereby the day-spring from on high hath vis –	it –	ed	us;
12.	and to guide our feet into the	way	of	peace.
13.	As it was in the beginning, is now, and ever shall be,			
	world without	end.	A –	men.

260. Break Thou the Bread of Life

Text: Mary A. Lathbury, 1841-1913, alt.

Tune: Bread of Life, 64. 64. 64. 64.
William F. Sherwin, 1826-1888

1. Break thou the bread of life, Dear Lord, to me,
2. Bless thou the truth, dear Lord, To me, to me,
3. Thou art the bread of life, O Lord, to me.
4. Oh, send thy Spir – it, Lord, Now un – to me,

1. As thou didst brake the loaves Be – side the sea.
2. As thou didst bless the bread By Gal – i – lee.
3. Thy ho – ly word the truth That sav – eth me.
4. That he may touch my eyes And make me see.

1. Be – yond the sa – cred page I seek thee, Lord;
2. Then shall all bon – dage cease, All fet – ters fall;
3. Give me to eat and live With thee a – bove;
4. Show me the truth con – cealed With – in thy Word,

1. My spir – it pants for thee, O liv – ing Word.
2. And I shall find my peace, My All – in – All!
3. Teach me to love thy truth, For thou art love.
4. And in thy book re – vealed, I see the Lord.

261. Breathe on Me, Breath of God

Text: Edwin Hatch, 1835-1889

Tune: Trentham, S. M.
Robert Jackson, 1842-1914

1. Breathe on me, breath of God,
2. Breathe on me, breath of God,
3. Breathe on me, breath of God,
4. Breathe on me, breath of God,

1. Fill me with life a – new,
2. Un – til my heart is pure,
3. Till I am whol – ly thine,
4. So shall I nev – er die,

1. That I may love what thou dost love,
2. Un – til with thee, I will one will,
3. Un – til this earth – ly part of me
4. But live with thee the per – fect life,

1. And do what thou wouldst do.
2. To do and to en – dure.
3. Glows with thy fire di – vine.
4. Of thine e – ter – ni – ty.

262. By the Blood that Flowed from Thee

Text: Fredrick Faber, 1814-1863
or Cecilia M. Caddell, 1814-1877

Tune: Dix, 77. 77. 77.
Conrad Kocher, 1786-1872

1. By the blood that flowed from thee In thy bit – ter
2. By the thorns that crowned thy head; By thy sce – pter
3. By the nails and poin – ted spear; By thy peo – ple's
4. By the dark – ness thick as night Blot – ting out the
5. By thy weep – ing Moth – er's woe; By the sword that

1. ag – o – ny; By thy scourge so meek – ly borne;
2. of a reed; By thy foot – steps faint and slow,
3. cru – el jeer; By thy dy – ing prayer which rose
4. sun from sight; By the cry with which in death
5. pierced her through, When, in an – guish stand – ing by,

1. By thy pur – ple robe of scorn:
2. Weighed be – neath thy Cross of woe,
3. Beg – ging mer – cy for thy foes.
4. Thou didst yield thy part – ing breath.
5. On the Cross she saw thee die.

Refrain:

Je – sus, Sav – ior, hear our cry!

Thou wert suff – 'ring once as we;

Hear the lov – ing lit – an – y

We thy chil – dren sing to thee.

263. Christ Is the King! O Friends Rejoice!

Text: G.K.A. Bell, 1883-1958, alt.

Tune: St. Catherine, 88. 88. 88.
Henry F. Hemy, 1818-1888

1. Christ is the King! O friends re – joice;
2. O mag – ni – fy the Lord, and raise
3. O Chris – tian wo – men, Chris – tian men,
4. Let love's un – con – quer – a – ble might

1. Broth – ers and sis – ters, with one voice
2. An – thems of joy and ho – ly praise
3. All the world o – ver, seek a – gain
4. Your scat – tered com – pan – ies u – nite

1. Make the world know he is your choice.
2. For Christ's brave saints of an – cient days,
3. The Way dis – ci – ples fol – lowed then.
4. In ser – vice to the Lord of light:

1. Ring out ye bells, give tongue, give tongue;
2. Who with a faith for ev – er new
3. Christ through all a – ges is the same:
4. So shall God's will on earth be done,

1. Let your most mer – ry peal be rung,
2. Fol – lowed the King, and round him drew
3. Place the same hope in his great name,
4. New lamps be lit, new tasks be – gun,

1. While our ex – ul – tant song is sung.
2. Thou – sands of faith – ful peo – ple true.
3. With the same faith his word pro – claim.
4. And the whole Church at last be one.

264. Christians, to the Paschal Victim

Text: *Victimae Paschali*, Wipo of Burgundy, c. 995-1050   Tune: Victimae Paschali, irregular
Tr. *The English Hymnal*, 1906   Chant, Mode I

1. Chris– tians, to the pas – chal vic – tim, Of – fer your thank – ful

prais – es! **2.** A Lamb the sheep re – deem– ing: Christ who on – ly

is sin – less, Re – con – cil – ing sin – ners to the Fa – ther.

3. Death and life have con – tend–ed, in that com– bat stu – pen – dous;

The prince of life, who died, Reigns im– mor– tal. **4.** Speak Ma – ry,

de – clar – ing, What you saw when way – far – ing. **5.**"The tomb of Christ

who is liv – ing, The glo –ry of Je – sus' res – ur – rec – tion;

6. Bright an – gels at – test– ing, The shroud and nap – kin rest – ing.

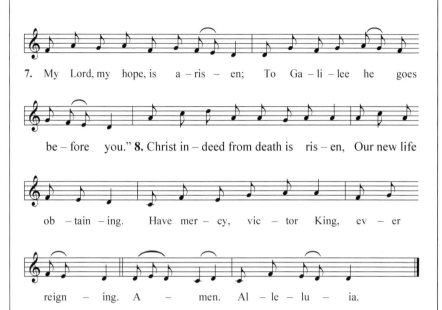

7. My Lord, my hope, is a – ris – en; To Ga – li – lee he goes

be – fore you." **8.** Christ in – deed from death is ris – en, Our new life

ob – tain – ing. Have mer – cy, vic – tor King, ev – er

reign – ing. A – men. Al – le – lu – ia.

265. Come, Holy Ghost, Creator Blest

Text: *Veni Creator Spiritus*, Rabanus Maurus, 776-856   Tune: Veni Creator Spiritus, 88. 88. [8]
Tr. Edward Caswall, 1814-1878   Louis Lambilotte, 1796-1855

1. Come, Ho – ly Ghost, Cre – a – tor blest,
2. O, Com – fort – er, to thee we cry,
3. O Ho – ly Ghost, through thee a – lone,
4. Praise we the Lord, Fa – ther and Son,

1. And in our hearts take up thy rest;
2. Thou heav'n – ly gift of God Most High;
3. Know we the Fa – ther and the Son;
4. And Ho – ly Spi – rit with them one;

1. Come with thy grace and heav'n – ly aid
2. Thou Fount of Life, and Fire of Love,
3. Be this our firm un – chang – ing creed,
4. And may the Son on us be – stow

1. To fill the hearts which thou hast made,
2. And sweet a – noint – ing from a – bove,
3. That thou dost from them both pro – ceed,
4. All gifts that from the Spir – it flow,

1. To fill the hearts which thou hast made.
2. And sweet a – noint – ing from a – bove.
3. That thou dost from them both pro – ceed.
4. All gifts that from the Spir – it flow. A – men.

266. Come, My Soul, Thy Suit Prepare

John Newton, 1725-1807

Tune: Redhead, 77. 77.
Richard Redhead, 1820-1901

1. Come, my soul, thy suit pre – pare,
2. With my bur – den I be – gin:
3. Lord, I come to thee for rest;
4. Show me what I have to do,

1. Je – sus loves to an – swer prayer;
2. Lord, re – move my load of sin!
3. Take pos – ses – sion of my breast;
4. Ev – 'ry hour my strength re – new;

1. He him – self has bid thee pray;
2. Let thy blood, for sin – ners spilt,
3. There thy sov – 'reign right main – tain
4. Let me live a life of faith,

1. Rise and ask with – out de – lay.
2. Set my con – science free from guilt.
3. And with – out a ri – val reign.
4. Let me die thy peo – ple's death.

267. Come, My Way, My Truth, My Life

George Herbert, 1593-1632

Tune: The Call, 77. 77.
Ralph Vaughan Williams, 1872-1958

1. Come, my way, my truth, my life:
2. Come, my light, my feast, my strength:
3. Come, my joy, my love, my heart:

1. Such a way as gives us breath;
2. Such a light as shows a feast;
3. Such a joy as none can move;

1. Such a truth as ends all strife;
2. Such a feast as mends in length;
3. Such a love as none can part;

1. Such a life as kill — — — eth death.
2. Such a strength as makes — — — his guest.
3. Such a heart as joys — — — in love.

268. Come, Thou Almighty King

Anonymous, c. 1757

Tune: Italian Hymn, 664. 6664.
Felice de Giardini, 1716-1796

1. Come, thou al – might – y King, Help us thy name to sing,
2. Come, thou In – car – nate Word, Gird on thy might – y sword,
3. Come, ho – ly Com – fort – er, Thy sa – cred wit – ness bear,
4. To the great One in Three, E – ter – nal prais – es be,

1. Help us to praise. Fa – ther all glo – ri – ous,
2. Our prayer at – tend. Come and thy peo – ple bless,
3. In this glad hour. Thou, who al – might – y art,
4. Hence ev – er – more! His sov – 'reign maj – es – ty,

1. O'er all vic – to – ri – ous, Come and reign o – ver us,
2. And give thy Word suc – cess; Stab – lish thy right – eous–ness,
3. Now rule in ev – 'ry heart, And ne'er from us de –part,
4. May we in glo – ry see, And to e – ter – ni –ty,

1. An – cient of Days.
2. Sav – ior and Friend!
3. Spir – it of Pow'r!
4. Love and a – dore! A – men.

269. Come, Thou Fount of Every Blessing

Robert Robinson, 1735-1790

Tune: Nettleton, 87. 87. D.
John Wyeth, *Repository of Sacred Music*, 1813

1. Come, thou Fount of ev–'ry bless–ing, Tune my heart to
2. Here I raise my Eb – en – e – zer, Hith – er by thy
3. Oh, to grace how great a debt – or, Dai – ly I'm con –

1. sing thy grace; Streams of mer – cy, nev – er ceas – ing,
2. help I'm come; And I hope, by thy good plea – sure,
3. strained to be; Let thy good – ness, like a fet – ter,

1. Call for songs of loud – est praise. Teach me some me –
2. Safe – ly to ar – rive at home. Je – sus sought me
3. Bind my wan – d'ring heart to thee. Prone to wan – der,

1. lo – dious son – net, Sung by flam – ing tongues a – bove,
2. when a strang – er, Wan – d'ring from the fold of God;
3. Lord, I feel it; Prone to leave the God I love.

1. Here's the Mount! I'm fixed up – on it,
2. He, to res – cue me from dan – ger,
3. Here's my heart, O, take and seal it;

1. Mount of thy re – deem – ing love.
2. In – ter – posed his pre – cious blood.
3. Seal it for thy courts a – bove.

270. Come, Thou Holy Spirit, Come

Text: *Veni Sancte Spiritus*, Pope Innocent III, 1160-1216
Tr. Edward Caswall, 1814-1878

Tune: Veni Sancte Spiritus, 7. 7. 7.
Chant, Mode I

1. Come, thou Ho — ly Spir – it, come! And from thy ce –
2. Come, thou Fa – ther of the poor! Come, thou Source of

1. les – tial home, Shed a ray of light div – ine!
2. all our store! Come, with – in our bos – oms shine!

3. Thou, of com – for – ters the best; Thou, the soul's most
4. In our la – bor, rest most sweet; Grate – ful cool – ness

3. wel – come Guest; Sweet re – fresh – ment here be – low;
4. in the heat; Sol – ace in the midst of woe.

5. O most bless – èd Light div – ine, Shine with – in these
6. Where thou art not, man hath naught, Noth – ing good in

5. hearts of thine, And our in – most be – ing fill!
6. deed or thought, Noth – ing free from taint of ill.

7. Heal our wounds, our strength re – new; On our dry – ness
8. Bend the stub – born heart and will; Melt the fro – zen,

7. pour thy dew; Wash the stains of guilt a – way;
8. warm the chill; Guide the steps that go a – stray.

9. On the faith – ful, who a – dore And con – fess thee,
10. Give them vir – tue's sure re – ward Give them thy sal –

9. ev– er – more In thy sev'n–fold gift de–scend;
10. va–tion, Lord; Give them joys that nev– er end. A – men. Al–le–lú – ia.

271. Come, Thou Long-Expected Jesus

Charles Wesley, 1707-1788

Tune: Jefferson 87. 87. D.
William Walker, 1809-1875

1. Come, thou long ex – pect – ed Je – sus,
2. Born thy peo – ple to de – liv – er;

1. Born to set thy peo – ple free;
2. Born a child and yet a king!

1. From our fears and sins re – lease us;
2. Born to reign in us for – ev – er,

1. Let us find our rest in thee.
2. Now thy gra – cious king – dom bring.

1. Is – rael's Strength and Con – so – la – tion,
2. By thine own e – ter – nal Spir – it,

1. Hope of all the earth thou art,
2. Rule in all our hearts a – lone;

1. Dear De – sire of ev – ery na – tion,
2. By thine all suf – fi – cient mer – it,

1. Joy of ev – 'ry long – ing heart.
2. Raise us to thy glo – rious throne.

272. Comfort, Comfort Ye My People

Text: *Tröstet Tröstet*, Johan Olearius, 1611-1684
Tr. Catherine Winkworth, 1827-1878

Tune: Freu Dich Sehr, 87. 87. 77. 88.
Trente Quatre Pseaumes de David, Geneva, 1551

1. Com – fort, com – fort ye my peo – ple, Speak ye peace, so
2. Hark, the voice of one that cri – eth, In the des – ert
3. Make ye straight what long was crook – ed, Make the rough – er

1. says our God; Com – fort those who sit in dark – ness,
2. far and near, Bid – ding all earth to re – pent – ance
3. plac – es plain; Let your hearts be true and hum – ble,

1. Mourn– ing 'neath their sor – rows' load. Speak ye to Je –
2. Since the king – dom now is here. O that warn – ing
3. As be – fits his ho – ly reign. For the glo – ry

1. ru – sa – lem Of the peace that waits for them;
2. cry o – bey! Now pre – pare for God a – way;
3. of the Lord Now o'er earth is shed a – broad;

1. Tell her of the sins I cov – er,
2. Let the val – leys rise to meet him
3. And all flesh shall see the to – ken

1. And her war – fare now is o – ver.
2. And the hills bow down to greet him.
3. That his word is nev – er bro – ken.

273. Cor Arca Legem

Text: Anonymous, 17th Century
ENGLISH: "O Heart, Thou Ark"

Tune: Alta Trinita Beata, Irregular
Laudi Spirituali, 14th Century

1. Cor, ar – ca le – gem cón – ti – nens,
2. Cor san – ctu – á – ri – um no – – vi
3. Te vul – ne – rá – tum cá – ri – tas
4. Hoc sub a – mó – ris sým – bo – lo
5. Quis non a – mán – tem ré – da – met?
6. Je – su, ti – bi sit gló – ri – a,

1. Non ser – vi – tú – tis vé – te – ris.
2. In – te – me – rá – tum foé – de – ris,
3. I – ctu pa – tén – ti vó – lu – it,
4. Pas – sus cru – én – ta et mý – sti – ca,
5. Quis non re – dém – ptus dí – li – gat,
6. Qui Cor – de fun – dis grá – ti – am

1. Sed grá – ti – ae, Sed vé – ni – ae,
2. Tem – plum ve – tú – sto sán – cti – us,
3. A – mó – ris in – vi – sí – bi – lis
4. U – trúm – que sa – cri – fĭ – ci – um
5. Et Cor – de in i – sto sé – li – gat
6. Cum Pa – tre et al – mo Spí – ri – tu

1. Sed et mi – se – ri – cór – di – ae.
2. Ve – lúm – que scis – so u – tí – li – us.
3. Ut ve – ne – ré – mur vul – né – ra.
4. Chri – stus sa – cér – dos ób – tu – lit.
5. Ae – tér – na ta – ber – ná – cu – la?
6. In sem – pi – tér – na sáe – cu – la.

274. Creator Alme Siderum

Chant, 9th Century
ENGLISH: "Creator of the Stars of Night"

Tune: Conditor Alme Siderum, L. M.
Chant, Mode IV

1. Cre — á — tor   al — me   sí — de — rum,
2. Qui   dáe — mo — nis   ne   fráu — di — bus
3. Com — mú — ne   qui   mun — di   ne — fas,
4. Cu — jus   po — tés — tas   gló — ri — ae,
5. Te   de — pre — cá — mur,   úl — ti — mae,
6. Vir — tus,   ho — nor,   laus,   gló — ri — a

1. Ae — tér — na   lux   cre — dén — ti — um,
2. Pe — rí — ret   or — bis,   ím — pe — tu
3. Ut   ex — pi — á — res,   ad   cru — cem,
4. No — mén — que   cum   pri — mum   so — nat,
5. Ma — gnum   di — é — i   Jú — di — cem,
6. De — o   Pa — tri   cum   Fí — li — o,

1. Je — su   Re — dém — ptor   ó — mni — um,
2. A — mó — ris   a — ctus,   lán — gui — di,
3. E   Vír — gi — nis   sa — crá — ri — o
4. Et   cáe — li — tes   et   ín — fer — i
5. Ar — mis   su — pér — nae   grá — ti — ae,
6. San — cto   si — mul   Pa — rá — cli — to,

1. In — tén — de   vo — tis   súp — pli — cum.
2. Mun— di   me — dé — la   fa — ctus   es,
3. In — tá — cta   pro — dis   ví — cti — ma.
4. Tre — mén — te   cur — ván — tur   ge — nu.
5. De — fén — de   nos   ab   hós — ti — bus.   *(After last verse:)*
6. In   sae — cu — ló — rum   sáe — cu — la.   A — men.

287

275. Creator of the Stars of Night

Text: Creator Alme Siderum, Chant, 9th Century
Tr. John Mason Neale, 1818-1866

Tune: Conditor Alme Siderum, L. M.
Chant, Mode IV

1. Cre – a – tor of the stars of night,
2. As once through Ma – ry's flesh you came,
3. And when on that last judg – ment day,

1. The peo – ple's e – ver – las – ting light,
2. To save us from our sin and shame,
3. We rise to glo – ry from de – cay,

1. Je – sus, Re – deem – er of us all,
2. So now, Re – deem – er, by your grace,
3. Then come a – gain, O Sav – ior blest,

1. O hear your ser – vants when they call.
2. Come, heal a – gain our fal – len race. *(After last verse:)*
3. And bring us to e – ter – nal rest. A – men.

276. Creator Spirit, Heavenly Dove

Text: *Veni Creator Spiritus*, Rabanus Maurus, 776-856
Tr. Composite

Tune: Veni Creator, L. M.
Chant, Mode VIII

1. Cre – a – tor Spir – it, heav'n – ly dove,
2. To you, the Com – fort – er, we cry,
3. In you, with grac – es sev – en – fold,
4. Your light to ev – 'ry sense im – part,
5. Keep far from us our cru – el foe,
6. Oh, make to us the Fa – ther known;
7. Praise we the Fa – ther and the Son

1. De – scend up – on us from a – bove;
2. To you, the gift of God most high,
3. We God's al – might – y hand be – hold
4. And shed your love in ev – 'ry heart;
5. And peace from your own hand be – stow;
6. Teach us th' e – ter – nal son to own;
7. And Ho – ly Spir – it, with them one;

1. With gra – ces man – i – fold re – store
2. True fount of life, the fire of love,
3. While you with tongues of fire pro – claim
4. Your own un – fail – ing might sup – ply
5. If you be our pro – tect – ing guide,
6. And you, whose name we ev – er bless,
7. And may the Son on us be – stow

1. Your crea – tures as they were be – fore.
2. The soul's a – noin – ting from a – bove.
3. To all the world his ho – ly name.
4. To strength–en our in – firm – i – ty.
5. No e – vil can our steps be – tide.
6. Of both the Spir – it, to con – fess. *(After last verse:)*
7. The gifts that from the Spir – it flow. A – men.

277. Crown Him with Many Crowns

Text: Matthew Bridges, 1800-1894; Godfrey Thring, 1823-1903

Tune: Diademata, S. M. D.
George J. Elvey, 1816-1903

1. Crown him with man – y crowns, The Lamb up –
2. Crown him the Lord of life, Who tri – umphed
3. Crown him the Lord of love, Be – hold his
4. Crown him the Lord of peace, Whose pow'r a
5. Crown him the Lord of years, The Po – ten –

1. on his throne; Hark! how the heav'n – ly
2. o'er the grave, And rose vic – to – rious
3. hands and side, Rich wounds yet vis – i –
4. scep – tre sways From pole to pole, that
5. tate of time, Cre – a – tor of the

1. an – them drowns All mu – sic but its own.
2. in the strife For those he came to save.
3. ble a – bove In beau – ty glo – ri – fied.
4. wars may cease, Ab – sorbed in prayer and praise.
5. roll – ing spheres, In – ef – fa – bly sub – lime.

1. A – wake,   my   soul,   and   sing   Of   him   who
2. His   glo – ries   now   we   sing,   Who   died   and
3. No   an – gel   in   the   sky   Can   ful – ly
4. His   reign   shall   know   no   end,   And   round   his
5. All   hail,   Re – deem – er,   hail!   For   thou   hast

1. died   for   thee,   And   hail   him   as   thy
2. rose   on   high,   Who   died,   e – ter – nal
3. bear   that   sight,   But   down – ward   bends   his
4. pierc – éd   feet   Fair   flow'rs   of   Par – a –
5. died   for   me;   Thy   praise   and   glo – ry

1. match – less   King   Through   all   e – ter – ni – ty.
2. life   to   bring,   And   lives   that   death   may   die.
3. burn – ing   eye   At   mys – ter – ies   so   bright.
4. dise   ex – tend   Their   fra – grance   ev – er   sweet.
5. shall   not   fail   Through – out   e – ter – ni – ty.

278. Day of Wrath and Doom Impending

Text: *Dies Irae Dies Illa*, Thomas of Celano, c. 1200-1265
Tr. William Josiah Irons, 1812-1883

Tune: Dies Irae, irregular
Chant, Mode I

1. Day of wrath and doom im- pen- ding, Da -vid's word with
2. O what fear man's bo- som rend-eth, When from hea-ven the
7. What shall I, frail man, be plea-ding? Who for me be
8. King of maj - es - ty tre - men-dous, Who dost free sal-
13. Through the sin - ful wo - man shriv-en, Through the dy - ing
14. Worth-less are my prayers and sigh -ings, Yet, good Lord, in

1. Sy- bil blen-ding: Hea- ven and earth in ash - es end-ing.
2. Judge de - scend-eth, On whose sen - tence all de - pend-eth!
7. in - ter - ce - ding? When the just are mer-cy need-ing?
8. va - tion send us, Fount of pit - y, then be - friend us.
13. thief for - giv - en, Thou to me a hope hast giv - en.
14. grace com - ply - ing, Res - cue me from fires un - dy - ing.

3. Won-drous sound the trum - pet fling-eth, Through earth's se- pul-
4. Death is struck and na - ture qua- king, All cre - a - tion
9. Think, kind Je - sus, my sal - va - tion, Caused Thy won-drous
10. Faint and wear - y Thou hast sought me, On the Cross of
15. With Thy sheep a place pro - vide me, From the goats a-
16. When the wick - ed are con- found-ed, Doomed to flames of

3. chres it ring-eth, All be - fore the throne it bring-eth.
4. is a - wa - king, To its Judge an an - swer ma - king.
9. In - car – na - tion, Leave me not to re - pro - ba - tion.
10. suff - 'ring bought me, Shall such grace be vain -ly brought me?
15. far di - vide me, To Thy right hand do Thou guide me.
16. woe un - bound-ed, Call me with Thy Saints sur - round-ed.

5.   Lo, the   book ex - act - ly   word - ed,   Where - in   all   hath
6.   When the   Judge his   seat at - tain - eth,   And   each hid - den
11.   Right-eous Judge, for   sin's pol - lu   - tion   Grant   Thy gift of
12.   Guil-ty   now I   pour my moan - ing,   All   my shame with
17.   Low I   kneel with heart's sub - mis - sion,   See,   like ash - es,

5.   been re - cord- ed,   Thence shall judg-ment be a - ward- ed.
6.   deed ar - raign-eth: No- thing un - a -venged re -main - eth.
11.   ab - so - lu -tion,   Ere that day of re - tri - bu - tion.
12.   an -guish own - ing.   Spare, O   God, Thy sup- pliant groan-ing.
17.   my con - tri - tion,   Help me in   my last con – di - tion.

18.   Ah! that day of tears and mourn-ing, From the dust of earth   re - turn-ing,

19.   Man for judg-ment must pre-pare him, Spare, O God, in mer - cy spare him.

20. Lord, all-pit-y-ing, Je-sus blest, Grant to them e - ter -nal rest. A-   men.

279. Dear Shepherd of Thy People, Hear

Text: John Newton, 1725-1807

Tune: Mendip, C. M.
English Traditional Melody

1. Dear Shep – herd of thy peo – ple, hear;
2. With – in these walls let ho – ly peace
3. May we in faith re – ceive thy Word,
4. The feel – ing heart, the melt – ing eye,

1. Thy pre – sence now dis – play;
2. And love and con – cord dwell;
3. In faith pre – sent our prayers;
4. The hum – ble mind be – stow;

1. As thou hast giv'n a place for prayer,
2. Here give the trou – bled con – science ease,
3. And, in the pre – sence of our Lord,
4. And shine up – on us from on high,

1. So give us hearts to pray.
2. The wound – ed spir – it heal.
3. Un – bo – som all our cares.
4. To make our grac – es grow!

280. Depth of Mercy

Text: Charles Wesley, 1707-1788

Tune: Buckland, 77. 77.
Leighton G. Hayne, 1836-1883

1. Depth of mer – cy! Can there be
2. I have long with – stood His grace,
3. Je – sus, an – swer from a – bove,
4. Now in – cline me to re – pent,

1. Mer – cy still re – served for me?
2. Long pro – voked Him to His face,
3. Is not all Thy na – ture love?
4. Let me now my sins la – ment,

1. Can my God His wrath for – bear,
2. Would not hear – ken to His calls,
3. Wilt Thou not the wrong for – get,
4. Now my foul re – volt de – plore,

1. Me, the chief of sin – ners, spare?
2. Grieved Him by a thou – sand falls.
3. Per – mit me to kiss Thy feet?
4. Weep, be – lieve, and sin no more.

281. Dies Irae, Dies Illa

Text: Thomas of Celano, c. 1200-1265   Tune: Dies Irae, 88. 88. 88. with irregular stanzas
ENGLISH: "Day of Wrath and Doom Inpending"   Chant, Mode I

1.	Di - es i - rae, di - es il - la,	Sol - vet sae - clum
2.	Quan-tus tre- mor est fu - tu - rus,	Quan-do ju - dex
7.	Quid sum mi - ser tunc di - ctu - rus?	Quem pa - tro - num
8.	Rex tre- men- dae ma - je - sta - tis,	Qui sal - van - dos
13.	Qui Ma – ri - am ab - sol - vi - sti,	Et la - tro - nem
14.	Pre - ces me - ae non sunt di - gnae:	Sed tu bo - nus

1.	in fa - vil - la:	Tes - te Da - vid cum Si - byl - la
2.	est ven – tu - rus,	Cun - cta stri - cte dis - cus - su - rus!
7.	ro - ga - tu - rus?	Cum vix ju - stus sit se - cu - rus?
8.	sal - vas gra- tis,	Sal - va me, fons pi - e - ta - tis.
13.	ex - au - di - sti,	Mi - hi quo - que spem de - di - sti.
14.	fac be - ni - gne,	Ne per - en - ni cre - mer i - gne.

3.	Tu - ba mi - rum spar - gens so - num,	Per se - pul - cra
4.	Mors stu- pe - bit et na - tu - ra,	Cum re - sur - get
9.	Re - cor- da - re Je - su pi - e,	Quod sum cau - sa
10.	Quae-rens me, se - di - sti las- sus:	Red – e - mi - sti
15.	In - ter o - ves lo - cum prae- sta,	Et ab hoe- dis
16.	Con - fu - ta - tis ma - le - di - ctis,	Flam-mis a - cri-

3.	re - gi - o - num,	Co - get o - mnes an - te thro- num.
4.	cre - a - tur - a,	Ju - di - can - ti re - spon- su - ra.
9.	tu - ae vi - ae:	Ne me per - das il - la di - e.
10.	cru - cem pas- sus:	Tan- tus la - bor non sit cas - sus.
15.	me se - que- stra,	Sta -tu - ens in par- te dex - tra.
16.	bus ad - di - ctis:	Vo - ca me cum be - ne - di - ctis.

5. Li - ber scri- ptus pro - fe - re - tur, In quo to - tum
6. Ju - dex er - go cum se - de - bit, Quid - quid la - tet
11. Ju - ste ju - dex ul - ti - o - nis, Do - num fac re-
12. In - ge - mi - sco, tam- quam re - us: Cul - pa ru - bet
17. O - ro sup-plex et ac - cli - nis, Cor con - tri - tum

5. con- ti - ne - tur, Un - de mun-dus ju - di - ce - tur.
6. ap - pa - re - bit: Nil in - ul - tum re - ma - ne - bit.
11. mis- si - o - nis; An - te di - em ra - ti - o - nis.
12. vul - tus me - us; Sup- pli - can - ti par - ce De- us.
17. qua - si ci - nis. Ge - re cu - ram me - i fi - nis.

18. La - cri-mo- sa di - es il - la, Qua re - sur-get ex fa - vil - la.

19. Ju - di-can- dus ho - mo re - us: Hu- ic er-go par - ce de- us.

20. Pi- e Je-su Do-mi-ne, do-na e- is re- qui- em. A- men.

282. Down in Adoration Falling

Text: *Tantum Ergo Sacramentum*, St. Thomas Aquinas, 1227-1274   Tune: St. Thomas, 87. 87. 87.
Tr. Edward Caswall, 1814-1878   *Cantus Diversi*, John Francis Wade, c. 1711-1786

1. Down   in   ad – or – a – tion   fall – ing,
2. To   the   ev – er – last – ing   Fa – ther,

1. Lo!   the   sa – cred   Host   we   hail;
2. And   the   Son   who   reigns   on   high,

1. Lo!   o'er   an – cient   forms   de – part – ing,
2. With   the   Spir – it   Blest   pro – ceed – ing

1. New – er   rites   of   grace   pre – vail;
2. Forth   from   each   e – ter – nal – ly,

1. Faith   for   all   de – fects   sup – ply – ing
2. Be   sal – va – tion,   hon – or,   bless – ing,

1. Where   the   fee – ble   sen – ses   fail.
2. Might   and   end – less   maj – es – ty.   A – men.

"Tantum ergo sacramentum, veneremur cernui."

"Et antiquum documentum, novo cedat ritui!"

283. Earth Was Waiting

Text: Walter Chalmers Smith (1824-1908)

Tune: Picardy 87. 87. 87.
Traditional French Melody

1.	Earth	was	wait – ing,	spent	and	rest – less,
2.	Still	the	gods	were	in	their	tem – ples,
3.	In	the	sa – cred	courts	of	Zi – on,
4.	Then	the	Spir – it	of	the	High – est
5.	Earth	for	him	had	groaned and	tra – vailed

1.	With	a	min – gled	hope	and	fear;
2.	But	the	an – cient	faith	had	fled;
3.	Where	the	Lord	had	his	a – bode,
4.	On	a	vir – gin	meek	came	down,
5.	Since	the	a – ges	first	be – gan;

1.	And	the	faith – ful	few	were	sigh – ing,
2.	And	the	priests	stood	by	their	al – tars
3.	There	the	mo – ney – chan – gers	traf – ficked,
4.	And	he	bur – den'd	her	with	bles – sing,
5.	For	in	him	was	hid	the	se – cret

1.	"Sure – ly,	Lord,	the	day	is	near;
2.	On – ly	for	a	piece	of	bread;
3.	And	the	sheep	and	ox – en	trod;
4.	And	he	pained	her	with	re – nown;
5.	That	through	all	the	a – ges	ran:

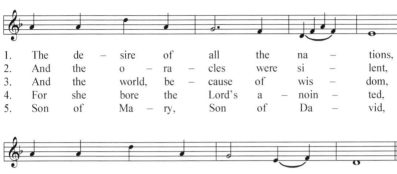

1.	The	de – sire	of	all	the	na –	tions,
2.	And	the	o – ra – cles	were	si –	lent,
3.	And	the	world,	be – cause	of	wis –	dom,
4.	For	she	bore	the	Lord's	a – noin –	ted,
5.	Son	of	Ma – ry,	Son	of	Da –	vid,

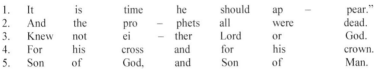

1.	It	is	time	he	should	ap –	pear."
2.	And	the	pro – phets	all	were	dead.
3.	Knew	not	ei – ther	Lord	or	God.
4.	For	his	cross	and	for	his	crown.
5.	Son	of	God,	and	Son	of	Man.

284. Eternal Father, Strong to Save

Text: William Whiting, 1825-1878

Tune: Melita 88. 88. 88.
John Bacchus Dykes, 1823-1876

1. E – ter – nal Fa – ther, strong to save, Whose
2. O Christ, the Lord o'er hill and plain, O'er
3. O Spi – rit whom the Fa – ther sent, To
4. O Tri – ni – ty of love and pow'r, Our

1. arm has bound the rest – less wave,
2. which our traf – fic runs a – main;
3. spread a – broad the fir – ma – ment;
4. breth – ren shield in dan – ger's hour;

1. Who bids the might – y o – cean deep, Its
2. By moun– tain pass or val – ley low; Where
3. O Wind of hea – ven, by thy might, Save
4. From rock and tem – pest, fire and foe, Pro –

1. own ap – point – ed lim – its keep;
2. ev – er, Lord, thy breth – ren go,
3. all who dare the ea – gle's flight,
4. tect them where – so – e'er they go;

1. O hear us when we cry to thee, For
2. Pro – tect them by thy guard – ing hand, From
3. And keep them by thy watch – ful care, From
4. Thus ev – er – more shall rise to thee, Glad

1. those in per – il on the sea.
2. ev – 'ry per – il on the land.
3. ev – 'ry per – il in the air.
4. praise from air and land and sea. A – men.

285. Faith of Our Fathers

Text: Fredrick William Faber, 1814-1863, alt.

Tune: St. Catherine, 88. 88. 88.
Henry F. Hemy, 1818-1888

1. Faith of our fa – thers! Liv – ing still,
2. Our fa – thers, chained in pris – ons dark,
3. Faith of our fa – thers! Ma – ry's prayers
4. Faith of our fa – thers! We will love

1. In spite of dun – geon, fire and sword:
2. Were still in heart and con – science free:
3. Shall win our coun – try back to thee;
4. Both friend and foe in all our strife:

1. O how our hearts beat high with joy,
2. And tru – ly blest would be our fate,
3. And through the truth that comes from God,
4. And preach thee, too, as love knows how,

1. When – e'er we hear that glo – rious word:
2. If we, like them, should die for thee.
3. The world* shall then in – deed be free.
4. By kind – ly deeds and vir – tuous life.

Refrain:

Faith of our fa – thers, ho – ly faith!

We will be true to thee till death.

* Original line: "England shall then indeed be free." *(Altered because of context.)*

286. Father of Mercies, in Your Word

Anne Steele, 1716-1778

Tune: Detroit, C. M.
The Sacred Harp, Philadelphia, 1844

1. Fa – ther of mer – cies, in your Word, What
2. Here springs of con – so – la – tion rise To
3. Oh, may these heav'n–ly pag – es be My
4. Di – vine in – struc – tor, gra – cious Lord, May

1. end – less glo – ry shines! For –
2. cheer the faint – ing mind, And
3. ev – er dear de – light; And
4. you be al – ways near; Teach

1. ev – er be your name a – dored For
2. thirst – y souls re – ceive sup – plies And
3. still new beau – ties may I see And
4. me to love your sa – cred Word And

1. these ce – les – tial lines.
2. sweet re – fresh – ment find.
3. still in – creas – ing light.
4. find my Sav – ior here.

287. Father, Son, and Holy Ghost

Text: Charles Wesley, 1707-1788

Tune: Dix, 77. 77. 77.
Conrad Kocher, 1786-1872

1. Fa — ther, Son, and Ho — ly Ghost,
2. Take my soul and bod — y's pow'rs,
3. Now, O God, thine own I am;

1. One in Three and Three in One,
2. Take my mem — 'ry, mind, and will,
3. Now I give thee back thine own;

1. As by the ce — les — tial host,
2. All my goods and all my hours,
3. Free — dom, friends and health and fame,

1. Let thy will on earth be done!
2. All I know and all I feel;
3. Con — se — crate to thee a — lone;

1. Praise by all to thee be giv'n,
2. All I think, or speak, or do;
3. Thine I live, thrice hap — py I!

1. Glo — rious Lord of earth and heav'n.
2. Take my heart, but make it new!
3. Hap — pier still if thine I die.

288. For All Your Saints, O Lord

Richard Mant, 1776-1848, alt.

Tune: Festal Song, S. M.
William H. Walter, 1825-1893

1. For all your saints, O Lord,
2. For all your saints, O Lord,
3. They all in life and death,
4. For this, your name we bless
5. To God the Fa – ther, Son,

1. Who strove in you to live,
2. Who strove in you to die,
3. With you, their Lord, in view,
4. And hum – bly pray a – new
5. And Spir – it, ev – er blest,

1. Who fol – lowed you, o – beyed, a – dored,
2. Who count – ed you their great re – ward,
3. Learned from your Ho – ly Spir – it's breath
4. That we like them in ho – li – ness
5. The One in Three, the Three in One,

1. Our grate – ful hymn re – ceive.
2. Ac – cept our thank – ful cry.
3. To suf – fer and to do.
4. May live and die in you.
5. Be end – less praise ad – dressed.

289. For the Beauty of the Earth

Text: Folliot S. Pierpoint, 1835-1917

Tune: Dix, 77. 77. 77.
Conrad Kocher, 1786-1872

1. For the beau – ty of the earth,
2. For the joy of hu – man love,
3. For thy Church, that ev – er – more
4. For thy – self, best Gift Di – vine!

1. For the glo – ry of the skies,
2. Bro – ther, sis – ter, par – ent, child,
3. Lift – eth ho – ly hands a – bove,
4. To our race so free – ly giv'n;

1. For the love which from our birth
2. Friends on earth, and friends a – bove;
3. Of – f'ring up on ev – 'ry shore
4. For that great, great love of thine,

1. O – ver and a – round us lies:
2. For all gen – tle thoughts and mild:
3. Her pure sac – ri – fice of love:
4. Peace on earth and joy in heav'n.

1-4. Lord of all, to thee we raise,

1-4. This our hymn of grate – ful praise.

290. Forty Days and Forty Nights

Text: George Hunt Smyttan, 1822-1870

Tune: Heinlein, 77. 77.
Nürnbergisches Gesanbuch, 1676

1. For – ty days and for – ty nights,
2. Shall not we thy sor – row share,
3. Then if Sa – tan on us press
4. So shall we have peace di – vine:
5. Keep, O keep us, Sa – vior dear,

1. Thou wast fast – ing in the wild;
2. And from world – ly joys ab – stain,
3. Flesh or spi – rit to as – sail,
4. Ho – lier glad – ness ours shall be;
5. Ev – er con – stant by thy side;

1. For – ty days and for – ty nights,
2. Fast – ing with un – ceas – ing prayer,
3. Vic – tor in the wil – der – ness,
4. Round us, too, shall an – gels shine,
5. That with thee we may ap – pear,

1. Temp t– ed and yet un – de – filed.
2. Strong with thee to suf – fer pain?
3. Grant we may not faint nor fail!
4. Such as min – is – tered to thee.
5. At the e – ter – nal Eas – ter – tide. A – men.

291. From God the Father, Virgin-Born

Text: *A Patre Unigenitus*, Anonymous, 11th Century Tune: Deus Tuorum Militum (Grenoble), L. M.
Tr. John Mason Neale, 1818-1866   *Grenoble Antiphoner*, 1753

1. From   God   the   Fa – ther,   vir –   gin   born
2. Be – gin – ning from   his   home   on   high,
3. Glide   on,   O   glo – rious   Sun,   and   bring
4. A – bide with   us,   O   Lord, we   pray;
5. Lord,   once   you   came   to   earth's do – main
6. To   you,   O   Lord,   all   glo –   ry   be

1. To   us   the   on – ly   Son   came   down;
2. In   hu – man flesh   he   came   to   die;
3. The   gift   of   heal – ing   on   your   wing;
4. The   gloom   of   dark – ness   chase a –   way;
5. And,   we   be – lieve,   shall   come   a –   gain;
6. For   this,   your   blest   E – pi – pha – ny;

1. By   death   the   font   to   con – se – crate,
2. Cre – a – tion   by   his   death re – stored,
3. To   ev – 'ry dull   and   cloud – ed   sense
4. Your   work   of   heal – ing,   Lord, be – gin,
5. Be   with   us   on   the   bat – tle – field,
6. To   God   whom   all   his   hosts a –   dore,

1. The   faith – ful   will   re – gen – er – ate.
2. And   shed   new   joys   of   life   a –   broad.
3. The   clear – ness   of   your   light dis – pense.
4. And   take   a – way the   stain of   sin.
5. From   ev – 'ry harm   your   peo – ple   shed.
6. And   Ho – ly Spir – it   ev – er – more.

292. Gloria, Laus et Honor

Text: Theodulph of Orleans, c. 760-820
ENGLISH: "All Glory, Laud, and Honor"

Tune: Gloria Laus et Honor, Irregular
Chant, Mode I

*Refrain: (sung whenever a bold "**R.**" appears in the text)*

Gló– ri – a, laus et ho – nor, ti – bi sit, Rex Chri– ste Red – ém–ptor:

Cu – i pu –é – ri – le de – cus prom–psit Ho–sán – na pi –um.

1. Is – ra – el es tu Rex, Da – ví – dis et

1. et ín – cly – ta pro – les: Nó – mi – ne qui in

1. Dó – mi – ni, Rex be – ne dí – cte, ve – nis. **R.**

2. Coe – tus in ex – cél – sis te lau – dat cáe –

2. li – cus o – mnis. Et mor – tá – lis ho – mo

2. et cun – cta cre – á – ta si – mul. **R.**

3. Plebs He – bráe – a ti – bi cum pal – mis

3. ób – vi – a ve – nit: Cum pre – ce, vo – to,

3. hy – mnis, ád – su – mus ec – ce ti – bi. **R.**

4. Hi ti – bi pas – sú – ro sol – vé – bant

4. mú – ni – a lau – dis: Nos ti – bi re – – gnán –

4. ti pán – gi – mus ec – ce me – los. **R.**

5. Hi pla – cu – é – re ti – bi, plá – ce – at

5. de – vó – ti – o no – stra. Rex bo – ne, Rex

5. cle – mens cu – i bo – na cun – cta pla – cent. **R.**

293. Go, Tell It on the Mountain

Text: African-American Spiritual
Compiled by John Wesley Work, Jr., 1872-1925

Tune: Go Tell It on the Mountain, 76. 76. with Refrain
African-American Spiritual

Refrain:

Go, tell it on the moun – tain, O – ver the hills and ev – 'ry – where; Go, tell it on the moun – tain, That Je – sus Christ is born!

1. While shep – herds kept their watch – ing, O'er
2. The shep – herds feared and trem – bled, When
3. Down in a low – ly man – ger, The

1. si – lent flocks by night, Be – hold through–out the
2. lo! a – bove the earth, Rang out the an – gel
3. hum– be Christ was born, And God sent us sal –

1. heav – ens, There shone a ho – ly light.
2. cho – rus, That hailed our Sav – ior's birth.
3. va – tion, That bless – ed Christ – mas morn.

294. God, Whose Almighty Word

Text: John Marriott, 1780-1825

Tune: Italian Hymn, 664. 6664.
Felice de Giardini, 1716-1796

1. God, whose al – might – y word Cha – os and
2. Sav – ior, you came to give Those who in
3. Spir – it of truth and love, Life giv – ing,
4. Gra – cious and ho – ly Three, Glo – ri – ous

1. dark – ness heard, And took their flight:
2. dark – ness live Heal – ing and sight,
3. ho – ly dove, Speed on your flight!
4. Tri – ni – ty, Wis – don, love, might:

1. Hear us, we hum – bly pray, And where the
2. Health to the sick in mind, Sight to the
3. Move on the wa – ter's face Bear – ing the
4. Bound – less as o – cean's tide Roll – ing in

1. gos – pel day Sheds not its glo – rious ray,
2. in – ward blind: Now to all hu – man –kind
3. lamp of grace And in earth's dark – est place,
4. full – est pride Through the world far and wide,

1. Let there be light!
2. Let there be light!
3. Let there be light!
4. Let there be light! A – men.

295. Godhead Here in Hiding

Text: *Adoro Te Devote*, St. Thomas Aquinas, 1227-1274   Tune: Adoro Te Devote 11. 11. 11. 11.
Tr. Gerard Manley Hopkins, 1844-1889   Chant, Mode V

1. God – head here in hid – ing, thee I do a – dore;
2. See – ing, touch –ing, tast – ing, are in thee de – ceived;
3. On the cross thy god – head made no sign to see,
4. I am not like Thom – as, wounds I can – not see,
5. O thou our re – mind – er of Christ cru – ci – fied,
6. Je – sus, whom I look at shroud– ed here be– low,

1. Masked by these bare shad – ows, shape and noth – ing more,
2. How says trust – y hear – ing? That shall be be – lieved;
3. Here thy ve – ry man – hood hides it – self from me:
4. But can plain – ly call thee Lord and God as he;
5. Liv – ing Bread, the life of us for whom he died,
6. I be – seech thee send me what I thirst for so,

1. See, Lord, at thy ser – vice, low lies here a heart;
2. What God's Son has told me, take for truth I do:
3. Both are my con – fes – sion, both are my be – lief,
4. Let me to a deep – er faith dai – ly near – er move,
5. Lend this life to me then: feed and feast my mind,
6. Some day to gaze on thee face to face in light

1. Lost, all lost in won – der, at the God thou art.
2. Truth him – self speaks tru – ly, or there's noth – ing true.
3. And I too pray the prayer of the dy – ing thief.
4. Dai – ly make me firm – er hope and dear – er love.
5. There be thou the sweet – ness all are meant to find.
6. And be blest for ev – er with thy glo – ry's sight.

296. Good Lord, Now Let Your Servant

Text: St. 1-3, Ernest Edwin Ryden, 1886-1981

Tune: St. Theodulph (Teschner) 76. 76. D.
Melchior Teschner, 1584-1635

1. Good Lord, now let your ser – vant De – part from
2. How pre – cious is the vi – sion Of your re –
3. Then grant that I may fol – low Your ray of
4. Glo – ry be to the Fa – ther, And al – so

1. here in peace, As one whose heart is glad – dened
2. deem – ing Love, But still my spir – it's yearn – ing
3. heav'n – ly Light, Till earth – ly shad – ows van – ish
4. to the Son, And to the Ho – ly Spir – it,

1. By grace with – out sur – cease; The Light of all
2. To see your grace a – bove, Where, clad in robes
3. And faith is changed to sight; Till all your saints
4. E – ter – nal Three in One. As 'twas in the

1. the Na – tions, Show them the way of life,
2. ce – les – tial, I too shall join the throng
3. shall gath – er, Up – on that bliss – ful shore,
4. be – gin – ning, Is now and e'er shall be:

1. That they with all your peo – ple
2. Of ran – somed souls in glo – ry
3. Where Christ, the ra – diant Day – star,
4. For – ev – er, world with – out end,

1. May dwell with – in your Light.
2. And sing the Lamb's new song.
3. Shall light them ev – er – more.
4. E – ter – nal One in Three.

315

297. Hail! Holy Queen Enthroned Above

Text: *Salve Regina Coelitum*, Anonymous, c. 1080   Tune: Salve Regina Coelitum 84. 84. w. Refrain
Tr. Anonymous, c. 1884   *Choralmelodien zum Heiligen Gesänge*, 1808

1. Hail! ho – ly Queen en – throned a – bove, O Ma – rí – a!
2. The cause of joy to us be – low, O Ma – ri – a!
3. O gen – tle, lov – ing, ho – ly one, O Ma – ri – a!

1. Hail! Queen of mer – cy and of love, O Ma – rí – a!
2. The spring through which all grac – es flow, O Ma – ri – a!
3. The God of light be – came your Son, O Ma – ri – a!

1. Tri – umph all ye Che – ru – bim, Sing with us
2. An – gels, all your prais – es bring, Earth and heav –
3. Tri – umph all ye Che – ru – bim, Sing with us

1. ye Se – ra – phim, Heav'n and earth re – sound the hymn:
2. en, with us sing, All cre – a – tion ech – o – ing:
3. ye Se – ra – phim, Heav'n and earth re – sound the hymn:

1. Sal – ve, Sal – ve, Sal – ve Re – gi – na!
2. Sal – ve, Sal – ve, Sal – ve Re – gi – na!
3. Sal – ve, Sal – ve, Sal – ve Re – gi – na!

298. Hark! a Thrilling Voice Is Sounding!

Text: *Vox Clara Ecce Intonat*, 6th Century
Tr. Edward Caswall, 1814-1878

Tune: Freuen Wir Uns All In Ein, 87. 87.
Michael Weisse, c. 1480-1534

1. Hark! A thrill – ing voice is sound – ing!
2. Star – tled at the sol – emn warn – ing,
3. See the Lamb, so long ex – pec – ted,
4. So, when next he comes in glo – ry
5. Hon – or, glo – ry, might, do – min – ion

1. "Christ is near," we hear the cry.
2. Let the earth – bound soul a – rise;
3. Comes with par – don down from heav'n.
4. And the world is wrapped in fear,
5. To the Fa – ther and the Son

1. "Cast a – way the works of dark – ness,
2. Christ, its sun, all sloth dis – pell – ing,
3. Let us haste, with tears of sor – row,
4. He will shield us with his mer – cy
5. With the ev – er – liv – ing Spir – it

1. All you chil – dren of the day!"
2. Shines up – on the morn – ing skies.
3. Once and all, to be for – giv'n;
4. And with words of love draw near.
5. While e – ter – nal a – ges run!

299. Hark! The Herald Angels Sing

Text: Charles Wesley, 1707-1788   Tune: Mendelssohn, 77. 77. 77. 77. with Refrain
                                                             Felix Mendelssohn, 1808-1847

1. Hark! The her – ald an – gels sing, "Glo – ry to
2. Christ, by high – est heav'n a – dored, Christ, the ev –
3. Hail the heav'n–born Prince of peace! Hail the Sun

1. the new – born King; Peace on earth and mer – cy mild –
2. er – last – ing Lord; Late in time be – hold him come,
3. of right – eous – ness! Light and life to all he brings,

1. God and sin – ners re – con – ciled!" Joy – ful all ye na –
2. Off – spring of the Vir – gin's womb. Veiled in flesh the God –
3. Ris'n with heal – ing in his wings. Mild he lays his glo –

1. tions rise, Join the tri – umph of the skies; With the an–
2. head see; Hail the in– car – nate De – i – ty, Pleased as
3. ry by, Born that we no more may die, Born to

1. gel – ic hosts pro – claim, "Christ is born in Beth – le – hem!"
2. man with us to dwell, Je – sus our Em – man – u – el.
3. raise the sons of earth, Born to give them sec – ond birth.

Refrain:

Hark! The her – ald an – gels sing, "Glo – ry to the new–born King!"

300. Have Mercy, Lord, on Us

Text: Nahum Tate, 1652-1715, and Nicholas Brady, 1659-1726

Tune: Southwell, S. M.
Damon's *Psalmes*, 1579

1. Have mer – cy, Lord, on us,
2. Lord, wash a – way our guilt,
3. The joy your grace can give,

1. For you are ev – er kind;
2. And cleanse us from our sin;
3. Let us a – gain ob – tain,

1. Though we have sinned be – fore you, Lord,
2. For we con – fess our wrongs, and see
3. And may your Spir – it's firm sup – port

1. Your mer – cy let us find.
2. How great our guilt has been.
3. Our spir – its then sus – tain.

301. Have Mercy, O Lord

Text: *Parce Domine*, St. Gregory the Great, 540-604   Tune: Parce Domine, Irregular
Tr. Refrain and St. 1-3, Agostino Taumaturgo, b. 1974; St. 4-5, Thomas A. Lacey, 1853-1931

Refrain:

Have mer – cy, O Lord, Par– don un –to thy peo – ple,
Do not for – ev – er, fix thy wrath up – on us.

1. Kneel – ing be – fore the a – ven – ger,
2. By our sins have we of – fend – ed,
3. Now is, the ac – cept – a – ble time,
4. O kind Cre – a – tor, bow thine ear
5. Our hearts are o – pen, Lord, to thee:

1. Be – fore the Judge we shed our tears;
2. A – gainst thy mer – cy and thy love
3. That we cry out our tears in streams
4. To mark the cry, to know the tear
5. Thou know – est our in – fir – mit – y;

1. Let us hum – bly cry out to him,
2. Pour out up – on us from heav – en
3. May they wash our heart's sac – ri – fice,
4. Be – fore thy throne of mer – cy spent
5. Pour out on all who seek thy face

1. Pros – trate we pour forth all our prayers:
2. Thy kind for – give – ness from a – bove.
3. May we be made hap – py and clean.
4. In this thy ho – ly fast of Lent.
5. A – bun – dance of thy lov – ing grace.

302. He Is Risen, He Is Risen

Text: Cecil F. Alexander, 1818-1895

Tune: Picardy 87. 87. 87.
Traditional French Melody

1. He is ris – en, he is ris – en!
2. Come, ye sad and fear – ful hear – ted,
3. Come, with high and ho – ly hymn – ing,
4. He is ris – en, he is ris – en!

1. Tell it out with joy – ful voice:
2. With glad smile and ra – diant brow!
3. Chant our Lord's tri – um – phant day;
4. He has o – pened Heav – en's gate:

1. He has burst his three days' pris – on;
2. Death's long shad – ows have de – par – ted;
3. Not one dark – some cloud is dim – ming
4. We are free from sin's dark pris – on,

1. Let the whole wide earth re – joice:
2. All our woes are o – ver now,
3. Yon – der glo – rious mor – ning ray,
4. Ris – en to a ho – lier state;

1. Death is o – ver – come, we are free,
2. Due to the suf – f'ring that he bore
3. Break – ing o – ver the pur – ple east:
4. And a mar – vel – lous Eas – ter beam

1. Christ has won the vic – to – ry.
2. Sin and pain can vex no more.
3. Bright – er far our Eas – ter feast.
4. On our long – ing eyes shall stream.

303. He 'Rose

Text: African-American Spiritual

Tune: Ascensius, 13. 13. 13. 9. with Refrain
Traditional African-American Spiritual

Refrain:

He   'rose,   He   'rose,   He   'rose   from the

dead, He   'rose,   He   'rose,   He   'rose   from the

dead, He   'rose,   He   'rose,   He   'rose   from the

dead,   and   the   Lord shall   bear   my   spir – it   home.

1.	They cru– ci – fied my	Sav– ior	and nailed him to	the	cross,
2.	And Jo– seph begged his	bod – y	and	laid it	in the	tomb,
3.	Sister Ma–ry, she came run – ning a –	look–ing for my	Lord,
4.	An an – gel came from heav – en,	and rolled the stone a –	way,

1. They cru– ci – fied my   Sav– ior and nailed him to the   cross,
2. And Jo– seph begged his bod – y and   laid it in the   tomb,
3. Sister Ma–ry, she came run – ning a –   look–ing for my   Lord,
4. An   an – gel came from heav – en, and rolled the stone a – way,

1. They cru– ci – fied my   Sav– ior and nailed him to the   cross,
2. And Jo– seph begged his bod – y and   laid it in the   tomb,
3. Sister Ma–ry, she came run – ning a –   look–ing for my   Lord,
4. An   an – gel came from heav – en, and rolled the stone a – way,

1. And the   Lord   will   bear   my   spir – it   home.
2. And the   Lord   will   bear   my   spir – it   home.
3. And the   Lord   will   bear   my   spir – it   home.
4. And the   Lord   will   bear   my   spir – it   home.

304. He Leadeth Me

Text: Joseph H. Gilmore, 1834-1918

Tune: He Leadeth Me L. M. D.
William Bradbury, 1816-1868

1. He lead – eth me! O bless – ed thought! O
2. Some– times 'mid scenes of deep – est gloom, Some–
3. Lord, I would clasp thy hand in mine, Nor
4. And when my task on earth is done, When

1. words with heav'n–ly com–fort fraught! What–e'er I do, wher–
2. times where E – den's bow–ers bloom, By wa – ters still, o'er
3. ev – er mur – mur nor re – pine; Con – tent, what–ev–er
4. by thy grace the vic –t'ry's won, E'en death's cold wave I

1. e'er I be, Still 'tis God's hand that lead– eth me.
2. trou– bled sea, Still 'tis his hand that lead – eth me!
3. lot I see, Since 'tis my God that lead – eth me!
4. will not flee, Since God thru Jor – dan lead – eth me.

Refrain:

He lead-eth me, he lead-eth me, By his own hand he lead-eth me;

His faith-ful fol-l'wer I would be, For by his hand he lead-eth me;

305. Heart of Jesus! Golden Chalice

Text: Louis C. Casartelli, 1852-1925

Tune: St. Thomas, 87. 87. 87.
Cantus Diversi, John Francis Wade, c. 1711-1786

1. Heart of Je - sus! gold - en chal - ice
2. Heart of Je - sus! Comb of hon - ey
3. Heart of Je - sus! Rose of Shar - on
4. Heart of Je - sus! Brok - en Vi - al

1. Brimm - ing with the rud - dy Wine,
2. From the cleft of Cal - vary's rock,
3. Glist - 'ning with the dew of tears,
4. Full of prec - ious spi - ken - ard!

1. Trod - den in the press of fu - ry,
2. Sweet - ness com - ing from the Strong One,
3. All a - mong the thorn - y prick - les
4. Al a - bas - ter vase of oint - ment!

1. Pur - est juice of tru - est vine,
2. Dripp - ing from the green - wood stock;
3. Lo! Thy blood - stained head ap - pears!
4. See, our souls are sore and hard:

1. From the Vine - yards of En - ged - di,
2. Fam - ish - ing of death is on us:
3. Spread thy fra - grance all a - round us,
4. Let thy heal - ing vir - tue touch them,

1. Quench this thirs - ty heart of mine.
2. Feed, oh, feed thy hun - gry flock!
3. Swee - tly lull - ing all our fears!
4. And from sin's cor - rup - tion guard! A - men.

306. Holy God, We Praise Thy Name

Text: *Grosser Gott, Wir Loben Dich*, Ignaz Franz, 1719-1790   Tune: Grosser Gott 78. 78. 77. 77.
Tr. Clarence Walworth, 1820-1900   *Katholisches Gesangbuch*, Vienna, c. 1774

1. Ho – ly   God,   we   praise   thy   Name!
2. Hark!   The   loud   ce – les – tial   hymn,
3. Lo!   The   a – pos – tol – ic   train
4. Ho – ly   Fa – ther,   Ho – ly   Son,

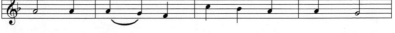

1. Lord   of   all,   we   bow   be – fore   thee;
2. An – gel   choirs   a – bove   are   rais – ing;
3. Join   the   sa – cred   name   to   hal – low;
4. Ho – ly   Spir – it,   Three   we   name   thee,

1. All   on   earth   thy   scep – ter   claim,
2. Cher – u – bim   and   Ser – a – phim,
3. Proph – ets   swell   the   loud   re – frain,
4. While   in   es – sence   on – ly   One,

1. All   in   heav'n   a – bove   a – dore   thee;
2. In   un – ceas – ing   cho – rus   prais – ing,
3. And   the   white – robed   mar – tyrs   fol – low;
4. Un – di – vid – ed   God   we   claim   thee,

1. In – fi – nite   thy   vast   do – main,
2. Fill   the   heav'ns   with   sweet   ac – cord:
3. And   from   morn   to   set   of   sun,
4. And   a – dor – ing   bend   the   knee,

1. Ev – er – last – ing   is   thy   reign.
2. Ho – ly,   Ho – ly,   Ho – ly   Lord!
3. Through the   Church   the   song   goes   on.
4. While we   own   the   mys – ter – y.

1. In – fi – nite   thy   vast   do – main,
2. Fill   the   heav'ns   with   sweet   ac – cord:
3. And   from   morn   to   set   of   sun,
4. And   a – dor – ing   bend   the   knee,

1. Ev – er – last – ing   is   thy   reign.
2. Ho – ly,   Ho – ly,   Ho – ly   Lord!
3. Through the   Church   the   song   goes   on.
4. While we   own   the   mys – ter – y.

5. Thou art King of glory, Christ:
Son of God, yet born of Mary;
For us sinners sacrificed,
And to death a tributary:
First to break the bars of death,
Thou has opened Heaven to faith.

6. From thy high celestial home,
Judge of all, again returning,
We believe that thou shalt come
In the dreaded doomsday morning;
When thy voice shall shake the earth,
And the startled dead come forth.

7. Therefore do we pray thee, Lord:
Help thy servants whom, redeeming
By thy precious blood out-poured,
Thou hast saved from Satan's scheming.
Give to them eternal rest
In the glory of the blest.

8. Spare thy people, Lord, we pray,
By a thousand snares surrounded:
Keep us without sin today,
Never let us be confounded.
Lo, I put my trust in thee;
Never, Lord, abandon me.

307. Holy, Holy, Holy

Text: Reginald Heber, 1783-1826

Tune: Nicaea 11. 12. 12. 10.
John Bacchus Dykes, 1823-1876

1. Ho – ly, Ho – ly, Ho – ly! Lord God Al – migh – ty!
2. Ho – ly, Ho – ly, Ho – ly! All the saints a – dore thee,
3. Ho – ly, Ho – ly, Ho – ly! Though the dark – ness hide thee,
4. Ho – ly, Ho – ly, Ho – ly! Lord God Al – migh – ty!

1. Ear – ly in the morn – ing our song shall rise to thee:
2. Cast – ing down their gold – en crowns a – round the glass– y sea;
3. Though the eye of sin – ful man thy glo – ry may not see,
4. All thy works shall praise thy name, in earth, and sky, and sea;

1. Ho – ly, Ho – ly, Ho – ly! mer – ci – ful and migh –ty,
2. Cher – u – bim and ser – a –phim fall – ing down be – fore thee,
3. On – ly thou art ho – ly; there is none be – side thee,
4. Ho – ly, Ho – ly, Ho – ly! mer – ci – ful and migh –ty,

1. God in three Per – sons, bless – ed Tri – ni – ty.
2. Which wert, and art, and ev – er – more shalt be.
3. Per – fect in pow'r, in love, and pu – ri – ty.
4. God in three Per – sons, bless – ed Tri – ni – ty. A – men.

308. Holy Spirit, Lord of Love

William D. Maclagen, 1826-1910

Tune: Abertswyth, 77. 77. D.
Joseph Parry, 1841-1903

1. Ho — ly Spir — it, Lord of love,
2. When the sa — cred vow is made,

1. Thou who cam — est from a — bove,
2. When the hands are on them laid,

1. Gifts of bless — ing to be — stow
2. Come in this most sol — emn hour

1. On your wait — ing Church be — low,
2. With your strength — 'ning gift of pow'r.

1. Once a — gain in love draw near
2. Give them light thy truth to see:

1. To thy ser — vants gath — ered here.
2. Give them life to live for thee,

1. From their bright bap — tis — mal day
2. Dai — ly pow'r to con — quer sin,

1. Thou hast led them on their way.
2. Pa — tient faith, the crown to win.

309. Hosanna, Loud Hosanna

Text: Jeanette Threlfall, 1821-1880

Tune: Ellacombe, 76. 76. D.
Gesangbuch der Herzogl, Würtemberg, 1784

1. Ho – san – na, loud ho – san – na, The lit – tle chil –dren sang;
2. From O – li – vet they fol – lowed Mid an ex – ul – tant crowd,
3. "Ho – san – na in the high – est!" That an – cient song we sing,

1. Thru pil – lared court and tem – ple, The love – ly an – them rang.
2. The vic – tor palm branch wav – ing, And chan – ting clear and loud.
3. For Christ is our Re – deem – er, The Lord of heav'n our King.

1. To Je – sus, who had blest them Close fol – ded to his breast,
2. The Lord of men and an – gels Rode on in low – ly state,
3. O may we ev – er praise him With heart and life and voice,

1. The chil – dren sang their prais– es, The sim – plest and the best.
2. Nor scorned that lit – tle chil – dren Should on his bid– ding wait.
3. And in his bliss – ful pre – sence E – ter – nal – ly re – joice!

310. How Sweet the Name of Jesus Sounds

Text: John Newton, 1725-1807

Tune: St. Peter, C. M.
Alexander R. Reinagle, 1799-1877

1.	How	sweet	the	name	of	Je – sus	sounds
2.	It	makes	the	wound – ed		spir – it	whole,
3.	Dear	name!	The	rock	on	which	I	build,
4.	Je – sus,	my	shep – herd,		hus – band,		friend,
5.	Weak	is	the	ef – fort		of	my	heart,

1.	In	a	be – liev – er's			ear!	
2.	And	calms	the	trou – bled		breast;	
3.	My	shield	and	hid – ing		place;	
4.	My	proph – et,		priest,	and	king;	
5.	And	cold	my	warm – est		thought;	

1.	It	soothes	his	sor – rows,		heals	his	wounds,
2.	'Tis	man – na		to	the	hun – gry		soul,
3.	My	nev – er – fail – ing				trea – sure,		filled,
4.	My	Lord,	my	life,	my	way,	my	end,
5.	But	when	I	see	thee	as	thou	art,

1.	And	drives	a – way		all		fear.
2.	And	to	the	wea – ry,			rest.
3.	With	bound – less		stores	of		grace!
4.	Ac – cept		the	praise	I		bring.
5.	I'll	praise	thee	as	I		ought.

311. I Know That My Redeemer Lives

Text: Samuel Medley, 1738-1799

Tune: Duke Street, L. M.
John Hatton, c. 1710-1793

1. I know that my Re – deem – er lives;
2. He lives, to bless me with his love;
3. He lives, and grants me dai – ly breath;
4. He lives, all glo – ry to his name;

1. What joy the blest as – sur – ance gives!
2. He lives, to plead for me a – bove;
3. He lives, and I shall con – quer death;
4. He lives, my Sav – ior, still the same;

1. He lives, he lives, who once was dead;
2. He lives, my hun – gry soul to feed;
3. He lives, my man – sion to pre – pare;
4. What joy the blest as – sur – ance gives;

1. He lives, my ev – er – last – ing Head!
2. He lives, to help in time of need.
3. He lives, to bring me safe – ly there.
4. I know that my Re – deem – er lives!

312. I Lay My Sins on Jesus

Text: Horatius Bonar, 1808-1889

Tune: Aurelia 76. 76. D.
Samuel S. Wesley, 1810-1876

1. I lay my sins on Je – sus, The spot – less Lamb of God;
2. I lay my wants on Je – sus; All full – ness dwells in him;
3. I long to be like Je – sus, Meek, lov – ing, low – ly, mild;

1. He bears them all, and frees us From the ac – cur – sed load:
2. He heals all my dis – eas – es, He doth my soul re – deem:
3. I long to be like Je – sus, The Fa – ther's ho – ly Child:

1. I bring my guilt to Je – sus, To wash my crim – son stains
2. I lay my griefs on Je – sus, My bur – dens and my cares;
3. I long to be with Je – sus, A – mid the heav'n–ly throng,

1. Cleansed by his blood most pre – cious, Till not a stain re – mains.
2. He from them all re – leas – es, He all my sor – rows shares.
3. To sing with saints his prais– es, To learn the an – gel's song.

313. Immortal, Invisible, God Only Wise

Text: Walter Chambers Smith, 1824-1908

Tune: St. Denio, 11. 11. 11. 11.
Welsh Melody, John Roberts' *Canaidau y Cyssegr*, 1839

1. Im – mor –tal, in –vis – i – ble, God on – ly
2. Un – rest – ing, un –hast –ing, and si – lent as
3. Great Fa – ther of glo – ry, pure Fa – ther of

1. wise, in light in – ac – ces – si – ble
2. light, Nor want – ing, nor was – ting, thou
3. light, Thine an – gels a – dore thee, all

1. hid from our eyes, Most bless – ed, most
2. rul – est in might; Thy jus – tice like
3. veil – ing their sight; All praise we would

1. glo – rious, the An – cient of Days, Al –
2. moun – tains high soar – ing a – bove Thy
3. ren – der: O help us to see 'Tis

1. might – y, vic – to – rious, thy great name we praise.
2. clouds which are foun – tains of good – ness and love.
3. on – ly the splen – dor of light hid – eth thee.

314. In Christ There Is No East or West

Text: William A. Dunkerley (alias John Oxenham), 1852-1941

Tune: St. Peter, C. M.
Alexander R. Reinagle, 1799-1877

1. In Christ there is no East or West, In him no
2. In him shall true hearts ev – 'ry – where Their high com –
3. Join hands, then, mem –bers of the faith, What–ev'r your
4. In Christ now meet both East and West, In him meet

1. South or North; But one great fel – low –
2. mu – nion find; His ser – vice is the
3. race may be! Who serves my Fa – ther
4. North and South; All Christ – ly souls are

1. ship of love Through –out the whole wide earth.
2. gol – den cord, Close bind – ing hu – man – kind.
3. as his child Is sure – ly kin to me.
4. one in him Through –out the whole wide earth.

335

315. It May Not Be On The Mountain's Height

Text: St. 1, Mary Brown, 1856-1918
St. 2 and 3, Charles Pryor, 1856-1927

Tune: Manchester, 96. 96. 96. 98. with refrain
Carrie E. Rounsefell, 1861-1930

1. It may not be on the moun–tain's height, Or
2. Per – haps to – day there are lov – ing words Which
3. There's sure – ly some – where a low – ly place In

1. o – ver the storm – y sea; It
2. Je – sus would have me speak; There
3. earth's har – vest fields so wide, Where

1. may not be at the bat – tle's front My
2. may be now, in the paths of sin, Some
3. I may la – bor through life's short day, For

1. Lord will have need of me; But
2. wan – d'rer whom I should seek; O
3. Je – sus the cru – ci – fied; So,

1. if by a still, small voice he calls To
2. Sav – ior, if thou wilt be my guide, Though
3. trust – ing my all un – to thy care, I

1. paths I do not know, I'll
2. dark and rug – ged the way, My
3. know thou lov – est me, I'll

1. an–swer, dear Lord, with my hand in thine, I'll
2. voice shall ech – o the mes – sage sweet, I'll
3. do thy will with a heart sin – cere, I'll

1. go where you want me to go.
2. say what you want me to say.
3. be what you want me to be.

Refrain:

I'll go where you want me to go, dear Lord, O'er

moun – tain or plain or sea; I'll

say what you want me to say, dear Lord, I'll

be what you want me to be.

316. Jerusalem, My Happy Home

Text: Joseph Bromehead, 1747-1826

Tune: Land of Rest, C. M.
Traditional American Melody

1.	Je	– ru	– sa	– lem,	my	hap	– py	home,
2.	Thy	saints	are	crowned	with	glo	– ry	great;
3.	There	Da	– vid	stands	with	harp	in	hand
4.	Our	La	– dy	sings	Mag	– ni	– fi	– cat
5.	There	Mag	– da	– len	hath	left	her	moan,
6.	Je	– ru	– sa	– lem,	Je	– ru	– sa	– lem,

1.	When	shall	I	come	to	thee?
2.	They	see	God	face	to	face;
3.	As	mas	– ter	of	the	choir:
4.	With	tune	sur	– pass	– ing	sweet;
5.	And	cheer	– ful	– ly	doth	sing
6.	God	grant	that	I	may	see

1.	When	shall	my	sor	– rows	have	an	end?
2.	They	tri	– umph	still,	they	still	re	– joice:
3.	Ten	thou	– sand	times	that	man	were	blest
4.	And	all	the	vir	– gins	bear	their	part,
5.	With	bless	– ed	saints,	whose	har	– mo	– ny
6.	Thine	end	– less	joy,	and	of	the	same

1.	Thy	joys	when	shall	I	see?
2.	Most	hap	– py	is	their	case.
3.	That	might	his	mu	– sic	hear.
4.	Sit	– ting	a	– bout	her	feet.
5.	In	ev	– 'ry	street	doth	ring.
6.	Par	– tak	– er	ev	– er	be!

317. Jesu, Dulcis Memoria

Text: St. Bernard of Clairvaux, 1090-1153
ENGLISH: "Jesus, the Very Thought of Thee"

Tune: Jesu Dulcis Memoria, L. M.
Chant, Mode I

1. Je – su, dul – cis me – mo – ri – a,
2. Nil ca – ni – tur su – a – vi – us,
3. Je – su, spes pae – ni – ten – ti – bus,
4. Nec lin – gua va – let di – ce – re,
5. Sis Je – su no – strum gau – di – um,

1. Dans ve – ra cor – dis gau – di – a:
2. Nil au – di – tur ju – cun – di – us,
3. Quam pi – us es pe – ten – ti – bus!
4. Nec lit – te – ra ex – pri – me – re:
5. Qui es fu – tu – rus prae – mi – um:

1. Sed su – per mel et o – mni– a,
2. Nil co – gi – ta – tur dul – ci – us,
3. Quam bo – nus te quae – ren – ti – bus!
4. Ex – per – tus po – test cre – de – re,
5. Sit no – stra in te glo – ri – a,

1. E – jus dul – cis prae – sen – ti – a.
2. Quam Je – sus De – i Fi – li – us.
3. Sed quid in – ve – ni – en – ti – bus?
4. Quid sit Je – sum di – li – ge – re.
5. Per cun – cta sem – per sae – cu – la.

After the Last verse:

A – – men.

318. Jesus Calls Us

Text: Cecil F. Alexander, 1818-1895

Tune: Galilee (Jude), 87. 87.
William H. Jude, 1851-1922

1. Je – sus calls us, o'er the tu – mult,
2. Je – sus calls us, from the wor – ship,
3. In our joys and, in our sor – rows,
4. Je – sus calls us; by thy mer – cies,

1. Of our life's wild, rest – less sea,
2. Of the vain world's gold – en store,
3. Days of toil and hours of ease,
4. Sav – ior, may we hear thy call,

1. Day by day his sweet voice sound – eth,
2. From each I – dol that would keep us,
3. Still he calls, in cares and pleas – ures,
4. Give our hearts to thy o – be – dience,

1. Say – ing, "Chris – tian, fol – low me."
2. Say – ing, "Chris – tian, love me more."
3. "Chris – tian, love me more than these."
4. Serve and love thee best of all.

319. Jesus Christ is Risen Today

Text: St. 1-3, *The Compleat Psalmodist*, c. 1750
St. 4, Charles Wesley, 1707-1788

Tune: Easter Hymn, 77. 77. with Alleluia
Lyra Davidica, 1708

1. Je – sus Christ is   ris'n to – day,   Al –   le –   lu –   ia!
2. Hymns of   praise then let   us   sing,   Al –   le –   lu –   ia!
3. But   the   pains which he   en– dured,   Al –   le –   lu –   ia!
4. Sing   we to   our   God a – bove,   Al –   le –   lu –   ia!

1. Our tri – um – phant ho – ly   day,   Al –   le –   lu –   ia!
2. Un –to   Christ, our heav'n–ly King,   Al –   le –   lu –   ia!
3. Our sal – va – tion   have pro–cured;   Al –   le –   lu –   ia!
4. Praise e – ter – nal   as   his   love;   Al –   le –   lu –   ia!

1. Who did once up – on   the   cross, Al –   le –   lu –   ia!
2. Who en–dured the   cross and grave, Al –   le –   lu –   ia!
3. Now a – bove the   sky   he's King, Al –   le –   lu –   ia!
4. Praise him, all   ye heav'n–ly host, Al –   le –   lu –   ia!

1. Suf – fer   to re – deem our loss.   Al –   le –   lu –   ia!
2. Sin – ners to re – deem and save.   Al –   le –   lu –   ia!
3. Where the   an–gels ev – er   sing.   Al –   le –   lu –   ia!
4. Fa – ther, Son, and Ho – ly   Ghost.   Al –   le –   lu –   ia!

320. Jesus, in Thy Dying Woes

Text: Thomas Benson Pollock, 1836-1896

Tune: Litany, 77. 76.
St. Alban's Tune Book, 1866

1. Je – sus in thy dy – ing woes, E – ven while thy
2. Sav – ior, for our par – don sue, When our sins thy
3. O may we, who mer– cy need, Be like thee in

1. life – blood flows, cra – ving par – don for thy foes:
2. pangs re – new, For we know not what we do:
3. heart and deed, When with wrong our spir – its bleed:

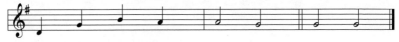

1. hear us, ho – ly Je – sus.
2. hear us, ho – ly Je – sus.
3. hear us, ho – ly Je – sus. A – men.

4. Jesus Pitying the sighs
Of the thief, who near thee dies,
Promising him paradise:
Hear us, holy Jesus.

5. May we in our guilt and shame
Still thy love and mercy claim,
Calling humbly on thy name:
Hear us, holy Jesus.

6. May our hearts to thee incline,
Looking from our cross to thine.
Cheer our souls with hope divine:
Hear us, holy Jesus.

7. Jesus, loving to the end
Her whose heart thy sorrows rend,
And thy dearest human friend:
Hear us, holy Jesus.

8. May we in thy sorrows share,
For thy sake all peril dare,
And enjoy thy tender care:
Hear us, holy Jesus.

9. May we all thy loved ones be,
All one holy family,
Looking for the Love of thee:
Hear us, holy Jesus.

10. Jesus, whelmed in fears unknown,
With our evil left alone,
While no light from heav'n is shown:
Hear us, holy Jesus.

11. When we seem in vain to pray
And our hope seems far away,
In the darkness be out stay:
Hear us, holy Jesus.

12. Though no Father seem to hear,
Though no light our spirits cheer,
May we know that God is near:
Hear us, holy Jesus.

13. Jesus in thy thirst and pain,
While thy wounds thy lifeblood drain,
Thirsting more our love to gain:
Hear us, holy Jesus.

14. Thirst for us in mercy still;
All thy holy work fulfill;
Satisfy thy loving will:
Hear us, holy Jesus.

15. May we thirst thy love to know;
Lead us in our sin and woe
Where the healing waters flow:
Hear us, holy Jesus.

16. Jesus, all our ransom paid,
All thy Father's will obeyed;
By thy suff'rings perfect made:
Hear us, holy Jesus.

17. Save us in our soul's distress;
Be our help to cheer and bless,
While we grow in holiness:
Hear us, holy Jesus.

18. Brighten all our heav'nward way
With an ever holier ray
Till we pass to perfect day:
Hear us, holy Jesus.

19. Jesus, all thy labor vast,
All thy woe and conflict past;
Yielding up thy soul at last:
Hear us, holy Jesus.

20. When the death shades round us low'r
Guard us from the tempter's pow'r
Keep us in that trial hour:
Hear us, holy Jesus.

21. May thy life and death supply
Grace to live and grace to die,
Grace to reach the home on high:
Hear us, holy Jesus.

321. Jesus, Lord, Be Thou Mine Own

Text: *Mondo, Più Per Me Non Sei*, St. Alphonsus Liguori, 1696-1787   Tune: Mondo Più, 77. 77.
Tr. E. Vaughan, 1827-1908   Don Lorenzo Perosi, 1872-1956

1. Je – sus, Lord, be thou mine own;
2. Life with – out thy Love would be
3. Thou, O God, my heart in – flame,
4. God of beau – ty, Lord of Light,

1. Thee I long for, thee a – lone;
2. Death, O Sov'r – eign Good, to me;
3. Give that love which thou dost claim;
4. Thy good will is my de – light;

1. All my – self I give to thee;
2. Bound and held by thy dear chains
3. Pay – ment I will ask for none;
4. Now hence – forth thy will di – vine

1. Do what – e'er thou wilt with me.
2. Cap – tive now my heart re – mains.
3. Love de – mands but love a – lone.
4. Ev – er shall in all be mine.

322. Jesus, My Lord, My God, My All

Text: Fredrick Faber, 1814-1863

Tune: Sweet Sacrament, L. M. with refrain
Romischkatholisches Gesanbuchlein, 1826

1. Je - sus, my Lord, my God, my all,
2. Had I but Ma - ry's sin - less heart,
3. Sound, sound His prais - es high - er still,

1. How can I love thee as I ought?
2. To love thee with, my dear - est King;
3. And come ye an - gels to our aid;

1. And how re - vere this won - d'rous gift,
2. O with what bursts of fer - vent praise,
3. 'Tis God, 'tis God, the ver - y God,

1. So far sur - pas - sing hope or thought.
2. Thy good - ness, Je - sus, would I sing!
3. Whose pow'r both man and an - gels made.

Refrain:

Sweet Sac - ra - ment, we thee a - dore.

O make us love thee more and more!

O make us love thee more and more!

323. Jesus, Savior, Wondrous Mild

Text: Benjamin Schmolck, 1672-1737
Tr. Herman Brueckner, 1866-1942

Tune: Nuremburg, 78. 78. 88.
Johann R. Ahle, 1625-1673

1. Je – sus, Sav – ior, won – drous mild, On thy ten – der
2. Nor should we thy war – ning scorn, That by wa – ter
3. So we has – ten, Lord, to thee, In our arms this
4. Now up – on thy heart we lay That which from the

1. grace re – ly – ing, We pre – sent this in – fant child,
2. and the Spir – it Man must needs be new – ly born
3. in – fant bear – ing; Pledged to thee O let it be,
4. heart pro – ceed – ed; Hear our sigh – ings, Lord, we pray,

1. With thy plain be – hest com – ply – ing: Chil – dren shall to
2. If his soul would fain in – her – it, As thy king–dom's
3. All thy ten – der mer – cies shar – ing; Own it as thy
4. Let our deep de – sires be heed – ed; Write the name that

1. me be giv – en; Theirs the king – dom is of heav – en.
2. sa – cred treas – ure; Grace and peace in full – est meas – ure.
3. child for – ev – er; Naught from thee its soul shall sev – er.
4. we have giv – en In the book of life in heav – en.

324. Jesus, the Very Thought of Thee

Text: *Jesu Dulcis Memoria*, St. Bernard of Clairvaux, 1090-1153   Tune: Jesu Dulcis, L. M.
Tr. Edward Caswall, 1814-1878, alt.   Chant, Mode I

1. Je – sus, the ve – ry thought of thee
2. No voice can sing, no heart can frame,
3. O Hope of ev – 'ry con – trite heart,
4. But what to those who find? Ah! this
5. Je – sus, our on – ly Joy be thou,

1. With sweet – ness fills the-en – ti – re breast;
2. Nor can the frail me – mo – ry find
3. O Joy of all the poor and meek,
4. Nor tongue nor pen can tru – ly show;
5. As thou our Prize wilt ev – er be:

1. But sweet – er far thy Face to see,
2. A sweet – er sound than Jes – us' name,
3. To those who ask how kind thou art,
4. The love of Jes – us, what it is
5. In thee be all our glo – ry now,

1. And in thy pre – sence take my rest.
2. The Sa – vior of all hu – man – kind.
3. How good to those who thee they seek!
4. None oth – er than his loved ones know.
5. And through – out all e – ter – ni – ty.

After the Last verse:

A – – men.

325. Jesus Took the Babes and Blessed Them

Text: Matthias Loy, 1828-1915

Tune: Regent Square, 87. 87. 87.
Henry Smart, 1813-1879

1. Je – sus took the babes and blessed them,
2. Je – sus calls them still with kind – ness
3. Je – sus, we would not for – bid them,

1. Brought to him in days of old;
2. Pass – ing ev – 'ry mor – tal thought;
3. We would have them brought to thee;

1. Fond – ly in his arms ca – ressed them,
2. Bids them come, though hu – man blind – ness
3. Thou of all their guilt dost rid them,

1. Bade them wel – come in his fold;
2. Still would chide when they are brought;
3. From the curse dost set them free;

1. Warm – ly wel – comed, warm – ly wel – comed,
2. Takes and bless – es, takes and bless – es,
3. Thine dost make them, thine dost make them,

1. When dis – ci – ples hearts were cold.
2. Whom he hath so dear – ly bought.
3. Thine let them for – ev – er be. A – men.

326. Jesus, What a Friend for Sinners

Text: John Wilbur Chapman, 1859-1918

Tune: Hyfrydol, 87. 87. D
Rowland H. Prichard, 1811-1887

1. Je – sus! what a Friend for sin – ners!
2. Je – sus! what a Strength in weak – ness!
3. Je – sus! I do now a – dore him,

1. Je – sus! Lov – er of my soul;
2. Let me hide my – self in him.
3. More than all in him I find.

1. Friends may fail me, foes as – sail me,
2. Tempt – ed, tried, and some – times fail – ing,
3. He hath grant – ed me for – give – ness,

1. He, my Sav – ior, makes me whole.
2. He, my Strength, my vic – t'ry wins.
3. I am his, and he is mine.

Refrain:

Hal–le–lu – jah! What a Sav – ior! Hal – le –lu – jah! What a Friend!

Sav – ing, help – ing, keep– ing, lov – ing, He is with me to the end.

327. Joy to the World

Text: Isaac Watts, 1674-1748

Tune: Antioch, C. M.
George Fredrick Handel, 1685-1759, Arr. By Lowell Mason, 1792-1872

1. Joy to the world! The Lord is come:
2. Joy to the world! The Sav – ior reigns:
3. No more let sins and sor – rows grow,
4. He rules the world, with truth and grace,

1. Let earth re – ceive her King;
2. Let all their songs em – ploy;
3. Nor thorns in – fest the ground;
4. And makes the na – tions prove,

1. Let ev – 'ry heart, pre – pare him room,
2. While fields and floods, rocks, hills, and plains,
3. He comes to make his bles – sings flow
4. The glo – ries of his right – eous – ness,

1. And heav'n and na – ture sing, And heav'n and na –
2. Re – peat the sound – ing joy, Re – peat the sound–
3. Far as the curse is found, Far as the curse
4. And won – ders of his love, And won – ders of

1. ture sing, And heaven, and heaven and na – ture sing.
2. ing joy, Re – peat, re – peat the sound – ing joy.
3. is found, Far as, far as the curse is found.
4. his love, And won – ders, won – ders of his love.

328. Joyful, Joyful We Adore Thee

Text: Henry van Dyke, 1852-1933

Tune: Hymn to Joy, 87. 87. D.
Adapted from Ludwig van Beethoven, 1770-1827

1. Joy – ful, joy – ful, we a – dore thee,
2. All thy works with joy sur – round thee,
3. Thou art giv – ing and for – giv – ing,
4. Mor – tals join the might – y cho – rus,

1. God of glo – ry, God of love; Hearts un – fold like
2. Earth and heav'n re – flect thy rays, Stars and an – gels
3. Ev – er bless – ing, ev – er blest, Well – spring of the
4. Which the morn – ing stars be – gan; Fa – ther love is

1. flowers be – fore thee, Open – ing to the sun a – bove.
2. sing a – round thee, Cen – ter of un – bro – ken praise;
3. joy of liv – ing, O – cean depth of hap – py rest!
4. reign – ing o'er us, Broth – er love binds man to man.

1. Melt the clouds of sin and sad – ness;
2. Field and for – est, vale and moun – tain,
3. Thou our Fa – ther, Christ our broth – er,
4. Ev – er sing – ing, march we on – ward,

1. Drive the dark of doubt a – way; Giv – er of im –
2. Flow – ery mead – ow, flash – ing sea, Chant – ing bird and
3. All who live in love are thine; Teach us how to
4. Vic – tors in the midst of strife; Joy – ful mu – sic

1. mor – tal glad – ness, Fill us with the light of day!
2. flow – ing foun – tain, Call us to re – joice in thee.
3. love each oth – er, Lift us to the joy di – vine.
4. leads us sun – ward, In the tri – umph song of life.

329. Lauda Sion Salvatorem

Text: St. Thomas Aquinas, 1227-1274   Tune: Psalm Tone VII-d
ENGLISH: "Zion, Praise Thy Savior"   Music Binder, Holy Family Church, Dayton, OH, 1995

1.	Lau –	da	Sion Salvató –	rem,	Lauda ducem
2.			Quantum potes, tantum au –	de:	Quia major
3.	Lau –	dis	thema speciá –	lis,	Panis vivus
4.			Quem in sacrae mensa ce –	nae,	Turbae fratrum
5.	Sit	laus	plena, sit sonó –	ra,	Sit jucúnda,
6.			Dies enim solemnis ági –	tur,	In qua mensae
7.	In	hac	mensa novi re –	gis,	Novum pascha
8.			Vetustátem nóvi –	tas,	Umbram
9.	Quod	in	coena Christi ges –	sit,	Faciendum
10.			Docti sacris institú –	tis,	Panem, vinum
11.	Dog –	ma	datur christiá –	nis,	Quod in
12.			Quod non capis, quod non vi –	des,	Animósa
13.	Sub	di –	vérsis specie –	bus,	Signis
14.			Caro cibus, sanguis po –	tus:	Manet tamen,
15.	A	su –	ménte non conclú –	sus,	Non contráctus
16.			Sumit unus, sumunt mil –	le;	Quantum isti,
17.	Su –	munt	boni sumunt ma –	li:	Sorte tamen
18.			Mors est malis, vita bo –	nis:	Vide paris
19.	Frac –	to	demum		
20.			Tantum esse		
21a.	Nul –	la	rei fit		
21b.			Qua nec status, ...		
22a.	**Ec –**	**ce**	**panis . . . .**		
22b.			**Vere panis . . . .**		
23a.	**In**	**fi –**	**gúris . . . .**		
23b.			**Agnus paschae . . . .**		
24a.	**Bo –**	**ne**	**Pastor, ...**		
24b.			**Tu nos pasce, nos tué –**	**re,**	**Tu nos bona**
25a.	**Tu**	**qui**	**cuncta . . . .**		
25b.			**Tuos ibi commensá –**	**les,**	**Coherédes**

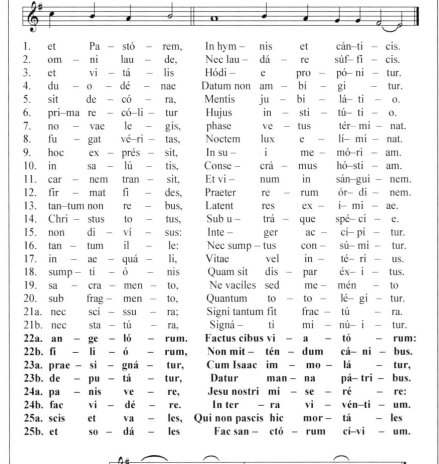

1.	et	Pa – stó – rem,	In hym –	nis	et	cán–ti – cis.
2.	om – ni	lau – de,	Nec lau –	dá –	re	súf– fi – cis.
3.	et	vi – tá – lis	Hódi –	e	pro –	pó–ni – tur.
4.	du – o – dé – nae	Datum non	am –	bí –	gi –	tur.
5.	sit	de – có – ra,	Mentis	ju –	bi –	lá–ti – o.
6.	pri–ma re – có–li – tur	Hujus	in –	sti –	tú–ti – o.
7.	no – vae	le – gis,	phase	ve –	tus	tér– mi – nat.
8.	fu – gat	vé–ri – tas,	Noctem	lux	e –	lí– mi – nat.
9.	hoc	ex – prés – sit,	In su –	i	me –	mó–ri – am.
10.	in	sa – lú – tis,	Conse –	crá –	mus	hó–sti – am.
11.	car – nem tran – sit,	Et vi –	num	in	sán–gui – nem.
12.	fir – mat	fi – des,	Praeter	re –	rum	ór– di – nem.
13.	tan–tum non	re – bus,	Latent	res	ex –	í – mi – ae.
14.	Chri – stus	to – tus,	Sub u –	trá –	que	spé–ci – e.
15.	non	di – ví – sus:	Inte –	ger	ac –	cí– pi – tur.
16.	tan – tum	il – le:	Nec sump – tus	con –	sú– mi – tur.
17.	in – ae – quá – li,	Vitae	vel	in –	té– ri – us.
18.	sump – ti – ó – nis	Quam sit	dis –	par	éx– i – tus.
19.	sa – cra – men – to,	Ne vacíles sed	me –	mén –	to
20.	sub	frag – men – to,	Quantum	to –	to –	lé– gi – tur.
21a.	nec scí – ssu – ra;	Signi tantum fit	frac –	tú –	ra.
21b.	nec sta – tú – ra,	Signá –	ti	mi –	nú– i – tur.
22a.	**an – ge – ló – rum.**	**Factus cibus vi – a – tó – rum:**
22b.	**fi – li – ó – rum,**	**Non mit – tén – dum cá– ni – bus.**
23a.	**prae – si – gná – tur,**	**Cum Isaac im – mo – lá – tur,**
23b.	**de – pu – tá – tur,**	**Datur man – na pá– tri – bus.**
24a.	**pa – nis ve – re,**	**Jesu nostri mi – se – ré – re:**
24b.	**fac vi – dé – re.**	**In ter – ra vi – vén–ti – um.**
25a.	**scis et va – les,**	**Qui non pascis hic mor – tá – les**
25b.	**et so – dá – les**	**Fac san – ctó – rum cí–vi – um.**

After Last verse:

A – men. Al – le – lú – ia.

* The verses in bold (22a-25b) are also known as the "Ecce Panis Angelorum," and may be sung as a separate hymn.

330. Let All Mortal Flesh Keep Silence

Text: Σιγησάτο παρα σὰρξ βροτεία, Liturgy of St. James, 5th Century
Para. Gerard Moultrie, 1829-1885

Tune: Picardy, 87. 87. 87.
Traditional French Melody

1. Let all mor – tal flesh keep si – lence,
2. King of kings, yet born of Ma – ry,
3. Rank on rank the host of hea – ven
4. At his feet the six wing ser – aph;

1. and with fear and trem – bling stand;
2. as of old on earth he stood,
3. spreads its van – guard on the way,
4. cher – u – bim with sleep – less eye,

1. Pon – der noth – ing earth – ly mind – ed,
2. Lord of lords in hu – man ves – ture,
3. As the Light of Light de – scend – eth
4. Veil their fac – es to the Pres – ence,

1. for with bless – ing in his hand
2. in the Bod – y and the Blood
3. from the realms of end – less day,
4. as with cease – less voice they cry,

1. Christ our God to earth de – scend – eth,
2. He will give to all the faith – ful
3. That the pow'rs of hell may van – ish
4. "Al – le – lu – ia, Al – le – lu – ia,

1. our full hom – age to de – mand.
2. his own self for heav'n – ly food.
3. as the dark – ness clears a – way.
4. Al – le – lu – ia, Lord most high!"

331. Let Me Be Thine Forever

Text: *Lass mich dein*, Nicolaus Selnecker, 1532-1592
Tr. Matthias Loy, 1828-1915

Tune: Commit Thy Way, 76. 76. D.
German Melody

1. Let me be thine for – ev – er, My gra – cious God and Lord;
2. Lord Je – sus, boun – teous Giv – er Of light and life di – vine,
3. O Ho – ly Ghost, who pour– est Sweet peace in – to my heart,

1. May I for – sake thee nev – er, Nor wan – der from thy Word:
2. Thou didst my soul de – liv – er; To thee I all re – sign.
3. And all my soul re – stor – est, Thy com – fort, ne'er de – part.

1. Pre – serve me from the maz – es Of er – ror and dis – trust,
2. Thou hast in mer – cy bought me With blood and bit – ter pain;
3. Let me, his name con – fess – ing, Whom I by faith have known,

1. And I shall sing thy prais – es For – ev – er with the just.
2. Let me, since thou hast sought me, E – ter – nal life ob – tain.
3. Re – ceive thy con – stant bless – ing And be in death thine own.

332. Lift up Your Heads, Ye Mighty Gates

Text: *Macht Hoch die Tür*, Georg Weissel, 1590-1635
Tr. Catherine Winkworth, 1827-1878

Tune: Truro, L. M.
Psalmodia Evangelica, 1789

1. Lift up your heads, ye might – y gates; Be –
2. O blest the land, the cit – y blest, Where
3. Fling wide the por – tals of your heart; Make
4. So come, my Sov – 'reign; en – ter in! Let

1. hold the King of glo – ry waits!
2. Christ the rul – er is con – fest!
3. it a tem – ple, set a – part
4. new and no – bler life be – gin;

1. The King of kings is draw – ing near; The
2. O hap – py hearts and hap – py homes, To
3. From earth – ly use for heav'n's em – ploy, A –
4. Thy Ho – ly Spir – it guide us on, Un –

1. Sa – vior of the world is here.
2. whom this King of tri – umph comes!
3. dorned with prayer and love and joy.
4. til the glo – rious crown be won.

333. Look Ye Saints, the Sight is Glorious

Text: Thomas Kelly, 1769-1855

Tune: Bryn Calfaria, 87.87.444.77.
William Owen, 1814-1893

1. Look, ye saints, the sight is glo – rious, See the Man
2. Crown the Sav – ior, an – gels, crown him Rich the tro –
3. Sin – ners in de – ri – sion crowned him, Mock–ing thus
4. Hark! Those bursts of ac – cla – ma – tion! Hark! Those loud

1. of Sor – rows now; From the fight re – turned vic – to – rious,
2. phies Je – sus brings; In the seat of pow'r en – throne him,
3. the Sav – ior's claim; Saints and an – gels crowd a – round him,
4. tri – um – phant chords! Je – sus takes the high – est sta – tion;

1. Ev – 'ry knee to him shall bow: Crown him! Crown him!
2. While the vault of heav – en rings: Crown him! Crown him!
3. Own his ti – tle, praise his name: Crown him! Crown him!
4. O what joy the sight af – fords! Crown him! Crown him!

1-4. Crown him! Crown him! Crown him! Crown him!

1. Crowns be – come the vic – tor's brow.
2. Crown the Sav – ior King of kings.
3. Spread a – broad the Vic – tor's fame!
4. King of kings, and Lord of lords.

1. Crowns be – come the vic – tor's brow.
2. Crown the Sav – ior King of kings.
3. Spread a – broad the Vic – tor's fame!
4. King of kings, and Lord of lords.

334. Lord, Dismiss Us with Your Blessing

Text: St. 1-2, John Fawcett, 1740-1817
St. 3, Godfrey Thring, 1823-1903, alt.

Tune: Sicilian Mariners, 87. 87. 87.
Derived from "O Sanctissima," Sicilian Melody

1. Lord, dis – miss us with your bless – ing,
2. Thanks we give and ad – o – ra – tion
3. Sav – ior, when your love shall call us

1. Fill our hearts with joy and peace;
2. For your Gos – pel's joy – ful sound.
3. From our strug – gling pil – grim way,

1. Let us each, your love pos – sess – ing,
2. May the fruits of your sal – va – tion
3. Let no fear of death ap – pall us,

1. Tri – umph in re – deem – ing grace.
2. In our hearts and lives a – bound.
3. Glad your sum – mons to o – bey.

1. Oh, re – fresh us, oh, re – fresh us,
2. Ev – er faith – ful, ev – er faith – ful
3. May we ev – er, may we ev – er

1. Trav – 'ling through this wil – der – ness.
2. To your truth may we be found.
3. Reign with you in end – less day.

335. Lord, Who Throughout These 40 Days

Text: Claudia F. Hernaman, 1838-1898

Tune: St. Flavian, C. M.
John Day's Psalter, 1562

1. Lord, who through-out these for - ty days,
2. As thou with Sa – tan didst con – tend,
3. As thou didst hun – ger bear and thirst,
4. A – bide with us, that so, this life

1. for us didst fast and pray,
2. And didst the vic – t'ry win,
3. So teach us, gra – cious Lord,
4. Of suf – f'ring o – ver – past,

1. Teach us with thee to mourn our sins,
2. O give us strength in thee to fight,
3. To die to self, and chief – ly live
4. An East – er of un – end – ing joy

1. And close by thee to stay.
2. In thee to con – quer sin.
3. By thy most ho – ly word.
4. We may at – tain at last!

336. Love Consecrates the Humblest Act

Text: Silas Bettes McManus, 1845-1917

Tune: Twenty-Fourth, C. M.
Attr. Lucius Chapin, 1760-1842

1. Love con — se — crates the hum — blest act,
2. When in the shad — ow of the cross,
3. Love serves and will — ing stoops to serve;

1. And ha — loes mer — cy's deeds;
2. Christ knelt and washed the feet,
3. What Christ in love so true,

1. It sheds a ben — e — dic — tion sweet,
2. Of his dis — ci — ples, he gave us,
3. Has free — ly done for one and all,

1. And hal — lows hu — man needs.
2. A sign of love com — plete.
3. Let us now glad — ly do!

337. Love Divine, All Loves Excelling

Text: Charles Wesley, 1707-1788

Tune: Hyfrydol, 87. 87. D.
Rowland H. Prichard, 1811-1887

1. Love di – vine, all loves ex – cel – ling,
2. Come, al – might – y, to de – liv – er,
3. Fin – ish then thy new cre – a – tion,

1. Joy of heav'n to earth come down!
2. Let us all thy life re – ceive;
3. Pure and spot – less let us be;

1. Fix in us thy hum – ble dwel – ling,
2. Sud–den – ly re – turn and nev – er,
3. Let us see thy great sal – va – tion,

1. All thy faith – ful mer – cies crown.
2. Nev – er more thy tem – ples leave.
3. Per – fect – ly re – stored in thee!

1. Je – sus, thou art all com – pas – sion,
2. Thee we would be al – ways bless – ing,
3. Changed from glo – ry in – to glo – ry,

1. Pure un – bound – ed love thou art;
2. Serve thee as thy hosts a – bove,
3. Till in heaven we take our place,

1. Vis – it us with thy sal – va – tion,
2. Pray, and praise thee with – out ceas – ing,
3. Till we cast our crowns be – fore thee,

1. En – ter ev – ery trem – bling heart.
2. Glo – ry in thy prec – ious love.
3. Lost in won – der, love, and praise.

338. Low in the Grave He Lay

Text: Robert Lowry, 1826-1899

Tune: Christ Arose, 6. 5. 6. 4. with Refrain
Robert Lowry, 1826-1899

1. Low in the grave he lay, Je – sus my Sav – ior!
2. Vain – ly they watch his bed, Je – sus my Sav – ior!
3. Death can – not keep his prey, Je – sus my Sav – ior!

1. Wait – ing the com – ing day, Je – sus my Lord!
2. Vain – ly they seal the dead, Je – sus my Lord!
3. He tore the bars a – way, Je – sus my Lord!

Refrain

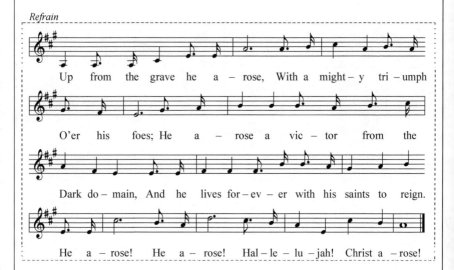

Up from the grave he a – rose, With a might – y tri – umph

O'er his foes; He a – rose a vic – tor from the

Dark do – main, And he lives for – ev – er with his saints to reign.

He a – rose! He a – rose! Hal – le – lu – jah! Christ a – rose!

339. Magnificat Anima Mea Dominum

Text: Blessed Virgin Mary, Luke 1:46-55
ENGLISH: "My Soul Magnifies the Lord"

Tune: Chant, Psalm Tone VIII

Ant. Ma - gní - fi - cat * á - ni - ma me - a Dó - mi - num.

1. Et   ex - sultávit spíritus   me - us   *
2. Qui - a   respéxit humilitátem ancíllae   su - ae;   *
3. Qui - a   fecit mihi magna qui   potens est,   *
4. Et   mi - sericórdia ejus a progénie in pro - géni - es,   *
5. Fe - cit   poténtiam in bráchio   su - o,   *
6. De - pó - suit poténtes de   se - de,   *
7. E - su - riéntes implévit   bo - nis,   *
8. Sus - cé - pit Israel púerum   su - um,   *
9. Si - cut   locútus est ad patres   no - stros: *
10. Gló - ri - a Patri et   Fíli - o,   *
11. Si - cut   erat in princípio, et nunc, et   sem - per,   *

1. in Deo salu   - tá - ri me - o.
2. ecce enim beátam me dicent omnes gene - ra - ti - ó - nes.
3. et sanctum   no - men e - jus.
4. timén   - ti - bus e - um.
5. dispérsit supérbos mente   cor - dis su - i.
6. et exal -   távit hú - mi - les.
7. et dívites dimí   - sit in - á - nes.
8. recordátus misericór   - di - ae su - ae.
9. Abraham et sémini ejus   in saé - cu - la.
10. et Spirí   - tu - i San - cto.
11. et in sáecula saecu   - ló - rum. A - men.

After the Last Stanza (Gloria Patri/Sicut Erat):

Ant. Ma - gní - fi - cat * á - ni - ma me - a Dó - mi - num.

340. Man of Sorrows! What a Name

Text: Philip Paul Bliss, 1838-1876
Lenten acclamation is alt.

Tune: Bliss, 77. 78.
Philip Paul Bliss, 1838-1876

1. Man of Sor – rows! what a   name   For the Son of
2. Bear–ing shame and scoff– ing rude,   In my place con –
3. Guil– ty, vile, and help – less we;   Spot– less Lamb of
4. Lift – ed up was he to die; "It is fin – ished!"
5. When he comes, our glo – rious King, All his ran – somed

1. God who came Ru – ined sin – ners to   re – claim.
2. demned he stood; Sealed my par – don with His blood.
3. God was he: "Full a – tone– ment!" can it be?
4. was his cry; Now in Heav'n ex – al – ted high.
5. home to bring, Then a – new His song we'll sing:

Outside Lent and Passiontide:
1-5. Hal – le – lu – jah! What a Sav – ior!

During Lent and Passiontide:
1-5. What a Sav– ior! What a Sav – ior!

341. Many and Great, O God, Are Thy Things

Text: *Wakantanka Taku Nitawa*, Joseph Renville, 1779-1846   Tune: Lac Qui Parle, 96. 98. 96.
Para. St 1 & 4, Philip Frazier, 1892-1964; St 2-3, Agostino Taumaturgo   Native American Melody

1. Man – y   and   great,   O   God,   are   thy   things,
2. By   thy   great   will,   both   ho – ly   and   strong,
3. Ad – am   thou   made,   the   first   of   our   race,
4. Grant   un – to   us   com – mu – nion   with   thee,

1. Mak – er   of   earth   and   sky;
2. All   the   world   hast   thou   made;
3. Him   one   com – mand   thou   gave;
4. Thou   star   a – bid – ing   One;

1. Thy   hands   have   set   the   heav – ens   with   stars;
2. All   that   we   have,   and   all   that   we   wear,
3. That   com – mand   our   first   fa – ther   trans – gressed,
4. Come   un – to   us   and   dwell   with   us;

1. Thy   fin – gers   spread   the   moun – tains   and   plains.
2. Thou,   too,   hast   made   our   food   and   drink,
3. I   strug – gle   now,   be – cause   of   his   sin,
4. With   thee   are   found   the   gifts   of   life,

1. Lo,   at   thy   Word   the   wa – ters   were   formed;
2. Thee,   God,   we   praise,   be – cause   thou   a – lone,
3. Then   Je – sus   came,   and   showed   me   his   grace,
4. Bless   us   with   life   that   has   no   end,

1. Deep   seas   o – bey   thy   voice.
2. Hast   brought   us   to   each   day.
3. He   blott – ed   out   my   sins.
4. E – ter – nal   life   with   thee.

367

342. May the Grace of Christ

Text: John Newton, 1725-1807

Tune: Stuttgart, 87. 87.
C. F. Witt, 1660-1716

1. May the grace of Christ our Sa – vior
2. So they may a – bide in un – ion
3. Now with all the saints in hea – ven

1. And the Fa – ther's bound – less love,
2. With each oth – er and the Lord,
3. Thanks and prais – es do we sing;

1. With the Ho – ly Spir – it's fa – vor
2. And pos – sess, in sweet com – mun – ion,
3. Fa – ther, Son, and Ho – ly Spir – it,

1. Rest up – on them from a – bove.
2. Joys which earth can – not af – ford.
3. Three in One, our Tri – une King. A – men.

343. Must Jesus Bear the Cross Alone

Text: Thomas Shepherd, 1665-1739

Tune: Maitland, C. M.
George N. Allen, 1812-1877

1. Must Je – sus bear the cross a – lone,
2. How hap – py are the saints a – bove,
3. The con – se – cra – ted cross I'll bear

1. And all the world go free?
2. Who once went sor – rowing here!
3. Till death shall set me free;

1. No, there's a cross for ev – 'ry one,
2. But now they taste un – min – gled love
3. And then go home my crown to wear,

1. And there's a cross for me.
2. And joy with – out a tear.
3. For there's a crown for me. A – men.

344. My Country, 'Tis of Thee

Text: Samuel F. Smith, 1805-1895

Tune: America, 664. 6664.
Thesaurus Musicus, 1740

1. My coun – try, 'tis of thee, Sweet land of lib – er – ty,
2. My na – tive coun – try, thee, Land of the no – ble free,
3. Let mu – sic swell the breeze, And ring from all the trees
4. Our fa – thers' God, to thee, Au – thor of lib – er – ty,

1. Of thee I sing; Land where my fa – thers died,
2. Thy name I love; I love thy rocks and rills,
3. Sweet free – dom's song; Let mor – tal tongues a – wake;
4. To thee we sing; Long may our land be bright

1. Land of the pil – grims' pride, From ev – 'ry
2. Thy woods and tem – pled hills; My heart with
3. Let all that breathe par – take; Let rocks their
4. With free – dom's ho – ly light. Pro – tect us

1. moun – tain – side Let free – dom ring.
2. rap – ture thrills Like that a – bove.
3. si – lence break, The sound pro – long.
4. by thy might, Great God, our King.

345. My Faith Looks Up to Thee

Text: Ray Palmer, 1808-1887

Tune: Olivet 664. 6664.
Lowell Mason, 1792-1872

1. My faith looks up to thee, Thou Lamb of Cal – va – ry,
2. May thy rich grace im – part, Strength to my faint – ing heart,
3. While life's dark maze I tread, And grief's a – round me spread,
4. When ends life's si – lent dream, When death's cold, sul – len stream

1. Sav – ior di – vine! Now hear me while I pray, Take all my
2. My zeal in – spire; As thou hast died for me, O may my
3. Be thou my guide; Bid dark – ness turn to day, Wipe sor – row's
4. Shall o'er me roll; Blest Sav – ior, then, in love, Fear and dis –

1. guilt a – way, O let me from this day, Be whol – ly thine!
2. love to thee; Pure, warm and change– less be, A liv – ing fire.
3. tears a – way, Nor let me ev – er stray, From thee a – side.
4. trust re – move; O bear me safe a – bove, A ran – somed soul!

346. My Lord and My God! I Have Trusted in Thee

Text: *O Domine Deus*, Mary Queen of Scots, 1542-1587
Tr. Agostino Taumaturgo, b. 1974

Tune: German Melody, P.M.
German, c. 1669

My Lord and my God! I have trus – ted in thee; O my dear–est

Je – sus! De – liv – er now me: In harsh – est of chains and in

mis –'ra – ble pains, I have long –ed for thee; Weak–'ning and

weep – ing, and on bend–ed knee, I a – dore and im – plore thee, de –

liv – er thou me! My Lord and my God! I have trus– ted in thee; O

My dear – est Je – sus! De – liv – er now me. A – men.

347. My Soul Magnifies the Lord

Text: *Magnificat*, Blessed Virgin Mary, Luke 1:46-55
Tr. *Confraternity Bible*, 1957

Tune: Chant, Psalm Tone VIII

Ant. My soul mag - ni - fies the Lord.

```
1. And   my     spirit re -                              - joi  - ces  *
2. Be  - cause  he has regarded the lowliness of his     hand - maid; *
3. Be  - cause  he who is mighty has done great things   for    me,   *
4. And  his     mercy is from generation to gener - -    a    - tion  *
5. He   has     shown might with                         his    arm,  *
6. He   has     put down the mighty from                 their  thrones,*
7. He   has     filled the hungry with                   good   things, *
8. He   has     given help to Israel, his                ser  - vant,  *
9. Ev - en      as he spoke to our                       fa   - thers  *
10. Glo -ry     be to the Father and to                  the    Son,   *
11. As  it      was in the beginning, is now, and ever   shall  be,    *
```

```
1. in                              God   my    Sa  - vior.
2. for, behold, from henceforth all
                 generations shall call  me    bles - sed.
3. and ho -                        ly    is    his    name.
4. on                              those who   fear   him.
5. he has scattered the proud in the con  - ceit  of    their heart.
6. and has exal -                  - ted   the   low - ly.
7. and the rich he has sent         a    - way  em  - pty.
8. mindful                          of    his   mer - cy.
9. to Abraham and to his posterit - - y    for - ev - er.
10. and to the                      Ho  - ly   Spi - rit.
11. world with -                    - out  end. A  - men.
```

After the Last Stanza (Glory be to the Father/As it was in the beginning):

Ant. My soul mag - ni - fies the Lord.

348. Now Let The Vault of Heaven Resound

Text: Paul Zeller Strodach, 1876-1947

Tune: Lasst Uns Erfreuen, 88. 88. 88. with alleluias
Geistliche Kirchengesange, Cologne, 1623

1. Now let the vault of Heav'n re – sound In praise of love
2. E – ter – nal is the gift He brings, Where–fore our heart
3. O fill us, Lord, with daunt – less love; Set heart and will
4. A – dor – ing prais–es now we bring And with the heav'n–

1. that doth a – bound, "Christ hath tri –umphed, Al – le – lu – ia!"
2. with rap – ture sings, "Christ hath tri –umphed, Al – le – lu – ia!"
3. on things a – bove That we con – quer Thro' thy tri – umph,
4. ly bles – sed sing, "Christ hath tri –umphed, Al – le – lu – ia!"

1. Sing, choirs of an – gels, loud and clear, Re – peat their song
2. Now doth He come and give us life, Now doth His pres –
3. Grant grace suf – fi – cient for life's day That by our life
4. Be to the Fa – ther, and our Lord, To Spir – it blest,

1. of glo – ry here, "Christ hath tri – umphed, Christ hath tri –umphed!"
2. ence still all strife Through his tri – umph; Je – sus reign – eth!
3. we ev – er say, "Christ hath tri – umphed, And he liv – eth!"
4. most ho – ly God, Thine the glo – ry, Nev–er end – ing!

1-4. Al – le – lu – ia! Al – le – lu – ia! Al – le – lu – ia!

349. Now Thank We All Our God

Text: *Nun Danket Alle Gott*, Martin Rinkart, 1586-1649   Tune: Nun Danket, 67. 67. 66. 66.
Tr. Catherine Winkworth, 1827-1878   Johann Crüger, 1598-1662

1. Now   thank   we   all   our   God   With
2. O   may   this   gra – cious   God   Through
3. All   praise   and   thanks   to   God   The

1. heart   and   hands   and   voic – es,   Who won – drous things hath
2. all   our   life   be   near us,   With ev – er   joy – ful
3. Fa – ther   now   be   giv – en,   The Son, and   Spir – it

1. done,   In   whom   his   world   re – joic – es;
2. hearts   And   bless – ed   peace   to   cheer   us;
3. blest,   Who   reigns   in   high – est   heav – en;

1. Who,   from   our   moth – ers'   arms,   Hath
2. Pre – serve   us   in   his   grace,   And
3. E – ter – nal,   Tri – une   God,   Whom

1. blessed   us   on   our   way   With   count– less   gifts   of
2. guide   us   in   dis – tress,   And   free   us   from   all
3. earth   and heav'n a – dore;   For   thus   it   was,   is

1. love,   And   still   is   ours   to – day.
2. sin,   Till   heav – en   we   pos – sess.
3. now,   And   shall   be   ev – er – more.   A – men.

350. O Bread of Angels

Text: *Panis Angelicus*, St. Thomas Aquinas, 1227-1274   Tune: Sacris Solemniis, 12. 12. 12. 8.
Tr. Claude G. Arnold, date unknown   Louis Lambilotte, 1796-1855

1. O Bread of an – gels made Bread for us be – low!
2. O God– head Three in One, we one to – ge – ther pray

1. All gifts of an – cient times this Bread will now be – stow.
2. That as we come to you, you too will come and stay,

1. O won–der un – sur– passed! Poor, hum–ble, peo – ple all
2. And by your ho – ly ways lead us un – to the day

1. Eat the Flesh of the Lord, their God.
2. Where you dwell in e – ter – nal light.

351. O Christ, Thou Art Our Joy Alone

Text: *Tu Christe Nostrum*, Anon., 5th Century   Tune: Deus Tuorum Militum (Grenoble), L. M.
Tr. John Mason Neale, 1818-1866   *Grenoble Antiphoner*, 1753

1. O Christ, thou art our joy a – lone,
2. We sup – pliants, there – fore, ask of Thee
3. Be Thou our joy, and Thou our guard,

1. Ex – al – ted on thy glo – rious throne:
2. To par – don our in – i – qui – ty:
3. As Thou wilt be our great re – ward:

1. To thee all pow'r in earth and heav'n
2. And lift up ev – 'ry Chris – tian heart
3. So shall the light that springs from thee

1. As vic – tor o'er the world is giv'n.
2. By grace to find thee where thou art.
3. Be ours through all e – ter – ni – ty.

352. O Come, All Ye Faithful

Text: *Adeste Fideles*, John Francis Wade, c. 1711-1786
Tr. Frederick Oakeley, 1802-1880 and others

Tune: Adeste Fideles – Irr. with Refrain
John Francis Wade, c. 1711-1786

1. Oh, come, all ye faith–ful, Joy–ful and tri – um – phant!
2. The high–est, most ho – ly, Light of Light e – ter – nal,
3. Sing, choirs of an – gels, Sing in ex – ul – ta – tion,
4. Yea, Lord, we greet thee, Born this hap – py morn – ing;

1. Oh, Come ye, oh, come . ye to Beth – le – hem;
2. Born of a vir – gin, a mor – tal he comes;
3. Sing, all ye cit – i – zens of hea – ven a – bove!
4. Je – sus, to thee... be...... glo – ry giv'n!

1. Come and be – hold him, Born the king of an – gels:
2. Son of the Fa – ther, Now in flesh ap – pear – ing!
3. Glo – ry to God . . In . . . the . . high – est:
4. Word of the Fa – ther, Now in flesh ap – pear – ing:

Refrain:

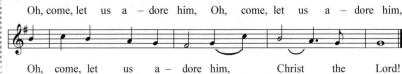

Oh, come, let us a – dore him, Oh, come, let us a – dore him,

Oh, come, let us a – dore him, Christ the Lord!

353. O Come, O Come, Emmanuel

Text: *Veni Veni Emmanuel*, Chant, 9th Century
Tr. Thomas Helmore, 1811-1890

Tune: Veni, Veni, Emmanuel L. M.
Chant, Mode I

1. O come, O come, Em – man – nu – el!
2. O come, thou rod of Jes – se's stem,
3. O come, thou Day – spring from on high
4. O come, thou key of Da – vid, come,

1. And ran – som cap – tive Is – ra – el,
2. From ev – 'ry foe de – li – ver them.
3. And cheer us by thy draw – ing nigh;
4. And o – pen wide our heav'n – ly home;

1. That mourns in lone – ly ex – ile here;
2. That trust thy might – y pow'r to save,
3. Dis – perse the gloom – y clouds of night,
4. Make safe the way that leads on high,

1. Un – til the Son of God ap – pear.
2. And give them vic – t'ry o'er the grave.
3. And death's dark shad – ow put to flight.
4. That we no more have cause to sigh.

Refrain:

Re – joice! Re – joice! Em – man – nu – el!

Shall come to thee, O Is – ra – el!

354. O Domine Deus, Speravi in Te

Text: Mary Queen of Scots, 1542-1587
ENGLISH: "My Lord and My God"

Tune: German Melody, P.M.
German, c. 1669

O Dó – mi – ne De – us! Spe – rá – vi in te; O ca – re mi

Je – su! Nunc lí – be – ra me: In du – ra ca – té – na, In

mí – se – ra pue – na, De – sí – de – ro te; Lan – guén – do, ge –

mén – do, et ge – nu – fle – ctén – do, A – dó – ro, im – pló – ro, Ut

lí – be – res me! O Dó – mi – ne De – us! Spe – rá – vi in te; O

Ca – re mi Je – su! Nunc lí – be – ra me. A – men.

355. O Filii et Filiae

Text: Jean Tisserand, 15th Century
ENGLISH: "Ye Sons and Daughters"

Tune: O Filii et Filiae, 8. 8. 8. with Alleluias
Solesmes, 15th Century

Refrain

Al – le – lu – ia,   al – le – lu – ia,   al – le – lu – ia!

1. O   Fí – li – i   et   Fí – li – ae,
2. Et   Ma – rí – a   Mag – da – lé – ne,
3. In   al – bis se –   dens, án – ge – lus
4. In   hoc   fe – sto   san – ctís – si – mo
5. De   qui – bus nos   hu – mí – li – mas,

1. Rex   cae – lé – stis,   Rex   gló – ri – ae
2. Et   Ja – có – bi   et   Sa – ló – me
3. Prae – dí – xit   mu –   li – é – ri – bus:
4. Sit   laus   et   ju –   bi – lá – ti – o,
5. De – vó – tas   at –   que   dé – bi – tas

1. Mor – te sur – ré – xit hó – di – e,   al – le – lú – ia!
2. Ve – né – runt cor – pus ún – ge – re, al – le – lú – ia!
3. In Ga – li – laé – a est Dó – mi – nus, al – le – lú – ia!
4. Be – ne – di – cá – mus Dó – mi – no,   al – le – lú – ia!
5. De – o   di – cá – mus grá – ti – as, al – le – lú – ia!

356. O, For a Thousand Tongues to Sing

Text: Charles Wesley, 1707-1788

Tune: Azmon, C. M.
Carl G. Gläser, 1784-1829

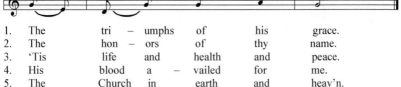

1. O   for   a   thou – sand   tongues to   sing,
2. My   gra – cious   Mas – ter   and   my   God,
3. Je – sus!   The   name   that   charms   our   fears,
4. He   breaks   the   pow'r   of   can – celled   sin,
5. Glo – ry   to   God   and   praise   and   love,

1. My   great   Re – deem – er's   praise,
2. As – sist   me   to   pro – claim,
3. That   bids   our   sor – rows   cease,
4. He   sets   the   pris' – ner   free,
5. Be   ev – er,   ev – er   giv'n,

1. The   glo – ries   of   my   God   and   King,
2. To   spread   through   all   the   earth   a – broad,
3. 'Tis   mu – sic   in   the   sin – ner's   ears,
4. His   blood   can   make   the   foul – est   clean,
5. By   saints   be – low   and   saints   a – bove,

1. The   tri – umphs   of   his   grace.
2. The   hon – ors   of   thy   name.
3. 'Tis   life   and   health   and   peace.
4. His   blood   a – vailed   for   me.
5. The   Church   in   earth   and   heav'n.

357. O God of Earth and Altar

Text: Gilbert Keith Chesterton, 1874-1936

Tune: King's Lynn, 76. 76. D
English Folk Melody, arr. By Ralph Vaughan Williams, 1872-1958

1. O   God   of   earth   and   al – tar,   Bow   down   and
2. From   all   that   ter – ror   teach – es,   From   lies   and
3. Tie   in   a   liv – ing   teth – er,   The   prince   and

1. hear   our   cry,   Our   earth – ly   ru – lers   fal – ter,
2. tongue   and   pen,   From   all   the   eas – y   speech – es
3. priest   and   thrall,   Bind   all   our   lives   to – geth – er,

1. Our   peo – ple   drift   and   die;   The   walls   of   gold
2. That   com – fort   cru – el   men,   From   sale   and   prof –
3. Smite   us   and   save   us   all;   In   ire   and   ex –

1. en – tomb   us,   The   swords   of   scorn   di – vide,
2. a – na – tion   Of   hon – or   and   the   sword,
3. ul – ta – tion   A – flame   with   faith,   and   free,

1. Take   not   thy   thun – der   from   us,
2. From   sleep,   and   from   dam – na – tion,
3. Lift   up   a   liv – ing   na – tion,

1. But   take   a – way   our   pride.
2. De – liv – er   us,   good   Lord!
3. A   sin – gle   sword   to   thee.

358. O Heart, Thou Ark

Text: *Cor Arca Legem*, Anonymous
Tr. J. Fitzpatrick, *The Raccolta*, 1957

Tune: Alta Trinita Beata, Irregular
Laudi Spirituali, 14th Century

1. O   Heart!   Thou   ark   where   lies   the   law,
2. O   Heart,   the   pure   and   stain – less   shrine
3. With   such   a   wound   as   must   ap –   pear
4. 'Neath   this,   love's   sym – bol,   suff – 'ring   twice,
5. Who   would   not   love   for   love   re –   pay?
6. Je – sus,   to   thee   be   glo – ry   giv'n,

1. Not   of   the   ser – vi –   tude   of   old.
2. Where   that   new   co – ven –   ant   has   lain:
3. Love   willed   that   Thou   shouldst   wound – ed   be,
4. Things   mys – tic – al   and   blood – y   both
5. What   man,   re – deemed, could   love   re – fuse
6. Whom   from   thy   Heart   dost   grace   out – pour;

1. But   that   from   which we   par – don   draw,
2. Tem – ple   than   Sa – lem's   more   div – ine;
3. That   we   might   all   the   wounds   re – vere,
4. Christ,   as   a   priest,   in   sac – ri – fice
5. To   this   Heart,   or   here – in,   for   aye,
6. To   Fath – er   and   to   Pa – ra – clete

1. And   grace and   mer – cies   man – i – fold.
2. Veil,   bet – ter   than   its   veil   in   twain.
3. Which   love   doth   bear   in – vis – ib – ly.
4. To   Heav'n up – lift – ed,   noth – ing   loth.
5. His   Tab – er – na – cle   fail   to   choose?
6. Be   end – less   praise   for   ev – er – more.

359. O Heavenly Word, Eternal Light

Text: *Verbum Supernum Prodiens*, Anonymous, 7th Century   Tune: O Heiland, Reiss, L. M.
Tr. John Mason Neale, 1818-1866   *Rheinfelsisches Deutsches Catholisches Gesangbuch*, 1666

1. O   heav'n – ly   Word,   e – ter – nal   Light,
2. Our   hearts   en – light – en   from   a – bove,
3. And   when   as   Judge   thou   draw – est   nigh,
4. O   let   us   not,   for   e – vil   past,
5. To   God   the   Fa – ther,   God   the   Son,

1. Be – got – ten   of   the   Fa – ther's   might,
2. And   kin – dle   with   thine   own   true   love,
3. The   se – crets   of   all   hearts   to   try,
4. Be   driv – en   from   thy   face   at   last,
5. And   God   the   Spi – rit,   Three   in   One,

1. Who   in   these   lat – ter   days   art   born
2. That   we,   who   hear   thy   call   to – day,
3. When   sin – ners   meet   their   aw – ful   doom,
4. But   with   the   bless – ed   ev – er – more
5. Praise,   hon – or,   might,   and   glo – ry   be

1. For   suc – cor   to   a   world   for – lorn;
2. May   cast   earth's   van – i – ties   a – way;
3. And   saints   at – tain   their   heav'n – ly   home;
4. Be – hold   thee,   love   thee,   and   a – dore.
5. From   age   to   age   e – ter – nal – ly.

360. O Jesus Christ, Within Me Grow

Text: *O Jesus Christus Wachs in Mir*, J. C. Lavater, 1741-1801
Tr. Elizabeth L. Smith, 1817-1877, alt.

Tune: Martyrdom, C. M.
Hugh Wilson, 1766-1824

1. O Je - sus Christ, with - in me grow
2. Each day may your sup - port - ing might
3. Make this poor self grow less and less,
4. Dai - ly more filled with love my heart,
5. Fill me with glad - ness from a - bove,

1. And all things else re - cede;
2. My weak - ness still em - brace;
3. Be both my life and aim;
4. Dai - ly from self more free;
5. Hold me by strength di - vine;

1. More of your na - ture may I know,
2. My dark - ness van - ish in your light,
3. And make me dai - ly through your face,
4. Lord to whom prayer did strength im - part,
5. Lord, let the glow of your great love

1. From sin be dai - ly freed.
2. Your life my death ef - face.
3. More fit to bear your name.
4. Of my prayer hear - er be.
5. Through my whole be - ing shine.

361. O Jesus, I Have Promised

John E. Bode, 1816-1874

Tune: Angel's Story, 76. 76. D
Arthur H. Mann, 1850-1929

1. O Je – sus, I have prom – ised, To serve thee
2. O Je – sus, thou hast prom – ised, To all who
3. O let me feel thee near me! The world is
4. O let me hear thee speak – ing In ac – cents

1. to the end; Be thou for – ev – er near me,
2. fol – low thee, That where thou art in glo – ry
3. ev – er near; I see the sights that daz – zle,
4. clear and still, A – bove the storms of pas – sion,

1. My Mas – ter and my friend; I shall not
2. There shall thy ser – vant be; And Je – sus,
3. The tempt – ing sounds I hear; My foes are
4. The mur – murs of self – will. O speak to

1. fear the bat – tle If thou art by my side,
2. I have prom – ised To serve thee to the end;
3. ev – er near me, A – round me and with – in;
4. re – as – sure me, To has – ten or con – trol!

1. Nor wan – der from the path – way
2. O give me grace to fol – low
3. But, Je – sus, draw thou near – er
4. O speak, and make me lis – ten,

1. If thou wilt be my guide.
2. My Mas – ter and my friend!
3. And shield me from my sin.
4. Thou guard – ian of my soul!

362. O Kind Creator, Bow Thine Ear

Text: *Audi Begnine Conditor*, St. Gregory the Great, 540-604
Tr. Thomas A. Lacey, 1853-1931

Text: Audi Begnine, L.M.
Chant, Mode II

1.	O	Kind	Cre – a – tor,	bow	thine	ear
2.	Our	hearts	are o – pen,	Lord,	to	thee:
3.	Our	sins	are man – y,	this	we	know;
4.	Give	us	the self – con – trol	that	springs
5.	We	pray	thee, Ho – ly	Trin – i – ty,

1.	To	mark	the	cry,	to	know	the	tear
2.	Thou	know – est	our	in – fir – mit – y;
3.	Spare	us,	good	Lord,	thy	mer – cy	show;
4.	From	dis – cip – line	of	out – ward	things,
5.	One	God,	un – chang – ing	U – nit – y,

1.	Be – fore	thy	throne	of	mer – cy	spent
2.	Pour	out	on	all	who	seek	thy	face
3.	And	for	the	hon – or	of	thy	name,
4.	That	fast – ing	in – ward	se – cret – ly
5.	That	we	from	this	our	ab – stin – ence

1.	In	this	thy	ho – ly	fast	of	Lent.
2.	A – bun – dance	of	thy	par – don – ing	grace.
3.	Our	faint – ing	souls	to	life	re – claim.
4.	The	soul	may	pure – ly	dwell	with	thee.
5.	May	reap	the	fruits	of	pen – i – tence.

363. O Little Town of Bethlehem

Phillips Brooks, 1835-1893

Tune: St. Louis, 76. 86. D
Lewis H. Redner, 1831-1908

1. O lit – tle town of Beth – le – hem, How still we
2. For Christ is born of Ma – ry, And gath – ered
3. O hol – ly Child of Beth – le – hem! De – scend to

1. see thee lie! A – bove thy deep and dream – less sleep,
2. all a – bove, While mor – tals sleep, the an – gels keep,
3. us, we pray; Cast out our sin and en – ter in,

1. The si – lent stars go by; Yet in the
2. Their watch of won – d'ring love. O morn – ing
3. Be born in us to – day. We hear the

1. dark streets shin – eth, The ev – er – last – ing Light;
2. stars, to – geth – er, Pro – claim the ho – ly birth!
3. Christ – mas an – gels, The great glad ti – dings tell;

1. The hopes and fears of all the years,
2. And prais – es sing to God the King,
3. O come to us, a – bide with us,

1. Are met in thee to – night.
2. And peace to men on earth.
3. Our Lord Em – man – u – el!

364. O Lord, I Am Not Worthy

Text: St 1. *O Herr Ich Bin Nicht Würdig*, Landshuter Gesanbuch, 1777   Tune: Non Dignus, 76. 76.
Tr. And St. 2-4. Anonymous   *Catholic Youth Hymnal*, 1871

1. O Lord, I am not wor – thy,
2. Oh, come all you who la – bor,
3. O Je – sus, we a – dore Thee,
4. O sac – ra – ment most ho – ly,

1. That thou shouldst come to me
2. In sor – row and in pain,
3. Our Vic – tim and our Priest,
4. O sac – ra – ment di – vine,

1. But speak the words of com – fort,
2. Come, eat this bread from heav – en,
3. Whose pre – cious Blood and Bo – dy
4. All praise and all thanks – giv – ing,

1. My spir – it healed shall be.
2. Your peace and strength re – gain.
3. Be – come our sa – cred Feast.
4. Be ev – 'ry mo – ment thine.

365. O Lord, Now Let Your Servant Go in Peace
(Nunc Dimittis)

Text: *Nunc Dimittis Servum Tuum Domine*, Luke 2:29-32   Tune: Modern Psalm Tone
Adapted from the *Confraternity Bible*, 1957   *Prepared for this Hymnal*

1. O, Lord, now let your servant   go in peace; *
2. My own eyes have seen the   sal – va – tion *
3. A light to reveal you to   the na – tions *
4. Glory be to the Father, and   to the Son, *
5. As it was in the beginning, is now, and ev – er shall be, *

1. your word   has been ful – filled.
2. which you prepared in the sight of all peo – ple:
3. and the glory of your peo – ple Is – ra – el.
4. and to the   Ho – ly Spir – it.
5. world with-   out end. A – men.

* At Compline, the Antiphon may be sung thusly:

1. Guide us wa – king, O Lord, * and   guard us sleep – ing;
2. that awake we may watch with Christ, * and asleep we may rest in peace.

366. Oh, Love, How Deep

Text: *O Amor Quam*, Thomas a Kempis, 1380-1471
Tr. Benjamin Webb, 1819-1885

Tune: Agincourt (Deo Gratias), L. M.
The Agincourt Song, English, 15th Century

1. Oh, love, how deep, how broad, how high,
2. He sent no an – gel to our race,
3. For us bap – tized, for us he bore
4. For us he prayed; for us he taught;

1. Be – yond all thought and fan – ta – sy,
2. Of high – er or of low – er place,
3. His ho – ly fast and hun – gered sore;
4. For us his dai – ly works he wrought,

1. That God, the Son of God, should take
2. But wore the robe of hu – man frame,
3. For us temp – ta – tion sharp he knew;
4. By words and signs and ac – tions thus

1. Our mor – tal form for mor – tal's sake!
2. And to this world him – self he came.
3. For us the temp – ter o – ver – threw.
4. Still seek – ing not him – self, but us.

367. O Master, Let Me Walk with Thee

Text: Washington Gladden, 1836-1918

Tune: Maryton L. M.
H. Percy Smith, 1825-1898

1. O Mas – ter, let me walk with thee,
2. Help me the slow of heart to move,
3. Teach me thy pa – tience! Still with thee,
4. In hope that sends a shin – ing ray,

1. In low – ly paths of ser – vice free;
2. By some clear, win – ning word of love;
3. In clos – er dear – er com – pa – ny,
4. Far down the fu – ture's broad' – ning way,

1. Tell me thy se – cret, help me bear,
2. Teach me the way – ward feet to stay,
3. In work that keeps faith sweet and strong,
4. In peace that on – ly thou canst give,

1. The strain of toil, the fret of care.
2. And guide them in the home – ward way.
3. In trust that tri – umphs o – ver wrong.
4. With thee, O Mas – ter, let me live.

368. O Most Holy One

Text: *O Sanctissima*, Anonymous, 18th Century
Tr. J. M. Raker, *The Saint Gregory Hymnal*, 1920

Tune: Sicilian Hymn, 5. 5. 7. D
Traditional Sicilian Melody

1. O most ho – ly one, O most low – ly one,
2. Help in sad – ness drear, Port of glad – ness near,
3. Call we fear – ful – ly, Sad – ly, tear – ful – ly,
4. Moth – er, Maid – en fair, Look with lov – ing care,

1. Dear – est Vir – gin *Ma – rí – a!*
2. Vir – gin Moth – er, *Ma – rí – a!*
3. Save us now O *Ma – rí – a!*
4. Hear our prayer, O *Ma – rí – a!*

1. Moth – er of fair Love, Home of the Spir– it Dove,
2. In pit – y heed – ing, Hear thou our plead – ing,
3. Let us not lan – guish, Heal thou our an – guish,
4. Our sor – row feel – ing, Send us thy heal – ing,

1. *O – ra, o – ra pro no – bis.*
2. *O – ra, o – ra pro no – bis.*
3. *O – ra, o – ra pro no – bis.*
4. *O – ra, o – ra pro no – bis.*

369. O Queen of the Holy Rosary

Text: Emily Shapcote, 1828-1909

Tune: Ellacombe, 96.76.76.76.
Gesangbuch der Herzogl, Würtemberg, 1784

1. O Queen of the Ho – ly Ro – sa – ry, Oh, bless us
2. O Queen of the Ho – ly Ro – sa – ry, Each mys – t'ry
3. O Queen of the Ho – ly Ro – sa – ry, We share thy

1. as we pray, And of – fer thee our ros – es
2. blends with thine The sa – cred life of Je – sus
3. joy and pain, And long to see the glo – ry

1. In gar – lands day by day, While from our
2. In ev – 'ry step di – vine. Thy soul was
3. Of Christ's tri – um – phant reign. Oh, teach us

1. Fa – ther's gar – den With lov – ing hearts and bold,
2. his fair gar – den, Thy vir – gin breast his throne,
3. ho – ly Ma – ry, To live each mys – te – ry,

1. We gath – er to thine hon – or
2. Thy thoughts his faith – ful mir – ror
3. And gain by pa – tient suf – f'ring

1. Buds white and red and gold.
2. Re – flect – ing him a – lone.
3. The glo – ry won by thee.

370. O Sacred Head, Surrounded

Text: *O Haupt voll Blut*, Paulus Gerhardt, 1607-1676
Tr. Composite

Tune: Passion Chorale, 76. 76. D
Hans Leo Hassler, 1564-1612

1. O   Sa – cred   Head   sur – round – ed,   By   crown   of
2. I   see   thy   strength and   vig – or,   All   fad – ing
3. In   this,   thy   bit – ter   pas – sion,   Good   Shep – herd,

1. pierc – ing   thorn!   O   bleed – ing   Head,   so   wound – ed,
2. in   the   strife,   And death   with   cru – el   rig – or,
3. think   of   me;   With thy   most   sweet   com – pas – sion,

1. Re – viled   and   put   to   scorn!   Death's pal – lid   hue
2. Be – reav – ing   thee   to   life;   O   ag – o – ny
3. Un – worth – y   though   I   be: Be – neath   thy   cross

1. comes   o'er   thee,   The   glow   of   love   de – cays,
2. and   dy – ing!   O   love   to   sin – ners   free!
3. a – bid – ing,   For – ev – er   would   I   rest,

1. Yet   an – gel   hosts   a – dore   thee,
2. Je – sus,   all   grace   sup – ply – ing,
3. In   thy   dear   love   con – fid – ing,

1. And   trem – ble   as   they   gaze.
2. O   turn   thy   face   on   me.
3. And   with   thy   pres – ence   blest.

371. O Salutaris Hostia

Text: St. Thomas Aquinas, 1227-1274   Music by Alajos Werner, 1905-1978
ENGLISH: "O Saving Victim"

1. O sa – lu – tá – ris Hós – ti – a,
2. U – ni – tri – nó – que Dó – mi – no,

1. Quae cae – li pan – dis ó – sti – um,
2. Sit sem – pi – tér – na gló – ri – a:

1. Bel – la prae – munt ho – stí – li – a,
2. Qui vi – tam si – ne tér – mi – no,

1. Da ro – bur fer au – xí – li – um.
2. No – bis do – net in pá – tri – a. A – men.

372. O Sanctissima, O Piissima

Text: Anonymous, 18th Century
ENGLISH: "O Most Holy One"

Tune: Sicilian Hymn, 5. 5. 7. D
Traditional Sicilian Melody

1. O San – ctís – si – ma, O Pi – ís – si – ma,
2. Tu so – lá – ti – um, Et re – fú – gi – um,
3. Ec – ce dé – bi – les, Per – quam flé – bi – les,
4. Vir – go ré – spi – ce, Ma – ter, ád – spi – ce,

1. Dul – cis Vir – go Ma – rí – a!
2. Vir – go Ma – ter Ma – rí – a!
3. Sal – va nos, Ma – rí – a!
4. Au – di nos, Ma – rí – a!

1. Ma – ter a – má – ta, In – te – me – rá – ta,
2. Quid – quid o – ptá – mus, Per te spe – rá – mus;
3. Tol–le lan – gu – ó – res, Sa – na do – ló – res,
4. Tu me – di – cí – nam, Por – tas di – ví – nam;

1. O – ra, o – ra pro no – bis.
2. O – ra, o – ra pro no – bis.
3. O – ra, o – ra pro no – bis.
4. O – ra, o – ra pro no – bis.

373. O Saving Victim, Opening Wide

Text: *O Salutaris Hostia*, St. Thomas Aquinas, 1227-1274   Music by Alajos Werner, 1905-1978
Tr. Edward Caswall, 1814-1878, alt.

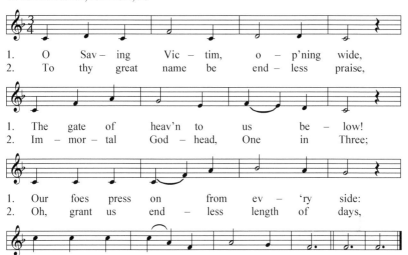

1. O Sav – ing Vic – tim, o – p'ning wide,
2. To thy great name be end – less praise,

1. The gate of heav'n to us be – low!
2. Im – mor – tal God – head, One in Three;

1. Our foes press on from ev – 'ry side:
2. Oh, grant us end – less length of days,

1. Thine aid sup – ply, thy strength be – stow.
2. When our true na – tive land we see. A – men.

374. O Savior, Precious Savior

Text: Frances R. Havergal, 1836-1879

Tune: Angel's Story, 76. 76. D
Arthur H. Mann, 1850-1929

1. O Sav – ior, pre – cious Sav – ior, Whom yet un –
2. O Bring – er of sal – va – tion, Who won – drous –
3. In thee all full – ness dwell – eth, All grace and
4. Oh, grant the con – sum – ma – tion, Of this our

1. seen we love; O name of might and fa – vor,
2. ly hast wrought, Thy – self the rev – e – la – tion,
3. pow'r di – vine; The glo – ry that ex – cel – leth,
4. song a – bove, In end – less ad – o – ra – tion,

1. All oth – er names a – bove:
2. Of love be – yond our thought:
3. O Son of God, is thine.
4. And ev – er – last ing love;

Refrain:

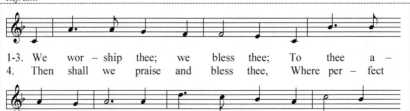

1-3. We wor – ship thee; we bless thee; To thee a –
4. Then shall we praise and bless thee, Where per – fect

1-3. lone we sing; We praise thee and con – fess thee,
4. prais – es ring, And ev – er – more con – fess thee,

1-3. Our ho – ly Lord and King.
4. Our Sav – ior and our King!

375. Oh, Wondrous Type! Oh, Vision Fair

Text: *Coelestis Formam*, Sarum Office Hymn, 15th Century   Tune: Agincourt (Deo Gratias), L.M.
Tr. John Mason Neale, 1818-1866, alt.   The Agincourt Song, English, 15th Century

1. Oh, won – drous type! Oh, vi – sion fair
2. With Mo – ses and E – li – jah nigh
3. With shin – ing face and bright ar – ray,
4. And faith – ful hearts are raised on high
5. O Fa – ther with the e – ter – nal Son

1. Of glo – ry that the Church may share,
2. The in – car – nate Lord holds con – verse high;
3. Christ deigns to man – i – fest that day
4. By this great vi – sion's mys – ter – y;
5. And Ho – ly Spir – it ev – er one,

1. Which Christ up – on the moun – tain shows,
2. And from the cloud, the Ho – ly One
3. What glo – ry shall be theirs a – bove
4. For which in joy – ful strains we raise
5. We pray you, bring us by your grace

1. Where bright – er than the sun he glows!
2. Bears rec – ord to the on – ly Son.
3. Who joy in God with per – fect love.
4. The voice of prayer, the hymn of praise.
5. To see your glo – ry face to face.

376. On Jordan's Bank

Text: *Jordanis Oras Praevia*, Charles Coffin, 1676-1749
Tr. John Chandler, 1806-1876

Tune: Winchester New, L. M.
Musikalisches Handbuch, Hamburg, 1690

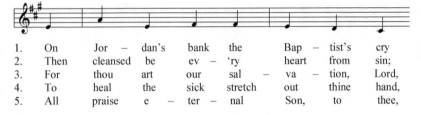

1. On   Jor – dan's   bank   the   Bap – tist's   cry
2. Then   cleansed   be   ev – 'ry   heart   from   sin;
3. For   thou   art   our   sal – va – tion,   Lord,
4. To   heal   the   sick   stretch   out   thine   hand,
5. All   praise   e – ter – nal   Son,   to   thee,

1. An – noun – ces   that   the   Lord   is   nigh;
2. Make   straight   the   way   of   God   with – in,
3. Our   ref – uge,   and   our   great   re – ward;
4. And   bid   the   fall – en   sin – ner   stand;
5. Whose   ad – vent   doth   thy   peo – ple   free;

1. A – wake   and   heark – en,   for   he   brings
2. And   let   each   heart   pre – pare   a   home
3. With – out   thy   grace   we   waste   a – way
4. Shine   forth,   and   let   thy   light   re – store
5. Whom   with   the   Fa – ther   we   a – dore

1. Glad   ti – dings   of   the   King   of   kings.
2. Where   such   a   might – y   guest   may   come.
3. Like   flow'rs   that   with – er   and   de – cay.
4. Earth's   own   true   love – li – ness   once   more.
5. And   Ho – ly   Ghost   for   ev – er – more.

377. Open My Eyes That I May See

Text: Clara H. Scott, 1841-1897

Tune: Scott, 88. 98. with refrain
Clara H. Scott, 1841-1897

1. O – pen my eyes, that I may see, Glimps–es of truth
2. O – pen my ears, that I may hear, Voic – es of truth
3. O – pen my mouth, and let me bear Glad – ly the warm

1. thou hast for me; Place in my hands the
2. thou send – est clear; And while the wave – notes
3. truth ev – 'ry – where; O – pen my heart, and

1. won–der–ful key That shall un – clasp, and set me free.
2. fall on my ear, Ev – 'ry – thing false will dis – ap – pear.
3. let me pre – pare Love with thy chil – dren thus to share.

Refrain:

Si – lent – ly now I wait for thee,

Read – y, my God, thy will to see;

O – pen my eyes, il – lu – mine me, Spir – it di – vine!

After the Last verse:

A – men.

378. Out of the Depths I Cry to Thee

Text: *Aus Tiefer Not*, Martin Luther, 1483-1546 Tune: De Profundis (Aus Tiefer Not), 87. 87. 88. 7.
Tr. Catherine Winkworth, 1827-1878   Martin Luther, 1483-1546

1. Out   of   the   depths   I   cry   to   thee;
2. Thy   par –   don,   Lord,   is   gained through grace:
3. My   hope   is,   there – fore,   in   the   Lord,
4. And   though I   tar – ry   till   the   night
5. Though great   our   sins   and   sore   our   woes,

1. Lord,   hear   me,   I   im – plore   thee.
2. It   can   a – lone   a – vail   us.
3. And   not   in   mine   own   mer – it;
4. And   till   the   morn   a – wak – en.
5. His   grace   much   more   a – bound – eth;

1. In – cline   thy   gra – cious   ear   to   me
2. Our   works   can   ne'er   our   guilt   ef – face,
3. I   rest   up – on   his   faith – ful   word
4. My   heart   shall   not   mis – trust   his   might
5. His   help – ing   love   no   lim – it   knows,

1. As   I   ap – pear   be – fore   thee.
2. The   strict – est   life   must   fail   us.
3. To   them   of   con – trite   spir – it;
4. Nor   count   it – self   for – sak – en.
5. Our   ut – most   need   it   sound – eth.

1. If thou re – mem – ber each mis – deed
2. Be – fore thee none can boast of aught;
3. That he is mer – ci – ful and just,
4. Do thus, o ye of Is – rael's seed,
5. Our Shep – herd good and true is he,

1. And give to each his right – ful meed,
2. To fear thee we are right – ly taught,
3. This is my com – fort and my trust:
4. Ye of the Spir – it born in – deed,
5. Who will at last set Is – rael free

1. Who can a – bide thy pres – ence?
2. On grace a – lone de – pend – ing.
3. I wait for him in pa – tience.
4. Wait for your God's ap – pear – ing.
5. From all their sin and sor – row.

379. Pange Lingua, Gloriosi Corporis

Text: St. Thomas Aquinas, 1227-1274
ENGLISH: "Sing My Tongue, the Savior's Glory"

Tune: Pange Lingua Gloriosi, 87. 87. 87.
Chant, Mode III

1. Pan – ge lin – gua, glo – ri – o – si
2. No – bis da – tus, no – bis na – tus
3. In su – pre – mae no – cte coe – nae,
4. Ver – bum ca – ro, pa – nem ve – rum
5. **Tan – tum er – go sa – cra – men – tum**
6. **Ge – ni – to – ri, Ge – ni – to – que**

1. Cor – po – ris my – ste – ri – um
2. Ex in – ta – cta Vir – gi – ne,
3. Re – cum – bens cum fra – tri – bus,
4. Ver – bo car – nem ef – fi – cit:
5. **Ve – ne – re – mur cer – nu – i:**
6. **Laus et ju – bi – la – ti – o,**

1. San – gui – nis – que pre – ti – o – si,
2. Et in mun – do con – ver – sa – tus,
3. Ob – ser – va – ta le – ge ple – ne
4. Fit – que san – guis Chri – sti me – rum,
5. **Et an – ti – quum do – cu – men – tum**
6. **Sa – lus, ho – nor, vir – tus quo – que**

1. Quem in mun – di pre – ti – um
2. Spar – so ver – bi se – mi – ne,
3. Ci – bis in le – ga – li – bus,
4. Et si sen – sus de – fi – cit,
5. **No – vo ce – dat ri – tu – i;**
6. **Sit et be – ne – di – cti – o:**

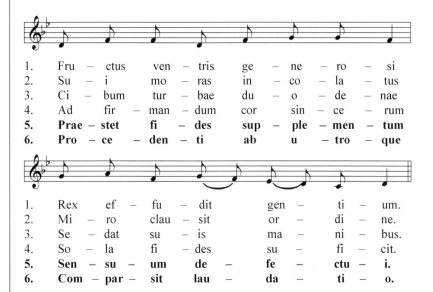

1. Fru – ctus ven – tris ge – ne – ro – si
2. Su – i mo – ras in – co – la – tus
3. Ci – bum tur – bae du – o – de – nae
4. Ad fir – man – dum cor sin – ce – rum
5. **Prae – stet fi – des sup – ple – men – tum**
6. **Pro – ce – den – ti ab u – tro – que**

1. Rex ef – fu – dit gen – ti – um.
2. Mi – ro clau – sit or – di – ne.
3. Se – dat su – is ma – ni – bus.
4. So – la fi – des su – fi – cit.
5. **Sen – su – um de – fe – ctu – i.**
6. **Com – par – sit lau – da – ti – o.**

After the Last verse:

A – – men.

*Verses 5 and 6 are also known as the "Tantum Ergo," and may be sung as a separate hymn.

380. Panis Angelicus

St. Thomas Aquinas, 1227-1274
ENGLISH: "O Bread of Angels"

Tune: Sacris Solemniis, 12. 12. 12. 8.
Louis Lambilotte, 1796-1855

1. Pa – nis an – ge – li – cus fit pa – nis ho – mi – num,
2. Te, tri – na De – i – tas, u – na – que po – sci – mus,

1. Dat pa – nis cae – li – cus fi – gu – ris ter – mi – num:
2. Sic nos tu vi – si – ta si – cut te co – li – mus:

1. O res mi – ra – bi – lis! Man–du – cat Do – mi – num
2. Per tu – as se – mi – tas duc nos quo ten – di – mus

1. Pau – per, ser – vus et hu – mi – lis.
2. Ad lu – cem quam in – ha – bi – tas.

381. Parce, Domine

Text: St. Gregory the Great, 540-604
ENGLISH: "Have Mercy, O Lord"

Tune: Parce Domine, Irregular
Chant, Mode I

Refrain:

Par – ce Dó – mi – ne Par – ce pó – pu – lo tu – o,

Ne in ae – tér – num i – ras – ca – ris no – bis.

1. Fle – ctá – mus i – ram vín – di – cem,
2. No – stris ma – lis of – fén – di – mus
3. Dans tem – pus ac – cep – tá – bi – le,
4. Au – di, be – ní – gne Cón – di – tor,
5. Scru – tá – tor al – me cór – di – um,

1. Plo – ré – mus an – te Jú – di – cem;
2. Tu – am De – us cle – mén – ti – am
3. Da la – cri – má – rum rí – vu – lis
4. No – stras pre – ces cum flé – ti – bus
5. In – fir – ma tu scis ví – ri – um;

1. Cla – mé – mus o – re súp – pli – ci,
2. Ef – fún – de no – bis dé – su – per
3. La – vá – re cor – dis ví – cti – mam,
4. In hoc sa – cro je – jú – ni – o
5. Ad te re – vér – sis éx – hi – be,

1. Di – cá – mus o – mnes cér – nu – i:
2. Re – mís – sor in – dul – gén – ti – am.
3. Quam laeta a – dú – rat cá – ri – tas.
4. Fu – sas qua – dra – ge – ná – ri – o.
5. Re – mis – si – ó – nis grá – ti – am.

382. Praise God from Whom All Blessings Flow (#1)

Text: Thomas Ken, 1637-1711

Tune: Old Hundredth, L. M.
Louis Bourgeois, c. 1510-1561

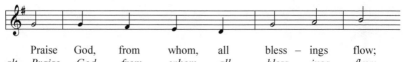

| | Praise | God, | from | whom, | all | bless – ings | flow; |
| *alt.* | *Praise* | *God,* | *from* | *whom,* | *all* | *bless – ings* | *flow;* |

| Praise | him, | all | crea – tures | here | be – low; |
| *Praise* | *God,* | *all* | *crea – tures* | *here* | *be – low;* |

| Praise | him | a – bove, | ye | heav'n – ly | host; |
| *Praise* | *God* | *a – bove,* | *ye* | *heav'n – ly* | *host;* |

| Praise | Fa – ther, | Son, | and | Ho – ly | Ghost. |
| *Cre – a – tor,* | | *Son,* | *and* | *Ho – ly* | *Ghost.* |

383. Praise God from Whom All Blessings Flow (#2)

Text: Thomas Ken, 1637-1711

Tune: Lasst Uns Erfreuen, 88. 88. 88. with alleluias
Geistliche Kirchengesange, Cologne, 1623

Praise God, from whom, all bless – ings flow;
alt. *Praise God, from whom, all bless – ings flow;*

Praise him, all crea – tures here be – low;
Praise God, all crea – tures here be – low;

Al – le – lu – ia! Al – le – lu – ia!

Praise him a – bove, ye heav'n – ly host;
Praise God a – bove, ye heav'n – ly host;

Praise Fa – ther, Son, and Ho – ly Ghost.
Cre – a – tor, Son, and Ho – ly Ghost.

Al – le – lu – ia! Al – le – lu – ia! Al – le – lu – ia!

Al – le – lu – ia! Al – le – lu – ia!

384. Quem Terra, Pontus, Aethera

Text: Venantius Fortunatus, 530-609
ENGLISH: "The God Whom Earth and Sea and Sky"

Tune: Eisenach, L. M.
Johann H. Schein, 1586-1630

1. Quem te – ra, pon – tus, aé – the – ra
2. Cui Lu – na, Sol, et ó – mni – a
3. Be – á – ta Ma – ter, mú – ne – re,
4. Be – á – ta cae – li nún – ti – o,
5. Je – su, ti – bi sit gló – ri – a,

1. Co – lunt, a – dó – rant, praé – di – cant,
2. De – sér – vi – unt per tém – po – ra,
3. Cu – jus su – pér – nus Ár – ti – fex,
4. Fe – cún – da San – cto Spí – ri – tu,
5. Qui na – tus es de Vír – gi – ne,

1. Tri – nam re – gén – tem má – chi – nam
2. Per – fu – sa cae – li grá – ti – a,
3. Mun – dum pú – gil – lo cón – ti – nens,
4. De – si – de – rá – tus Gén – ti – bus,
5. Cum Pa – tre-et al – mo Spí – ri – tu,

1. Clau – strum Ma – rí – ae bá – ju – lat.
2. Ge – stant Pu – él – lae ví – sce – ra.
3. Ven – tris sub ar – ca clau – sus est.
4. Cu – jus per al – vum fu – sus est.
5. In sem – pi – tér – na saé – cu – la.

385. Raise Your Voices, Vales and Mountains

Text: *Causa Nostrae Laetitiae*, St. Alphonsus Liguori, 1696-1787 Tune: Old English Hymn
Tr. E. Vaughan, 1827-1908 *St. Basil Hymnal*, 1918 Edition

1. Raise your voi – ces vales and moun – tains,
2. Murm – 'ring brooks your tri – bute bring – ing,
3. Say sweet Vir – gin, we im – plore thee,

1. Flow – 'ry mead – ows, streams and foun – tains,
2. Lit – tle birds with joy – ful sing – ing,
3. Say what beau – ty God sheds o'er thee;

1. Praise, O praise, the lov – liest maid – en
2. Come with mirth – ful prais – es la – den,
3. Praise and thanks to him be giv – en,

1. Ev – er the Cre – a – tor made.
2. To your Queen be hom – age paid.
3. Who in love cre – a – ted thee.

Refrain:

Lau – dá – te, Lau – dá – te, Lau – dá – te Ma – rí – am;

Lau – dá – te, Lau – dá – te, Lau – dá – te Ma – rí – am!

386. Rejoice Now, You Angelic Choirs

Text: *Exsultet Jam Angelica Turba*, Roman Missal
Para. by Agostino Taumaturgo, b. 1974

Tune: Vexilla Regis, L. M.
Chant, Mode I

1. Re – joice now, you an – ge – lic choi – rs.
2. Re – joice, O earth, made ra – di – ant;
3. Re – joice, O ho – ly moth – er Church;
4. And you, dear friends, all stand – ing here
5. He called us to be saved in him,
6. Thru' Je – sus Christ, his Son, our Lord,

1. Peo – ple re – joice a – round Christ's throne.
2. You're made brill – iant by such spleen – dor.
3. You are made ra – diant by this light.
4. Near the flame of this sa – cred light,
5. Weak and un – wor – thy tho' we be.
6. Who lives and reigns with the Fa – ther,

1. This might – y King is vic – tor – ious.
2. Dark – ness ev – 'ry – where is o'er – come
3. Let this place ring with re – joic – ing,
4. Pray with me to al – might – y God.
5. Pray that he may shed light on us,
6. With the Ho – ly Spir – it, one God,

1. Sound, O trum – pet, our sal – va – tion.
2. By the bright – ness of this our King.
3. With the song of those gath – er'd here.
4. Let us ask that he show mer – cy.
5. And may we praise his ho – ly light.
6. For ev – er and ev – er. A – men.

387. Rock of Ages, Cleft for Me

Text: Augustus M. Toplady, 1740-1778

Tune: Toplady, 77. 77. 77.
Thomas Hastings, 1784-1872

1. Rock of A – ges, cleft for me,
2. Could my tears for – ev – er flow,
3. While I draw this fleet – ing breath,

1. Let me hide my – self in thee;
2. Could my zeal no lan – guor know,
3. When my eyes shall close in death,

1. Let the wa – ter and the blood,
2. These for sin could not a – tone,
3. When I rise to worlds un – known,

1. From thy wound – ed side which flowed,
2. Thou must save, and thou a – lone:
3. And be – hold thee on thy throne,

1. Be of sin the dou – ble cure,
2. In my hand no price I bring,
3. Rock of A – ges, cleft for me,

1. Save from wrath and make me pure.
2. Sim – ply to thy cross I cling.
3. Let me hide my – self in thee;

388. Salve Regina Coelitum

Text: Anonymous, c. 1080   Tune: Salve Regina Coelitum 84. 84. with Refrain
ENGLISH: "Hail! Holy Queen, Enthroned Above"   *Choralmelodien zum Heiligen Gesänge*, 1808

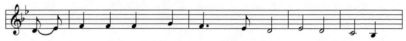

1. Sal – ve Re – gí – na coé – li – tum, O Ma – rí – a!
2. Spes no – stra, sal – ve, Dó – mi – na, O Ma – rí – a!

1. Sors ú – ni – ca ter – rí – ge – num, O Ma – rí – a!
2. Ex – stín – gue no – stra crí – mi – na! O Ma – rí – a!

Refrain:

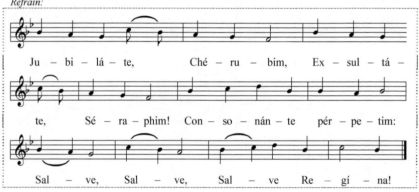

Ju – bi – lá – te, Ché – ru – bim, Ex – sul – tá –

te, Sé – ra – phim! Con – so – nán – te pér – pe – tim:

Sal – ve, Sal – ve, Sal – ve Re – gí – na!

389. Savior of the Nations, Come

Text: *Veni Redemptor Gentium*, St. Ambrose of Milan
Tr. William Reynolds, 1812-1876

Tune: Nun Komm der Heiden Heiland
Johann Walther, 1524

1.	Sav – ior	of	the	na –	tions,	come;
2.	Not	by	hu – man	flesh	and	blood,
3.	Won – drous	birth!	O	won –	drous	Child
4.	From	the	Fa – ther	forth	he	came
5.	Thou,	the	Fa – ther's	on –	ly	Son,
6.	Bright – ly	doth	thy	man –	ger	shine,
7.	Praise	to	God	the	Fa –	ther	sing,

1.	Show	the	glo – ry	of	the	Son!
2.	By	the	Spir – it	of	our	God
3.	Of	the	Vir – gin	un – de –	filed!
4.	And	re – turn – eth	to	the	same,
5.	Hast	o'er	sin	the	vic –	t'ry	won.
6.	Glo – rious	is	its	light	di –	vine.
7.	Praise	to	God	the	Son,	our	King,

1.	Mar – vel	now,	O	heav'n	and	earth,
2.	Was	the	Word	of	God	made	flesh
3.	Though	by	all	the	world	dis –	owned,
4.	Cap – tive	lead – ing	death	and	hell
5.	Bound – less	shall	thy	king –	dom	be;
6.	Let	not	sin	o'er –	cloud	this	light;
7.	Praise	to	God	the	Spir –	it	be

1.	That	our	Lord	chose	such	a	birth!
2.	Wo – man's	off – spring,	pure	and	fresh.
3.	Still	to	be	in	heav'n	en –	throned.
4.	High	the	song	of	tri –	umph	swell!
5.	When	shall	we	its	glo –	ries	see?
6.	Ev – er	be	our	faith	thus	bright.
7.	Ev – er	and	e –	ter –	nal –	ly.

390. Savior, When in Dust to You

Text: Robert Grant, 1779-1838

Tune: Abertswyth, 77. 77. D.
Joseph Parry, 1841-1903

1. Sav – ior, when in dust to you, Low we bow in
2. By your help – less in – fant years, By your life of
3. By your hour of dire de – spair, By your ag – o –
4. By your deep ex – pir – ing groan, By the sad se –

1. hom – age due; When, re – pen – tant, to the skies
2. want and tears, By your days of deep dis – tress
3. ny of prayer, By the cross, the nail, the thorn,
4. pul – chral stone, By the vault whose dark a – bode

1. Scarce we lift our weep – ing eyes; Oh, by all your
2. In the sav – age wil – der – ness, By the dread, mys –
3. Pierc – ing spear and tor – turing scorn, By the gloom that
4. Held in vain the ris – ing God, Oh, from earth to

1. pains and woe, Suf – fered once for us be – low,
2. te – rious hour Of the-in – sult – ing tempt – er's pow'r,
3. veiled the skies O'er the dread – ful sac – ri – fice,
4. heav'n re – stored, Might – y, re – as – cend – ed Lord,

1. Ben – ding from your throne on high,
2. Turn, oh, turn a fa – v'ring eye;
3. Lis – ten to our hum – ble sigh;
4. Bend – ing from your throne on high,

1. Hear our pen – i – ten – tial cry!
2. Hear our pen – i – ten – tial cry!
3. Hear our pen – i – ten – tial cry!
4. Hear our pen – i – ten – tial cry!

391. Silent Night

Joseph Mohr, 1792-1849
Tr. John F. Young, 1820-1885

Tune: Stille Nacht, 66. 88. 66.
Franz Gruber, 1787-1863

1. Si – lent night, ho – ly night, All is calm,
2. Si – lent night, ho – ly night, Shep– herds quake,
3. Si – lent night, ho – ly night, Son of God,

1. all is bright Round yon Vir – gin Moth– er and Child.
2. at the sight Glo – ries stream from heav– en a – far,
3. love's pure light Ra – diant beams from thy ho – ly face,

1. Ho – ly In – fant, so ten – der and mild, Sleep in heav–en – ly
2. Heav'n–ly hosts sing, Al – le – lu – ia, Christ the Sav–ior is
3. With the dawn of re – deem – ing grace, Je – sus, Lord at thy

1. peace, Sleep in heav – en – ly peace.
2. born! Christ the Sav – ior is born!
3. birth. Je – sus, Lord at thy birth.

392. Sing My Tongue, the Savior's Glory

Text: *Pange Lingua*, St. Thomas Aquinas, 1227-1274
Tr. Edward Caswall, 1814-1878

Tune: Pange Lingua Gloriosi, 87. 87. 87.
Chant, Mode III

1. Sing my tongue, the Sav – ior's glo – ry,
2. Of a pure and spot – less Vir – gin
3. On the night of that last sup – per
4. Word made Flesh, the bread of na – ture
5. **Down in a – do – ra – tion fall – ing,**
6. **To the ev – er – las – ting Fa – ther,**

1. Of his Flesh the mys – t'ry sing:
2. Born for us on earth be – low,
3. Seat – ed with his cho – sen band,
4. By his word to Flesh he turns;
5. **Lo! The sa – cred Host we hail;**
6. **And the Son who reigns on high,**

1. Of the Blood all price ex – ceed – ing,
2. He, as one of us con – ver – sing,
3. He, the Pas – chal Vic – tim eat – ing,
4. Wing in – to his Blood he chan – ges,
5. **Lo! o'er an – cient forms de – part – ing,**
6. **With the Spir – it Blest pro – ceed – ing**

1. Shed by our im – mor – tal King,
2. Stayed, the seeds of truth to sow;
3. First ful – fills the Law's com – mand;
4. What though sense no change dis – cerns?
5. **new – er rites of grace pre – vail;**
6. **Forth from each e – ter – nal – ly,**

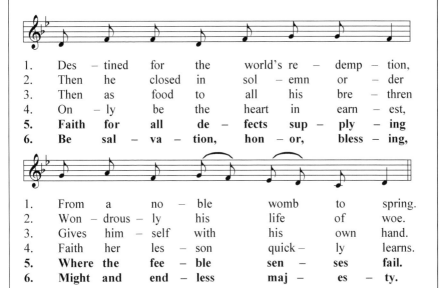

1. Des – tined for the world's re – demp – tion,
2. Then he closed in sol – emn or – der
3. Then as food to all his bre – thren
4. On – ly be the heart in earn – est,
5. Faith for all de – fects sup – ply – ing
6. Be sal – va – tion, hon – or, bless – ing,

1. From a no – ble womb to spring.
2. Won – drous – ly his life of woe.
3. Gives him – self with his own hand.
4. Faith her les – son quick – ly learns.
5. Where the fee – ble sen – ses fail.
6. Might and end – less maj – es – ty.

After the Last verse:

A – – men.

*Verses 5 and 6 are also known as the "Tantum Ergo," and may be sung as a separate hymn.

393. Sing with All the Saints in Glory

Text: William J. Irons, 1812-1883, alt.

Tune: Hymn to Joy, 87. 87. D.
Adapted from Ludwig van Beethoven, 1770-1827

1. Sing with all the saints in glo – ry,
2. O what glo – ry, far ex – ceed – ing
3. Life e – ter – nal! Heav'n re – joi – ces:
4. Life e – ter – nal! O what won – ders

1. Sing the res – ur – rec – tion song! Death and sor – row,
2. All that eye has yet per – ceived! Ho – liest hearts for
3. Je – sus lives who once was dead; Shout with joy, O
4. Crown of faith; what joy un – known, When, a – midst earth's

1. earth's dark sto – ry, To the for – mer days be – long.
2. a – ges plead – ing, Nev– er that full joy con – ceived.
3. death – less voic – es! Child of God, lift up your head!
4. clo – sing thun – ders, Saints shall stand be – fore the throne!

1. All a – round the clouds are break – ing,
2. God has prom – ised, Christ pre – pares it,
3. Pa – tri – archs from dis – tant a – ges,
4. O to en – ter that bright por – tal,

1. Soon the storms of time shall cease; In God's like– ness
2. There on high our wel – come waits; Ev – 'ry hum–ble
3. Saints all long – ing for their heav'n, Proph–ets, psalm–ists,
4. See that glow – ing fir – ma – ment, Know, with you, O

1. we a – wak – en, Know–ing ev – er – last– ing peace.
2. spir – it shares it, Christ has passed the–e– ter – nal gates.
3. seers, and sag – es, All a – wait the glo – ry giv'n.
4. God im – mor – tal, "Je – sus Christ whom you have sent!"

394. Songs of Thankfulness and Praise

Text: Christopher Wordsworth, 1807-1885

Tune: Salzburg, 77. 77. D
Jakob Hintze, 1622-1702

1. Songs of thank – ful – ness and praise, Je – sus, Lord, to
2. Man – i – fest at Jor – dan's stream, Proph– et, Priest, and
3. Man – i – fest in mak – ing whole Pal – sied limbs and
4. Grant us grace to see thee, Lord, Pres – ent in thy

1. thee we raise; Man – i – fest – ed by the star
2. King su – preme; And at Ca – na wed – ding guest
3. faint – ing soul; Man – i – fest in val – iant fight,
4. ho – ly Word; Grace to im – i – tate thee now

1. To the sag – es from a – far, Branch of roy – al
2. In thy God – head man – i – fest; Man – i – fest in
3. Quell – ing all the dev – il's might; Man – i – fest in
4. And be pure, as pure art thou; That we might be –

1. Da – vid's stem In thy birth at Beth – le – hem:
2. pow'r di – vine, Chang– ing wa – ter in – to wine;
3. gra – cious will, Ev – er bring – ing good from ill:
4. come like thee At thy great e – piph – a – ny,

1. An – thems be to thee ad – dressed,
2. An – thems be to thee ad – dressed,
3. An – thems be to thee ad – dressed,
4. And may praise thee, ev – er blest,

1-4. God in man made man – i – fest!

395. Spirit Divine, Attend Our Prayers

Text: Andrew Reed, 1788-1862

Tune: Graffenberg, C. M.
Johann Crüger, 1598-1662

1. Spir – it di – vine, at – tend our prayers,
2. Come as the light; to us re – veal
3. Come as the fire, and purge our hearts
4. Come as the dove, and spread thy wings,
5. Spir – it di – vine, at – tend our prayers,

1. And make this place thy home;
2. Our emp – ti – ness and woe,
3. Like sac – ri – fi – cial flame;
4. The wings of peace – ful love;
5. Make a lost world thy home;

1. De – scend with all thy gra – cious pow'rs,
2. And lead us in those paths of life
3. Let our whole soul an of – f'ring be
4. And let thy Church on earth be – come
5. De – scend with all thy gra – cious pow'rs,

1. O come, great Spir – it, come!
2. Where – on the right – eous go.
3. To our Re – deem – er's Name.
4. Blest as the Church a – bove.
5. O come, great Spir – it, come!

396. Spirit of Mercy, Truth and Love

Text: Anonymous
London Foundling Hospital Collection, 1774

Tune: Germany, L. M.
William Gardiner, 1770-1853

1. Spir – it of mer – cy, truth and love,
2. In ev – 'ry clime, by ev – 'ry tongue,
3. Un – fail – ing Com – fort, heav'n – ly Guide,

1. O shed thy pow – er from a – bove
2. Be God's sur – pass – ing glo – ry sung;
3. Still o'er thy ho – ly Church pre – side;

1. And still from age to age con – vey
2. Let all the list – 'ning earth be taught
3. Let hu – man – kind thy bless – ings prove,

1. The won – ders of this sa – cred day!
2. The won – ders by our Sav – ior wrought.
3. Spir – it of mer – cy, truth, and love.

397. Spread, O Spread, Thou Mighty Word

Text: *Walte Fürder*, Jonathan Friedrich Bahnmaier, 1774-1841   Tune: Freylinghausen, 77. 77.
Tr. Catherine Winkworth, 1827-1878   Johann A. Freylinghausen, 1670-1739

1. Spread, O spread, thou might – y Word,
2. Tell them how the Fa – ther's will
3. Tell of our Re – deem – er's love,
4. Tell them of the Spir – it giv'n
5. Word of life, most pure and strong,
6. Lord of har – vest, let there be

1. Spread the king – dom of the Lord,
2. Made the world, and keeps it still,
3. Who for – ev – er doth re – move
4. Now to guide us up to heav'n,
5. Lo! for thee the na – tions long,
6. Joy and strength to work for thee,

1. That on earth's re – mot – est bound,
2. How he sent his Son to save
3. By his ho – ly sac – ri – fice
4. Strong and ho – ly, just and true,
5. Spread, till from its drear – y night
6. Till the na – tions, far and near,

1. All may hear thy joy – ful sound.
2. all who help and com – fort crave.
3. all the guilt that on us lies.
4. work – ing both to will and do.
5. all the world a – wakes to light.
6. see thy light, and learn thy fear.

398. Stabat Mater Dolorosa

Text: Ascribed to Pope Innocent III or Jacopone da Todi　　　Tune: Stabat Mater, 8. 8. 7.
ENGLISH: "At the Cross Her Station Keeping"　　　*Mainz Gesanbuch*, 1661

1. Sta – bat ma – ter do – lo – ró – sa, Ju – xta cru – cem

1. la – cri – mó – sa, Dum pen – dé – bat Fí – li – us.

2. Cuius ánimam geméntem,
contristátam et doléntem
pertransívit gládius.

3. O quam tristis et afflícta
fuit illa benedícta,
mater Unigéniti!

4. Quae moerébat et dolébat,
pia Mater, dum vidébat
nati poenas inclýti.

5. Quis est homo qui non fleret,
matrem Christi si vidéret
in tanto supplício?

6. Quis non posset contristári
Christi Matrem contemplári
doléntem cum Fílio?

7. Pro peccátis suae gentis
vidit Iesum in torméntis,
et flagéllis súbditum.

8. Vidit suum dulcem Natum
moriéndo desolátum,
dum emísit spíritum.

9. Eia, Mater, fons amóris
me sentíre vim dolóris
fac, ut tecum lúgeam.

10. Fac, ut árdeat cor meum
in amándo Christum Deum
ut sibi compláceam.

11. Sancta Mater, istud agas,
crucifíxi fige plagas
cordi meo válide.

12. Tui Nati vulneráti,
tam dignáti pro me pati,
poenas mecum dívide.

13. Fac me tecum pie flere,
crucifixo condolére,
donec ego víxero.

14. Juxta Crucem tecum stare,
et me tibi sociáre
in planctu desídero.

15. Virgo vírginum praeclára,
mihi iam non sis amára,
fac me tecum plángere.

399. Take My Life and Let It Be

Text: Frances R. Havergal, 1836-1879

Tune: Patmos, 77. 77.
William H. Havergal, 1793-1870

1. Take my life, and let it be
2. Take my hands, and let them move
3. Take my voice, and let me sing
4. Take my sil – ver and my gold,
5. Take my will and make it thine;
6. Take my love; my Lord, I pour

1. Con – se – cra – ted, Lord, to thee;
2. At the im – pulse of thy love;
3. Al – ways, on – ly, for my King;
4. Not a mite would I with – hold;
5. It shall be no lon – ger mine;
6. At thy feet its trea – sured store;

1. Take my mo – ments and my days,
2. Take my feet, and let them be
3. Take my lips, and let them be
4. Take my in – tel – lect, and use
5. Take my heart, it is thine own;
6. Take my – self, and I will be,

1. Let them flow in cease – less praise.
2. Swift and beau – ti – ful for thee.
3. Filled with mes – sag – es from thee.
4. Ev – 'ry pow'r as thou shalt choose.
5. It shall be thy roy – al throne.
6. Ev – er, on – ly, all, for thee.

428

400. Take the Name of Jesus with You

Text: Lydia Baxter, 1809-1874

Tune: Precious Name, 87. 87. with Refrain
William H. Doane, 1832-1915

1. Take the name of Je – sus with you, Child of sor – row
2. Take the name of Je – sus ev – er, As a shield from
3. O the pre – cious name of Je – sus! How it thrills our
4. At the name of Je – sus bow– ing, Fall – ing pros–trate

1. and of woe; It will joy and com–fort give you –
2. ev – 'ry snare; If temp– ta – tions 'round you gath– er,
3. souls with joy, When his lov – ing arms re – ceive us,
4. at his feet, King of kings in heav'n we'll crown him,

Refrain:

1. Take it then wher – e'er you go.
2. Breathe that ho – ly name in prayer. Pre – cious name,
3. And his songs our tongues em – ploy!
4. When our jour –ney is com – plete.

O how sweet! Hope of earth and joy of heav'n; Pre – cious name,

O how sweet! Hope of earth and joy of heav'n.

401. Take Time to Be Holy

Text: William D. Longstaff, 1822-1894

Tune: Holiness, 65. 65. D
George C. Stebbins, 1846-1945

1. Take time to be ho – ly, Speak oft with the Lord;
2. Take time to be ho – ly, The world rush–es on;
3. Take time to be ho – ly, Let him be thy guide,
4. Take time to be ho – ly, Be calm in thy soul

1. A – bide in him al – ways And feed on his Word.
2. Spend much time in se – cret With Je – sus a – lone.
3. And run not be – fore him, What – ev – er be – tide.
4. Each thought and each mo – tive Be – neath his con – trol.

1. Make friends of God's chil – dren, Help those who are weak,
2. By look – ing to Je – sus, Like him thou shalt be;
3. In joy or in sor – row Still fol – low the Lord,
4. Thus led by his Spir – it To foun – tains of love,

1. For – get – ting in noth – ing His bless– ing to seek.
2. Thy friends in thy con – duct His like – ness shall see.
3. And, look – ing to Je – sus, Still trust in his Word.
4. Thou soon shalt be fit – ted For ser – vice a – bove.

402. Tantum Ergo Sacramentum

Text: St. Thomas Aquinas, 1227-1274
ENGLISH: "Down in Adoration Falling"

Tune: St. Thomas, 87. 87. 87.
Cantus Diversi, John Francis Wade, c. 1711-1786

1. Tan – tum er – go Sa – cra – mén – tum
2. Ge – ni – tó – ri, Ge – ni – tó – que

1. Ve – ne – ré – mur cér – nu – i:
2. Laus et ju – bi – lá – ti – o,

1. Et an – tí – quum do – cu – mén – tum
2. Sa – lus, ho – nor vir – tus quo – que

1. No – vo ce – dat rí – tu – i:
2. Sit et be – ne – dí – cti – o:

1. Prae – stet fi – des sup – ple – mén – tum
2. Pro – ce – dén – ti ab u – tró – que

1. Sén – su – um de – féc – tu – i.
2. Com – par sit lau – dá – ti – o. A – men.

403. That Day of Wrath, That Dreadful Day

Text: Sir Walter Scott, 1771-1832. Adapted from the *Dies Irae*.

Tune: Windham, L. M.
Daniel Read, 1757-1836

1. That day of wrath, that dread – ful day,
2. When, shriv – 'ling like a parch – éd scroll,
3. Lord, on that day, that wrath – ful day,

1. When heav'n and earth shall pass a – way!
2. The flam – ing heav'ns to – geth – er roll;
3. When man to judg – ment wakes from clay,

1. What pow'r shall be the sin – ner's stay?
2. When loud – er yet, and yet more dread,
3. Be thou the trem – bling sin – ner's stay,

1. How shall he meet that dread – ful day?
2. Swells the high trump that wakes the dead:
3. Though heav'n and earth shall pass a – way.

404. That Easter Day with Joy Was Bright

Text: *Claro Paschali Gaudio*, Office Hymn, 5th century
Tr. John Mason Neale, 1818-1866

Tune: Puer Nobis, L. M.
Michael Praetorius, 1571-1621

1. That Eas – ter Day with joy was
2. O Je – sus, King of gen – tle –
3. O Lord of all, with us a –
4. All praise, O ris – en Lord, we

1. bright; The sun shone out with
2. ness, Do thou thy – self our
3. bide, In this our joy – ful
4. give, To thee, who, dead, a –

1. fair – er light, When to their long – ing
2. hearts pos – sess, That we may give thee
3. Eas – ter – tide; From ev – 'ry wea – pon
4. gain dost live; To God the Fa – ther

1. eyes re – stored, The-a – pos – tles saw their
2. all our days, The will – ing trib – ute
3. death can wield, Thine own re – deemed for –
4. e – qual praise, And God the Ho – ly

1. ris – en Lord.
2. of our praise.
3. ev – er shield.
4. Ghost, we raise. A – men.

405. The Advent of Our God

Text: *Instantis Adventum Dei*, Charles Coffin, 1676-1749
Tr. John Chandler, 1806-1876

Tune: Franconia S. M.
Johann B. König, 1691-1758

1. The advent of our God
2. The everlasting Son,
3. Come, Zion's daughter, rise,
4. As judge, on clouds of light,
5. All glory to the Son,

1. Shall be our theme for prayer;
2. Incarnate stoops to be,
3. To meet your lowly king,
4. He soon will come again,
5. Who comes to set us free,

1. Come, let us meet him on the road
2. Himself the servant's form puts on
3. Nor let your faithless heart despise
4. And all his scattered saints unite
5. With Father, Spirit, ever one

1. And place for him prepare.
2. To set his people free.
3. The peace he comes to bring.
4. With him on high to reign.
5. Through all eternity.

406. The Ancient Law Departs

Text: Debilis Cessent Elementa Legis, Sebastien Besnault, d. 1724
Tr. *Hymns Ancient and Modern*, 1861

Tune: St. Michael, S. M.
Louis Bourgeois, c. 1510-1561

1. The an – cient law de – parts, And
2. The Light of Light di – vine, True
3. His in – fant bod – y now Be –
4. To – day the Name is thine, At

1. All its ter – rors cease; For
2. bright – ness un – de – filed, He
3. gins our pains to feel; Those
4. which we bend the knee; They

1. Je – sus makes with faith – ful hearts A
2. bears for us the shame of sin, A
3. pre – cious drops of blood that flow For
4. call thee Je – sus, Child di – vine! Our

1. cov – en – ant of peace.
2. ho – ly, spot – less Child.
3. death the vic – tim seal.
4. Je – sus deign to be.

407. The Church's One Foundation

Text: Samuel J. Stone, 1839-1900

Tune: Aurelia 76. 76. D.
Samuel S. Wesley, 1810-1876

1. The Church's one foun – da – tion Is Je – sus
2. 'Mid toil and trib – u – la – tion, And tu – mult
3. Yet she on earth hath un – ion With God, the

1. Christ her Lord; She is his new cre – a – tion
2. of her war, She waits the con – sum – ma – tion
3. three in One, And mys – tic sweet com – mun – ion

1. By wa – ter and the Word; From heav'n he
2. Of peace for – ev – er – more; Till with the
3. With those whose rest is won. O hap – py

1. came and sought her To be the ho – ly bride;
2. vi – sion glo – rious, Her long – ing eyes are blest,
3. ones and ho – ly! Lord, give us grace that we

1. With his own blood he bought her,
2. And the great Church vic – to – rious
3. Like them, the meek and low – ly,

1. And for her life he died.
2. Shall be the Church at rest.
3. On high may dwell with thee.

408. The Day of Resurrection

Text: *Αναστάσεως ἡμέρα*, John of Damascus, 675-749
Tr. John Mason Neale, 1818-1866

Tune: Passion Chorale, 76. 76. D
Hans Leo Hassler, 1564-1612

1. The day of re – sur – rec – tion! Earth, tell it
2. Our hearts be pure from e – vil, That we may
3. Now let the heav'ns be joy – ful! Let earth her

1. out a – broad; The Pass – o – ver of glad – ness,
2. see a – right The Lord in rays e – ter – nal
3. song be – gin! The round world keep high tri – umph,

1. The Pass – o – ver of God. From death to life
2. Of re – sur – rec – tion light; And list – 'ning to
3. And all that is there – in! Let all things seen

1. e – ter – nal, From earth un – to the sky,
2. his ac – cents, May hear so calm and plain
3. and un – seen Their notes in glad – ness blend,

1. Our Christ hath brought us o – ver,
2. His own "All hail!" and, hear – ing,
3. For Christ the Lord hath ris – en,

1. With hymns of vic – to – ry.
2. May raise the vic – tor strain.
3. Our joy that hath no end.

409. The Glory of These Forty Days

Text: *Clarum Decus Jejunii*, St. Gregory the Great, 540-604
Tr. Maurice Bell, 1862-1947

Tune: Erhalt Uns Herr, L. M.
Joseph Klug, 1523-1552

1. The glo – ry of these for – ty days
2. A – lone and fast – ing Mo – ses saw
3. So Dan – iel trained his mys – tic sight,
4. Then grant us, Lord, like them to be
5. O Fa – ther, Son, and Spir – it blest,

1. We cel – e – brate with songs of praise;
2. The lov – ing God who gave the law;
3. De – liv – er'd from the li – on's might;
4. Full oft in fast and prayer with thee;
5. To thee be ev – 'ry prayer ad – drest;

1. For Christ, by whom all things were made,
2. And to E – li – jah, fast – ing, came
3. And John, the Bride – groom's friend, be – came
4. Our spir – its strength – en with thy grace,
5. Who art in three – fold name a – dored,

1. Him – self has fast – ed and has prayed.
2. The steeds and char – i – ots of flame.
3. The her – ald of Mes – si – ah's name.
4. And give us joy to see thy face.
5. From age to age, the on – ly Lord. A – men.

410. The God Whom Earth and Sea and Sky

Text: *Quem Terra Pontus Aethera*, Venantius Fortunatus, 530-609
Tr. John Mason Neale, 1818-1866

Tune: Eisenach, L. M.
Johann H. Schein, 1586-1630

1. The God whom earth and sea and sky
2. The God whose will by moon, and sun,
3. O Moth – er blest! the cho – sen shrine
4. Blest in the mes – age Ga – briel brought;
5. O Lord, the Vir – gin – born, to you

1. A – dore and laud and mag – ni – fy,
2. And all things in due course is done,
3. Where in the ar – chi – tect di – vine,
4. Blest in the work the Spir – it wrought;
5. E – ter – nal praise and laud are due,

1. Whose might they claim, whose love they tell,
2. Is borne up – on a Maid – en's breast,
3. Whose hand con – tains the earth and sky,
4. Most blest, to bring to hu – man birth
5. Whom with the Fa – ther we a – dore

1. In Ma – ry's bod – y comes to dwell.
2. By full – est heav'n – ly grace pos – sessed.
3. Has come in hu – man form to lie:
4. The long de – sired of all the earth.
5. And Spir – it blest for ev – er – more.

411. The Head That Once Was Crowned with Thorns

Text: Thomas Kelley, 1789-1854

Tune: St. Magnus, C. M.
Jeremiah Clark, c. 1670-1707

1. The head that once was crowned with thorns
2. The high – est place that heav'n af – fords
3. The joy of all who dwell a – bove,
4. To them the cross with all its shame,
5. They suf – fer with their Lord be – low;
6. The cross he bore is life and health,

1. Is crowned with glo – ry now;
2. Be – longs to him by right;
3. The joy of all be – low,
4. With all its grace, is giv'n;
5. They reign with him a – bove;
6. Though shame and death to him,

1. A roy – al di – a – dem a – dorns
2. The King of kings, and Lord of lords,
3. To whom he man – i – fests his love,
4. Their name an ev – er – last – ing name;
5. Their prof – it and their joy to know
6. His peo – ple's hope, his peo – ple's wealth,

1. The might – y vic – tor's brow.
2. And heav'n's e – ter – nal light.
3. And grants his name to know.
4. Their joy the joy of heav'n.
5. The mys – t'ry of his love.
6. Their ev – er – last – ing theme.

412. The King of Love My Shepherd Is

Text: Henry W. Baker, 1821-1877

Tune: St. Columba, 87. 87.
Traditional Gaelic Melody

1.	The	King	of	love	my	shep – herd	is,
2.	Where	streams	of	liv – ing	wa – ter	flow,
3.	Per –	verse	and	fool – ish	oft	I	strayed,
4.	In	death's	dark	vale	I	fear	no	ill,
5.	Thou	spreadst	a	ta – ble	in	my	sight
6.	And	so,	through	all	the	length	of	days

1.	Whose	good –	ness	fail –	eth	nev –	er;
2.	My	ran –	somed	soul	he	lead –	eth
3.	But	yet	in	love	he	sought	me,
4.	With	thee,	dear	Lord,	be –	side	me,
5.	Thine	unc –	tion	grace	be –	stow –	eth;
6.	Thy	good –	ness	fail –	eth	nev –	er.

1.	I	noth –	ing	lack	if	I	am	his
2.	And,	where	the	ver –	dant	pas –	tures	grow,
3.	And	on	his	shoul –	der	gen –	tly	laid,
4.	Thy	rod	and	staff	my	com –	fort	still;
5.	And,	oh,	what	trans –	port	of	de –	light
6.	Good	Shep –	herd,	may	I	sing	thy	praise

1.	And	he	is	mine	for –	ev –	er.
2.	With	food	ce –	les –	tial	feed –	eth.
3.	And	home,	re –	joic –	ing,	brought	me.
4.	Thy	cross	be –	fore	to	guide	me.
5.	From	thy	pure	chal –	ice	flow –	eth!
6.	With –	in	thy	house	for –	ev –	er.

413. The Master Hath Come

Text: Sarah Doudney, 1841-1926

Tune: The Ash Grove, 12. 11. 12. 11. D.
Welsh Folk Melody

1. The Mas –ter hath   come, and he calls us   to   fol – low   The
2. The Mas –ter hath   called us; the road may be   drear – y,   And
3. The Mas –ter hath   called us,   in   life's ear – ly   morn – ing,   With

1. track of   the   foot – prints he   leaves on   our   way;   Far
2. dan–gers and   sor – rows are   strewn on   the   track;   But
3. spir–its   as   fresh as   the   dew on   the   sod: We

1. o – ver   the   moun–tain and through the   deep   hol – low,   The
2. God's Ho–ly   Spir – it   shall com – fort   the   wea– ry;   We
3. turn from the   world, with its   smiles   and   its   scorn–ing,   To

1. path leads   us   on   to   the   man –sions of   day: The
2. fol – low   the   Sa –vior and   can – not   turn   back;   The
3. cast in   our   lot with the   peo – ple   of   God: The

1. Mas– ter   hath   called us, the   chil – dren who   fear   him,   Who
2. Mas– ter   hath   called us: though doubt and   temp – ta – tion   May
3. Mas– ter   hath   called us, his   sons   and   his   daugh – ters,   We

1. march 'neath Christ's ban –ner, his own lit – tle band; We
2. com –pass our jour –ney, we cheer–ful – ly sing: "Press
3. plead for his bles –sing and trust in his love; And

1. love him and seek him, we long to be near him, And
2. on – ward, look up – ward," thro' much trib –u – la – tion; The
3. through the green pas–tures, be – side the still wa – ters, He'll

1. rest in the light of his beau – ti – ful land.
2. chil – dren of Zi – on must fol – low their King.
3. lead us at last to his king – dom a – bove.

414. The Morning Sun Illumes the Skies

Text: Nicolaus Hermann, 1500-1561
Tr. Herman Brueckner, 1866-1942

Tune: Canonbury, L. M.
Robert Alexander Schumann, 1810-1856

1. The mor – ning sun il – lumes the skies,
2. Lord Je – sus, be our shield this day
3. Make thou our hearts o – be – di – ent
4. Grant that our work may pros – per well,

1. And we from peace – ful slum – bers rise;
2. And keep us on the nar – row way;
3. To do thy will till life is spent,
4. While we be – neath thy shad – ow dwell.

1. All praise to God, who hath this night
2. To us thy ho – ly an – gels send
3. To heed thy Word, what – e'er be – tide,
4. Let all that we be – gin with thee

1. Pro – tect – ed us from Sa – tan's might.
2. And let them to our needs at – tend.
3. And fol – low thee, our faith – ful Guide.
4. To thine own praise ac – com – plished be.

415. The Old Year Now Hath Passed Away

Text: *Das Alte Jahr Vergangen Ist*, Johann Steuerlein, 1546-1613   Tune: Old Hundredth, L. M.
Tr. Catherine Winkworth, 1827-1878   Louis Bourgeois, c. 1510-1561

1. The old year now hath passed away,
2. O thou, the Father's only Son,
3. Take not thy saving Word away,
4. O grant that we, renouncing sin,
5. Thus as true Christians may we live,

1. And we would thank thee, Lord, today
2. Be with us till our course is run.
3. The soul's true comfort, staff, and stay;
4. A better life may now begin;
5. And may thy peace sweet comfort give

1. That thou wast nigh our hearts to cheer
2. Guard thou and rule thy Christendom
3. Abide with us that we may be
4. Hide from the old year's guilt thy face
5. When we shall leave this world of strife

1. When danger and distress drew near.
2. Through all the ages yet to come.
3. From grievous errors ever free.
4. And for the new year lend thy grace.
5. And pass through death to blissful life.

416. The People Who in Darkness Walked

Text: John Morison, 1749-1798

Tune: Dundee, C. M.
Scottish Psalter, 1615

1. The peo – ple who in dark – ness walked
2. To hail thy ris – ing, Sun of life,
3. To us the prom – ised Child is born,
4. His name shall be the Prince of Peace
5. His pow'r in – creas – ing still shall spread,

1. Have seen a glo – rious light;
2. The ga – th'ring na – tions come,
3. To us the Son is giv'n;
4. For – ev – er – more a – dored,
5. His reign no end shall know;

1. On them broke forth the heav'n – ly dawn
2. Joy – ous as when the reap – ers bear
3. Him shall the tribes of earth o – bey,
4. The Won – der – ful, the Coun – sel – lor,
5. Jus – tice shall guard his throne a – bove,

1. Who dwelt in death and night.
2. Their har – vest trea – sures home.
3. And all the hosts of heav'n.
4. The might – y God and Lord.
5. And peace a – bound be – low.

417. The Royal Banners Forward Go

Text: *Vexilla Regis Prodeunt*, Venantius Fortunatus, 530-609
Tr. John Mason Neale, 1818-1866

Tune: Vexilla Regis, L. M.
Chant, Mode I

1. The roy – al ban – ners for – ward go,
2. Where deep for us the spear was dyed,
3. O cross, our one re – li – ance, hail!
4. To thee, e – ter – nal Three in One,

1. The cross shines forth in mys – tic glow;
2. Life's tor – rent rush – ing from his side,
3. Still may thy pow'r with us a – vail
4. Let hom – age meet by all be done:

1. Where he in flesh, our flesh who made,
2. To wash us in that pre – cious flood,
3. To give new vir – tue to the saint,
4. As by the cross thou dost re – store,

1. Our sen – tence bore, our ran – som paid.
2. Where min – gled wa – ter flowed, and blood.
3. And par – don to the pen – i – tent.
4. So rule and guide us ev – er – more.

After the Last verse:

A – – men.

418. The Star-Spangled Banner

Text: Francis Scott Key. 1779-1843

Tune: Star-Spangled Banner, irregular
John Stafford Smith, 1750-1836

1. O say can you see, by the dawn's ear – ly light,
2. O thus be it ev – er, when free men shall stand

1. What so proud – ly we hailed at the twi – light's last gleam – ing,
2. Be – tween their loved homes and the war's des – o – la – tion!

1. Whose broad stripes and bright stars, thru the per – il – ous fight,
2. Blest with vic – t'ry and peace, may the heav'n res – cued land

1. O'er the ram – parts we watched, were so gal – lant – ly stream–ing?
2. Praise the Pow'r that hath made and pre– served us a na –tion!

1. And the rock–ets' red glare, the bombs burst – ing in air,
2. Then con – quer we must, when our cause it is just;

1. Gave proof thru the night that our flag was still there.
2. And this be our mot – to: "In God is our trust!"

1. O say does that star – span – gled ban – ner yet wave
2. And the star– span – gled ban – ner in tri – umph shall wave

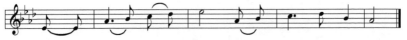

1. O'er the land of the free and the home of the brave?
2. O'er the land of the free and the home of the brave!

419. The Sun's Bright Rays Are Lost to Sight

Text: Nicolaus Hermann, 1500-1561
Tr. Herman Brueckner, 1866-1942

Tune: Compline Hymn, L. M.
Prepared for this Hymnal

1. The sun's bright rays are lost to sight,
2. To thee our fer – vent thanks we pay,
3. Our sins and faults do thou ef – face,
4. Thine an – gel guards from heav – en send,

1. A – round us spreads the gloom of night;
2. Whose mer – cy crowned us all this day;
3. Vouch – safe to us thy bound – less grace;
4. A – gainst the foe pro – tec – tion lend;

1. Lord Je – sus Christ, thou light di – vine,
2. For thou didst send thine an – gels fair,
3. By thy for – give – ness tru – ly blest,
4. O gra – cious Lord, from per – ils sore

1. Let not our souls in dark – ness pine.
2. Who kept us in their ten – der care.
3. May we in sleep find peace and rest.
4. Shield us to – night and ev – er more.

After the Last verse:

A – – men.

420. There Is a Green Hill Far Away

Text: Cecil F. Alexander, 1823-1895

Tune: Windsor, C. M.
Booke of Musicke, 1591

1. There is a green hill far a – way,
2. We may not know, we can – not tell,
3. He dies that we might be for – giv'n;

1. Out – side a cit – y wall,
2. What pains he had to bear,
3. He died to make us good,

1. Where the dear Lord was cru – ci – fied,
2. But we be – lieve it was for us
3. That we might go at last to heav'n,

1. Who died to save us all.
2. He hung and suf – fered there.
3. Saved by his pre – cious blood.

421. 'Tis Good, Lord, to Be Here

Text: Joseph A. Robinson, 1858-1933

Tune: Swabia, S. M.
Johann M. Spiess, 1715-1766

1. 'Tis good, Lord, to be here!
2. 'Tis good, Lord, to be here!
3. Ful – fill – er of the past!
4. Be – fore we taste of death,
5. 'Tis good, Lord, to be here!

1. Thy glo – ry fills the night;
2. Thy beau – ty to be – hold,
3. Prom – ise of things to be!
4. We see thy king – dom come;
5. Yet we may not re – main;

1. Thy face and gar – ments, like the sun,
2. Where Mo – ses and E – li – jah stand,
3. We hail thy bod – y glo – ri – fied,
4. We fain would hold the vi – sion bright,
5. But since thou bidst us leave the mount,

1. Shine with un – bor – rowed light.
2. Thy mes – sen – gers of old.
3. And our re – demp – tion see.
4. And make this hill our home.
5. Come with us to the plain. A – men.

422. Tu Christe Nostrum Gaudium

Text: Anonymous, 5th Century   Tune: Deus Tuorum Militum (Grenoble), L. M.
ENGLISH: "O Christ, Thou Art Our Joy Alone"   *Grenoble Antiphoner*, 1753

1. Tu, Chri — ste, no — strum gaú — di — um,
2. Hinc te pre — cán — tes quaé — su — mus,
3. Tu e — sto no — strum gaú — di — um,

1. Ma — nens o — lým — po praé — di — tum,
2. I — gnó — sce cul — pis ó — mni — bus,
3. Qui es fu — tú — rus praé — mi — um;

1. Mun — di re — gis qui fá — bri — cam,
2. Et cor — da sur — sum súb — le — va
3. Sit no — stra in te gló — ri — a

1. Mun — dá — na vin — cens gaú — di — a.
2. Ad te su — pér — na grá — ti — a.
3. Per cun — cta sem — per saé — cu — la.

452

423. Veni, Creator Spiritus

Text: Rabanus Maurus, 776-856
ENGLISH: "Come Holy Ghost" and "Creator Spirit"

Tune: Veni Creator, L. M.
Chant, Mode VIII

1. Ve – ni Cre – á – tor Spí – ri – tus,
2. Qui di – cé – ris Pa – rá – cli – tus,
3. Tu se – pti – fór – mis mú – ne – re,
4. Ac – cén – de lu – men sén – si – bus,
5. Ho – stem re – pél las lón – gi – us,
6. Per te sci – á – mus da Pa – trem,
7. De – o Pa – tri sit gló – ri – a,

1. Men – tes tu – ó – rum ví – si – ta:
2. Al – tís – si – mi do – num De – i,
3. Dí–gi – tus pa – tér – nae déx – te – rae,
4. In – fún – de-a mó – rem cór – di – bus,
5. Pa – cém – que do – nes pró – ti – nus:
6. No – scá – mus at – que Fí – li – um,
7. Et Fí – li – o, qui-a mór – tu – is

1. Im – ple su – pér – na grá – ti – a,
2. Fons vi – vus, i – gnis, cá – ri – tas,
3. Tu ri – te pro – mís – sum Pa – tris,
4. In – fír – ma no – stri cór – po – ris
5. Du – ctó – re sic te praé – vi – o
6. Te – que u – tri – ús – que Spí – ri – tum
7. Sur – ré – xit, ac Pa – rá – cli – to,

1. Quae tu cre – á – sti pé – cto – ra.
2. Et spi – ri – tá – lis ún – cti – o.
3. Ser – mó – ne di – tans gút – tu – ra.
4. Vir – tú – te fir – mans pér – pe – ti.
5. Vi – té – mus o – mne nó – xi – um.
6. Cre – dá – mus o – mni tém – po – re. *(After last verse:)*
7. In sae – cu – ló – rum saé – cu – la. A – men.

424. Veni, Sancte Spiritus

Text: Pope Innocent III, 1160-1216, or Stephen Langton, 1150-1228   Tune: Veni Sancte Spiritus
ENGLISH: "Come, Thou Holy Spirit, Come"   Chant, Mode I

1. Ve – ni, San – cte, Spí – ri – tus, Et e – mít – te
2. Ve – ni, Pa – ter páu – pe – rum, Ve – ni, da – tor

1. cae – li – tus, Lu – cis tu – ae rá – di – um.
2. mú – ne – rum, Ve – ni Lu – men cór – di – um.

3. Con – so – lá – tor ó – pti – me, Dul – cis ho – spes
4. In la – bó – re ré – qui – es, In ae – stu tem –

3. á – ni – mae, Dul – ce re – fri – gé – ri – um.
4. pé – ri – es, In fle – tu so – lá – ti – um.

5. O Lux be – a – tís – si – ma, Re – ple cor – dis
6. Si – ne tu – o nú – mi – ne, Ni – hil est in

5. ín – ti – ma, Tu – ó – rum fi – dé – li – um.
6. hó – mi – ne, Ni – hil est in – nó – xi – um.

7. La – va quod est sór – di – dum, Ri – ga quod est
8. Fle – cte quod est rí – gi – dum, Fo – ve quod est

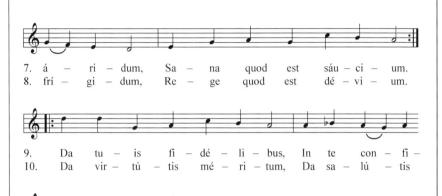

7. á – ri – dum, Sa – na quod est sáu – ci – um.
8. frí – gi – dum, Re – ge quod est dé – vi – um.

9. Da tu – is fi – dé – li – bus, In te con – fi –
10. Da vir – tú – tis mé – ri – tum, Da sa – lú – tis

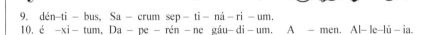

9. dén–ti – bus, Sa – crum sep – ti – ná – ri – um.
10. é –xi – tum, Da – pe – rén – ne gáu– di – um. A – men. Al– le–lú – ia.

425. Veni, Veni, Emmanuel

Text: Anonymous, 9th Century
ENGLISH: "O Come, O Come Emmanuel"

Tune: Veni, Veni, Emmanuel L. M.
Chant, Mode I

1. Ve — ni, ve — ni, Em — man — nu — el!
2. Ve — ni, O Jes — se Vir — gu — la!
3. Ve — ni, ve — ni O Ó — ri — ens!
4. Ve — ni Cla — vis Da — ví — di — ca!

1. Cap — ti — vum sol — ve Is — ra — el;
2. Ex hos — tis tu — os un — gu — la:
3. So — lá — re nos ad vé — ni — ens:
4. Re — gna, re — clú — de coé — li — ca

1. Qui ge — mit in e — xi — li — o,
2. De spe — cu tu — os tar — ta — ri,
3. No — ctis de — pél — le né — bu — las,
4. Fac i — ter tu — tum su — pér — num

1. Pri — va — tus De — i Fi — li — o.
2. E — duc, et an — tro ba — rath — ri.
3. Di — rás — que no — ctis té — ne — bras.
4. Et clau — de vi — as ín — fe — rum.

Refrain:

Gau — de, Gau — de, Em — mán — nu — el!

Na — scé — tur pro te, Ís — ra — el.

426. Vexilla Regis Prodeunt

Text: Venantius Fortunatus, 530-609
ENGLISH: "The Royal Banners Forward Go"

Tune: Vexilla Regis, L. M.
Chant, Mode I

1. Ve – xíl – la Re – gis pró – de – unt:
2. Quae vul – ne – rá – ta lán – ce – ae
3. O Crux a – ve, spes ú – ni – ca,
4. Te, fons sa – lú – tis Trí – ni – tas,

1. Ful – get Cru – cis my – sté – ri – um,
2. Mu – cró – ne di – ro, crí – mi – num
3. *Hoc Pas – si – ó – nis tém – po – re;
4. Col – laú – det o – mnis spí – ri – tus:

1. Qua vi – ta mor – tem pér – tu – lit,
2. Ut nos la – vá – ret sór – di – bus,
3. Pi – is ad – aú – ge grá – ti – am,
4. Qui – bus Cru – cis vi – ctó – ri – am

1. Et mor – te vi – tam pró – tu – lit.
2. Ma – ná – vit un – da-et sán – gui – ne.
3. Re – ís – que de – le crí – mi – na.
4. Lar – gí – ris, ad – de praé – mi – um.

After the Last verse:

A – – men.

* *During Paschaltide:* **Paschále quae fers gaúdium.**
 Outside both Paschaltide and Passiontide: **In hac triúmphi glória.**

427. Victimae Paschali Laudes

Text: Wipo of Burgundy, c. 995-1050
ENGLISH: "Christians, to the Paschal Victim"

Tune: Victimae Paschali, irregular
Chant, Mode I

1. Vic – ti – mae Pas – cha – li lau – des, im – mo – lent Chris – ti –

a – ni. **2.** A – gnus re – de – mit o – ves: Chri – stus in – no –

cens Pa – tri re – con – ci – li – a – vit pec – ca – tor – es.

3. Mors et vi – ta du – el – lo con – fli – xe – re mi – ran – do:

dux vi – tae mor – tu – us re – gnat vi – vus. **4.** Dic no – bis

Ma – ri – a, quid vi – di – sti in vi – a? **5.** Se – pul – chrum Chri –

sti vi – ven – tis, et glo – ri – am vi – di re – sur – gen – tis.

6. An – ge – li –cos te –stes, su –da – ri – um et ve – stes.

7. Sur – re –xit Chri–stus spes me – a: prae–ce – det su – os in Ga –

li – le – am. **8.** Sci – mus Chri–stum sur– re –xis – se a mor–tu –

is ve – re: tu no – bis vic – tor Rex, mi – se –

re – re. A – men. Al – le – lu – ia.

428. We Gather Together

Text: Theodore Baker, 1851-1934

Tune: Kremser, 12. 11. 12. 11.
Dutch Folk Melody, arr. By Edward Kremser, 1838-1914

1. We gath – er to – geth – er to ask the Lord's bless–ing;
2. Be – side us to guide us, our God with us join – ing,
3. We all do ex – tol thee, thou, lead –er tri – um – phant,

1. He chast – ens and hast – ens his will to make known;
2. Or – dain – ing, main – tain – ing his king – dom di – vine;
3. And pray that thou still our de – fend – er wilt be.

1. The wick – ed op – press–ing now cease from dis – tress –ing:
2. So from the be – gin –ning the fight we were win – ing:
3. Let thy con –gre – ga – tion es – cape trib – u – la – tion:

1. Sing prais–es to his name; he for – gets not his own.
2. Thou, Lord, wast at our side: all glo – ry be thine!
3. Thy name be ev– er praised! O Lord, make us free!

429. We Give Thee But Thine Own

Text: William W. How, 1823-1897

Tune: Heath, S. M.
Cantica Lauda, 1850

1. We give thee but thine own, What —
2. May we thy boun – ties thus As
3. O hearts are bruised and dead, And
4. To com – fort and to bless, To
5. The cap – tive to re – lease, To

1. e'er the gift may be; All
2. stew – ards true re – ceive; And
3. homes are bare and cold, And
4. find a balm for woe, To
5. God the lost to bring, To

1. that we have is thine a – lone, A
2. glad – ly as thou bless – est us, To
3. lambs for whom the Shep – herd bled Are
4. tend the lone and fa – ther – less Is
5. teach the way of life and peace? It

1. trust, O Lord, from thee.
2. thee our first – fruits give.
3. stray – ing from the fold.
4. an – gels' work be – low.
5. is a Christ – like thing.

430. We Praise Thee, O God (Te Deum)

Text: *Te Deum Laudamus*, St. Ambrose of Milan, 340-397 Tune: Chant, Psalm Tone VII
Tr. *Book of Common Prayer*, 1928

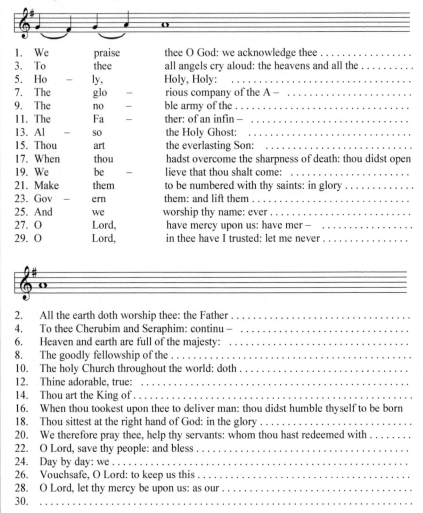

1. We	praise	thee O God: we acknowledge thee . . . .
3. To	thee	all angels cry aloud: the heavens and all the . . . .
5. Ho – ly,		Holy, Holy: . . . .
7. The glo –		rious company of the A – . . . .
9. The no –		ble army of the . . . .
11. The Fa –		ther: of an infin – . . . .
13. Al – so		the Holy Ghost: . . . .
15. Thou	art	the everlasting Son: . . . .
17. When	thou	hadst overcome the sharpness of death: thou didst open
19. We	be –	lieve that thou shalt come: . . . .
21. Make	them	to be numbered with thy saints: in glory . . . .
23. Gov – ern		them: and lift them . . . .
25. And	we	worship thy name: ever . . . .
27. O	Lord,	have mercy upon us: have mer – . . . .
29. O	Lord,	in thee have I trusted: let me never . . . .

2. All the earth doth worship thee: the Father . . . .
4. To thee Cherubim and Seraphim: continu – . . . .
6. Heaven and earth are full of the majesty: . . . .
8. The goodly fellowship of the . . . .
10. The holy Church throughout the world: doth . . . .
12. Thine adorable, true: . . . .
14. Thou art the King of . . . .
16. When thou tookest upon thee to deliver man: thou didst humble thyself to be born
18. Thou sittest at the right hand of God: in the glory . . . .
20. We therefore pray thee, help thy servants: whom thou hast redeemed with . . . .
22. O Lord, save thy people: and bless . . . .
24. Day by day: we . . . .
26. Vouchsafe, O Lord: to keep us this . . . .
28. O Lord, let thy mercy be upon us: as our . . . .
30. . . . .

1.	....	to	be	the	Lord.
3.	....	pow –	ers	there –	in.
5.	....	Lord	God	of	Hosts;
7.	....	pos –	tles:	praise	thee.
9.	....	Mar –	tyrs:	praise	thee.
11.	....	ite	maj – es –		ty;
13.	....	the	Com –	for –	ter.
15.	....	of	the	Fa –	ther.
17.	the kingdom of heaven to	all	be –	lieve –	ers.
19.	....	to	be	our	Judge.
21.	....	ev –	er –	last –	ing.
23.	....	up	for –	ev –	er.
25.	....	world	with –	out	end.
27.	....	cy	up –	on	us.
29.	....	be	con –	found –	ed.

2.	....	ev –	er –	last –	ing.
4.	....	al –	ly	do	cry,
6.	....	of	thy	glo –	ry.
8.	....	Proph –	ets:	praise	thee.
10.	....	ac –	knowl –	edge	thee;
12.	....	and	on –	ly	Son;
14.	....	Glo –	ry:	O	Christ.
16.	....	of	a	Vir –	gin.
18.	....	of	the	Fa –	ther.
20.	....	thy	pre –	cious	blood.
22.	....	thine	her –	it –	age,
24.	....	mag –	ni –	fy	thee.
26.	....	day	with –	out	sin.
28.	....	trust	is	in	thee.
30.	....	A –	–	–	men.

431. We Three Kings of Orient Are

Text: John Henry Hopkins, Jr., 1820-1891

Tune: Kings of Orient, 88. 84.6. with Refrain
John Henry Hopkins, Jr., 1820-1891

1. We three kings of O – ri – ent are, Bear– ing gifts we
2. Born a Babe on Beth – le – hem's plain, Gold we bring to
3. Frank–in – cense to of – fer have I; In – cense owns a
4. Myrrh is mine; its bit – ter per – fume Breathes a life of
5. Glo – rious now be – hold – him rise, King and God and

1. trav – erse a – far Field and foun – tain, moor and
2. crown him a – gain; King for – ev – er, ceas – ing
3. de – i – ty nigh, Prayer and prais – ing all men
4. gath – 'ring gloom; Sor – r'wing, sigh – ing, bleed – ing,
5. sac – ri – fice; Heav'n sing "Hal – le – lu – jah!"

1. moun – tain, Fol – low – ing yon – der Star.
2. nev – er, O – ver us all to reign.
3. rais – ing, Wor – ship God on high.
4. dy – ing, Sealed in the stone cold tomb.
5. "Hal – le – lu – jah!" earth re – plies.

Refrain:

Oh, star of won – der, star of night, Star with roy – al

beau–ty bright, West – ward lead – ing, still pro – ceed – ing,

Guide us to the per – fect Light.

432. Were you There

Text: African-American Spiritual

Tune: Were You There, 10. 10. 14. 10.
African-American Spiritual

1. Were you there when they cru – ci – fied my Lord? Were you
2. Were you there when they nailed him to the tree? Were you
3. Were you there when they laid him in the tomb? Were you
4. Were you there when God raised him from the tomb? Were you

1. there when they cru – ci – fied my Lord? Oh,
2. there when they nailed him to the tree? Oh,
3. there when they laid him in the tomb? Oh,
4. there when God raised him from the tomb? Oh,

1. some – times it caus– es me to trem – ble, trem – ble, trem – ble.
2. some – times it caus– es me to trem – ble, trem – ble, trem – ble.
3. some – times it caus– es me to trem – ble, trem – ble, trem – ble.
4. some – times it caus– es me to trem – ble, trem – ble, trem – ble.

1. Were you there when they cru – ci – fied my Lord?
2. Were you there when they nailed him to the tree?
3. Were you there when they laid him in the tomb?
4. Were you there when God raised him from the tomb?

465

433. What a Friend We Have in Jesus

Text: Joseph Scriven, 1820-1886

Tune: Converse, 87. 87. D.
Charles C. Converse, 1832-1918

1. What a friend we have in Je – sus, All our
2. Have we tri – als and temp – ta – tions? Is there
3. Are we weak and heav – y – lad – en, Cum – bered

1. sins and griefs to bear! What a priv – i – lege to
2. trou – ble an – y – where? We should nev – er be dis –
3. with a load of care? Pre – cious Sav – ior, still our

1. car – ry Ev – 'ry – thing to God in prayer!
2. cour – aged – Take it to the Lord in prayer.
3. ref – uge – Take it to the Lord in prayer.

1. Oh, what peace we of – ten for – feit; Oh, what
2. Can we find a friend so faith – ful Who will
3. Do your friends de – spise, for – sake you? Take it

1. need – less pain we bear – All be – cause we do not
2. all our sor – rows share? Je – sus knows our ev – 'ry
3. to the Lord in prayer. In his arms he'll take and

1. car – ry Ev – 'ry – thing to God in prayer!
2. weak – ness – Take it to the Lord in prayer.
3. shield you; You will find a so – lace there.

434. What Child is This

Text: William Chatterton Dix (1837-1898)

Tune: Greensleeves 87. 87. with Refrain
English Ballad, 16th Century

1. What child is this, who, laid to rest, On Ma – ry's
2. Why lies he in such mean es – tate, Where ox and
3. So bring him in – cense, gold, and myrrh, Come peas–ant,

1. lap is sleep – ing? Whom an – gels greet with an –
2. ass are feed – ing? Good Chris– tian, fear; for sin –
3. king, to own him; The King of kings sal – va –

1. thems sweet, While shep – herds watch are keep – ing?
2. ners here, The si – lent Word is plead – ing.
3. tion brings, Let lov – ing hearts en – throne him.

1. This, this is Christ the King, Whom shep – herds
2. Nail, spear shall pierce him through, The cross be
3. Raise, raise a song on high, The Vir – gin

1. guard and an – gels sing; Haste, haste to bring
2. borne for me, for you. Hail, hail the Word
3. sings her lull – a – by. Joy, joy for Christ

1. him laud, The Babe, the Son of Ma – ry.
2. made flesh, The Babe, the Son of Ma – ry.
3. is born, The Babe, the Son of Ma – ry.

435. With Broken Heart and Contrite Sigh

Text: Cornelius Elven, 1791-1873

Tune: St. Cross, L. M.
John Bacchus Dykes, 1823-1876

1. With bro – ken heart and con – trite sigh,
2. I smite up – on my troub – led breast,
3. Far off I stand with tear – ful eyes,
4. Nor alms, nor deeds that I have done,
5. And when, re – deemed from sin and hell,

1. A trem – bling sin – ner, Lord, I cry; Thy
2. With deep and con – scious guilt op – pressed, Christ
3. Nor dare up – lift them to the skies; But
4. Can for a sin – gle sin a – tone; To
5. With all the ran – somed throng I dwell, My

1. par – d'ning grace is rich and free:
2. and His cross my on – ly plea:
3. Thou dost all my an – guish see:
4. Cal – va – ry a – lone I flee:
5. rap – tured song shall ev – er be,

1. O God, be mer – ci – ful to me.
2. O God, be mer – ci – ful to me.
3. O God, be mer – ci – ful to me.
4. O God, be mer – ci – ful to me.
5. God has been mer – ci – ful to me.

436. Ye Sons and Daughters of the King

Text: Jean Tisserand, 15th Century
Tr. John Mason Neale, 1818-1866

Tune: O Filii et Filiae, 8. 8. 8. with Alleluias
Solesmes, 15th Century

Refrain

Al – le – lu – ia,   al – le – lu – ia,   al – le – lu – ia!

1. Ye   sons   and   daugh – ters   of   the   King,
2. On   that   first   mor – ning   of   the   week,
3. An   an – gel   bade   their   sor – row   flee,
4. On   this   most   ho – ly   day   of   days,
5. And   we   with   ho – ly   Church   u – nite,

1. Whom   heav'n – ly   hosts   in   glo – ry   sing,
2. Be – fore   the   day   be – gan   to   break,
3. For   thus   he   spake   un – to   the   three:
4. To   God   your   hearts   and   voic – es   raise
5. As   ev – er – more   is   just   and   right,

1. To – day   the   grave   hath lost   its   sting,   al – le – lu – ia!
2. The Ma – rys   went   their   Lord   to   seek,   al – le – lu – ia!
3. "Your Lord is   gone   to   Ga – li – lee,"   al – le – lu – ia!
4. In   laud, and   ju – bi – lee,   and   praise,   al – le – lu – ia!
5. In   glo – ry   to   the   King   of   Light,   al – le – lu – ia!

437. Ye Watchers and Ye Holy Ones

Text: John Athelstan Riley, 1858-1945

Tune: Lasst Uns Erfreuen, L. M. with alleluias
Geistliche Kirchengesange, Cologne, 1623

1. Ye watch – ers and ye ho – ly ones,
2. O high – er than the cher – u – bim,
3. Re – spond, ye souls in end – less rest,
4. O friends, in glad – ness let us sing,

1. Bright ser – aphs, cher – u – bim, and thrones,
2. More glo – rious than the ser – a – phim,
3. Ye pa – tri – archs and proph – ets blest,
4. Su – per – nal an – thems ech – o – ing,

1. Raise the glad strain, Al – le – lu – ia!
2. Lead their prais – es, Al – le – lu – ia!
3, 4. Al – le – lu – ia! Al – le – lu – ia!

1. Cry out, do – min – ions, prince – doms, pow'rs,
2. Thou bear – er of the'e – ter – nal Word,
3. Ye ho – ly twelve, ye mar – tyrs strong,
4. To God the Fa – ther, God the Son,

1. Vir – tues, arch – an – gels, an – gels' choirs,
2. Most gra – cious, mag – ni – fy the Lord,
3. All saints tri – um – phant, raise the song,
4. And God the Spir – it, Three in One,

Al – le – lu – ia! Al – le – lu – ia! Al – le – lu – ia!

Al – le – lu – ia! Al – le – lu – ia!

438. Yield Not to Temptation

Text: Horatio R. Palmer, 1834-1907

Tune: Palmer, 65. 65. D with Refrain
Horatio R. Palmer, 1834-1907

1. Yield not to temp–ta – tion, for yield–ing is sin;
2. Shun e – vil com –pan– ions, bad lan –guage dis – dain,
3. To him that o'er –com– eth, God giv – eth a crown;

1. Each vic – t'ry will help you some oth – er to win;
2. God's Name hold in rev – 'rence, nor take it in vain;
3. Through faith we shall con – quer, though of – ten cast down;

1. Fight man –ful – ly on – ward, dark pas – sions sub – due,
2. Be thought–ful and earn – est, kind – heart–ed and true,
3. He who is our Sav – ior our strength will re – new;

1-3. Look ev – er to Je – sus, He'll car – ry you through.

Refrain:

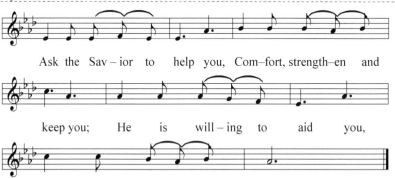

Ask the Sav – ior to help you, Com–fort, strength–en and

keep you; He is will – ing to aid you,

He will car – ry you through.

439. Zion, Praise Thy Savior, Singing (Part 1)

Text: *Lauda Sion*, St. Thomas Aquinas, 1227-1274
Tr. Henry Weman, 1937

Tune: Quem Pastores New #1, 8.8.7 D
Traditional German Melody

Part 1, *Lauda Sion Salvatorem*

1. Zi – on, praise thy Sa – vior, sing – ing,
2. Let the Bread, life – giv – ing, liv – ing,
3. What he did, at sup – per seat – ed,

1. Hymns with ex – ul – ta – tion ring – ing,
2. Be our theme of glad thanks – giv – ing,
3. Christ or – dained to be re – peat – ed,

1. Praise thy King and Shep – herd true.
2. Now in – deed be – fore thee set;
3. His mem – or – ial ne'er to cease;

1. Hon – or him, thy voice up – rais – ing,
2. As of old the Lord pro – vid – ed
3. His com – mand for guid – ance tak – ing,

1. Who sur – pas – seth all thy prais – ing:
2. When the twelve, div – ine – ly guid – ed,
3. Bread and wine we hal – low, mak – ing

1. Nev – er canst thou reach his due.
2. At the ho – ly ta – ble met.
3. Thus our sac – ri – fice of peace.

440. Zion, Praise Thy Savior, Singing (Part 2)

Text: *Lauda Sion*, St. Thomas Aquinas, 1227-1274
Tr. unknown

Tune: Quem Pastores New #2, 88.87
Traditional German Melody

Part 2, *Ecce Panis Angelorum*

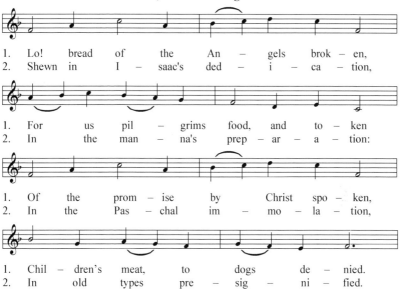

1. Lo!   bread   of   the   An — gels   brok — en,
2. Shewn   in   I — saac's   ded — i — ca — tion,

1. For   us   pil — grims   food,   and   to — ken
2. In   the   man — na's   prep — ar — a — tion:

1. Of   the   prom — ise   by   Christ   spo — ken,
2. In   the   Pas — chal   im — mo — la — tion,

1. Chil — dren's   meat,   to   dogs   de — nied.
2. In   old   types   pre — sig — ni — fied.

441. Zion, Praise Thy Savior, Singing (Part 3)

Text: *Lauda Sion*, St. Thomas Aquinas, 1227-1274
Tr. Roman Missal, 1964

Tune: Quem Pastores New #3, 88. 88. 7
Traditional German Melody

Part 3, *Bone Pastor, Panis Vere*

1. Ve – ry   Bread,   Good   Shep – herd,   tend   us,
2. Thou   who   all   things   canst   and   know – est,

1. Je – sus,   of   thy   love   be – friend   us,
2. Who   on   earth   such   Food   be – stow – est,

1. Thou   re – fresh   us,   thou   de – fend   us,
2. Grant   us   with   thy   saints,   though   low – est,

1. Thine   e – ter – nal   good – ness   send   us
2. Where   the   heav'n – ly   feast   thou   show – est,

1. In   the   land   of   life   to   see.
2. Fel – low   heirs   and   guests   to   be.

After Last Verse: A – men.   Al – le – lu – ia.

XIII. Sunday Prayers and Historic Lectionary

442. Season of Advent

First Sunday of Advent

O Lord, stir up your might and come! Be our protector and liberator; rescue us from the dangers that threaten us because of our sins, and lead us to our salvation: You who live and reign with God the Father in the unity of the Holy Spirit, God, forever and ever.

Rom. 13:11-14a   *Luke 21:25-33*

Second Sunday of Advent

O Lord, stir up our hearts to prepare the way of your only-begotten Son, so that, through his coming on earth, we may serve you always with a pure intention: You who live and reign with God the Father in the unity of the Holy Spirit, God, forever and ever.

Rom. 15:4-13   *Matt. 11:2-10*

Third Sunday of Advent

Hear our prayers, O Lord, and enlighten the darkness of our minds by your coming on earth: You who live and reign with God the Father in the unity of the Holy Spirit, God, forever and ever.

Philippians 4:4-7   *John 1:19b-28*

Fourth Sunday of Advent

O Lord, stir up your might and come. Aid us with your powerful assistance so that, through your grace and merciful forgiveness, we may attain salvation, which now is hindered by our sins: You who live and reign with God the Father in the unity of the Holy Spirit, God, forever and ever.

1 Cor. 4:1-5   *Luke 3:1-6*

443. Season of Christmas

Christmas: First Mass at Midnight
O God, you have made this most holy night radiant with your own true brightness. Grant that we who have known the mystery of Christ's light on earth may also enjoy his happiness in heaven: Who lives and reigns with you in the unity of the Holy Spirit, God, forever and ever.

Tit. 2:11-15   *Luke 2:1-14*

Christmas: Second Mass at Dawn
Almighty God, now that we have been newly enlightened by the Word made flesh, grant that our deeds may reveal the light of faith that shines in our hearts. Through Jesus Christ, your Son, our Lord, who lives and reigns with you in the unity of the Holy Spirit, God, forever and ever.

Tit. 3:4-7   *Luke 2:15-20*

Christmas: Third Mass during the Day
O almighty God, free us from the old bondage and yoke of sin by your only-begotten Son's new birth as man. Through Jesus Christ, your Son, our Lord, who lives and reigns with you in the unity of the Holy Spirit, God, forever and ever.

Heb. 1:1-12   *John 1:1-14*

Sunday in the Octave of Christmas
O almighty and eternal God, direct our actions according to your holy will, so that, in the name of your beloved Son, we may lead lives that are marked by good deeds: Who lives and reigns with you in the unity of the Holy Spirit, God, forever and ever.

Gal. 4:1-7   *Luke 2:33-40*

Circumcision of the Lord (Jan. 1)
O God, it was through the motherhood of the blessed virgin Mary that you bestowed the gift of eternal life upon mankind. Grant that we may feel the powerful intercession of Mary, through whom we were privileged to receive the giver of life, Jesus Christ, your Son, our Lord: Who lives and reigns with you in the unity of the Holy Spirit, God, forever and ever.

Tit. 2:11-15   *Luke 2:21*

Holy Name (Sunday after Jan. 1, or Jan. 2)
O God, it was you who conferred the name of Jesus upon your only-begotten Son, the Savior of the world. Grant that by venerating his holy name on earth we may enjoy his presence in heaven. Through Jesus Christ, your Son, our Lord, who lives and reigns with you in the unity of the Holy Spirit, God, forever and ever.

Acts 4:8-12   *Luke 2:21*

444. Season of Epiphany

Epiphany of Our Lord (Jan. 6)

O God, who by the star this day revealed your only-begotten Son to all nations, grant that we, who know you now by faith, may be brought one day before the vision of your majesty. Through Jesus Christ, your Son, our Lord, who lives and reigns with you in the unity of the Holy Spirit, God, forever and ever.

Isa. 60:1-6   *Matt. 2:1-12*

Holy Family (First Sunday after the Epiphany)

O Lord Jesus Christ, you sanctified home life with untold virtues by being subject to Mary and Joseph. May they assist us to imitate the example of your holy family, so that we may share with them their eternal happiness: You who live and reign, with God the Father in the unity of the Holy Spirit, God, forever and ever.

Col. 3:12-17   *Luke 2:42-52*

Second Sunday after the Epiphany

Almighty and eternal God, who govern all things in heaven and on earth, mercifully hear the prayers of your people and grant us your peace in our days. Through Jesus Christ, your Son, our Lord, who lives and reigns with you in the unity of the Holy Spirit, God, forever and ever.

Rom. 12:6-16a   *John 2:1-11*

Third Sunday after the Epiphany

Almighty and eternal God, look mercifully upon our weakness, and stretch forth the right hand of your power to protect us. Through Jesus Christ, your Son, our Lord, who lives and reigns with you in the unity of the Holy Spirit, God, forever and ever.

Rom. 12:16c-21   *Matt. 8:1-13*

Fourth Sunday after the Epiphany

O God, you know that our weakened nature cannot withstand the dangers that surround us. Make us strong in mind and body, so that with your help we may be able to overcome the afflictions that our own sins have brought upon us. Through Jesus Christ, your Son, our Lord, who lives and reigns with you in the unity of the Holy Spirit, God, forever and ever.

Rom. 13:8-10   *Matt. 8:23-27*

Fifth Sunday after the Epiphany

O Lord, watch over your household with constant loving care. Let your protection forever shield those who rely solely on the hope of your heavenly grace. Through Jesus Christ, your Son, our Lord, who lives and reigns with you in the unity of the Holy Spirit, God, forever and ever.

Col. 3:12-17   *Matt. 13:24-30*

Sixth Sunday after Epiphany

Almighty God, let our minds always be fixed on your truths, so that, in every word and deed, we may do what is pleasing to you. Through Jesus Christ, your Son, our Lord, who lives and reigns with you in the unity of the Holy Spirit, God, forever and ever.

1 Thes. 1:2-10   *Matt. 13:31-35*

Transfiguration Sunday (Optional for Last Sunday after Epiphany)

O God, in the glorious transfiguration of your only-begotten Son you confirmed the mysteries of faith by the testimony of the prophets, and you wondrously foreshadowed our adoption as your sons by the voice speaking through the resplendent cloud. Grant us in your mercy that we may be co-heirs with the King of glory and sharers in that very glory that is his. Through Jesus Christ, your Son, our Lord, who lives and reigns with you in the unity of the Holy Spirit, God, forever and ever.

2 Pet. 1:16-21   *Matt. 17:1-9*

445. Season of Septuagesima

Septuagesima Sunday

O Lord, in your kindness hear the prayers of your people. We are being justly punished for our sins, but be merciful and free us for the glory of your name. Through Jesus Christ, your Son, our Lord, who lives and reigns with you in the unity of the Holy Spirit, God, forever and ever.

1 Cor. 9:24-10:5a   *Matt. 20:1-16a*

Sexagesima Sunday

O God, you see that we place no trust in our own actions. May the power of your mighty arm defend us against all adversity. Through Jesus Christ, your Son, our Lord, who lives and reigns with you in the unity of the Holy Spirit, God, forever and ever.

2 Cor. 11:19-12:9   *Luke 8:4b-15*

Quinquagesima Sunday

Hear our prayers, we beg you, O Lord. Free us from the slavery of our sins, and protect us against all adversity. Through Jesus Christ, your Son, our Lord, who lives and reigns with you in the unity of the Holy Spirit, God, forever and ever.

1 Cor. 13:1-13   *Luke 18:31-43*

446. Season of Lent

Ash Wednesday
O Lord, may the faithful begin the solemn season of fast with fitting piety, and may they continue through to its end with unwavering devotion. Through Jesus Christ, your Son, our Lord, who lives and reigns with you in the unity of the Holy Spirit, God, forever and ever.

Joel 2:12b-19   *Matt. 6:16-21*

First Sunday of Lent
O God, each year you purify the Church through the Lenten observance. May the good works of your Church obtain for us the grace we ask for through our self-denial. Through Jesus Christ, your Son, our Lord, who lives and reigns with you in the unity of the Holy Spirit, God, forever and ever.

2 Cor. 6:1-10   *Matt. 4:1-11*

Second Sunday of Lent
O God, you see that we are completely powerless of ourselves. Protect us from bodily and spiritual dangers, so that we may not be harmed by physical misfortunes and evil thoughts. Through Jesus Christ, your Son, our Lord, who lives and reigns with you in the unity of the Holy Spirit, God, forever and ever.

1 Thes. 4:1-7   *Matt. 17:1-9*

Third Sunday of Lent
O almighty God, fulfill the petitions of the humble; and stretch forth the right hand of your power to defend us. Through Jesus Christ, your Son, our Lord, who lives and reigns with you in the unity of the Holy Spirit, God, forever and ever.

Eph. 5:1-9   *Luke 11:14-28*

Fourth Sunday of Lent
O almighty God, we are being justly punished for our sins, but comfort us with your grace, that we may live. Through Jesus Christ, your Son, our Lord, who lives and reigns with you in the unity of the Holy Spirit, God, forever and ever.

Gal. 4:22-31   *John 6:1-15*

Passion Sunday
O almighty God, look with mercy upon your family. Guide and guard us in body and soul by your bounteous grace and protection. Through Jesus Christ, your Son, our Lord, who lives and reigns with you in the unity of the Holy Spirit, God, forever and ever.

Heb. 9:11-15a   *John 8:46-59*

Palm Sunday

O almighty and eternal God, it was your will that our Savior should become man and suffer upon the cross as a model of humility for all mankind. Grant that we may follow the example of his patience and share in his resurrection. Through Jesus Christ, your Son, our Lord, who lives and reigns with you in the unity of the Holy Spirit, God, forever and ever.

Phil. 2:5-11   *Matt. 21:1-9 and Matt. 26:36-27:66*

447. Season of Easter

Easter Sunday

On this day, O God, you overcame death through your only-begotten Son, and opened to us the gate of everlasting life. Help us continually to carry out by our actions the desires that you put into our hearts. Through Jesus Christ your Son, our Lord, who lives and reigns with you in the unity of the Holy Spirit, God, forever and ever.

1 Cor. 5:7-8   *Mark 16:1-7*

Quasi Modo or Low Sunday. First Sunday after Easter

O almighty God, let our conduct and our lives always be guided by the Easter feast we have just celebrated. Through Jesus Christ your Son, our Lord, who lives and reigns with you in the unity of the Holy Spirit, God, forever and ever.

1 John 5:4-10a   *John 20:19-31*

Second Sunday after Easter

You raised up our fallen world, O God, by the humiliation of your own Son. May we, your faithful people, whom you have rescued from the danger of eternal death, be always joyful on earth and come to everlasting happiness in heaven. Through Jesus Christ your Son, our Lord, who lives and reigns with you in the unity of the Holy Spirit, God, forever and ever.

1 Pet. 2:21b-25   *John 10:11-16*

Third Sunday after Easter

Show us the light of your truth, O God, which guides the sinner back to the path of justice. Let those who profess to be Christians avoid whatever will endanger their profession, and follow those things which will help it. Through Jesus Christ your Son, our Lord, who lives and reigns with you in the unity of the Holy Spirit, God, forever and ever.

1 Pet. 2:11-19a   *John 16:16-22*

Fourth Sunday after Easter

O God, in whom all the faithful are united in one mind, let your people everywhere love your commandments and yearn for what you promise, so that, even amid the changes of this world, their hearts may always be fixed upon true happiness. Through Jesus Christ your Son, our Lord, who lives and reigns with you in the unity of the Holy Spirit, God, forever and ever.

James 1:17-21   *John 16:5-14*

Fifth Sunday after Easter

O God, the source of all good, grant us your inspiration that we may have proper thoughts, and your guidance that we may carry them into practice. Through Jesus Christ your Son, our Lord, who lives and reigns with you in the unity of the Holy Spirit, God, forever and ever.

James 1:22-27   *John 16:23b-30*

Ascension Thursday

O almighty God, we firmly believe that your only-begotten Son, our Redeemer, ascended this day into heaven. May our minds dwell always on this heavenly home. Through Jesus Christ your Son, our Lord, who lives and reigns with you in the unity of the Holy Spirit, God, forever and ever.

Acts 1:1-11   *Mark 16:14-20*

Sunday within the Octave of the Ascension

O almighty and eternal God, make our wills devoted to you so that our hearts may sincerely serve your majesty. Through Jesus Christ your Son, our Lord, who lives and reigns with you in the unity of the Holy Spirit, God, forever and ever.

1 Pet. 4:7b-11   *John 15:26-16:4*

448. Season of Pentecost

Pentecost Sunday

O God, on this day by the light of the Holy Spirit you taught the hearts of the faithful; grant us by the same Spirit to relish what is right, and always to rejoice in his comfort. Through Jesus Christ your Son, our Lord, who lives and reigns with you in the unity of the Holy Spirit, God, forever and ever.

Acts 2:1-11   *John 14:23-31*

Trinity Sunday (First Sunday after Pentecost)

Almighty and everlasting God, you have given your servants, in the confession of the true faith, to acknowledge the glory of the Eternal Trinity, and to adore the unity in the power of your majesty; grant that by steadfastness in this faith we may ever be defended from all adversities. Through Jesus Christ your Son, our Lord, who lives and reigns with you in the unity of the Holy Spirit, God, forever and ever.

Rom. 11:33-36   *Matt. 28:18-20*

Corpus Christi (Thursday after Trinity Sunday)

The Feast of Corpus Christi may be celebrated on the following Sunday.

O God, we possess a lasting memorial of your passion in this wondrous sacrament. Grant that we may so venerate the mysteries of your body and blood that we may always feel within ourselves the effects of your redemption. You who live and reign with the Father in the unity of the Holy Spirit, one God, forever and ever.

1 Cor. 11:23-29   *John 6:55-58*

449. Sundays after Pentecost

Second Sunday after Pentecost

O Lord, grant that we may always have a reverential fear and love of your holy name, for those who are firmly grounded in your love will ever be guided and governed by your grace. Through Jesus Christ your Son, our Lord, who lives and reigns with you in the unity of the Holy Spirit, God, forever and ever.

1 John 3:13-18   *Luke 14:16-24*

Sacred Heart of Jesus (Friday after the Second Sunday after Pentecost)

The Feast of the Sacred Heart may be celebrated on the following Sunday.

O God, through your mercy we posses the treasures of your love in the heart of your Son, the same heart we wounded by our sins. Grant that we may make reparation to him for our faults by offering him the worship of our devotion. Through Jesus Christ your Son, our Lord, who lives and reigns with you in the unity of the Holy Spirit, God, forever and ever.

Eph. 3:8-12, 14-19   *John 19:31-37*

Third Sunday after Pentecost

O God, you are the protector of all who trust in you, and without you nothing is strong, nothing is holy. Be even more merciful towards us, and rule and guide us that we may use the good things of this life in such a way as not to lose the blessings of eternal life. Through Jesus Christ your Son, our Lord, who lives and reigns with you in the unity of the Holy Spirit, God, forever and ever.

1 Pet. 5:6-11   *Luke 15:1-10*

Fourth Sunday after Pentecost

O Lord, let peace guide the course of world events, that your Church may serve you in joy and security. Through Jesus Christ your Son, our Lord, who lives and reigns with you in the unity of the Holy Spirit, God, forever and ever.

Rom. 8:18-23   *Luke 5:1-11*

Fifth Sunday after Pentecost

For those that love you, O God, joys beyond understanding are waiting. Fill our hearts with such a love that our desire for you in all things, and above all things, may lead us to what you have promised, which is far superior to anything we can desire. Through Jesus Christ your Son, our Lord, who lives and reigns with you in the unity of the Holy Spirit, God, forever and ever.

1 Pet. 3:8-15a   *Matt. 5:20-24*

Sixth Sunday after Pentecost

O mighty God, author of every good thing, implant in our hearts a deep love of your name. Support and protect us with your loving care so that we may be filled with a true spirit of devotion and sincere virtue. Through Jesus Christ your Son, our Lord, who lives and reigns with you in the unity of the Holy Spirit, God, forever and ever.

Rom. 6:3-11   *Mark 8:1-9*

Seventh Sunday after Pentecost

O God, whose ever-watchful providence rules all things, we humbly implore you to remove from us whatever is harmful, and to bestow on us only that which will be helpful. Through Jesus Christ your Son, our Lord, who lives and reigns with you in the unity of the Holy Spirit, God, forever and ever.

Rom. 6:19-23   *Matt. 7:15-21*

Eighth Sunday after Pentecost

O Lord, we cannot exist without you. Inspire us to think and act rightly, that we may always live as you would have us live. Through Jesus Christ your Son, our Lord, who lives and reigns with you in the unity of the Holy Spirit, God, forever and ever.

Rom. 8:12-17   *Luke 16:1-9*

Ninth Sunday after Pentecost

O Lord, in your mercy hear the prayers of those who call upon you. May they ask only what is pleasing to you, so that their requests may always be heard. Through Jesus Christ your Son, our Lord, who lives and reigns with you in the unity of the Holy Spirit, God, forever and ever.

1 Cor. 10:6b-13   *Luke 19:41-47a*

Tenth Sunday after Pentecost

O God, your almighty power is made most evident in your mercy and pity. Be even more merciful toward us, that we may seek the rewards you have promised and come to share in them. Through Jesus Christ your Son, our Lord, who lives and reigns with you in the unity of the Holy Spirit, God, forever and ever.

1 Cor. 12:2-11   *Luke 18:9-14*

Eleventh Sunday after Pentecost

Almighty and eternal God, your bounteous kindness exceeds the merits and fondest hope of our prayers. Shower your mercy upon us, forgive us the sins that strike fear in our consciences, and grant us the blessings we dare not presume to ask for. Through Jesus Christ your Son, our Lord, who lives and reigns with you in the unity of the Holy Spirit, God, forever and ever.

1 Cor. 15:1-10a   *Mark 7:31-37*

Twelfth Sunday after Pentecost

Almighty and merciful God, it is through your grace that the faithful are able to serve you fittingly and laudably. Grant that we may hurry, without faltering, toward the rewards you have promised to us. Through Jesus Christ your Son, our Lord, who lives and reigns with you in the unity of the Holy Spirit, God, forever and ever.

2 Cor. 3:4-9   *Luke 10:23-37*

Thirteenth Sunday after Pentecost

Almighty and eternal God, deepen our faith, our hope and our charity. Make us love what you have commanded so that we may attain what you have promised. Through Jesus Christ your Son, our Lord, who lives and reigns with you in the unity of the Holy Spirit, God, forever and ever.

Gal. 3:16-22   *Luke 17:11-19*

Fourteenth Sunday after Pentecost

Keep your Church, O Lord, in your everlasting mercy. Without your assistance our human nature is bound to fail, so help us to shun whatever is harmful and guide us toward those things that will aid our salvation. Through Jesus Christ your Son, our Lord, who lives and reigns with you in the unity of the Holy Spirit, God, forever and ever.

Gal. 5:16-24   *Matt. 6:24-33*

Fifteenth Sunday after Pentecost

O Lord, let your abiding mercy purify and defend the Church. Graciously govern her always, for without your assistance she cannot remain safe. Through Jesus Christ your Son, our Lord, who lives and reigns with you in the unity of the Holy Spirit, God, forever and ever.

Gal. 5:25-6:10   *Luke 7:11-16*

Sixteenth Sunday after Pentecost

O Lord, may your grace always be with us, to make us diligent in performing good deeds. Through Jesus Christ your Son, our Lord, who lives and reigns with you in the unity of the Holy Spirit, God, forever and ever.

Eph. 3:13-21   *Luke 14:1-11*

Seventeenth Sunday after Pentecost

O Lord, keep your people from falling under the influence of the devil and let them sincerely seek the only God. Through Jesus Christ your Son, our Lord, who lives and reigns with you in the unity of the Holy Spirit, God, forever and ever.

Eph. 4:1-6   *Matt. 22:34-46*

Eighteenth Sunday after Pentecost

O Lord, let your mercy direct our hearts, for without you we can do nothing to please you. Through Jesus Christ your Son, our Lord, who lives and reigns with you in the unity of the Holy Spirit, God, forever and ever.

1 Cor. 1:4-8   *Matt. 9:1-8*

Nineteenth Sunday after Pentecost

Almighty and merciful God, graciously shield us from all that is harmful, so that both in body and soul we may be free to do your will. Through Jesus Christ your Son, our Lord, who lives and reigns with you in the unity of the Holy Spirit, God, forever and ever.

Eph. 4:23-28   *Matt. 22:1-14*

Feast of Christ the King

This Feast is celebrated on the Last Sunday in October.

Almighty and eternal God, you have renewed all creation in your beloved Son, the king of the whole universe. May all the peoples of the earth, now torn apart by the wound of sin, become subject to the gentle rule of your only-begotten Son: Who lives and reigns with you in the unity of the Holy Spirit, one God, forever and ever.

Col. 1:12-20   *John 18:33-37*

Twentieth Sunday after Pentecost

O Lord, grant your faithful pardon and peace, that they may be cleansed from their sins and serve you without fear. Through Jesus Christ your Son, our Lord, who lives and reigns with you in the unity of the Holy Spirit, God, forever and ever.

Eph. 5:15-21   *John 4:46b-53*

Twenty-First Sunday after Pentecost

Keep your family under your continual care, O Lord. Shelter it with your protection from all adversity, that it may be zealous in doing good for the honor of your name. Through Jesus Christ your Son, our Lord, who lives and reigns with you in the unity of the Holy Spirit, God, forever and ever.

Eph. 6:10-17   *Matt. 18:23-35*

Twenty-Second Sunday after Pentecost

O God, our refuge and out strength, source of all good, hear the earnest prayers of your Church, and grant us the requests we confidently make of you. Through Jesus Christ your Son, our Lord, who lives and reigns with you in the unity of the Holy Spirit, God, forever and ever.

Phil. 1:6-11   *Matt. 22:15-21*

Twenty-Third Sunday after Pentecost

When the Last Sunday after Pentecost falls on this day, the Prayer and Readings for the Last Sunday shall be used.

Forgive the offenses of your people, O Lord, so that through your merciful goodness we may be freed from the bondage of sin into which we were led by our own weakness. Through Jesus Christ your Son, our Lord, who lives and reigns with you in the unity of the Holy Spirit, God, forever and ever.

Phil. 3:17-4:3   *Matt. 9:18-26*

If there are additional Sundays between the 23rd and the Last Sunday after Pentecost, the Prayers and Readings for the remaining Sundays after Epiphany are to be used on those days.

Twenty-Fourth and Last Sunday after Pentecost

O Lord, stir up the wills of the faithful that they may be more eager to seek the fruits of divine grace, and to discover in your mercy greater healing for their sinfulness. Through Jesus Christ, our Lord, your Son, who lives and reigns with you in the unity of the Holy Spirit, one God, forever and ever.

Col. 1:9-14   *Matt. 24:15-35*

XIV. Sunday Prayers and Three-Year Lectionary

450. Season of Advent

First Sunday of Advent

All-powerful God, increase our strength of will for doing good, that Christ may find an eager welcome at his coming and call us to his side in the kingdom of heaven, where he lives and reigns with you and the Holy Spirit, one God, for ever and ever.

Year A	*Isa. 2:1-5*	*Ps. 122:12,3-4, 4-5,6-7,8-9*	*Rom. 13:11-14*	*Matt. 24:37-44*
Year B	*Isa. 63:16-17, 64:2-7*	*Ps. 80:2-3, 15-16, 18-19*	*1 Cor. 1:3-9*	*Mark 13:33-37*
Year C	*Jer. 33:14-16*	*Ps. 25:4-5, 8-9, 10, 14*	*1 Thes. 3:12-4:2*	*Luke 21:25-28, 34-46*

Second Sunday of Advent

God of power and mercy, open our hearts in welcome. Remove the things that hinder us from receiving Christ with joy, so that we may share in his wisdom, and become one with him, when he comes in glory, for he lives and reigns with you and the Holy Spirit, one God, for ever and ever.

Year A	*Isa. 11:1-10*	*Ps. 71:1-2,7-8, 12-13, 17*	*Rom. 15:4-9*	*Matt. 3:1-12*
Year B	*Isa. 40:1-5, 9-11*	*Ps. 85:9-10, 11-12,13-14*	*2 Pet. 3:8-14*	*Mark 1:1-8*
Year C	*Bar. 5:1-9*	*Ps. 126:12,2-3, 4-5,6*	*Phil. 1:4-5, 8-11*	*Luke 3:1-6*

Third Sunday of Advent

Lord God, may we, your people, who look forward to the birthday of Christ experience the joy of salvation and celebrate that feast with love and thanksgiving. We ask this through Jesus Christ your Son, who lives and reigns with you and the Holy Spirit, one God, forever and ever.

Year A	*Isa. 35:1-6, 10*	*Ps. 146:6-7, 8-9, 9-10*	*James 5:7-10*	*Matt. 11:2-11*
Year B	*Isa. 61:1-2, 10-11*	*Luke 1:46-48, 49-50, 53-54*	*1 Thes. 5:16-24*	*John 1:6-8, 19-28*
Year C	*Zeph. 3:14-18*	*Isa. 2-3,4,5-6*	*Phil. 4:4-7*	*Luke 3:10-18*

Fourth Sunday of Advent

Lord, fill our hearts with your love, and as you revealed to us by an angel, the coming of your Son as man, so lead us through his suffering and death, to the glory of his resurrection. For he lives and reigns with you and the Holy Spirit, one God, for ever and ever.

Year A	*Isa. 7:10-14*	*Ps. 24:1-2, 3-4,5-6*	*Rom. 1:1-7*	*Matthew 1:18-24*
Year B	*2 Sam. 7:1-5, 8-11, 16*	*Ps. 89:2-3,4-5, 27, 29*	*Rom. 16:25-27*	*Luke 1:26-38*

Year C	Micah 5:1-4	Ps. 80:2-3, 15-16, 18-19	Heb. 10:5-10	Luke 1:39-45

451. Season of Christmas

Vigil of Christmas (Dec. 24)

God our Father, every year we rejoice as we look forward to this feast of our salvation. May we welcome Christ as our Redeemer, and meet him with confidence when he comes to be our judge, who lives and reigns with you and the Holy Spirit, one God, for ever and ever.

Years A, B, C	Isa. 62:1-5	Ps. 89:4-5, 16-17,27,29	Acts 13:16-17, 22-25	Matt. 1:1-25 or 1:18-25

Christmas at Midnight – Prayer

Father, you make this holy night radiant, with the splendor of Jesus Christ our light. We welcome him as Lord, the true light of the world. Bring us to eternal joy in the kingdom of heaven, where he lives and reigns with you and the Holy Spirit, one God, for ever and ever.

Years A, B, C	Isa. 9:1-6	Ps. 96:1-2,2-3, 11-12,13	Tit. 2:11-14	Luke 2:1-14

Christmas at Dawn

Father, we are filled with the new light, by the coming of your Word among us. May the light of faith, shine in our words and actions. Grant this through our Lord Jesus Christ, your Son, who lives and reigns with you and the Holy Spirit, one God, for ever and ever.

Years A, B, C	Isa. 62:11-12	Ps. 97:1, 6, 11-12	Tit. 3:4-7	Luke 2:15-20

Christmas During the Day

Lord God, we praise you for creating Man, and still more for restoring him in Christ. Your Son shared our weakness: may we share his glory, for he lives and reigns with you and the Holy Spirit, one God, for ever and ever.

Years A, B, C	Isa. 52:7-10	Ps. 98:1,2-3, 3-4,5-6	Heb. 1:1-6	John 1:1-18 or 1-5, 9-14

Holy Family (Sunday in the Octave of Christmas) – Prayer

Father, help us to live as the holy family, united in respect and love. Bring us to the joy and peace of your eternal home. Grant this through our Lord Jesus Christ, your Son, who lives and reigns with you and the Holy Spirit, one God, for ever and ever.

Year A	Sir. 3:2-6, 12-14	Ps. 128:1-2,3,4-5	Col. 3:12-21	Matthew 2:13-15, 19-23
Year B	Sir. 3:2-6, 12-14	Ps. 128:1-2,3,4-5	Col. 3:12-21	Lk 2:22-40 or 22, 39-40
Year C	Sir. 3:2-6, 12-14	Ps. 128:1-2,3,4-5	Col. 3:12-21	Luke 2:41-52

Solemnity of Mary (Jan. 1)

God our Father, may we always profit by the prayers of the Virgin Mother Mary, for you bring us life and salvation, through Jesus Christ her Son, who lives and reigns with you and the Holy Spirit, one God, for ever.

Years A, B, C	Num. 6:22-27	Ps. 67:2-3, 5, 6, 8	Gal. 4:4-7	Luke 2:16-21

Epiphany of Our Lord (Sunday between January 2 and 8)

Father, you revealed your Son to the nations, by the guidance of a star. Lead us to your glory in heaven, by the light of faith. We ask this through our Lord Jesus Christ, your Son, who lives and reigns with you and the Holy Spirit, one God, for ever and ever.

Years A, B, C	Isa. 60:1-6	Ps. 72:1-2,7-8, 10-11,12-13	Eph. 3:2-3, 5-6	Matt. 2:1-12

Baptism of the Lord (First Sunday after the Epiphany)

Almighty, eternal God, when the Spirit descended upon Jesus, at his baptism in the Jordan, you revealed him as your own beloved Son. Keep us, your children born of water and the Spirit, faithful to your calling. We ask this through our Lord Jesus Christ, your Son, who lives and reigns with you and the Holy Spirit, one God, for ever and ever.

Year A	Isa. 42:1-4, 6-7	Ps. 29:1-2,3-4, 3, 9-10	Acts 10:34-38	Matt. 3:13-17
Year B	Isa. 42:1-4, 6-7	Ps. 29:1-4, 3, 9-10	Acts 10:34-38	Mark 1:7-11
Year C	Isa. 42:1-4, 6-7	Ps. 29:1-4, 3, 9-10	Acts 10:34-38	Luke 2:15-16, 21-22

452. Season of Lent

Ash Wednesday

Lord, protect us in our struggle against evil. As we begin the discipline of Lent, make this day holy by our self-denial. Grant this through our Lord Jesus Christ, your Son, who lives and reigns with you and the Holy Spirit, one God, for ever and ever.

Years A, B, C	Joel 2:12-18	Ps. 51:3-6, 12-14, 17	2 Cor. 5:20-6:2	Matt. 6:1-6, 16-18

First Sunday of Lent

Father, through this observance of Lent, help us to understand the meaning, of your Son's death and resurrection, and teach us to reflect it in our lives. Grant this through our Lord Jesus Christ, your Son, who lives and reigns with you and the Holy Spirit, one God, for ever and ever.

Year A	Gen. 2:7-9, 3:1-7	Ps. 51:3-4,5-6, 12-13,14,17	Ro.5:12-19 or 12,17-19	Matt. 4:1-11
Year B	Gen. 9:8-15	Ps. 25:4-5,6-7,8-9	1 Pet. 3:18-22	Mark 1:12-15
Year C	Deut. 26:4-10	Ps. 91:1-2,10-11, 12-13, 14-15	Rom. 10:8-13	Luke 4:1-13

Second Sunday of Lent

God our Father, help us to hear your Son. Enlighten us with your word, that we may find the way to your glory. We ask this through our Lord Jesus Christ, your Son, who lives and reigns with you and the Holy Spirit, one God, for ever and ever.

Year A	*Gen. 12:1-4*	*Ps. 33:1-4,18-19, 20,22*	*2 Tim. 1:8-10*	*Matt. 17:1-9*
Year B	*Gen. 22:1-2, 9-13,15-18*	*Ps.116:10,15,16-17, 18-19*	*Rom. 8:31-34*	*Mark 9:2-10*
Year C	*Gen. 15:5-12, 17-18*	*Ps. 27:1,7-8,8-9, 13-14*	*Phil. 3:17-4:1*	*Luke 9:28-36*

Third Sunday of Lent

Father, you have taught us to overcome our sins, by prayer, fasting, and works of mercy. When we are discouraged by our weakness, give us confidence in your love. We ask this through our Lord Jesus Christ, your Son, who lives and reigns with you and the Holy Spirit, one God, for ever and ever.

Year A	*Exod. 17:3-7*	*Ps. 95:1-2, 6-7, 8-9*	*Rom. 5:1-2, 5-8*	*John 4:5-42*
Year B	*Exod. 20:1-17*	*Ps. 19:19, 8,9, 10,11*	*1 Cor. 1:22-25*	*John 2:13-25*
Year C	*Exod. 3:1-8, 13-15*	*Ps. 103:1-2,3-4, 6-7, 8,11*	*1 Cor. 10:1-6, 10-12*	*Luke 13:1-9*

Fourth Sunday of Lent

Father of peace, we are joyful in your Word, your Son Jesus Christ, who reconciles us to you. Let us hasten toward Easter, with the eagerness of faith and love. We ask this through our Lord Jesus Christ, your Son, who lives and reigns with you and the Holy Spirit, one God, for ever and ever.

Year A	*1 Sam. 16:1, 6-7, 10-13*	*Ps. 23:1-3,3-4, 5,6*	*Eph. 5:8-14*	*John 9:1-41*
Year B	*2 Chr. 36:14-17, 19-23*	*Ps. 137:1-2, 3, 4-5, 6*	*Eph. 2:4-10*	*John 3:14-21*
Year C	*Jos. 5:9, 10-12*	*Ps 34:2-3,4-5,6-7*	*2 Cor. 5:17-21*	*Lk 15:1-3,11-32*

Fifth Sunday of Lent

Father, help us to be like Christ your Son, who loved the world and died for our salvation. Inspire us by his love, guide us by his example, who lives and reigns with you and the Holy Spirit, one God, for ever and ever.

Year A	*Ezek. 37:12-14*	*Ps. 130:1-2,3-4, 5-6,7-8*	*Rom. 8:8-11*	*John 11:1-45*
Year B	*Jer. 31:31-34*	*Ps. 51:3-4,12-13, 14-15*	*Heb. 5:7-9*	*John 12:20-33*
Year C	*Isa. 43:16-21*	*Ps. 126:1-2,2-3, 4-5,6*	*Phil. 3:8-14*	*John 8:1-11*

Palm Sunday. The Sixth Sunday of Lent

Almighty, ever-living God, you have given the human race Jesus Christ our Savior as a model of humility. He fulfilled your will, by becoming man and giving his life on the cross. Help us to bear witness to you, by following his example of suffering, and make us worthy to share in his resurrection. We ask this through our Lord Jesus Christ, your Son, who lives and reigns with you and the Holy Spirit, one God, for ever and ever.

Year A	*Isa. 50:4-7*	*Ps. 22:8-9,17-18, 19-20,23-24*	*Phil. 2:6-11*	*Matt 26:14-27:66*
Year B	*Isa. 50:4-7*	*Ps. 22:8-9,17-18, 19-20,23-24*	*Phil. 2:6-11*	*Mark 14:1-15:47*
Year C	*Isa. 50:4-7*	*Ps. 22:8-9,17-18, 19-20,23-24*	*Phil. 2:6-11*	*Luke 22:14-23:56*

453. Season of Easter

Easter Sunday

God our Father, by raising Christ your Son you conquered the power of death and opened for us the way to eternal life. Let our celebration today raise us up and renew our lives by the Spirit that is within us. Grant this through our Lord Jesus Christ, your Son, who lives and reigns with you and the Holy Spirit, one God, for ever and ever.

Years A, B, C	*Acts 10:34, 37-43*	*Ps. 118:1-2, 16-17,22-23*	*Col. 3:1-4 or 1 Cor. 5:6-8*	*John 20:1-9*

Second Sunday of Easter

God of mercy, you wash away our sins in water, you give us new birth in the Spirit, and redeem us in the blood of Christ. As we celebrate Christ's resurrection increase our awareness of these blessings, and renew your gift of life within us. We ask this through our Lord Jesus Christ, your Son, who lives and reigns with you and the Holy Spirit, one God, for ever and ever.

Year A	*Acts 2:42-47*	*Ps. 118:2-4, 13-15, 22-24*	*1 Pet. 1:3-9*	*John 20:19-31*
Year B	*Acts 4:32-35*	*Ps. 118:2-4, 13-15, 22-24*	*1 John 5:1-6*	*John 20:19-31*
Year C	*Acts 5:12-16*	*Ps. 118:2-4, 13-15, 22-24*	*Apoc. 1:9-11, 12-13,17-19*	*John 20:19-31*

Third Sunday of Easter

God our Father, may we look forward with hope to our resurrection, for you have made us your sons and daughters, and restored the joy of our youth. We ask this through our Lord Jesus Christ, your Son, who lives and reigns with you and the Holy Spirit, one God, for ever and ever.

Year A	*Acts 2:14, 22-28*	*Ps. 16:1-2, 5, 7-8, 9-10, 11*	*1 Pet. 1:17-21*	*Luke 24:13-35*
Year B	*Acts 3:13-15, 17-19*	*Ps. 4:2,4, 7-8,9*	*1 John 2:1-5*	*Luke 24:35-48*
Year C	*Acts 5:27-32, 40-41*	*Ps. 30:2,4,5-6, 11-12, 13*	*Apoc. 5:11-14*	*John 21:1-19*

Fourth Sunday of Easter

Almighty and ever-living God, give us new strength from the courage of Christ our shepherd, and lead us to join the saints in heaven, where he lives and reigns with you and the Holy Spirit, one God, for ever and ever.

Year A	*Acts 2:14, 36-41*	*Ps. 23:1-3,3-4,5,6*	*1 Pet. 2:20-25*	*John 10:1-10*
Year B	*Acts 4:8-12*	*Ps. 118:1, 8-9, 21-23,26,21,29*	*1 John 3:1-2*	*John 10:11-18*
Year C	*Acts 13:14, 43-52*	*Ps. 100:1-2, 3, 5*	*Apoc. 7:9,14-17*	*John 10:27-30*

Fifth Sunday of Easter

God our Father, look upon us with love. You redeem us and make us your children in Christ. Give us true freedom and bring us to the inheritance you promised. We ask this through our Lord Jesus Christ, your Son, who lives and reigns with you and the Holy Spirit, one God, for ever and ever.

Year A	*Acts 6:1-7*	*Ps. 33:1-2, 4-5, 18-19*	*1 Pet. 2:4-9*	*John 14:1-12*
Year B	*Acts 9:26-31*	*Ps. 22:26-27, 28, 30, 31-32*	*1 John 3:18-24*	*John 15:1-8*
Year C	*Acts 14:21-17*	*Ps. 145:8, 9, 10-11, 12-13*	*Apoc. 21:1-5*	*John 13:31-35*

Sixth Sunday of Easter

Ever-living God, help us to celebrate our joy in the resurrection of the Lord and to express in our lives the love we celebrate. Grant this through our Lord Jesus Christ, your Son, who lives and reigns with you and the Holy Spirit, one God, for ever and ever.

Year A	*Acts 8:5-8, 14-17*	*Ps. 66:1-3,4-5, 6-7, 16, 20*	*1 Pet. 3:15-18*	*John 14:15-21*
Year B	*Ac10:25-26,34-35, 44-48*	*Ps. 98:1-2,3,3-4*	*1 John 4:7-10*	*John 15:9-17*
Year C	*Acts 15:1-2, 22-29*	*Ps. 67:2-3, 5, 6, 8*	*Apoc. 21:10-14, 22-23*	*John 14:23-29*

Ascension Thursday

In the United States and Canada, this Feast is commonly celebrated on the Sunday following.
God our Father, make us joyful in the ascension of your Son Jesus Christ. May we follow him into the new creation, for his ascension is our glory and our hope. We ask this through our Lord Jesus Christ, your Son, who lives and reigns with you and the Holy Spirit, one God, for ever and ever.

Year A	*Acts 1:1-11*	*Ps. 47:2-3, 6-7, 8-9*	*Eph. 1:17-23*	*Matt. 28:16-20*
Year B	*Acts 1:1-11*	*Ps. 47:2-3, 6-7, 8-9*	*Eph. 1:17-23*	*Mark 16:15-20*
Year C	*Acts 1:1-11*	*Ps. 47:2-3, 6-7, 8-9*	*Eph. 1:17-23*	*Luke 24:46-53*

Seventh Sunday of Easter

Father, help us keep in mind that Christ our Savior lives with you in glory, and promised to remain with us until the end of time. We ask this through our Lord Jesus Christ your Son, who lives and reigns with you and the Holy Spirit, one God, for ever and ever.

Year A	*Acts 1:12-14*	*Ps. 27:1, 4, 7-8*	*1 Pet. 4:13-16*	*John 17:1-11*
Year B	*Acts 1:15-17, 20-26*	*Ps. 103:1-2, 11-12, 19-20*	*1 John 4:11-16*	*John 17:11-19*
Year C	*Acts 7:55-60*	*Ps. 97:1-2, 6-7, 9*	*Ap. 22:12-14, 16-17, 20*	*John 17:20-26*

Pentecost Sunday

God our Father, let the Spirit you sent on your Church to begin the teaching of the gospel continue to work in the world through the hearts of all who believe. We ask this through our Lord Jesus Christ, your Son, who lives and reigns with you and the Holy Spirit, one God, for ever and ever.

Year A	*Acts 2:1-11*	*Ps. 104:1, 24, 29-30, 31, 34*	*1 Cor. 12:3-7, 12-13*	*John 20:19-23*
Year B	*Acts 2:1-11*	*Ps. 104:1,24, 29-30, 31, 34*	*Gal. 5:16-25*	*John 15:26-27; 16:12-15*
Year C	*Acts 2:1-11*	*Ps. 104:1,24, 29-30, 31, 34*	*Rom. 8:8-17*	*John 14:15-16, 23b-26*

454. Ordinary Time

First Week in Ordinary Time

The prayer is used on the weekdays following the Baptism of the Lord, with the weekday readings.
Father of love, hear our prayers. Help us to know your will and to do it with courage and faith. Grant this through our Lord Jesus Christ, your Son, who lives and reigns with you and the Holy Spirit, one God, for ever and ever.

Second Sunday in Ordinary Time (2nd Sunday after Epiphany)

Father of heaven and earth, hear our prayers, and show us the way to peace in the world. Grant this through our Lord Jesus Christ, your Son, who lives and reigns with you and the Holy Spirit, one God, for ever and ever.

Year A	*Isa. 49:3, 5-6*	*Ps. 40:2, 4, 7-8, 8-9, 10*	*1 Cor. 1:1-3*	*John 1:29-34*
Year B	*1 Sam 3:3-10, 19*	*Ps. 40:2, 4, 7-8, 8-9, 10*	*1 Cor. 6:13-15, 17-20*	*John 1:35-42*
Year C	*Isa. 62:1-5*	*Ps. 96:1-2, 2-3, 7-8, 9-10*	*1 Cor. 12:4-11*	*John 2:1-12*

Third Sunday in Ordinary Time (3rd Sunday after Epiphany)

All-powerful and ever-living God, direct your love that is within us, that our efforts in the name of your Son, may bring mankind to unity and peace. We ask this through our Lord Jesus Christ, your Son, who lives and reigns with you and the Holy Spirit, one God, for ever and ever.

Third Sunday in Ordinary Time – Readings

Year A	*Isa. 8:23-9:3*	*Ps. 27:1, 4, 13-14*	*1 Cor. 1:10-13, 17*	*Matt. 4:12-23 or 12-17*
Year B	*Jonah 3:1-5, 10*	*Ps. 25:4-5, 6-7, 8-9*	*1 Cor. 7:29-31*	*Mark 1:14-20*
Year C	*Neh. 8:2-6, 8-10*	*Ps. 19:8, 9, 10, 15*	*1 Cor. 12:12-30*	*Luke 1:1-4, 4:14-21*

Fourth Sunday in Ordinary Time (4th Sunday after Epiphany)

Lord our God, help us to love you with all our hearts, and to love all men as you love them. Grant this through our Lord Jesus Christ, your Son, who lives and reigns with you and the Holy Spirit, one God, for ever and ever.

Year A	*Zeph 2:3;3:12-13*	*Ps. 146:6-7, 8-9, 9-10*	*1 Cor. 1:26-31*	*Matt. 5:1-12*
Year B	*Deut. 18:15-20*	*Ps. 95:1-2, 6-7, 7-9*	*1 Cor. 7:32-35*	*Mark 1:21-28*
Year C	*Jer. 1:4-5, 17-19*	*Ps. 71:1-2, 3-4, 5-6, 15-17*	*1 Cor. 12:31-13:13*	*Luke 4:21-30*

Fifth Sunday in Ordinary Time (5th Sunday after Epiphany)

Father, watch over your family, and keep us safe in your care, for all our hope is in you. Grant this through our Lord Jesus Christ, your Son, who lives and reigns with you and the Holy Spirit, one God, for ever and ever.

Year A	*Isa. 58:7-10*	*Ps. 112:4-5, 6-7, 8-9*	*1 Cor. 2:1-5*	*Matt. 5:13-16*
Year B	*Job 7:1-4, 6-7*	*Ps. 147:1-2, 3-4, 5-6*	*1 Cor. 9:16-19, 22-23*	*Mark 1:29-39*
Year C	*Isa. 6:1-8*	*Ps. 138:1-2, 2-3, 4-5, 7-8*	*1 Cor. 15:1-11*	*Luke 5:1-11*

Sixth Sunday in Ordinary Time (Epiphany 6 or Proper 1)

God our Father, you have promised to remain for ever, with those who do what is just and right. Help us to live in your presence. We ask this through our Lord Jesus Christ, your Son, who lives and reigns with you and the Holy Spirit, one God, for ever and ever.

Year A	*Sir. 15:15-20*	*Ps. 119:1-2,4-5, 17-18, 33-34*	*1 Cor. 2:6-10*	*Matt. 5:17-37 or 5:20-22, 27-28, 33-34, 37*
Year B	*Lev. 13:1-2, 44-46*	*Ps. 32:1-2, 5, 11*	*1 Cor. 10:31-11:1*	*Mark 1:40-45*
Year C	*Jer. 17:5-8*	*Ps. 1:1-2, 3, 4, 6*	*1 Cor. 15:12, 16-20*	*Luke 6:17:20-26*

Seventh Sunday in Ordinary Time (Epiphany 7 or Proper 2)

Father, keep before us the wisdom and love, you have revealed in your Son. Help us to be like him, in word and deed, for he lives and reigns with you and the Holy Spirit, one God, for ever and ever.

Year A	*Lev. 19:1-2, 17-18*	*Ps. 103:1-2, 3-4, 10, 12, 12-13*	*1 Cor. 3:16-23*	*Matt. 5:38-48*
Year B	*Isa. 43:18-19, 21, 22, 24-25*	*Ps. 41:2-3, 4-5, 13-14*	*2 Cor. 1:18-22*	*Mark 2:1-12*
Year C	*1 Sam. 26:2, 7-9, 12-13, 22-23*	*Ps. 103:1-2, 3-4, 8, 10, 12-13*	*1 Cor. 15:45-49*	*Luke 6:27-38*

Eighth Sunday in Ordinary Time (Epiphany 8 or Proper 3)

Lord, guide the course of world events, and give your Church the joy and peace, of serving you in freedom. We ask this through our Lord Jesus Christ, your Son, who lives and reigns with you and the Holy Spirit, one God, for ever and ever.

Year A	*Isa. 49:14-15*	*Ps. 62:2-3, 6-7, 8-9*	*1 Cor. 4:1-5*	*Matt. 6:24-34*
Year B	*Hosea 2:16-17, 21-22*	*Ps. 103:1-2, 3-4, 8, 10, 12-13*	*2 Cor. 3:1-6*	*Mark 2:18-22*
Year C	*Sir. 27:4-7*	*Ps 92:2-3, 13-14, 15-16*	*1 Cor. 15:54-58*	*Luke 6:39-45*

Ninth Sunday in Ordinary Time (Epiphany 9 or Proper 4)

Father, your love never fails. Hear our call. Keep us from danger, and provide for all our needs. Grant this through our Lord Jesus Christ, your Son, who lives and reigns with you and the Holy Spirit, one God, for ever and ever.

Year A	*Deut. 11:18, 26-28*	*Ps. 31:2-3, 3-4, 17, 25*	*Rom. 3:21-25, 28*	*Matt. 7:21-27*
Year B	*Deut. 5:12-15*	*Ps. 81:3-4, 5-6, 6-8, 10-11*	*2 Cor. 4:6-11*	*Mark 2:23-3:6 or 2:23-28*
Year C	*1 Kgs. 8:41-43*	*Ps. 117:1, 2*	*Gal. 1:1-2, 6-10*	*Luke 7:1-10*

Tenth Sunday in Ordinary Time (Proper 5)

God of wisdom and love, source of all good, send your Spirit to teach us your truth and guide our actions in your way of peace. We ask this through our Lord Jesus Christ, your Son, who lives and reigns with you and the Holy Spirit, one God, for ever and ever.

Year A	*Hosea 6:3-6*	*Ps. 50:1, 8, 12-13, 14-15*	*Rom. 4:18-25*	*Matt. 9:9-13*
Year B	*Gen. 3:9-15*	*Ps. 130:1-2, 3-4, 5-6, 7-8*	*2 Cor. 4:13-5:1*	*Mark 3:20-35*
Year C	*1 Kgs. 17:17-24*	*Ps. 30:2, 4, 5-6, 11, 12, 13*	*Gal. 1:11-19*	*Luke 7:11-17*

Eleventh Sunday in Ordinary Time (Proper 6)

Almighty God, our hope and our strength, without you we falter. Help us to follow Christ and to live according to your will. We ask this through our Lord Jesus Christ, your Son, who lives and reigns with you and the Holy Spirit, one God, for ever and ever.

Year A	*Exod. 19:2-6*	*Ps. 100:1-2, 3, 5*	*Rom. 5:6-11*	*Matt. 9:36-10:8*
Year B	*Ezek. 17:22-24*	*Ps. 92:2-3, 13-14, 15-16*	*2 Cor. 5:6-10*	*Mark 4:26-34*
Year C	*2 Sam. 12:7-10, 13*	*Ps. 32:1-2, 5, 7, 11*	*Gal. 2:16, 19-21*	*Luke 7:36-8:3 or 7:36-50*

Twelfth Sunday in Ordinary Time (Proper 7)

Father, guide and protector of your people, grant us an unfailing respect for your name, and keep us always in your love. Grant this through our Lord Jesus Christ, your Son, who lives and reigns with you and the Holy Spirit, one God, for ever and ever.

Year A	*Jer. 20:10-13*	*Ps. 69:8-10, 14, 17, 33-35*	*Rom. 5:12-15*	*Matt. 10:26-33*
Year B	*Job 38:1, 8-11*	*Ps 107:23-24, 25-26, 28-29,30-31*	*2 Cor. 5:14-17*	*Mark 4:35-41*
Year C	*Zech. 12:10-11*	*Ps. 63:2, 3-4, 5-6, 8-9*	*Gal. 3:26-29*	*Luke 9:18-24*

Thirteenth Sunday in Ordinary Time (Proper 8)

Father, you call your children to walk in the light of Christ. Free us from darkness and keep us in the radiance of your truth. We ask this through our Lord Jesus Christ, your Son, who lives and reigns with you and the Holy Spirit, one God, for ever and ever.

Year A	*2 Kgs. 4:8-11, 14-16*	*Ps. 89:2-3, 16-17, 18-19*	*Rom. 6:3-4, 8-11*	*Matt. 10:37-42*
Year B	*Wis. 1:13-15, 2:23-24*	*Ps. 30:2, 4, 5-6, 11, 12, 13*	*2 Cor. 8:7, 9, 13-15*	*Mark 5:21-43 or 21-24,35-43*
Year C	*1 Kgs. 19:16, 19-21*	*Ps. 16:1-2, 5, 7-8, 9-10, 11*	*Gal. 5:1, 13-18*	*Luke 9:51-62*

Fourteenth Sunday in Ordinary Time (Proper 9)

Father, through the obedience of Jesus, your servant and your Son, you raised a fallen world. Free us from sin and bring us the joy that lasts for ever. We ask this through our Lord Jesus Christ, your Son, who lives and reigns with you and the Holy Spirit, one God, for ever and ever.

Year A	*Zech. 9:9-10*	*Ps. 144:1-2, 8-9, 10-11,13-14*	*Rom. 8:9, 11-13*	*Matt. 11:25-30*
Year B	*Ezek. 2:2-5*	*Ps. 123:1-2, 3-4*	*2 Cor. 12:7-10*	*Mark 6:1-6*
Year C	*Isa. 66:10-14*	*Ps. 66:1-3, 4-5, 6-7, 16-20*	*Gal. 6:14-18*	*Luke 10:1-12,17-20 or 10:1-9*

Fifteenth Sunday in Ordinary Time (Proper 10)

God our Father, your light of truth guides us to the way of Christ. May all who follow him reject what is contrary to the gospel. We ask this through our Lord Jesus Christ, your Son, who lives and reigns with you and the Holy Spirit, one God, for ever and ever.

Year A	*Isa. 55:10-11*	*Ps. 65:10, 11, 12-13, 14*	*Rom. 8:18-23*	*Matt. 13:1-23 or 13:1-9*
Year B	*Amos 7:12-15*	*Ps. 85:9-10, 11-12, 13-14*	*Eph. 1:3-14 or 1:3-10*	*Mark 6:7-13*
Year C	*Deut. 30:10-14*	*Ps. 69:14,17,30-31, 33-34,36,37*	*Col. 1:15-20*	*Luke 10:25-37*

Sixteenth Sunday in Ordinary Time (Proper 11)

Lord, be merciful to your people. Fill us with your gifts and make us always eager to serve you in faith, hope, and love. Grant this through our Lord Jesus Christ, your Son, who lives and reigns with you and the Holy Spirit, one God, for ever and ever.

Year A	*Wis. 12:13, 16-19*	*Ps. 86:5-6, 9-10, 15-17*	*Rom. 8:26-27*	*Matt. 13:24-43 or 13:24-30*
Year B	*Jer. 23:1-6*	*Ps. 23:1-3, 3-4, 5, 6*	*Eph. 2:13-18*	*Mark 6:30-34*
Year C	*Gen. 18:1-10*	*Ps 15:2-3, 3-4, 5*	*Col. 1:24-28*	*Luke 10:38-42*

Seventeenth Sunday in Ordinary Time (Proper 12)

God our Father and protector, without you nothing is holy, nothing has value. Guide us to everlasting life by helping us to use wisely the blessings you have given to the world. We ask this through our Lord Jesus Christ, your Son, who lives and reigns with you and the Holy Spirit, one God, for ever and ever.

Year A	*1 Kgs. 3:5, 7-12*	*Ps 119:57,72,76-77, 127-128, 129-130*	*Rom. 8:28-30*	*Matt. 13:44-52 or 13:44-46*
Year B	*2 Kgs. 4:42-44*	*Ps. 145:10-11, 15-16, 17-18*	*Eph. 4:1-6*	*John 6:1-15*
Year C	*Gen. 18:20-32*	*Ps. 138:1-2, 2-3, 6-7, 7-8*	*Col. 2:12-14*	*Luke 11:1-13*

Eighteenth Sunday in Ordinary Time (Proper 13)

Father of everlasting goodness, our origin and guide, be close to us and hear the prayers of all who praise you. Forgive our sins and restore us to life. Keep us safe in your love. Grant this through our Lord Jesus Christ, your Son, who lives and reigns with you and the Holy Spirit, one God, for ever and ever.

Year A	*Isa. 55:1-3*	*Ps. 145:8-9, 15-16, 17-18*	*Rom 8:35, 37-39*	*Matt. 14:13-21*
Year B	*Exod. 16:2-4, 12-15*	*Ps. 78:3-4, 23-24, 25, 54*	*Eph. 4:17, 20-24*	*John 6:24-35*
Year C	*Eccl. 1:2, 2:21-23*	*Ps. 95:1-2, 6-7, 8-9*	*Col. 3:1-5, 9-11*	*Luke 12:13-21*

Nineteenth Sunday in Ordinary Time (Proper 14)

Almighty and ever-living God, your Spirit made us your children, confident to call you Father. Increase your Spirit within us and bring us to our promised inheritance. Grant this through our Lord Jesus Christ, your Son, who lives and reigns with you and the Holy Spirit, one God, for ever and ever.

Year A	*1 Kgs. 19:9, 11-13*	*Ps. 85:9, 10, 11-12, 13-14*	*Rom. 9:1-5*	*Matt. 14:22-33*
Year B	*1 Kgs. 19:4-8*	*Ps. 34:2-3, 4-5, 6-7, 8-9*	*Eph. 4:30-5:2*	*John 6:41-51*
Year C	*Wis. 18:6-9*	*Ps. 33:1, 12, 18-19, 20-22*	*Heb. 11:1-2, 8-19 or 11: 1-2, 8-12*	*Luke 12:32-48 or 12:35-40*

Twentieth Sunday in Ordinary Time (Proper 15)

God our Father, may we love you in all things and above all things and reach the joy you have prepared for us beyond all our imagining. We ask this through our Lord Jesus Christ, your Son, who lives and reigns with you and the Holy Spirit, one God, for ever and ever.

Year A	Isa. 56:1, 6-7	Ps. 67:2-3, 5, 6, 8	Rom. 11:13-15, 29-32	Matt. 15:21-28
Year B	Prov. 9:1-6	Ps. 34:2-3,10-11,12-13,14-15	Eph. 5:15-20	John 6:51-58
Year C	Jer. 38:4-6, 8-10	Ps. 40:2, 3, 4, 18	Heb. 12:1-4	Luke 12:49-53

Twenty-First Sunday in Ordinary Time (Proper 16)

Father, help us to seek the values that will bring us lasting joy in this changing world. In our desire for what you promise make us one in mind and heart. Grant this through our Lord Jesus Christ, your Son, who lives and reigns with you and the Holy Spirit, one God, for ever and ever.

Year A	Isa. 22:15, 19-23	Ps 138:1-2, 2-3, 6, 8	Rom. 11:33-36	Matt. 16:13-20
Year B	Jos. 24:1-2, 15-17, 18	Ps. 34:2-3,16-17, 18-19, 20-21, 22-23	Eph. 5:21-32	John 6:60-69
Year C	Isa. 66:18-21	Ps. 117:1, 2	Heb. 12:5-7, 11-13	Luke 13:22-30

Twenty-Second Sunday in Ordinary Time (Proper 17)

Almighty God, every good thing comes from you. Fill our hearts with love for you, increase our faith, and by your constant care protect the good you have given us. We ask this through our Lord Jesus Christ, your Son, who lives and reigns with you and the Holy Spirit, one God, for ever and ever.

Year A	Jer. 20:7-9	Ps. 63:2, 3-4, 5-6, 8-9	Rom. 12:1-2	Matt. 16:21-27
Year B	Deut. 4:1-2, 6-8	Ps. 15:2-3, 3-4, 4-5	James 1:17-18, 21-22, 27	Mark 7:1-8, 14-15, 21-23
Year C	Sir. 3:17-18, 20, 28-29	Ps. 68:4-5, 6-7, 10-11	Heb. 12:18-19, 22-24	Luke 14:1, 7-14

Twenty-Third Sunday in Ordinary Time (Proper 18)

God our Father, you redeem us and make us your children in Christ. Look upon us, give us true freedom and bring us to the inheritance you promised. Grant this through our Lord Jesus Christ, your Son, who lives and reigns with you and the Holy Spirit, one God, for ever and ever.

Year A	Ezek. 33:7-9	Ps. 95:1-2, 6-7, 8-9	Rom. 13:8-10	Matt. 18:15-20
Year B	Isa. 35:4-7	Ps. 146:7, 8-9, 9-10	James 2:1-5	Mark 7:31-37
Year C	Wis. 9:13-18	Ps. 90:3-4,5-6, 12-13, 14, 17	Phil. 9-10, 12-17	Luke 14:25-33

Twenty-Fourth Sunday in Ordinary Time (Proper 19)

Almighty God, our creator and guide, may we serve you with all our heart and know your forgiveness in our lives. We ask this through our Lord Jesus Christ, your Son, who lives and reigns with you and the Holy Spirit, one God, for ever and ever.

Year A	*Sir. 27:30-28:1*	*Ps. 103:1-2, 3-5, 9-10, 11-12*	*Rom. 14:7-9*	*Matt. 18:21-35*
Year B	*Isa. 50:4-9*	*Ps. 115:1-2, 3-4, 5-6, 8-9*	*James 2:14-18*	*Mark 8:27-35*
Year C	*Exod. 32:7-1, 13-14*	*Ps. 51:3-4, 12-13, 17, 19*	*1 Tim. 1:12-17*	*Luke 15:1-32 or 15:1-10*

Twenty-Fifth Sunday in Ordinary Time (Proper 20)

Father, guide us, as you guide creation according to your law of love. May we love one another and come to perfection in the eternal life prepared for us. Grant this through our Lord Jesus Christ, your Son, who lives and reigns with you and the Holy Spirit, one God, for ever and ever.

Year A	*Isa. 55:6-9*	*Ps. 145:2-3, 8-9, 17-18*	*Phil. 1:20-24, 27*	*Matt. 20:1-16*
Year B	*Wis. 2:12, 17- 20*	*Ps. 54:3-4, 5, 6-8*	*James 3:16-4:3*	*Mark 9:30-37*
Year C	*Amos 8:4-7*	*Ps. 113:1-2, 4-6, 7-8*	*1 Tim. 2:1-8*	*Luke 16:1-13 or 16:10-13*

Twenty-Sixth Sunday in Ordinary Time (Proper 21)

Father, you show your almighty power in your mercy and forgiveness. Continue to fill us with your gifts of love. Help us to hurry towards the eternal life you promise and come to share in the joys of your kingdom. Grant this through our Lord Jesus Christ, your Son, who lives and reigns with you and the Holy Spirit, one God, for ever and ever.

Year A	*Ezek. 18:25-28*	*Ps. 25:4-5, 6-7, 8-9*	*Phil. 2:1-11 or 2:1-5*	*Matt. 21:28-32*
Year B	*Num. 11:25-29*	*Ps. 19:8, 10, 12-13, 14*	*James 5:1-6*	*Mark 9:38-43, 45, 47-48*
Year C	*Amos 6:1, 4-7*	*Ps. 146:7, 8-9, 9-10*	*1 Tim. 6:11-16*	*Luke 16:19-31*

Twenty-Seventh Sunday in Ordinary Time (Proper 22)

Father, your love for us surpasses all our hopes and desires. Forgive our failings, keep us in your peace and lead us in the way of salvation. We ask this through our Lord Jesus Christ, your Son, who lives and reigns with you and the Holy Spirit, one God, for ever and ever.

Year A	*Isa. 5:1-7*	*Ps. 80:9,12,13-14, 15-16,19-20*	*Phil. 4:6-9*	*Matt. 21:33-43*
Year B	*Gen. 2:18-24*	*Ps. 128:1-2, 3, 4-5, 6*	*Heb. 2:9-11*	*Mark 10:2-16 or 10:2-12*
Year C	*Hab. 1:2-3, 2:2-4*	*Ps. 95:1-2, 6-7, 8-9*	*2 Tim. 1:6-8, 13-14*	*Luke 17:5-10*

Twenty-Eighth Sunday in Ordinary Time (Proper 23)

Lord, our help and guide, make your love the foundation of our lives. May our love for you express itself in our eagerness to do good for others. Grant this through our Lord Jesus Christ, your Son, who lives and reigns with you and the Holy Spirit, one God, for ever and ever.

Year A	Isa. 25:6-10	Ps. 23:1-3, 3-4, 5, 6	Phil. 4:12-14, 19-20	Matt. 22:1-14 or 22:1-10
Year B	Wis. 7:7-11	Ps. 90:12-13, 14-15, 16-17	Heb. 4:12-13	Mark 10:17-30 or 10:17-27
Year C	2 Kgs. 5:14-17	Ps. 98:1, 2-3, 3-4	2 Tim. 2:8-13	Luke 17:11-19

Twenty-Ninth Sunday in Ordinary Time (Proper 24)

Almighty and ever-living God, our source of power and inspiration, give us strength and joy in serving you as followers of Christ, who lives and reigns with you and the Holy Spirit, one God, for ever and ever.

Year A	Isa. 45:1, 4-6	Ps. 96:1, 3, 4-5, 7-8, 9-10	1 Thes. 1:1-5	Matt. 22:15-21
Year B	Isa. 53:10-11	Ps. 33:4-5, 18-19, 20, 22	Heb. 4:14-16	Mark 10:35-45 or 10:42-45
Year C	Exod. 17:8-13	Ps. 121:1-2, 3-4, 5-6, 7-8	2 Tim. 3:14-4:2	Luke 18:1-8

Thirtieth Sunday in Ordinary Time (Proper 25)

Almighty and ever-living God, strengthen our faith, hope, and love. May we do with loving hearts what you ask of us and come to share the life you promise. We ask this through our Lord Jesus Christ, your Son, who lives and reigns with you and the Holy Spirit, one God, for ever and ever.

Year A	Exod. 22:20-26	Ps. 18:2-3, 3-4, 47, 51	1 Thes. 1:5-10	Matt. 22:34-40
Year B	Jer. 31:7-9	Ps. 126:1-2, 2-3, 4-5, 6	Heb. 5:1-6	Mark 10:46-52
Year C	Sir. 35:12-14, 16-18	Ps 34:2-3, 17-18, 19, 23	2 Tim. 4:6-8, 16-18	Luke 18:9-14

Thirty-First Sunday in Ordinary Time (Proper 26)

God of power and mercy, only with your help can we offer you fitting service and praise. May we live the faith we profess and trust your promise of eternal life. Grant this through our Lord Jesus Christ, your Son, who lives and reigns with you and the Holy Spirit, one God, for ever and ever.

Year A	Mal. 1:14-2:2, 8-10	Ps. 131:1, 2, 3	1 Thes. 2:7-9, 13	Matt. 23:1-12
Year B	Deut. 6:2-6	Ps. 18:2-3, 3-4, 47, 51	Heb. 7:23-28	Mark 12:28-34
Year C	Wis. 11:22-12:1	Ps. 145:1-2, 8-9, 10-11, 13, 14	2 Thes. 1:11-2:2	Luke 19:1-10

Thirty-Second Sunday in Ordinary Time (Proper 27)

God of power and mercy, protect us from all harm. Give us freedom of spirit and health in mind and body to do your work on earth. We ask this through our Lord Jesus Christ, your Son, who lives and reigns with you and the Holy Spirit, one God, for ever and ever.

Year A	*Wis. 6:12-16*	*Ps. 63:2, 3-4, 5-6, 7-8*	*1 Thes 4:13-18 or 4:13-14*	*Matt. 25:1-13*
Year B	*1 Kgs. 17:10-16*	*Ps. 146:7, 8-9, 9-10*	*Heb. 9:24-28*	*Mark 12:38-44 or 12:41-44*
Year C	*2 Mac. 7:1-2, 9-14*	*Ps. 17:1, 5-6, 8, 15*	*2 Thes. 2:16-3:5*	*Luke 20:27-38 or 20:27, 34-38*

Thirty-Third Sunday in Ordinary Time (Proper 28)

Father of all that is good, keep us faithful in serving you, for to serve you is our lasting joy. We ask this through our Lord Jesus Christ, your Son, who lives and reigns with you and the Holy Spirit, one God, for ever and ever.

Year A	*Prov. 31:10-13, 19-20, 30-31*	*Ps. 128:1-2, 3, 4-5*	*1 Thes. 5:1-6*	*Mat. 25:14-30 or 25:14-15, 19-20*
Year B	*Dan. 12:1-3*	*Ps. 16:5, 8, 9-10, 11*	*Heb 10:11-14, 18*	*Mark 13:24-32*
Year C	*Mal. 3:19-20*	*Ps. 98:5-6, 7-8, 9*	*2 Thes. 3:7-12*	*Luke 21:5-19*

Thirty-Fourth Week in Ordinary Time (Proper 29)

The prayer is used on the weekdays following Christ the King, with the weekday readings.
Lord, increase our eagerness to do your will and help us to know the saving power of your love. Grant this through our Lord Jesus Christ, your Son, who lives and reigns with you and the Holy Spirit, one God, for ever and ever.

455. Solemnities of the Lord during Ordinary Time

Trinity Sunday (First Sunday after Pentecost)

Father, you sent your Word to bring us truth and your Spirit to make us holy. Through them we come to know the mystery of your life. Help us to worship you, one God in three Persons, by proclaiming and living our faith in you. Grant this through our Lord Jesus Christ, your Son, who lives and reigns with you and the Holy Spirit, one God, for ever and ever.

Year A	*Exod. 34:4-6, 8-9*	*Dan. 3:52, 53, 54, 55, 56*	*2 Cor. 13:11-13*	*John 3:16-18*
Year B	*Deut. 4:32-34, 39-40*	*Ps. 33:4-5,6,9,18-19,20,22*	*Rom. 8:14-17*	*Matt.28:16-20*
Year C	*Prov. 8:22-31*	*Ps. 8:4-5, 6-7, 8-9*	*Rom. 5:1-5*	*John 16:12-15*

Corpus Christi (Thursday after Trinity Sunday) – Prayer

Lord Jesus Christ, in this most wonderful sacrament you have left us the memorial of your passion; deepen our reverence for the mystery of your body and blood, that we may experience within us the fruit of your redemption. You live and reign with the Father in the unity of the Holy Spirit, God for ever and ever.

Corpus Christi (Thursday after Trinity Sunday) – Readings

Year A	*Deut. 8:2-3, 14-16*	*Ps. 147:12-13, 14-15,19-20*	*1 Cor. 10:16-17*	*John 6:51-58*
Year B	*Exod. 24:3-8*	*Ps. 116:12-13, 15-16,17-18*	*Heb. 9:11-15*	*Mark 14:12-16, 22-26*
Year C	*Gen. 14:18-20*	*Ps. 110:1, 2, 3, 4*	*1 Cor. 11:23-26*	*Luke 9:11-17*

Sacred Heart of Jesus (Friday after the Second Sunday after Pentecost)

Father, we rejoice in the gifts of love we have received from the heart of Jesus your Son. Open our hearts to share his life and continue to bless us with his love. We ask this through our Lord Jesus Christ, your Son, who lives and reigns with you and the Holy Spirit, one God, for ever and ever.

OR:

Father, we have wounded the heart of Jesus your Son, but he brings us forgiveness and grace. Help us to prove our grateful love and make amends for our sins. We ask this through our Lord Jesus Christ, your Son, who lives and reigns with you and the Holy Spirit, one God, for ever and ever.

Year A	*Deut. 7:6-11*	*Ps. 1-3:1-2, 3-4, 6-7, 8, 10*	*1 John 4:7-16*	*Matt. 11:25-30*
Year B	*Hosea 11:1, 3-4, 8-9*	*Isa. 12:2-3, 4, 5-6*	*Eph. 3:8-12, 14-19*	*John 19:31-37*
Year C	*Ezek. 34:11-16*	*Ps. 23:1-3, 3-4, 5, 6*	*Rom. 5:5-11*	*Luke 15:3-7*

Feast of Christ the King (Last Sunday in Ordinary Time)

Almighty and merciful God, you break the power of evil and make all things new in your Son Jesus Christ, the King of the universe. May all in heaven and earth acclaim your glory and never cease to praise you. We ask this through Christ our Lord.

Year A	*Ezek. 34:11-12, 15-17*	*Ps. 23:1-2, 2-3, 5-6*	*1 Cor. 15:20-26, 28*	*Matt. 25:31-46*
Year B	*Dan. 7:13-14*	*Ps. 93:1, 1-2, 5*	*Apoc. 1:5-8*	*John 18:33-37*
Year C	*2 Sam. 5:1-3*	*Ps. 122:1-2, 3-4, 4-5*	*Col. 1:12-20*	*Luke 23:35-43*

Other Books from THAVMA Publications

Christian Candle Magic:
The Magic Use of Candles in the
Christian Home
Agostino Taumaturgo, © 2015

ISBN-10: 1523484152
ISBN-13: 978-1523484157
152 Pages. 5½ x 8½.

Available in Paperback and Kindle.

The Power of Fire!

Since the dawn of time, man has harnessed the awesome power of fire. Today the magic continues, with the power of fire harnessed in the light of a candle.

With this book, you'll learn:
- How candles form part of the Christian's life.
- The physical and psychological effects of color.
- How the Saints can make things happen.
- How to work the different types of candles.
- How to use the Rosary as a magical weapon.
- Rituals for Love, Money, Health, and Protection.
- How to read what your magic is doing.

The Paperback version also includes:
- 78 Prayers to contact the Saints.
- Oils and incenses to make your magic stronger.

Reading this book can be first step to changing your life!

**Ritual Magic
for Conservative Christians**
Brother A.D.A., © 2016

ISBN-10: 1523697067
ISBN-13: 978-1523697069

186 pages, 5½ x 8½.

Available in Paperback and Kindle.

MORE POWER FOR LIVING!

Christians have practiced magic since the first century, and almost all classic magical texts since the Middle Ages have Christian authors. With this book, you can tap into that power!

You'll learn:
- A theology of magic that embraces all mainstream Christian denominations.
- A curriculum for training yourself in the magic art.
- An organized method for calling the Choirs of Angels.
- How to consecrate, and use talismans and amulets.
- A powerful system for creating your own magical rituals.
- Multiple fully-functioning example rituals.
- Practical advice to make your magic even more effective!

Between these pages you'll find the most potent manual yet for Christian magicians who want to retain their orthodoxy and more deeply understand their faith as well as their practice.

Manifest with orthodoxy. Believe with power. Grow with awesomeness!

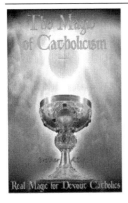

The Magic of Catholicism:
Real Magic for Devout Catholics
Brother A.D.A., © 2004 and 2015

ISBN-10: 1515126560
ISBN-13: 978-1515126560

264 Pages. 5½ x 8½.

Available in Paperback and Kindle.

THE HIDDEN FAITH

What is magic?
Is it wrong?
Can it help me?

Previously titled Occult Catholicism: Real Magic for Devout Catholics, this new edition is upwards of 90% rewritten and contains loads of new material.

With this book, you can learn:
- What magic is and how a Catholic can practice it.
- Catholicism as an initiatory magical system.
- How to set up a magical home altar.
- How to make prayers and novenas work for you.
- Using candles to bring good things into your life.
- How you can work with the Angels and the Saints.

Accompanied with copious footnotes and references to the Bible, the Early Fathers, the Council of Trent, and the Catechism of the Catholic Church, this book contains a guided tour of faith and spirituality in theory, in practice, and in power.

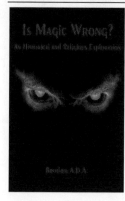

**Is Magic Wrong?
An Historical and Religious
Exploration**
Brother A.D.A., © 2015

ISBN-10: 1523497874
ISBN-13: 978-1523497874
36 Pages. 5½ x 8½.

Available in Paperback and Kindle.

IS MAGIC EVIL?

Many people believe it is.
But is it?

Inquiring minds want to know!

In this journey through history, language, religion, and practice, Brother A.D.A. puts to rest once and for all the question of whether magic is evil from a Christian perspective. Easy-to-read and accessible, Brother A.D.A. begins with remote antiquity and traces the laws against magic through Paganism and Judaism, paving the way for Christianity's own attitude on the subject.

So what does Christianity really think? Open this book and find out!

Get your free copy by going to http://thavmapub.com and registering for your free gift TODAY!

Made in United States
Orlando, FL
06 November 2023

38607901R00302